METHODOLOGY IN THE ACADEMIC TEACHING OF THE HOLOCAUST

Studies in Judaism

METHODOLOGY IN THE ACADEMIC TEACHING OF THE HOLOCAUST

Edited by Zev Garber

With
Alan L. Berger
and
Richard Libowitz

UNIVERSITY
PRESS OF
AMERICA

Lanham • New York • London

Copyright © 1988 by

University Press of America,® Inc.

4720 Boston Way
Lanham, MD 20706

3 Henrietta Street
London WC2E 8LU England

Printed in the United States of America

British Cataloging in Publication Information Available

Library of Congress Cataloging-in-Publication Data

Methodology in the academic teaching of the Holocaust / edited by
Zev Garber, with Alan L. Berger and Richard Libowitz.
p. cm.—(Studies in Judaism)
Includes bibliographies.
1. Holocaust, Jewish (1939–1945)—Study and teaching (Higher)
i. Garber, Zev. 1941–   . II. Berger, Alan L., 1939–
III. Libowitz, Richard, 1948–   . IV. Series.
D804.3.M48   1988
940.5315'03924—dc 19   88–5591 CIP
ISBN 0–8191–6961–7 (alk. paper)
ISBN 0–8191–6962–5 (pbk. : alk. paper)

All University Press of America books are produced on acid-free
paper which exceeds the minimum standards set by the National
Historical Publications and Records Commission.

Rabbi Tarfon taught:

... It is not thy duty to complete the work, but neither are thou free to desist from it...

(m. 'Avot 2.16)

Acknowledgements

Methodology in the Academic Teaching of the Holocaust is published with the partial support of the following institutions:

- International Center for Holocaust Studies
- 1939 Club, Inc.

The International Center for Holocaust Studies is chaired by Nat Kamedy and directed by Dr. Dennis B. Klein. It is a leading disseminator of Holocaust teaching and learning material in the U.S. and overseas. A new project of the Center is the Foundation to Sustain Righteous Christians, founded and chaired by Rabbi Harold M. Schulweis and directed by Dr. Eva Fogelman.

The 1939 Club, Inc., is a Los Angeles-based organization of 700 survivors of the Holocaust, founded in 1952, dedicated to the support of charitable endeavors, and devoted to preserving the memory of 6 million Jewish men, women, and children who perished in the Holocaust. One of the Club's legacies is to provide Holocaust education to future generations so that such an event will never happen again.

Additional assistance in the publication of this volume came from the following: Israel and Rose Gold, Ernie and Regina Goldberger, William and Marjorie Handel, The Lodzer Organization of California (Board of Directors; Sam Franen, President), Leopold Page, Dr. Herman and Gladys Sturman, and Dr. Auri and Deena Spigelman. Also, Mr. Roman Rakover, a survivor, lent concern and interest.

The editors are grateful for their support and encouragement.

Contents

Part I
Theory and Methods

Part II
Teaching Others

Part III
Literature and Arts

Part IV
Surveys and Reports

Contributors

LAWRENCE BARON is Professor of History, St. Lawrence University.

ALAN L. BERGER chairs the interdisciplinary Jewish Studies Program and teaches in the Religion Department at Syracuse University. He is the author of *Crisis and Covenant: The Holocaust in American Jewish Fiction* (1985).

LIVIA E. BITTON-JACKSON is Professor of Judaic Studies, Herbert H. Lehman College of the City University of New York.

RACHEL FELDHAY BRENNER teaches on the faculty of York University, and the Community Hebrew Academy of Toronto.

S. DANIEL BRESLAUER is Associate Professor of Religious Studies, University of Kansas.

HARRY JAMES CARGAS is Professor of Literature and Language, Webster University.

ARYE CARMON chairs The Israel-Diaspora Institute on the campus of Tel-Aviv University.

JOEL J. EPSTEIN is Professor of History, Olivet College.

MARILYN BONNER FEINGOLD teaches on the faculty of Rhode Island College.

ZEV GARBER is Professor of Jewish Studies, Los Angeles Valley College, and Visiting Professor of Religious Studies, University of California at Riverside. He also serves as President, National Association of Professors of Hebrew.

BJÖRN KRONDORFER, a German national, is a Ph.D. candidate in the Department of Religion, Temple University.

FRANKLIN H. LITTELL is Professor Emeritus, Temple University, and currently Professor, Hebrew University of Jerusalem. He is also President of The Hamlin Institute of Philadelphia.

RICHARD L. LIBOWITZ is Rabbi of Congregation Ner Tamid, Springfield, Pennsylvania. He also serves as Educational Director of the Anne Frank Institute of Philadelphia, and is on the faculty of Saint Joseph's University.

HUBERT G. LOCKE is Dean and Professor, Graduate School of Public Affairs, University of Washington, and Director and Senior Fellow, the William O. Douglas Institute of Seattle.

JAMES F. MOORE is Assistant Professor in the Department of Theology, Valparaiso University.

MOSHE PELLI is Director of Judaic Studies, University of Central Florida.

JOHN K. ROTH is Pitzer Professor of Philosophy, Claremont McKenna College.

RUTH ZERNER is a member of the Department of History, Herbert H. Lehman College of the City University of New York.

Abstracts

Chapter 1

The Holocaust and the Chosen People: A Methodological Paradox

S. DANIEL BRESLAUER, *Associate Professor of Religious Studies,*
University of Kansas

The academic study of Judaism takes as a basic assumption that Jewish studies as one of the humanities examines Jewish religion to discover certain universal principles of human religiosity. The content studied, however, represents the beliefs and practices of a living and vital group of people, among whom the professor of Jewish Studies is often to be counted. The emotional ties and vested interests of Jews present certain problems in the study of Judaica in an academic setting.

The study of the Nazi Holocaust represents a challenge for academics precisely because it is an emotionally charged subject. Jewish thinkers have emphasized the uniqueness of the Holocaust, its depth of meaning, and its significance for Jewish theology. A few, among whom Richard Rubenstein is most prominent, suggest that the Holocaust requires that Jews abandon their traditional views of God and the Jewish people. Other theologians, including Emile Fackenheim, find in the Holocaust a new divine missive, a directive that augments the traditional Jewish commandments. Both views evoke powerful responses from contemporary Jews that make the teaching of the Holocaust problematic in the academic setting. The proposed essay will begin by summarizing the methodological challenge it raises: how is it possible to treat in a dispassionate, academic way a passionately significant pathological event and how can one treat as an illustration of general religiousness what members of a religious group claim to be unique? After summarizing the difficulties of coping with the theological claims of Jewish thinkers about the Holocaust in an academic setting the introduction to the essay will examine how the theological relevance of the Holocaust can be studied in the context of the humanities as an illustration of certain general principles.

The search for those general principles will begin by placing the Holocaust and the questions it raises theologically in the context of Jewish thought broadly conceived. The challenge of the Holocaust to Jewish thinking can be understood as part of the general question of how Jewish suffering can be reconciled with Jewish choseness. Both concepts share an emphasis on Jewish uniqueness that cannot be accepted uncritically in an academic investigation and the study of the two in tandem will develop a theoretical approach appropriate for the academic setting. The essay, therefore, will perform two functions: that of creating a general theological framework within which to understand the meaning of the Holocaust and that of building a theoretical construct able to account for the impact of both the Holocaust and other Jewish tragedies on Judaism generally.

Chapter 2

Teaching the Holocaust: The Introductory Course

ZEV GARBER, *Professor of Jewish Studies, Los Angeles Valley College; Visiting Professor of Religious Studies, U.C. Riverside*

The experience of the Holocaust is truly unique. Nothing can compare to the enactment of absolute evil that attacked the Jewish people and other minorities during the 1930s and 1940s. Some say that all speaking about the

Holocaust and its consequences is thoroughly inadequate and sacrilegious to the memory of the millions murdered, maimed, and orphaned. Others say that silence is ultimately a posthumous victory to Hitlerism. However, all agree that education is the key to understanding the Great Catastrophe. But how to teach a subject that most educators believe is like no other course taught in the basic college curriculum of today?

The main thrust of this paper, an attempt at an objective presentation, is to provide some direction for possible standards in an introductory (i.e., lower division) class in Holocaust Studies. This article discusses background, objectives, methodology, theological responses, and limitations. It concludes with comments on the Written Assignment. Not the final word but a beginning, which perceives the material it teaches from a student's point of view, and attempts to make the Holocaust learning experience meaningful and academically responsible.

Chapter 3

Asking the Question:
Classroom Philosophies for Holocaust Study

RICHARD LIBOWITZ, *Rabbi of Congregation Ner Tamid, Springfield, PA; Educational Director, Anne Frank Institute; Faculty, St. Joseph's University*

The past decade has witnessed dramatic growth in interest about the Holocaust. Nowhere has this concern been greater than on college campuses, where courses pertaining to the *Shoah* have become expected components of "Jewish Studies" programs and are frequently the first to fill their enrollment quotas.

In more than one instance, the growing popularity of Holocaust studies has led to creation of such courses without consideration of purpose or methodology and/or their assignment to faculty members unprepared for the special demand of the subject.

The uniqueness of the Holocaust event renders insufficient a normative methodology in which theories are offered, cases presented, and outlines constructed into which data may be gathered and shaped. The end product of such efforts may trace patterns of destruction in a particular country, analyze German corporate complicity, or collate underground resistance efforts, without developing an understanding of the event's significance.

Authentic study of the Holocaust requires entry into the event. The instructor's primary task is one of revelation, rather than analytic examination. The successful course results in an intensity of meeting, the inherent painfulness of which must be noted with concern without becoming cause for rejection.

The risks inherent in revelation methodology fall upon tutor as well as students. The subjective approach rejects the instructor who instructs in favor of the professor who will profess. Department politics, decisions concerning tenure, promotion, and funding, argue for stances that are empirical and, ultimately, safe. Such stances can only lead one to "teach about" the Holocaust.

Chapter 4

Teaching the Holocaust in Israel: The Dilemma as a Disturbing Reality and Pedagogical Concept

ARYE CARMON, *Chair, Israel-Diaspora Institute, Tel Aviv University*

In Israel the Holocaust has a unique place in the collective consciousness from which it is virtually impossible to dissociate it in teaching. The Holocaust presents an unsolvable dilemma as there are no logical answers to the vast number of questions which it poses. Part of the dilemma stems from the ambiguity of Israeli attitudes towards the Holocaust. As a reality, then, the dilemma offers the challenge of becoming an educational concept; an educational goal to be coped with, so that students can learn that not all questions have answers.

While the story of the Holocaust was taught earlier at both high school and university levels, it was only in April 1979 — almost a generation after World War II — that it was introduced by the Ministry of Education as a compulsory subject. Thus a distinction was made between "knowing about" the Holocaust and "being aware of" the the Holocaust as a human phenomenon.

The chapter will be divided into three parts. The first part will deal with the history of the teaching of the Holocaust in Israel; the second with the failure of a specific pedagogical program introduced in the 1970s; and the third with teaching the lessons learnt from the Holocaust as a means of easing the tensions between universalism and particularism in Israel.

Holocaust education in the 1950s hardly existed. In this period it was influenced by the dual feelings of guilt and shame that characterized the founding fathers' generation and was expressed by emphasizing the active "Zionist" resistance in the annual event of *Yom Hashoa ve' hagvura* (Holocaust memorial and heroism day). In the 1960s, the Eichman trial exposed the macabre symmetry of dissociation by the Israeli public — from both the victims and the perpetrators of the Holocaust. They witnessed the testimony of the Holocaust survivors on the one hand and the presence of a human being in the glass cage on the other. This period saw the beginning of Holocaust education as part of the history classes.

The 1967 and Yom Kippur wars brought about a significant change in the perceptions of Israelis of their proper place in Jewish history. The initial notion that the Zionist revolution was not part of the continuum of Jewish history changed. This change was manifested in a transformation of the concept of *Gvura* (heroism). From being conceived as physical resistance only it was now expanded to include the maintaining of individual and communal life. The 1980s saw the rise of the ethos of *hisardut* (bare physical survival) as a result of the War in Lebanon and the advent of Kahanism. It also emphasized the role of the Holocaust in the collective consciousness. The conclusion of this section will expose the fallacy of the phrase "from Holocaust to rebirth," the awareness of which emerged in the mid-1980s.

The second section will concern the failure of a specific pedagogical program which was introduced in the 1970s. This program attempted to deal with the student and his needs rather than with the subject matter and its problematics. However, the program was initiated prematurely and it failed because of the unpreparedness of the teachers and the inadequacy of the environment in which they taught. In the experimental stage, whenever the teachers adhered strictly to given instructions, tremendous progress was made. An offshoot of this discussion will be the tracing of the link between the demand for this type of program and the simultaneous rise of Kahanism.

The last section will deal with the teaching of the lessons learnt from the Holocaust in attempting to ease the tension between universalism and particularism in Israel. The two major themes to be discussed are (a) the concept of orphanhood replacing that of "Holocaust to rebirth," which includes the impact on the collective consciousness of the void created in Jewish Europe and its effect on the teaching of Jewish history in general and the Holocaust in particular, and (b) the universal dimension of the Holocaust — the human aspect of the inhuman crime.

Chapter 5

Resistance and Submission: Teaching About Responses to Oppression

RUTH ZERNER, *Department of History, Herbert Lehman College, City University of New York*

This paper explores the complexity of teaching about those who submitted and those who resisted during the Nazi era. Often tendencies and actions which were outwardly submissive veiled spiritual or psychological resistance, which enhanced the strength, dignity, and life-affirmation of individuals, especially concentration camp inmates. Moreover, persons who actively participated in anti-Nazi resistance efforts usually orchestrated complicated rhythmic patterns of apparent submission to Nazi dictates, while plotting or committing actions aimed at the destruction of the Nazi system. Submission and resistance alternated in the behavior patterns of any one individual, as well as in profiles of groups opposing Nazi oppression.

Holocaust survivors, both in oral and written testimonies, have provided us with lessons concerning the efficacy of internal reservoirs of aesthetic and spiritual strength, tapped during or after the camp experiences. The distilled power of Elie Wiesel's novel *Night* rockets its readers to the "planet" Auschwitz. For many twentieth-century thinkers and artists the concentration camp or prison has become the central metaphor for modern life and society, with recent emphases shifting from anti-Nazi resistance to resistance to the power of death. Film art, one of the most powerful media of affective education, is central to contemporary teaching about the Holocaust and the rise of Nazi Germany.

Just as Dietrich Bonhoeffer, a Lutheran pastor executed by the Nazis for anti-Nazi activities, balanced strategies of resistance and submission, so teachers who focus on responses to modern oppression recreate the past most effectively by balancing their presentations of victims' experiences of suffering in the Holocaust with accounts of actions by individual bystanders (either supporting, undermining, or displaying indifference towards victims) and by the organized anti-Nazi resistance movement.

Chapter 6

What Can Anyone Do?

JOHN K. ROTH, *Pitzer Professor of Philosophy, Claremont McKenna College*

Modernized economic systems, technological capabilities, and political structures produce not only countless blessings but also surplus people, unique forms of human domination, and unprecedented quantities of mass murder. As the Holocaust exemplified, the modern political state may not flinch from putting its apparatus of destruction into action. If a ruling elite still retains control over this overwhelming power, the more ordinary man or woman seems to fall impotently before it.

The Holocaust dwarfed most individuals. Typically it showed them to be either defenseless victims, compliant cogs in the machinery of death, or bystanders, largely silent even if not incredulous or stunned, who did too little too late in opposing pressures that drove millions to extinction. Yet, however valid it may be, the impression that individuals and small groups were helpless to intervene effectively against that destruction process must be challenged.

As one teaches about the Holocaust, which unavoidably involves encountering the fact that twentieth-century states may progressively squeeze the individual into obedience devoid of dissent, it becomes more important than ever to appraise what individuals can and cannot do. Courageous resistance did from time to time save lives and prevent the Nazis from doing their worst. Countless Jews resisted. Some Gentiles did, too, including a few from deep within the German system itself. If Jewish losses did not exceed two-thirds of European Jewry and one-third of the Jewish people worldwide, the credit does not belong entirely to Allied military might. Persons acting as individuals or within small groups made their contributions as well.

"What Can Anyone Do?" — this paper argues that the immensity of the Holocaust becomes too impersonal and more inevitable than it really was if one overlooks the fact that individuals did make the decisions and obey the orders that destroyed millions. Buy exploring, moreover, what people did and could have done to thwart the destruction process, the essay also contends that the answer to its title-question can be hopeful and realistic at once.

Chapter 7

Teaching About the Holocaust: Theory and Method for Non-Jewish Audiences

HUBERT LOCKE, *Dean and Professor, Graduate School of Public Affairs, University of Washington; Director and Senior Fellow, William O. Douglas Institute*

The primary challenge in Holocaust education, four decades after the virtual destruction of European Jewry, is to make continuously clear its implication for the non-Jewish community. This challenge is heightened by the recent ADL survey which reports that four out of ten Americans "do not wish to hear any more about the Holocaust" — an indication both of fading memory and of increased insensitivity to the greatest human tragedy of the modern era.

This essay would explore approaches used by the author, both in university courses and adult education, in presenting the Holocaust to basically non-Jewish audiences. A principal focus on the role of the perpetrators (both actual and potential) and those who were by-standers (i.e., the role of leaders and citizens in Western Allied nations) is discussed as the pedagogical method of introducing Holocaust teaching, either comprehensively in a single course or as a mode of analysis for courses in ethics and the public service, as well as graduate courses in the professional field of law, education, social work, and other fields.

Chapter 8

Teaching About the Rescuers of Jews

LAWRENCE BARON, *Professor of History, St. Lawrence University*

Since the rescue of Jews in Nazi-occupied Europe was a relatively rate occurrence, Holocaust educators have tended either to neglect or minimize their coverage of this topic. When they do treat it, they usually employ approaches which fail to incorporate the findings of recent research into the ideological, psychological, situational, and sociological factors which prompted individuals and groups to save Jews.

The shortcomings of the following common methods of teaching about Jewish rescue are discussed: 1) usage of Anne Frank's diary, 2) usage of Raoul Wallenberg as an example of a heroic rescuer, 3) usage of the Danish experience as a model for mass rescue elsewhere.

To assist teachers in preparing units on rescue, current theories about which factors contributed to the decisions of rescuers to aid Jews are reviewed. These include: conditions which promoted rescue on the national and local levels, personal skills and circumstances which facilitated the rescue of Jews, prior positive relationships with Jews, social marginality, childhood relationships with parents, affective and intellectual socialization, and previous record of acting upon professed political and religious beliefs. This article concludes by describing two techniques to encourage students to draw on these theories when analyzing books by and about rescuers.

Chapter 9

Crossing the Experience Barrier: Teaching the Holocaust to Christian Students

JAMES F. MOORE, *Assistant Professor of Theology, Valparaiso University*

Drawing upon eight years of classroom experience in teaching the Holocaust to Christian students, this paper will examine both particular problems that teaching the Holocaust to Christian students poses and specific techniques that have been effectively used to help students cross over barriers that may seem at first insuperable. Two assumptions form the basic structure of the argument in this paper. First, Christian students think about and feel toward the Holocaust in clearly different ways than do Jewish students. Most Christian students have only an indirect relationship to the events of the Holocaust having no experience of the events except through second-hand reports and formal classroom experiences. They do not hear of the Holocaust in childhood nor do they know survivors or of victims (except by chance). Of course, this indirect relationship is not the case for all Christian students but it is the case for most American Christians. Thus, Christians approach the Holocaust with an experience barrier unlike the approach of a Jewish student. Likewise, Christian students because of their own Christianity can more easily detach themselves from events that do not directly affect them than can Jewish students. Second, the primary way to cross the experience barrier is through classroom techniques that are inherently experiential. This paper will examine four such techniques (in particular, the use of the journal), detail their success and limits, and suggest possible expanded use of these techniques for any class designed to teach about the Holocaust.

Chapter 10

Memory and Meaning:
The Holocaust in Second Generation Literature

ALAN L. BERGER, *Chair, Jewish Studies, Syracuse University*

Studying and teaching about the Holocaust through literature is an indispensable mode of approaching the unapproachable. Writings of the witnesses chronicle the Kingdom of Night in a manner unavailable to nonwitnesses. But the fact is that survivors are becoming fewer and their legacy is increasingly being assumed by their children. What the second generation writes of the Holocaust combines pedagogic and salvific value. Such literature reveals what Elie Wiesel terms an "example for the world of how to deal with evil and the memory of evil."

Students can be made aware of the reality that the Holocaust continues to plague both its survivors, their children, and the wider human community. My essay examines second generation Holocaust Literature by focusing on covenantal issues such as the meaning of chosenness and the role of historical memory. This literature has its own icons of Holocaust remembrance including positive elements primarily dealing with family solidarity.

This paper seeks to unfold what the Holocaust is in the lives of its secondary victims and, by extension, society at large. By reading contemporary literature many students may be better able to relate both to the fact that the Holocaust continues to wound and that its survivors and their children are crucial models of how to remain human in an inhuman world.

Chapter 11

"The Almost Meeting": The Quest for the Holocaust in Canadian Jewish Fiction

RACHEL FELDHAY BRENNER, *York University and Community Hebrew Academy, Toronto*

The study of the response to the Holocaust in North American Jewish literature becomes increasingly relevant to those who did not experience the tragedy directly. The critical exploration of the theme ensures that the tragedy will not be forgotten. At the same time, the understanding of the impact of the Holocaust upon the consciousness of the North American Jew is instrumental to the healing process of the traumatic sense of guilt and impotence that has haunted the vicarious witness of the tragedy.

The paper examines the representation of the Holocaust in three significant Canadian novels: Henry Kreisel's *The Rich Man*, A. M. Klein's *The Second Scroll*, and Mordecai Richler's *St. Urbain's Horseman*. Their treatment of the Holocaust is discussed in the context of the survivor's reluctance to write about the direct experience of the horror. Yet, despite the survivor's apprehension to impart the experience and thus separate from it, the unspeakable horror of the event inhibits fictional recreation of the survivor's tale. The recurring pattern of quest in the three novels demonstrates how the outsider gravitates toward the experience and, at the same time, withdraws from it. This ambivalence is manifest in the "almost meeting" motif — the repeatedly thwarted attempts to recapture the experience. The theme of the unsuccessful journey across the Atlantic, erects a metaphoric screen between the North American outsider and the naked reality of the European tragedy.

While history cannot be undone, the very attempt to rediscover the past manifests hope for restoration. "Quest is all" — the search for severed links with the lost heritage initiates the restorative journey to self-knowledge.

Chapter 12

Ka-Tzetnik's Literary Portrayal of Holocaust Experience

MOSHE PELLI, *Director of Judaic Studies, University of Central Florida*

This paper offers an analysis of a book by the Holocaust writer and survivor known as Ka-tzetnik as a model for discussion and literary probe into the uniqueness of Holocaust literature, especially that which is written in Hebrew.

The structure of the book, entitled *Star Eternal* (Hebrew: *Kochav Ha'efer*), attempts to achieve the "before (the Holocaust) and after" effect. It is further based on loosely connected fragmentary scenes. Chapters follow the course of a day — a day in Auschwitz.

Ka-tzetnik's style is said to be austere. Language seems to imitate the distorted reality of the Holocaust in its impoverishment, and in the treatment of time.

Certain literary devices are then analyzed, such as the use of second-person voice, use of present tense, lack of dialogues, and lack of personal identity, throughout most of the book.

Concept of death and its literary presentation by Ka-tzetnik is essayed. A general tone of paradox is said to represent the dominant feature of the Jewish catastrophe in this book. The motifs of sun, stars, and sparks are subsequently examined. The author finds a direct allusion to the biblical covenant between God and Abraham concerning the eternity of the Hebrew people which has been shattered in the universe of the Holocaust. Another biblical allusion, to the divine guidance, has now been replaced by the ashes of the Holocaust.

Perception and portrayal of people and reality are said to be linear and limited in the universe of the concentration camp.

Chapter 13

Experimental Drama and the Holocaust: The Work of the Jewish-German Dance Theatre and Its Application to the Teaching of the Holocaust

BJÖRN KRONDORFER, *Ph.D. Candidate in Religion, Temple University*

This article proposes the use of experimental drama techniques to teach the Holocaust, based on the work of The Jewish-German Dance Theatre in Philadelphia. This ensemble created a performance about the effects which the Holocaust had on their relations as Jews and Germans born after the war.

The article is divided into three parts: introduction, description of the collaborative work of the Jewish-German Dance Theatre, (JGDT), and its possible application to their educational contexts.

In the introduction, the relations of art and the Holocaust is discussed. Can art work do justice to the suffering endured by victims of the *Shoah?* Do aesthetic decisions distort the historical reality of the Holocaust? The author affirms that art has both a special responsibility in the task to remember the Holocaust, and the opportunity to find access to otherwise inexpressible horrors. Thus conclusion is then applied to drama and the Holocaust. A short survey provides information on theatrical activities in death camps, modern playwrights, dramatic use of Holocaust metaphors, and experimental drama.

In the second part, the Jewish and German collaboration is described. Special attention is given to the preparatory phase and rehearsal period of the project. The JGDT experimented with various methodological approaches such as required readings, sociodrama, meeting with survivors, questionnaires. Various experimental drama techniques, including movement exercises and groupdynamic situations, were introduced. Although the JGDT's rehearsals were designed for a future performance, their work provides many devices which assist and enrich the difficult task of teaching the Holocaust.

How their experience can be applied to a different educational context is the question posed in the last part of the article. It is assumed that the work of the

JGDT can provide a model for future projects which address the Holocaust. A concept of play including issues such as catharsis and protection will be introduced which can serve as tentative guidelines for teacher with courage.

Chapter 14

The Holocaust as Non-History: Coverage in College Western Civilization Textbooks

JOEL EPSTEIN, *Professor of History, Olivet College*

How much do students learn about Hitler's "Final Solution" by reading today's Standard Western and World Civilization textbooks? Is there significant focus in texts on the Holocaust as a major historical event? If there is not, then how may this best be explained? What suggestions for upgrading coverage of the important subject might be worth considering ?

This essay addresses these questions and concludes that while several texts have upgraded their treatment of the subject, even the best accounts fail to treat the Holocaust as a major historical event. It is still treated as a "sub event" and discussed within the framework of Nazism and World War II. Many historians still do not realize that anti-Semitism was at the very core of Nazism itself, and that the "Final Solution" was at the "center of Hitler's mental world" (footnote 26 in text).

A realistic suggestion for change is presented that shows how coverage of the subject can be redesigned for meaningful inclusion within the general textbook.

Chapter 15

Problems Related to Knowledge Utilization in Elementary and Secondary Schools

MARILYN B. FEINGOLD, Ed. D., *Faculty, Rhode Island College; Education Consultant to the U.S. Holocaust Memorial Council in Washington, D.C.*

This chapter examines the relevance of the current status of research on knowledge use and school improvement to teaching about the Holocaust at the elementary and secondary levels. Knowledge use as used here is information based on evidence derived from scientific research, from practice, or from both. Knowledge can reside in ideas, theories, explanations, advice (Sieber, 1974), or in "things," such as programs, materials or techniques (Yin, 1976). Knowledge use refers to policies or efforts to promote the applications of such knowledge in the practice setting. Educators in key positions in the change process and external agents promote the knowledge transfer. Several important questions need to be explored: What lessons for public policy can be drawn from the current research? In more specific terms, what does the research on diffusion mean to the Holocaust educator? How might we most effectively generate support for education about the Holocaust? The chapter further explores the role of the NDN (National Diffusion Network) plays as a key federal mechanism for promoting knowledge utilization in our schools.

Chapter 16

My Papal Encyclical

HARRY JAMES CARGAS, *Professor of Literature and Language, Webster University*

My encyclical letter from a pope to the Catholic faithful always has wide impact. After centuries of persecution of Jews by Christians, and particularly after the Holocaust, such a document condemning anti-Semitism, is needed. Since it has not been forthcoming, here is a suggested papal letter which is offered by way of suggestion to cover important areas of Christian activities and attitudes towards Jews. Adolf Hitler should be excommunicated. More homilies in churches should deal with the Holocaust. The errors of traditional Christian teachings about Jews should be corrected. An examination of scriptures and what they mean for Jewish-Christian relations must be undertaken and, in keeping with this, we must find new terms for what we now call Old and New Testaments. The essential Jewishness of Christianity must be emphasized, the Vatican historical archives will be opened up to 1975, and Catholic educational institutions are urged to study Judaism for its own sake and for the close relationship of Judaism to Christianity as well. Missionary activity towards Jews should be redirected towards spiritual self-perfection. Finally, the State of Israel is now recognized officially by the Vatican.

Chapter 17

The Nazi "Blood Myth" and the Holocaust

LIVIA BITTON-JACKSON, *Professor of Judaic Studies, Herbert H. Lehman College, City University of New York*

"They walk in Jewish blood up to their knees... the cries of Jewish babies pierce their ears, and they, without faltering for a second, proceed with their work. They indeed deserve a monument." With these words a Nazi "foreman" concluded his report. Professor Talmon comments: "The image of the Jew had not been merely dehumanized, he had become Satan incarnate... the butchers were no longer affected by signs of pain manifested by Jews."

The process of preparation for mass murder included an extensive literature which isolated the Jew, effectively surrounding him with an aura of evil magic. The "blood myth," a pivotal credo of Nazi ideology, became a potent weapon in this struggle.

Nazi literature utilized medieval myths which had isolated and targeted the Jews for centuries with the effective use of various blood accusations. The myth of the Jew as Christ-killer had been periodically revitalized by the ritual murder charge. In Nazi literature the ritual murderer became the parasite who sucks Aryan blood. The medieval poisoner-of-wells became poisoner-of-Aryan-blood; the desecrator-of-host became the defiler-of-German blood.

In the *"Blut und Ehre"* religion of the Nazis, this was a most powerful image. Hitler's description of the "black-haired Jew-boy" who "with satanic joy on his face" "lurks in wait for the unsuspecting girl whom he defiles with his blood" is but a recasting of earlier literary images. A. Dinter's *Sin Against the Blood* (1918), a German best-seller, focuses on the Jews' predilection for systematic blood-despoilation in order to subjugate the world. O. Spengler's *Decline of the West* (1918), A. Rosenberg's *The Mythos of the Twentieth Century* (1930), M. Bewer's *Der Deutsche Christus* (1907), the writings of D. Eckart, R. Wagner, H. S. Chamberlain, Streicher, H. Bluher, W. Stapel, W. Marr, E. Duhring and N. Junger are reiterations of the theme.

When, at the Wannsee Conference in January 1942, the blue-print for the "Final Solution" was unveiled, the mood had been set. The German psyche had been desensitized in preparation for the Holocaust: literature had a major share in the process.

Preface

Teaching and learning about the war against the Jews, 1933-1945, is an excruciating but necessary experience. But it is virtually impossible to know, let alone to master the rapidly growing body of material on the Holocaust. Thus, at the post-session meeting of the Post-Holocaust Reflection seminar (American Academy of Religion Annual Meeting in Anaheim, California, November 24,1985), we shared a sense of frustration with the task at hand coupled with a sense of hope that a group of us working independently and communally can give important direction to Holocaust teaching and education in American schools of higher learning. A number of us at the meeting agreed that the time is right and advantageous to publish a volume that will serve as a guide to all who tackle the question of "What can we learn?" and "How do we teach the Holocaust and its lessons?" We believe that our text is the first collective attempt in the Second Generation devoted to pedagogical issues arising in the academic teaching of the Holocaust. It is a sequel to Z. Garber, Editor, *Methodology in the Academic Teaching of Judaism* (UPA, 1987).

Methodology in the Academic Teaching of the Holocaust is a volume which seeks to address the central issues of human life and meaning in the post-Holocaust world. The essays it brings together are written by scholars who represent a variety of disciplines and religious orientations. Their formal concerns seem three-fold: literary, pedagogical, and theological. What unites these essays is, however, something very fundamental: the recognition that after the Holocaust the entire enterprise of being human has been called into serious question. These essays are all animated by the realization that the continuity of the human species is now at a great risk. Each of the authors attempts to pinpoint ways in which it is possible to remain human and seek meaning in an age of technologically administered mass death. This volume is offered as a meditation on human responsibility and theological possibility for those who come after the Great Catastrophe.

Structurally, the work is divided into four sections. The first section raises the questions of meaning and methodology within the discipline and goals of university education. The second section is concerned with the proper direction in presenting the Holocaust to basically non-Jewish audiences. The third section speaks on the teaching of Holocaust Studies from literature and the arts. The final part is designed as an "open end" section, and includes critical studies and personal ideologies suggesting a post-Auschwitz Second Generation committed to life, hope, and action.

The key to this volume is the diverse talent and scholarship provided by the contributors. We gratefully acknowledge their time and effort in providing the best volume possible. The presentation and style of the original essays are kept intact, though editing was provided to ensure a degree of conformity.

The clerical work was provided by my student, Wendy Hughes. I am deeply grateful for her efficient word-processing expertise. A special debt of gratitude to Associate Editors Alan L. Berger and Richard L. Libowitz, who read each chapter carefully and offered important criticism and helpful comments. Their conscientious devotion and cheerful *menschlikeit* exemplify scholarship and collegiality. Finally, my wife, Susan, assisted in the final editing of this volume. I am thankful for her devotion and support in the completion of this project.

We are honored that Professor Franklin H. Littell agreed to write the Foreword. His was one of the first voices of conscience raised in the First Generation to the plight of the Holocaust victims and its aftermath. His lessons on the implication of the Holocaust for the modern university provide direction for this work. We are indebted to his pioneering lead.

The contributors to this volume who teach, research, and write in the area of Holocaust Studies, know that the task at hand may not be completed, but that is no reason why it should not be attempted. We write in the spirit of the Sages of Israel: "It is not thy duty to complete the work, but neither are thou free to desist from it."

Zev Garber
For the Editors

Yom HaShoah 5748
April 14, 1988

Zev Garber
Jewish Studies Department
Los Angeles Valley College
Van Nuys, California

Alan L. Berger
Jewish Studies Program
Syracuse University
Syracuse, New York

Richard L. Libowitz
Congregation Ner Tamid
Springfield, Pennsylvania

Foreword

By Franklin H. Littell

In the dawn of our awakening to the tragedy of the Holocaust, the poets warned us that *silence* was the fit response. Silence at least observed the quality of respect for the dead. How could any form of words do justice to the sheer mass of the event? "Whichever word you speak, you owe to perdition" (Paul Celan).

The first responses were poems, musical compositions, plays and novels — attempting to find new forms to convey a message to those with ears to hear. Slowly prayers and liturgies emerged, and with the years *Yom Hashoah* became a national calendar day in Israel and America. The Days of Remembrance became a season for meditation, reflection, recollections of those who were lost and the civilization that was destroyed.

After the Scriptural "forty years in the wilderness" some of the numbness began to wear off. Survivors began to speak of what they knew, thinking of their children and grandchildren. Rescuers allowed themselves to be brought forward. Liberators convened and told the public of what their own eyes had seen, incidentally confirming the stories of the survivors in the teeth of the so-called historical revisionists. In Hubert Locke's essay in this book we are told of how scholars began to draw together in an Annual Conference, sharing what they had learned in studies of the *Shoah*, the *Kirchenkampf*, anti-semitism, the assault of the Nazi Third Reich on human liberty and religion.

In some ways the scholarly approach was more dangerous than telling the story, whatever the style of discourse. To stand back and report such a terrible thing objectively is to risk the same personal disengagement as that of the guilty by-stander, also complicit in the crime. Moreover, the scholars from different university disciplines had to remember what doctors, lawyers, sociologists, theologians, psychologists and psychiatrists — well trained in the world-rank German universities (before the Nazis ever took them over) — had so recently done.

The killing of 6,000,000 Jews in the heart of Christendom — without the audible opposition of Christian church leaders — was coming to be recognized as a credibility crisis for Christianity. Aware theologians in America and Europe were demanding a reworking and reconstruction of Christian preaching and teaching in the post-Auschwitz era. Among the congregations the concern was kept alive by the sign of *Yom Hashoah*.

There was a second credibility crisis for major institutions in the West, deriving from the fact that university men and women planned, rationalized, supervised and in most of the key positions staffed the *selexia* and the killing. The role of the "murderers of the desk" had to be confronted, and they were of the family of the campus, the Academe.

As Ruth Zerner points out in her essay, intensive intellectual work with the Holocaust inevitably changes one's personal history. Neither for churchmen nor for academics can the encounter with the story and its lessons be anything but life-changing. The churchmen must recall a mass apostasy among the believers and their leaders. The academics have their own *Anfechtungen* (agony of mind and spirit) when they deal honestly with the story. All witnesses testify: on this side of the mountain nothing looks the same.

Just as *Yom Hashoah* is a time of spiritual recovery, so *Kristallnacht* is a season for studying and communicating the lessons of the Holocaust. As the 50th anniversary of *Kristallnacht* approaches, more and more conferences and seminars are being announced to emphasize the lessons of the Holocaust on 9-11 November 1988.

Among the most important lessons emerging in recent years is one that has to do with Holocaust education itself: if Holocaust education is to go on, *nothing is more critical than the proper training of the teachers.*

Methodology in the Academic Teaching of the Holocaust is a book whose time has come. The time is right, the authors are right, and the need which it answers has grown with each passing semester.

Franklin H. Littell
Temple University and
Hebrew University of Jerusalem
3 December 1987

Part I

Theory and Methods

Chapter One
The Holocaust and the Chosen People: A Methodological Paradox

S. Daniel Breslauer

When explicating matters of depth-religious conviction, academics are caught in a dilemma. Which approach conveys the reality of the religious tradition better — one that takes an outsider's objective perspective, or one that projects the insider's passion and engagement? The first approach preserves academic rigor, but may distort the meaning of the tradition. The second remains true to the phenomenon studied but may distort the facts of the case. When seeking to understand such ideas as those of the chosen people and of the impact of the Nazi Holocaust on Jews, the choice of method is crucial.

Rabbi Nahman of Bratzlav, in a classic case of deriving archetypes from biblical stories, struggles to make sense out of the same dichotomy. He identifies the first approach with the third patriarch under the guise of Jacob and the second with that patriarch when known as Israel.[1] Rabbi Nahman clearly prefers Israel to Jacob and suggests that only the passionate scholar who reflects the tradition rather than subjects it to objective criticism should be allowed to teach others. As a tool in the hands of God such a teacher acts as a channel through which the divine power emanates into the world. Students of this type transmit learning rather than import meaning into the texts they study; as passive vehicles they allow Torah to flow through them.

Academics may well be shocked at Rabbi Nahman's views. As Jacob Neusner's review of *People of the Book* demonstrates, a gulf separates devotional, reflective 'lernen' and the academic pursuit of knowledge.[2] Those who teach Judaica expect to communicate a content, to enable students to understand, to provide a means for grappling with an unfamiliar world, not merely an experience of that world. When faced with the phenomena of the Nazi Holocaust, however, many of us fall back on Rabbi Nahman's dichotomy. Those who experienced the trauma know its meaning; the rest of us must respect their silence, must acknowledge our inability to articulate meaning. Some types of scholars find the task of teaching the Holocaust relatively easier; historians utilize a standard method for analyzing a crucial social or political event; scholars of literature apply the normative categories of their discipline to writings from or about the Holocaust. The student of religious studies, however, has a double task. While, together with all academic disciplines, the study of religion demands objective and universalized standards of interpretation, the phenomenon of religion must be appropriated, understood, and appreciated for its own sake. The double dangers of over sentimentalizing and presenting an insider's apology on the one hand and of over analyzing and reducing the religious phenomena to social, psychological, or historical causes on the other confront those investigating religious life.

The dangers are particularly critical for Jewish studies. The temptation to use the academic setting to further commitment to Jewish life tempts some teachers into an apologetic stance. They seek to communicate the depth and greatness of Jewish religious experience, but fail to utilize critical scholarly techniques of analysis. Like Rabbi Nahman's archetypal "Israel" such a teacher remains content to be a passive vehicle conveying the experience of Judaism. Other teachers, however, fall into the trap of reductionism. The history of Jewish religion becomes a tale of sociological, psychological, or historical determinism. Seemingly exemplifying the "Jacob" typology, teachers using this method often impose a foreign structure on what they study. As a humanistic discipline, however, the academic study of Judaism takes as a basic assumption that Jewish studies examines Jewish religion to discover certain universal principles of human religiosity. While the content studied represents the beliefs and practices of a living and vital group of people, among whom the professor of Jewish Studies is often to be counted, the method used must enable students to move beyond any specific conclusions to a general understanding of religion in human life and culture. The only acceptable approach can be one in which the datum of the "Israel" type forms the foundation of the conclusions drawn by "Jacob" since other options present certain problems in the study of Judaica in an academic setting.

This problem of method confronts the student of Judaism in almost every area of investigation. The study of the Nazi Holocaust, however, represents a special challenge for academics precisely because it is an emotionally charged subject. Jewish thinkers have emphasized the uniqueness of the Holocaust, its depth of meaning, and its significance for Jewish theology. A few, among whom

Richard Rubenstein is most prominent, suggest that the Holocaust requires that Jews abandon their traditional views of God and the Jewish people. Thus while Rubenstein admits that Jewish theology was at one time functional in Jewish life, he contends that more recent history demonstrates the danger of any ideological construction of human events. Other theologians, however, including Emil Fackenheim, find in the Holocaust a new divine missive, a directive that augments the traditional Jewish commandments. For Fackenheim the Holocaust confirms the Jewish will to exist and propels Jews into a new commandment, that of survival. The mythic significance of the Holocaust can also function positively. Eliezer Berkovits demonstrates how modern Orthodox Jews can find hope in the ashes of Auschwitz.[3] Before analyzing the meaning of the Holocaust for Jewish theology a student must somehow recognize the essential impact of the crisis despite the varying accounts different thinkers provide.

The teacher of contemporary Judaic thought can find the various views stimulating, and yet still be perplexed as to how the Holocaust should be presented. In a course on modern history the methods of study are traditional, only the subject matter has changed. Were the Holocaust to be integrated into a study of contemporary political science the teacher would find fewer problematic questions confronting the teaching of the subject. For the professor of Judaica, however, certain questions cannot be avoided. How is the Holocaust to be integrated into the general teaching of contemporary Jewish religious thought? How is that thought to be presented not as an insider's self-defense but in terms of objective academic analysis without at the same time falsifying the emotional content of the discussion?

Even if teachers remain theoretically neutral, endorsing none of the three alternatives noted above nor even offering a unique answer of their own, the teaching must progress from a specific point of departure, aim at a specific terminus, and project a specific perspective. Meeting these demands for a specific orientation must be achieved without compromising the academic mission — that of showing how a parochial subject matter suggests the universally human. As Jacob Neusner argues so persuasively, Jewish studies must provide a "universally accessible human experience" for students who engage in it. The study of Judaism in the university is not just for Jews but for all interested in human life; Jewish theology has a place only as an example of the universally human.[4] Such a judgment applies not only to the teaching of the Holocaust but to the other constituent elements of Jewish religious thought such as election, Torah, redemption, and religious leadership. The problem of adequately teaching the theology of the Holocaust can be linked with the more general problem of teaching Jewish theology as a whole. This present study focuses on the idea of election and its relationship to Holocaust theology. The interconnection of these two concepts has often been ignored; the study of the uniqueness of the Holocaust sometimes sheds little light on the uniqueness of the people of Israel. The importance of that interconnection, however, goes beyond the common methodological problem they pose and demands theological investigation.[5]

As theologians seek to understand the meaning of the Nazi slaughter of six million Jews, they are often overwhelmed by the magnitude of the event itself. Nowhere else, it seems, either in history or in geography has such a destructive program been carried out with as thoroughgoing and systematic resolve as that of the Nazis. Many thinkers succumb to the temptation to generalize from this feeling of overwhelming astonishment. The Holocaust, they claim, represents a unique historical and theological occurrence; its challenge lies as much in its astonishing uniqueness as in the horror it evokes. Thus, for example, Irving Greenberg compares the Holocaust to Sinai and post-exilic Judaism as a covenant event continuing the trend toward more and more recondite redemptive acts and together with Alvin H. Rosenfeld declares that "The Holocaust is an event of such magnitude that it creates an historical force field of its own."[6] The theological implications of this assertion of the uniqueness of the Holocaust extend to every aspect of Jewish religious life.[7]

The view that the Holocaust, as a unique event, demands radical rethinking of the entire Jewish tradition encounters resistance from a number of different perspectives. The traditional Jew notes that the Holocaust evoked a normative Jewish response, that of *halakhic* thinking, of *halakha*, Jewish legal decision-making. The normality of that response, it can be claimed, evolved from the historical situation of the Jews. Time and again the Jewish people confronted catastrophe and responded by utilizing traditional Jewish religious categories. The Holocaust, some contend, represents no distinct break in that tradition.[8] Others argue that theological reflection stimulated by catastrophe can be traced back to the biblical book of Lamentations. Jewish tradition offers theological paradigms of heroic faith and martyrdom appropriate for understanding the Holocaust; even if some writers such as Elie Wiesel move beyond those paradigms, the Holocaust need not be understood as a unique event.[9]

A third critique of the uniqueness theory suggests that such a view obscures the true lesson of the Holocaust. Since suffering, pain, and death are universal, the proper response to the Holocaust consists in reducing the possibilities of its recurrence and to avoid repeating its error. The Holocaust should be understood as as human tragedy that can recur if not prevented.[10]

Steven Katz contributes a valuable perspective in his investigation of the uniqueness of the Holocaust.[11] Katz notes that the claim of uniqueness can mean different things. He points, specifically, to two types of uniqueness: Historical and theological. While the Holocaust may represent a new type of historical possibility, a program of destruction without analogy in the human past, it may not thereby present a unique challenge to Jewish theological thinking. Katz criticizes Emil Fackenheim and Richard Rubenstein for confusing historical uniqueness with a radically new theological crisis. He also faults Eliezer Berkovits for overlooking the historical novum represented by the Holocaust even while applauding his recognition that theologically traditional Jewish thought has already confronted the problems raised by the Nazi persecutions.

The two-fold division of the category of uniqueness, while helpful, should be expanded to include three divisions. The Holocaust can be regarded as a unique historical event, as a unique theological problem, and also as a unique challenge to Jewish ideology as opposed to Jewish theology. That latter challenge needs to be taken with utter seriousness because Jewish thinking since at least the late nineteenth century has created a variety of ideological approaches, many associated with Zionism and some with secular humanism. Even the self-presentation of major religious groups within Judaism depend as much on ideological as on theological considerations. The different meanings attributable to the idea of "uniqueness" suggest the complexity not only of the challenge of the Holocaust but also of Jewish theology generally. When different Jews understand themselves as a unique people they may be indicating very different self-images. The student of Jewish religion must be careful to distinguish the various nuances involved in any claim for uniqueness or chosenness.

Merely noting the distinctiveness of different meanings given to the term unique, however, provides only a point of departure for study. The significance of that distinction needs investigation as well. A peculiar sense of Jewish chosenness accompanies each type of uniqueness stressed. In addition to investigating each nuance of uniqueness, then, one must discover how that nuance shapes the view of being Jewish held by a particular author. While some authors focus on only one aspect of the uniqueness of the Holocaust and thereby stress one primary element in Jewish existence, others look more broadly at the significance and implications of the Nazi destruction of Jewish life. The writings of Richard L. Rubenstein demonstrate that he is one of the latter type of thinkers. While his various books tend to look at one particular facet of the question raised by the Holocaust, taken in sum his writings illuminate the entire spectrum of meanings given to its uniqueness.

In his earliest essays Rubenstein confronts the basic theological presuppositions of Jewish thinking — the unity of God, the covenant of God with the Jews, the activity of God in history — and concludes that "The God who is the ground of being is not the transcendent, theistic God of Jewish patriarchal monotheism."[12] The rationale for this conclusion lies in Rubenstein's understanding of the nature of Judaism and the challenge of the Holocaust. Judaism, he contends, has always taken history seriously. That the God of Israel has been involved in acts of salvation forms the basis for Jewish belief in a covenant existence. Judaism provides a normative response to disaster — those who suffer deserve their punishment for having broken faith in the covenant. At the heart of covenantal thinking lies the doctrine of Israel's election: what happens to the Jewish people reflects God's response to the way Jews fulfill their obligations; both prosperity and adversity find their place within this theory of "perdition, redemption and salvation," a theory Rubenstein finds unacceptable after Auschwitz.[13]

Why did the death camps destroy the possibility of accepting traditional theodicy and the traditional doctrine of reward and punishment when earlier disasters did not? The answer lies in the process of demythologization to which the Holocaust added a definitive impetus and ultimacy. Modernization had undermined traditional Jewish and Christian theological values even before the Holocaust. What the Holocaust added, however, was a definitive illustration of the absence of a God of history. Rubenstein suggests that after Auschwitz the Jew faces a clear choice: either live in a world free from the old mythic perspective or "a return to an ideology which must end by praising God for the death of six million Jews. This we will never do."[14] That last point deserves particular stress. The Holocaust uniquely points up the absurdity of the modern Jewish choice: either affirm a demonic God or choose life; making such a decision is not a choice, but a forgone conclusion; the Holocaust makes an affirmation of traditional Jewish myth either naive or hypocritical.

At the heart of this critique of Jewish myth lies Rubenstein's concern about the doctrine of the chosen people, his restlessness with the idea of election. He contends that this idea itself may be responsible for Jewish suffering. His major contention is that "Jewish theology must be a theological anthropology more than a theology of history"[15] The focus must move from the Jews as a chosen people with a chosen and supernatural task to the generally human situation revealed by the realities of Jewish life. If the Holocaust sounds the death-knell for traditional Jewish myth and its theology, Rubenstein suggests that part of the new theology must be a Jewish self-understanding that rejects the idea of election.

While Rubenstein concludes that the Holocaust offers the definitive critique of traditional Jewish theology, other thinkers disagree. Steven Katz, as noted above, concludes that Rubenstein has confused historical uniqueness with theological uniqueness. Katz suggests that Rubenstein has, implicitly, accepted the empiricist critique of religion — religious language is literally non-sense since it does not make at least theoretically verifiable or falsifiable claims. Rubenstein's theory that the Holocaust falsifies Jewish mythic claims, however, cannot be sustained according to Katz. Traditional language need not be de-mythologized in order to meet the challenge of the Holocaust since the actual facts are too weak to shake the mythic claims being made.[16] Katz recognizes the positive as well as the negative elements in Rubenstein's thinking. He declares that the Israel-orientation Rubenstein displays demonstrates the deeply Jewish nature of his response.[17] This recognition, however, does not weaken his philosophical critique against Rubenstein's naturalistic and Zionist perspective. Katz reveals the philosophical limitations in Rubenstein's empirical method without confronting Rubenstein's application of that method to the meaning of Jewish election after the Holocaust.

While Katz offers a close refutation of Rubenstein's presuppositions and theological judgments, Eliezer Berkovits provides a living demonstration of how traditional Jewish thinking can continue in the face of the Holocaust. Berkovits does not deny the demoralizing effect of the Holocaust nor the need for contemporary Jews to respond in realistic, not merely theological ways to the challenge of Auschwitz. He suggests, however, that "while the holocaust is unique in the objective magnitude of its inhumanity, it is not unique as a problem of faith resulting from Jewish historical experience."[18] Berkovits is not perturbed by heretics, nor does he see them as uniquely modern. The talmudic period also saw its share of heresies, including the arch-unbeliever Elisha Ben Abuya whose rejection of Judaism seemed based on the same empirical arguments as that of Richard Rubenstein. Berkovits contends that the same answers that helped Jews respond to critics throughout the history of catastrophe marking Jewish life also solve the problem of traditional Jewish theology after the Holocaust.

The solution that traditional theology provides does not deny the overwhelming evidence of human destructiveness and Jewish suffering that occurred during the Holocaust. The empirical facts remain the same for both Berkovits and Rubenstein — the Holocaust and the essential necessity of the reborn State of Israel, but Berkovits uses these facts to establish the chosenness of the Jewish people. He suggests that both events show how Jews become "the point for the crystallization of moral direction in history. That is the ultimate significance of being the chosen people of God."[19] Jewish theology, from this perspective, need not interpret Jewish experience as either punishment or as accident. Between these two extremes comes the understanding of Jewish history as revelational: Jews perform a litmus test for human culture. Auschwitz proves that western culture failed that test; the modern State of Israel demonstrates that God will preserve Jews as a continual means of testing human civilization.

This view moves beyond a mechanistic understanding of covenant as promises and their fulfillment given by Rubenstein. The Holocaust is not interpreted as a definitive act of hostility brought by a vindictive deity against a recalcitrant people. Instead the Holocaust, together with all other catastrophes in the Jewish past, represents one arena in which Jews can perform their chosen duty. All of history, even its tragic moments, presents opportunities for Jews to fulfill their particular mission. For Berkovits this supernaturally imposed task entails bearing witness to the possibilities of transcendence, nobility, and divine struggle within humanity. The Jew demonstrates how to create values, how to realize the ideal. By so demonstrating, Jews give value to being human. Jews are chosen to bear witness before God to the transcendent potential within the human soul; they thereby justify the world of humanity before the divine judge: "Only when the chosen ones choose to accept 'the decree' does the world acquire the moral right to exist."[20] When Jews use their free will to transform even the worst of historical situations into a means of praising God, then all of humanity benefits. Here the point is not that Jews suffer because they have sinned. Rather Jewish suffering redeems the world through demonstrating the potential for transcendence that all human beings might have. Naturally Berkovits admits that many Jews did not live up to the high expectations of the convenant; they could not accept 'the decree.' Nevertheless, the fact that some of them did can be taken as proof of Jewish chosenness.

Berkovits' view is not without problems itself.[21] His presentation, however, shows an important alternative to Rubenstein's position. The experience of the Holocaust can be utilized to demonstrate how Jews transcend history. Nowhere else could such transcendence be accomplished in so dramatic a context. That Jewish theology can transform human suffering and transfigure it into a witness before God suggests the power of traditional mythology. Such a view harmonizes well with traditional understandings of the meaning of Jewish chosenness. Michael Wyschogrod, for example, contends that the Jewish people are the "incarnation of Torah," and that they embody the demands God makes upon all humanity. As such Israel's election consists in its universal mission of redemption, in its exemplification of values through the existence of Jews committed to their task.[22] Rather than contradict such a view the Holocaust shows how Jews exemplify such chosenness under extreme and inhuman conditions.

While Rubenstein's earliest writings on the Holocaust focus on the unique theological challenge it poses, his later writings see the Nazi program of extermination of Jews as an example of the unique possibilities of modernity. The Holocaust represents a unique stage in the development of humanity, one necessary step in the demonic rationalization process leading to a demythologized world controlled by abstract social forces. He contends that "something happened in the twentieth century that made it morally and psychologically possible to realize dreams of destructiveness that had previously been confined to fantasy."[23] Thus Rubenstein suggests that the Holocaust represents a new historical reality, a reality that permits human beings to commit legal genocide without qualms of legality or of conscience. He marshals the facts of the Holocaust in connection with descriptions of other twentieth century inhumanities to show how economic necessity, sociological imperatives, psychological pressures, and the process of rationality combine to undermine the restraining power of traditional values. In a world attuned to efficiency and expediency, human beings become expendable for the sake of social engineering.[24] The uniqueness of the Holocaust, from this perspective, offers a clue to the modern predicament as well as to that of Jews: modernity makes any minority radically vulnerable to ideological attack.

Jews reacting to this reality might well be expected to reaffirm Richard Rubenstein's rejection of the idea of the chosen people. Chosenness uses religious ideology to solve a practical problem and can never, therefore, cope with the problems of modernity. In a world characterized by the "collapse of every credible religious moral restraint," Rubenstein considers it folly — although certainly possible — to traditional affirmations about the "innate dignity of human beings." Rubenstein applauds Jews who move beyond religious ideology to political realism — a transition he associates with the Zionist movement. Zionists, he suggests have realized that the modern world is one in which efficiency rather than theology legitimates decisions. With Zionists he concludes that a rational and sophisticated approach to the realities of Judaism — by using the disciplines of economics, sociology, and psychology — offers the only valid perspective on Jewish life. Unlike the Zionists, however, his decision to focus on social, economic or psychological causation leads to a pessimistic prognosis for the Jewish future. Without theology, Jews must rely on the shaky structure of Western civilization for support, a structure that will not allow the luxury of a chosen people.[25]

The historical uniqueness of the Holocaust, however, may not mean that theology is irrelevant. Emil L. Fackenheim admits that the Holocaust provides Jews with a reason to reject theology, since "never within or without Jewish history have men anywhere had such a dreadful, such a horrifying reason for turning their backs on the God of history," but he concludes that theology takes on an even greater significance in the face of that challenge. Theology can provide an unprecedented human affirmation of survival in the face of the threat of destruction.[26] The fact of Auschwitz should lead, at least for the Jew, to a more dedicated commitment to the values and ideals of Jewish religion. Survival represents one such value that needs reaffirmation, not merely as a celebration of life but as a rejection of the philosophy of death.

Death in Auschwitz was horribly literal and real. Yet the Nazis made people into "living things before making them into dead things." Such a living dehumanization demands resistance no less than more palpable threats to survival. In the wake of Auschwitz, continuing the politics of efficiency, the exaltation of machines and mechanistic thinking, the degradation of human beings into things constitutes a betrayal "as much of the world as of the Jewish people." While Fackenheim sees the same processes of rationalization, sociological and psychological determinism, and mechanistic tyranny over human choice that Rubenstein discovers, he challenges contemporary women and men to triumph over them lest they let Hitler gain a posthumous victory.[27]

Fackenheim celebrates Jewish chosenness as a part of the task of redeeming the world from modernity. Fackenheim claims that Jews have the duty of "tikkun olam," reparation of the world, a duty that can be fulfilled by their continued survival as a living symbol of hope, of the possibility for moral transcendence in the world after the Holocaust. Jews survived the mechanistic genius of the Nazi genocide; they can survive today as a historical nation that demonstrates the moral primacy of life. Such a will to survive independently redeems not only Jews but the "whole post-Holocaust world."[28]

Since Jews experienced the hostility of the processes of rationalism and mechanism and survived, their continued existence serves a beneficent purpose, not merely for them but for all humanity. By affirming their identity and right to exist they demonstrate an alternative to Hitler's destructive bureaucracy and confirm the possibility of true human existence despite the tendencies of modernity.

Fackenheim's views have been criticized primarily because of his reliance upon Martin Buber's category of dialogue.[29] His approach, however, may be better understood as exemplifying one mythic construction of contemporary Jewish identity. Jacob Neusner has explored the meaning of the Holocaust as "a generative source of symbols and myths." He shows how American Jews utilize the images of the Holocaust to create a sense of self setting them apart from others "while giving them a claim upon those others."[30] Fackenheim suggests the possibility of legitimating a Jewish identity on the basis of the Holocaust event. While at first glance the Holocaust seems to show that religious ideals and values are irrelevant in a world of social, economic, and psychological determinism, he designs a mythic meaning for Jewish existence responding to that critique. Standing the criticism on its head, he declares that precisely because the Jew suffered the onslaught of modernity and survived, Jewish identity offers a viable alternative to deterministic thinking. This myth stresses the activity of the Jew in choosing Jewish consciousness rather than the activity of God in selecting the Jew.

Both the passivity of being chosen and the self-conscious act of affirming Jewish identity are needed. As Gunther Plaut suggests "The Jew is what he is because of a double choice: because of his choosing and his being chosen..."[31] Jewish survival demonstrates this active side of Jewish chosenness. Richard -

Rubenstein has noticed the duality of chosen and choosing and has identified them as two biblical models explaining Jewish history.[32] Unlike Plaut, Rubenstein does not see the complementary nature of these two aspects of Jewish experience as necessarily positive. One model, the covenantal model associated with the revelation at Mount Sinai, suggests divine control over the world and by subordinating human power to divine control helps explain disaster to a defeated people. Since Rubenstein sees the value of this Sinaitic model as "most likely to arise in the aftermath of a natural or social catastrophe" he credits it with enabling Judaism "to maintain its religious and communal integrity in the face of repeated military and political catastrophes."[33] Such an ideology might help in coping with the crisis of the Holocaust. One might argue, then, that the ideology of Sinai proves remarkably useful to the modern Jew by offering a means of coping with national helplessness.

Rubenstein doubts such utility, however, since the paradigm contains within it the seeds of its own destruction. The covenant model, by its very nature, thrives on social instability, undermines authority, and becomes dysfunctional in times when secure and predictable policies are needed. An alternative ideology arises to meet the new needs of more stable times. Rubenstein suggests that the biblical contention of sacral kingship came to replace covenantal thinking. Sacral kingship interpreted the community in terms of the power of the state and the divine stake in the existence of the state. Not insignificantly, the centrality of national existence in this paradigm parallels Rubenstein's own view of Zionism in the modern age.

The way in which Rubenstein analyzes Jewish ideas shows his distance from traditional Judaic thought. By putting both the paradigm of covenant and that of sacral kingship under the microscope of sociological investigation, he demonstrates that neither provides a compelling ideology for today. The light of objective study reveals that these patterns of self-presentation lack intrinsic merit and are valid only insofar as they serve a social use. Thus, unlike Elie Wiesel or Emil Fackenheim, Rubenstein cannot take comfort in a traditional language even if he recognizes its power. His rationalism unmasks its weaknesses. As one interpreter understands it, Rubenstein's work is marked by a distinctive alienation from traditional mythic language, his inability to utilize the inherited ideology setting him apart in the modern discussion of the Holocaust.[34] In his discussion of the idea of covenant and chosenness Rubenstein demonstrates why a modern Jew must reject the idea. Scholarly investigation uncovers that the only justification of the view is pragmatic; once the paradigm becomes unworkable an honest scholar must reject it out of hand. The Holocaust is unique because it undermines both the facticity of covenantal promises and, by illustrating the dominance of social, economic, and psychological causes, the naive ability to accept the supremacy of a transcendent God whose inscrutable ways cannot be questioned. The Holocaust leaves a unique legacy to those who innocently embrace ideology — they are condemned to repeat its horrors:

> If we fail to learn the simple lesson that the community of men is possible only through the encounter of persons rather than of myths or abstractions, we will only doom future generations to repeat the horrible deeds of our times...[35]

An uncritical acceptance of religious ideology, according to Rubenstein, leads to a repetition of the Holocaust. Unless humanity learns to live in a de-mythologized world, a world that suspects all ideology and myth, then hostility, primitive hatreds, and self-deception will lead to future holocausts.

In what appears to be an oblique response to Rubenstein, Israeli theologian David Hartman declares that "Those theologians who pronounced God dead or dethroned since Auschwitz misunderstood the source and staying power of covenantal theism."[36] Drawing on William James' willingness to accept the testimony of believers, Hartman suggests that since the mystery of covenant compels Jewish faith, it should be respected. This argument concludes a fascinating investigation of rabbinic responses to suffering. Hartman notes the varieties of ways in which traditional Judaism sought to cope with suffering. At times the response focused on guilt, retribution, and divine justice in punishing the wicked; at other times "chastisements of love" were exalted as means of drawing close to the divine. Sometimes covenantal obligation entailed arguing with God; sometimes it demanded submission before the indecipherable mystery of the divine will. Here Hartman suggests that the absorption of values need not follow the rigorous deterministic laws of cause and effect. The lesson of continued belief in Judaism despite the Holocaust is a lesson about the meaning of being human and of ways human beings respond to challenges.

Hartman does not argue that Jews alone have responded in such a multivalent way to critical situations. His point is neither "the superiority or the necessity of a covenantal orientation to life," but rather that a covenantal theology demonstrates an important truth about the way human beings interact with the world.[37] Jewish covenantal existence has more than parochial relevance because it shows how human beings move beyond mere facts. The variety of responses to suffering demonstrates that people look at the world not through any one set of perspectives but in diverse ways. Fact-finding represents one, legitimate, human response to the external environment. Theories of reward and punishment, of suffering for the sake of God, of radical human ignorance also play an important role in the way human beings make sense out of their existence. Were human beings limited to a scientific worldview, then the Holocaust might well be definitive evidence against covenantal belief. Since, however, the human being "is not only a fact seeking animal, but equally, and possibly more so, a value-hungry individual" the lesson of the Holocaust is not that ideology is worthless, but rather that its worth surpasses its translation into social, economic, or psychological utility. Hartman explicitly rejects theories that identify religious beliefs as proof of human irrationality, as mere indicators of normative judgments, or as self-deception. They are instead tokens of "a vision of life...more complex than some of our theories of truth and meaning can handle."[38] Judaism stands as a corrective to an approach to life that robs it of mystery, that explains all of experience, that avoids the unknown. While Rubenstein thinks that the Holocaust illuminates all existence with the cruel light of scientific knowledge, Hartman holds that post-Holocaust belief demonstrates the wonder that can still possess the human soul. Unlike Rubenstein he celebrates a combination of certainty and uncertainty as the true human condition.

The basic approaches to the uniqueness of the Holocaust correspond to specific views of Jewish chosenness. If the Holocaust is claimed as a unique theological challenge, then Jewish chosenness is understood in terms of a supernatural task and divine mission; if the uniqueness of the Holocaust is located in its historical role, then Jewish chosenness involves a specific historical task, a witness within history itself; when the uniqueness of the Holocaust is identified with its naturalistic refutation of religious ideology, then the meaning of Jewish identity becomes its fidelity to a truth beyond empirical evidence. Students of religions, however, learn to look more deeply and universally into the issues at hand. At first glance there are three views of the Holocaust and three understandings of Judaism. On closer inspection a more general pattern emerges. In every case catastrophe threatens to destroy a group's sense of self; that threat then engenders a response. In the first case the threat is answered by recourse to a theory of transcendence. Yes, members of the group in question suffer, that suffering, however, raises them to an exalted status. In the second case history seems to disconfirm the promises given to the group. The promises, however, are reinterpreted as imperatives: challenges to continued self-identification with the group confirm the nature of the religious commandment; self-identification as a member of the group is both the commandment and its reward. The final case suggests that identification with a despised group represents an ultimate defiance of rational categories. From empathy with the problems Jews face for continued belief in Judaism when confronted by the Holocaust, students can learn to utilize social scientific categories to make sense out of the data and can develop an intellectual humility when confronted by religious phenomena.

Students can generalize from the specific case of Jews responding to the challenge of the Holocaust to that of human beings in general when faced with historical evidence that disconfirms deeply held beliefs. Social scientists have devised a number of paradigms to help understand such reactions to disconfirmation which, when used with care, can help universalize the theologies studied. The variety of approaches indicated suggests that no simple answer will suffice; while any response can be reduced to a particular social or psychological cause, the fact of diverse responses precludes an uncritical acceptance of a univocal explanatory principle for all responses. A review of alternative scholarly interpretations of the data can help students sense some of the emotional as well as intellectual concerns stimulating theological investigation. Students learn an empathy with religious experience through universalizing findings without, at the same time, reducing the data to those findings.

Sociology offers one means of creating the needed empathy through the concept of cognitive dissonance that provides a bridge between the intellectual study of Holocaust theology and a more general human experience. The concept itself, while enjoying some sociological renown, may well be criticized as limited and simplistic.[39] The idea, at its most stark, suggests that when faced with evidence disconfirming deeply felt beliefs human beings are often plunged into confusion. They seek strategies for reconciling the challenged beliefs with the evidence at hand. A very popular and commonly recognized response to disconfirming evidence is that of changing the terms of the claim being made. The most direct assault made by disconfirming events is directed against Jewish self-understanding. Jews seeking to affirm their unique identity find it challenged by the vagaries of history.

Some theologians respond to that challenge by seeking to define the meaning of being a Jew. These thinkers emphasize that Jewish covenant refers to Jewish self-identification and often engage in a reinterpretation of traditional Jewish claims. Jewish chosenness, the task of affirming Jewish identity, becomes a reflex response to the disconfirmation of history.

In an interesting variation on this theme a recent study suggested how Emil Fackenheim and other contemporary Jewish theologians utilize the traditional technique of midrash for "biographic rehabilitation."[40] In the face of an untenable history, a "sinful" biography, Jews learn to reinterpret the past, to reconstruct its meaning in ways more profitable for life and survival. From studying this approach students should learn to understand how Emil Fackenheim reshapes Jewish tradition, how his use of Midrash and Jewish mysticism enables him to build new structures on an older foundation. They should also learn that this process did not begin with him and has a venerable pedigree. Finally they should learn to empathize with those who confront their inherited tradition in new, drastically altered circumstances. The point of their study should not be to debunk Fackenheim, but to catch a glimpse of how some people cope with realities that threaten to destroy their tradition, their system of values, and their sense of self. This understanding can become the basis for self-recognition; students may find in their own reactions to their studies, to their classmates, to their teachers, examples of the same process at work.

Naturally human beings employ more than one method for coping with cognitive dissonance. Not only do they redefine their beliefs, they also redefine reality itself. The deprivations of daily life find compensation in the transcendent realm.[41] The theory of deprivation as motivation for religious belief can be applied to those theologians who advocate Judaism as a means to transcendence. The transcendent task of Jewish peoplehood — understood as the result of a supernatural choice of the Jews — defuses the threat of disconfirming historical events — symbolized most dramatically by the Holocaust. The historical situation of the Jew hardly sustains belief in Jewish chosenness. By moving the relevant evidence from this historical realm to the transcendent, Jews find compensation for their suffering. When thinkers such as Eliezer Berkovits suggest that Israel's transcendent task places Jews in a unique category within the divine plan, they illustrate such a compensatory tendency. The chosenness of the Jewish people as witnesses to human transcendence compensates for their very real historical suffering and deprivation. By moving from promises of earthly reward to a theology of redemptive suffering for the sake of history and the earth, Jews can make sense out of their suffering and derive self-respect from it.

Once again it must be stressed that students should be discouraged from using this putative motivation as a basis for rejecting Berkovits' theology. Any human system of thought flows from a complex variety of sources and motivations; uncovering one such motivation should not discredit the system as a whole. On the other hand, students can be led to sympathize with and understand the impulse to leave behind the dross, painful facts of historical existence. Their own lives provide examples enough of discouraging incidents, of failures and setbacks, with which one can cope by seeing them as necessitated by a greater task.

Both strategies for coping with dissonance discussed so far — reinterpreting beliefs and compensating for disappointment — are susceptible to reductionism; taken as explanations for theories rather than as imaginative entries into the consciousness of believers, they trivialize theology by reducing it to one or another means of evading life's problems. The preceding discussion of Holocaust theology should leave students skeptical of any such reductionism. The sense of wonder, the willingness to suspend belief, and the inherent problems in every answer stand as witness to a complexity that cannot be explained away. It is at this point that Rabbi Nahman of Bratzlav's distinction between Jacob and Israel needs to be reinforced. The student struggles to understand, to master the material, to evoke the social and psychological motivations behind a religious tradition. At the same time, understanding a religion requires the ability to share the sense of wonder that the faithful often express. Critical analysis should prepare for, not replace, empathetic understanding. A hasidic tale born from the Holocaust tells how Yoav Kimmelman abandoned Jewish tradition after his liberation from the death camps. Finding no rationale for Jewish religious life unrefuted by the Holocaust, he rejected every precept of tradition. Once, however, he was induced to join a group at worship in order to fill out the required number for a prayer quorum. When forced by circumstances to read from the Torah scroll for the sake of others, he did so. At that point, he recounts, the letters of the Torah reached out to him. He gives no rational explanation for his return to tradition; he blames his renewed Jewishness on the inherent power of the Hebrew letters themselves.[42] Students of religion need not agree with Yoav Kimmelman about the inherent strength of the Hebrew alphabet to find in his story both an example of cognitive dissonance and an appreciation of the intangible power of religious experience. As a springboard for both intellectual analysis and the evocation of religious experience studies of post-Holocaust theology find an appropriate place in the humanistic studies of academe.

---

[1]Rabbi Nahman ben Simhah of Bratzlav, *Likutei MohHaRaN.* New York: Bratzlaver Foundation, 1969. 21:8.

[2]See Jacob Neusner, "Torah Today: *Lernen* and Learning" in Samuel C. Heilman's *People of the Book*, in his *Major Trends in Formative Judaism: Society and Symbol in Political Crisis.* Chico, California: Scholars Press, 1983, pp. 109-116.

[3]See the discussion of these and other views in Steven T. Katz, "Jewish Faith After the Holocaust, Four Approaches," in his *Post Holocaust Dialogues: Critical Studies in Modern Jewish Thought.* New York: New York University Press, 1983, pp. 141-173. The implication of Holocaust theology for the idea of Jewish uniqueness and chosenness is explored by Arnold M. Eisen in *The Chosen People in America: A Study of Jewish Religious Ideology*, pp. 149-170. Bloomington: Indiana University Press, 1985. See, in particular, his discussion of Emil Fackenheim, pp. 154ff., and of uniqueness, pp. 166-167.

[4]Jacob Neusner, "Jewish Students and the New Humanities," in his *New Humanities and Academic Disciples: The Case of Jewish Studies.* Madison, Wisconsin: University of Wisconsin Press, 1984, p. 171.

[5]See the theological discussion by Lewis S. Feuer, "The Reasoning of Holocaust Theology," *Judaism* 35 (1986): 198-210; compare Eisen as noted in footnote 3 and also David Polish, "Covenant — Jewish Universalism and Particularism," *Judaism* 34 (1985): 298-299.

[6]See Irving Greenberg and Alvin H. Rosenfeld, "Introduction," in their *Confronting the Holocaust: The Impact of Elie Wiesel.* Bloomington: Indiana University Press, 1978, p. xi, and compare Irving Greenberg, "Religious Values After the Holocaust, A Jewish View," in *Jews and Christians After the Holocaust,* edited by Abraham J. Peck. Philadelphia: Fortress Press, 1982, pp. 63-86 and his "Cloud of Smoke, Pillar of Fire: Judaism, Christianity, and Modernity After the Holocaust," in *Auschwitz: Beginning of a New Era?: Reflections on the Holocaust,* edited by Eva Fleischener. New York: Ktav Publishing House, 1977, pp. 7-55.

[7]See the discussions in Arthur H. Cohen, *The Tremendum: A Theological Interpretation of the Holocaust.* New York: Crossroad Press, 1981, and in Michael L. Morgan, "Jewish Ethics After the Holocaust," *Journal of Religious Ethics* 12:2 (1984), pp. 156-277.

[8]See Irving J. Rosenbaum, *The Holocaust and Halakhah.* New York: Ktav Publishing House, 1976.

[9]See Sidra Ezrahi, "The Holocaust Writer and the Lamentation Tradition: Responses to Catastrophe in Jewish Literature," in Rosenfeld and Greenberg, *Confronting the Holocaust,* pp. 133-149.

[10]See George M. Kren, "The Holocaust: Some Unresolved Issues." *Annals of Scholarship* III (1984) : 39-56.

[11]Steven Katz, "The Unique Intentionality of the Holocaust," in his *Post-Holocaust Dialogues,* pp. 287-317.

[12]Richard L. Rubenstein, *After Auschwitz: Radical Theology and Contemporary Judaism.* Indianapolis: Bobbs-Merrill Company, 1966, p. 238.

[13]See especially *ibid.,* pp. 47-58.

[14]*Ibid.,* p. 70.

[15]*Ibid.,* p. 188.

[16]Katz, *Post- Holocaust Dialogues,* pp. 186-191.

[17]*Ibid.,* p. 147.

[18]Eliezer Berkovits, *Faith After the Holocaust.* New York: Ktav Publishing House, 1973, p. 90.

[19]*Ibid.,* p. 36.

[20]*Ibid.,* p. 125.

[21]See Steven T. Katz, "Eliezer Berkovits's Post-Holocaust Jewish Theodicy," *Post-Holocaust Dialogues,* pp. 268-286.

[22]Michael Wyschogrod, *The Body of Faith: Judaism as Corporeal Election.* New York: Seabury Press, 1983, pp. 217-223.

[23]Richard L. Rubenstein, *The Cunning of History: The Holocaust and the American Future.* New York: Harper and Row, 1978, p. 6.

[24]See Richard L. Rubenstein, *The Age of Triage: Fear and Hope In an Overcrowded World.* Boston: Beacon Press, 1983; note especially pages 128-164.

[25]Rubenstein, *Cunning of History,* pp. 87, 90, 92.

[26]Emil L. Fackenheim, *God's Presence in History: Jewish Affirmations and Philosophical Reflections.* New York: New York University Press, (1970), p. 6; compare his *The Jewish Return into History: Reflections in the Age of Auschwitz and a New Jerusalem.* New York: Schocken Books, 1978.

[27]Fackenheim, *The Jewish Return into History,* pp. 89, 99.

[28]Emil L. Fackenheim, *To Mend the World: Foundations of Future Jewish Thought.* New York: Schocken Books, 1982, p. 303.

[29]See Katz, "Emil Fackenheim: On Jewish Life After Auschwitz," *Post Holocaust Dialogues,* 205-24.

[30]See Jacob Neusner, *Stranger at Home: "The Holocaust," Zionism and American Judaism,* Chicago: University of Chicago Press, 1981, pp. 62, 89.

[31]W. Gunther Plaut, *The Case for the Chosen People.* Garden City, New York: Doubleday and Company, 1965, p. 101.

[32]Richard L. Rubenstein, "Religion and History: Power, History and the Covenant at Sinai," in Jacob Neusner, editor, *Take Judaism for Example: Studies Toward the Comparison of Religions,* Chicago: University of Chicago Press, 1983, pp. 165-183.

[33]*Ibid.,* pp. 165, 176.

[34]See Michael Berenbaum, *The Vision of the Void: Theological Reflections on the Works of Elie Wiesel.* Middletown, Connecticut: Wesleyan University Press, 1979, pp. 160-171.

[35]Rubenstein, *After Auschwitz,* pp. 80-81.

[36]David Hartman, *A Living Covenant: The Innovative Spirit in Traditional Judaism.* New York: The Free Press, 1985, p. 203.

[37]*Ibid.,* p. 183.

[38]*Ibid.,* p. 203.

[39]On cognitive dissonance see Leon Festinger, *The Theory of Cognitive Dissonance.* Evanston: Row, Peterson, and Company, 1957; compare Jonathan Z. Smith in "No Need to Travel to the Indies: Judaism and The Study of Religion," in Neusner, *Take Judaism, For Example,* pp. 222-224.

[40]See Mordechai Rotenberg, "The 'Midrash' and Biographic Rehabilitation." *Journal for the Scientific Study of Religion* 25 (1986), pp. 41-55.

[41]See Charles Y. Glock, "The Role of Deprivation in the Origin and Evolution of Religious Groups," in Robert Lee and Martin Marty, editors, *Religion and Social Conflict.* New York: Oxford University Press, 1964, pp. 24-36.

[42]See Yaffa Eliach, *Hasidic Tales of the Holocaust.* New York: Oxford University Press, 1982, pp. 202-204.

Chapter Two

Teaching the Holocaust:
The Introductory Course

Zev Garber

The subject of the Holocaust *(Shoah)*, the destruction of the Jews of Europe, and others, at the hands of the Nazis and their collaborators, is one of great moral significance in the history of human civilization. Genocide, the obliteration of all members of a national group, is the most horrible of crimes and one of the most difficult to deal with in the field of social studies, revealing the human race in its worst perspective. After presenting a Course Outline (Part I), suggesting some direction for possible standards in an introductory (i.e., lower division) class in Holocaust Studies, this chapter will probe a number of theological responses to Judaism's perpetual dilemma and tragedy (Part II). The chapter concludes with comments on the Written Assignment, emphasizing a view of the Holocaust from a student's perspective (Part III).

I. Course Outline[1]

Purpose

A. To study the background, meaning, and practice of anti-Semitism.

B. To learn about, and analyze, the assault against the Jewish people waged by Nazi Germany between 1933 and 1945.

C. To consider, in their various implications, the results of the Holocaust in Europe and the rest of the world.

D. To examine how the Holocaust differs from other examples of Genocide.

E. To evaluate responses to the Holocaust from the following perspectives: Biblical, rabbinic, existentialist, literary, secular, Christian, etc.

F. Using the materials presented and discussed in this course, to consider whether a holocaust can happen again.

Objectives

A. To develop an awareness and understanding of racial and religious prejudice in the minds of our student body.

B. To clarify the unique nature of the Holocaust and its significance for Jews and non-Jews alike.

C.   To highlight the problems of Jewish-Christian relations and seek a better understanding of these problems.

D. To attempt to develop some insight into the motives and purposes of those responsible for the Holocaust.

E. To analyze the attitudes of the leaders of the democratic nations before, during, and after the event.

F. To consider the results of the Holocaust upon the Jewish communities in Europe and the rest of the world.

G. To study the relationship between the Holocaust and the attitude of world Jewry to Zionism and the concept of a Jewish state.

H. To study the Holocaust as background for the UN decision to support the reestablishment of a Jewish state.

I. To study the Holocaust as a factor in the national awakening of Soviet, Arab, and Ethiopian Jewry and as a force in the support of Israel by the Jewish people of the world.

J. To understand that the Holocaust and its aftermath represent a vast reservoir of feelings, thoughts, values, concerns, and actions preserved by victims and survivors in artifacts, signs, symbols, calendars, legal traditions, nature, history, persons, documents, and ideas.

K. To feel the personal and the group, the parochial and the universal, the legal and the mystic, the spiritual and secular dimensions of the Holocaust.

L. To discover the change and development of Jewish religious experiences and theology due to the Holocaust.

M. To develop a self-awareness in the relevancy and legitimacy of Holocaust Studies.

N. To acquire the basic vocabulary for study of, and oral and written presentations in, a basic introduction to Holocaust Studies.

O. To be made aware of the laborious work involved in a critical, disciplined study of origins, sources, and materials, and to obtain skills in oral and written presentations on a given problem in Holocaust Studies.

P. To enhance for the identifying Jewish student a self-concept and self-pride in the relevancy of Reb Dodye Feig's last charge in Spring, 1944, to his grandson, Elie Wiesel: "You are Jewish, your task is to remain Jewish"; to develop by all a sensitivity to the way of life, thought and faith of Holocaust victims and survivors.

Method

Analysis of historical experience; literature, newspapers, TV programs, movies, plays; linguistic and rhetorical evidence; reports from local survivors, liberators of the camps and their experiences; group discussions of this material and dilemmas involving choice; and written evaluation of quality and extent of thinking and reasoning demonstrated.

Topics

"Responses to the Holocaust" is a course designed to introduce students to Holocaust Studies. It is selective of, but influenced by, much that is written above. Suggested topics include:

Topic 1   *Defining the Subject*

Is the *Shoah* different only in degree, not in kind, from previous and contemporary acts of man's inhumanity to man?

Topic 2   *Understanding Anti-Semitism and the Nature of Prejudice*

The unifying link of anti-Semitism, yesterday, today and forever, is the "dislike of the unlike."

Topic 3   *The Biblical Response*

The structure and dimensions of the Bible have much to say about human suffering. What can Creation, *Akedah* ("Binding of Isaac"), "the Hidden Face," Test of Job, Valley of the Bones, Sinai and other biblical selections tell us about the silence of Auschwitz?

Topic 4   *The Rabbinic Response*

The Rabbis endured the destruction of the Temple and Jerusalem in the year 70 C.E. and the tragedy of the abortive revolution of Bar-Kochba in 135 C.E. How does the classical rabbinic mind respond to the Holocaust?

Topic 5   *The Mystical Response*

In every generation there have been those who contemplated the problem of evil in a context which, while not obliterating its reality, diminished its power by virtue of a cosmic or mythic perspective. What is a Kabbalistic response to the *Shoah?*

Topic 6   *The Hasidic Response*

Hutzpah and *Ahavat Yisrael* — courage bordering on the reckless and love of the Jewish people — are characteristics of the tales about R. Levi Yitzhak of Berditchev. How does Hasidic optimism prevail against impossible odds?

Topic 7   *The Literary Response*

The literary imagination does not merely deal with the Holocaust as *Historie:* controlled, objective facts of historiography. Rather it sees the Holocaust as *Geschichte:* a paradigm, above the historical; attached to history but by no means limited by it. What are some of the responses of the creative artist to "show what cannot be shown, to explain what is not to be explained, to recapture an experience that cannot be relived" (Elie Wiesel).

Topic 8   *Film Response*

In recent years, significant films on the destruction of European Jewry have been produced for television and theatre release, including *Sophie's Choice, Genocide, Night and Fog, Who Shall Live and Who Shall Die?, The Wall, Inside the Third Reich,*

Skokie, Shoah, Weapons of the Spirit, etc. How does filmography contribute to our understanding of the Holocaust?

Topic 9   *The Traditionalist Response*

Many notable rabbis endured the Nazi era. Leo Baeck commenced his study of *This People Israel* in Theresienstadt. Ignaz Maybaum contemplated the *Face of God After Auschwitz.* Ephraim Oshry wrote voluminous responsa in the ghetto of Kovno, in the midst of Lithuanian fascistic cruelty. Emil Fackenheim reaffirmed *God's Presence in History.* Eliezer Berkovits responded with *Faith After the Holocaust.* What is the quality of faith and Halachah in response to the Holocaust?

Topic 10   *The Humanist Response*

For the religious theist, responding to the Holocaust is intolerable. How could the Guardian of Israel have failed to intervene? For the religious humanist, responding is no less agonizing. How could Man have done it? What are the responses of Jewish humanists, e.g., Martin Buber, Mordecai Kaplan, Richard Rubenstein, and others, to the Holocaust?

Topic 11   *The Christian Response*

Whether or not we take the extreme view that there is a direct causal link between two thousand years of the "teaching of contempt" and the *Shoah,* Christian culpability for the Holocaust cannot be denied. What is the Christian response to the *Shoah?*

Topic 12   *The American Jewish Response*

How effective was the American Jewish response to the Holocaust? Why has a prestigious Holocaust fact-finding group, made up of prominent Jews and headed by former Supreme Court Justice

Arthur J. Goldburg, "split up in anger and dissension" *(New York Times,* week of January 2nd, 1983) while investigating the American Jewish community's response to the Nazi extermination program?

Topic 13   *A Dialogue Response*

For centuries the Jewish community in Poland prospered, but memories of the Holocaust have tainted the relationship. Can looking honestly at the past begin the healing? Or must it be resolved that anti-Jewish prejudice is very strong among Poles in and outside of Poland, the land of Auschwitz?

Topic 14   *An Israeli Response*

Never since 1948 has one campaign and one massacre — the summer of 1982 Peace for Galilee Operation and the Phalangist murder of Palestinian refugees at Sabra and Shatila on the eve of Rosh HaShannah 5743 (1982) — caused so many in and outside of Israel to raise the question of Israeliness and Jewishness, Israeli state and Jewish state, we are one versus we are many, and suggest that "Judaism does *not* need a political entity in the Land of Israel to survive worldwide. A State of Israel that can conspire with Phalangist thugs is *not* a proper response to the Holocaust. And we are *not* one people if that means condoning blatantly immoral Israeli acts" (Eugene B. Borowitz writing in *Sh'ma,* November 5, 1982.). Is Zionism deconstructed an effective response to living after the Holocaust in the land of Zion, which is continually existing under the threat of new tragedy?

Topic 15   *Can It Happen Again?*

The question of whether or not "it" could happen again depends for an answer upon our model of an "I and Thou" society. The major traits of Hitlerism — isolation, vilification, expulsion, slavery, and extermination — are not the will of heaven but the act of

Everyman, the bitter fruits of the freedom he has abused. Consequently, man can stamp out these evils if he so chooses by demonstrating intelligence, wisdom, and moral will. This then is the commandment after the Great Tragedy: All are made in the image of God, and the interdependence of humankind is the only rational road to survival.

Observations

A.   The subject of the Holocaust with its universal qualities of human nature is unusually broad. Can it encompass all within a course unit or even within one course alone?

B.   The effort would be not to cover *all* the history, sociology, psychology, philosophy, theology, etc., relating to the Holocaust. Rather, the introductory course provides a context for asking questions and providing a frame of reference through which insights would be provided and further applications would be suggested.

C.   The emphasis should be on tolerance, diversity, and understanding. It is important that an initial class in Holocaust (1)   represents a universal, humanistic approach; (2) focus on the student rather than the event, utilizing an interdisciplinary approach; and (3) endeavor to heighten the student's awareness of ethical themes and human tendencies toward prejudice.

D.   There are, of course, many examples of history's excesses being repeated and exceeded. However, there is also progress. We have changed. The United States of 1988 is significantly improved in many ways from the United States of 1958. The same can be said of Germany of January 1933 and West Germany today. Mankind is "improvable"; we must all be reminded of this and educators, above all, must believe it.

E.   The essence of Holocaust thinking is "dislike of the unlike." It is the recognition of this force in our lives that must be at the core of any Holocaust presentation. Also at the core must be the students' feelings and recognition of how this distrust of the unfamiliar often dominates our lives.

F.   The message of Holocaust for the generation after and for future generations is not survival alone. There is something more important than survival, and that is preventing moral bankruptcy. When Auschwitz (survival at any price) contends with Sinai (a moral standard), Sinai must prevail. Nazi Germany is an example of what can happen when Auschwitz prevails.

G.   A number of college, university, and seminary programs may lack the mechanism (staff, funding, sources, etc.) to offer a class in Holocaust Studies, or the subject matter may be limited in appeal. If so, themes from the Holocaust may be generalized within a topic such as "Studies in Human Values," "Civil Liberties," etc., or a one-day seminar can be given on "Moral Choices," etc. This should not be seen as *the* Holocaust course or symposium but should utilize the Holocaust experience and other comparable experiences as part of its context. The approach should be universal and interdisciplinary, and other examples of human "holocausts" should be included (American Indians, Armenians, etc.).

H.   Los Angeles Valley College, to my knowledge, is the only public community college which offers a class on the Holocaust on a regular/continuing basis. The method used is a "response" approach, which the writer feels is more effective than the "traditional" lecture presentation. There should be readings but not "difficult" ones, so that the students' feelings and, thus, interest should be engaged. The aim should be the transformation of values. A caring, understanding delivery is essential.

A final observation. A course such as "Teaching the Holocaust" is lacking in the social science curriculum of many State and University Schools of Education and many local teachers feel the lack of preparation to deal with the Holocaust issue knowledgeably and capably. This is especially true recently, given the publicity and success of Claude Lanzmann's film, *Shoah*, and a segment on the Holocaust as part of the very popular film series *Heritage: Civilization and the Jews*. Our attempt to discuss several approaches to Holocaust curricula represents an invitation to "learn Holocaust" for junior high or high school teachers in the social sciences and literature. Becoming capable in directing students through this historical, theological, and ethical problem will help one give a sharpened focus to the courses one teaches in the area.

II.   Thoughts on Theological Responses[2]

The theology from Jewish Tradition is that God is good, merciful, compassionate, omniscient, just, loving, etc. He is, above all, a redeemer God.

This theology has its origins in the Hebrew world view, conditioned by the wanderings of the Jewish people from place to place and environment to environment which, in contrast to the other cultures (stationary, static) of the Ancient Near East, sees God as incorporeal, ineffable and transcendent; neither restricted by nor embedded in nature; and whose fuller presence is immanent not in space but in time. Not cosmic phenomena but history is pregnant with meaning; history becomes a revelation of the divine will and the arena in which man acts out his responsibility in this encounter. In the Hebrew myth of origins, the interrelationship between history (Sinai) and nature (nomadic freedom) produces a religion (Judaism) which upholds man's power to reason and freedom of will. Without this power, man cannot be responsible for his actions and the fabric of society will dissolve into chaos and anarchy.

Yet traditional theology clashes with the Holocaust and all that the Jewish genocide of World War II represents: the silence of God and His nonintervention in the Nazi treatment of Europe's Jews and millions of non-Jews. How then to resolve the problem from a Jewish theological perspective?

Option One

If theology is tied to history then historical events can create and dislodge theological imperatives, doctrines and values. The historical events of the Exodus and Sinai created Jewish covenantal theology and its important corollary, the Jews are God's Chosen People.

From the earliest biblical record to the eve of Emancipation, Jews took seriously the belief that Israel is the firstborn of God (Exod. 4:22), a unique people, chosen from all the nations as God's treasured people (Deut 7:6; 14:2; 26:18, 19; 28:9, etc.), and singled out for the mission of bringing all life closer to the kinship of God on earth. The mission of Israel was cemented in a mutual covenant of love between God and Israel (Deut 6:5; 7:12, 13; 10:15, etc.). This belief helped compensate Jews for the hurts and humiliations of life in the exile.

Traditionally defined within and outside of the group as "a people that dwells alone, not reckoned among the nations" (Num 23:9), Jews sustained this role, for they believed they were part of "a kingdom of priests, and a holy nation" (Exod 19:6), divinely commissioned to advance the day that the "Lord shall be king over all the earth; on that day shall the Lord be one and His name be one" (Zech 14:9).

Enlightenment and Emancipation brought a radical departure from traditional thought patterns and aspirations. Emancipation destroyed the authority of the Jewish community and Enlightenment offered an ideological justification of surrendering the authority of Jewish tradition. The organic relationship of God-Torah-Israel (religion, culture, peoplehood) was now challenged by reason and egalitarianism. Count Clermont Tonnerre's declaration to the French National Assembly in 1791: "To the Jew as an individual — everything; to the Jew as a nation — nothing," and the positions adopted by the French Great Sanhedrin in February 1807, though bestowing equal civic rights upon Jews, began the process of redefining Jewish doctrines and values.

Unlike the national-religious identifying Jews in the Arab world and in Eastern Europe, Jews of the West now saw themselves as nationals of their countries of citizenship and worshippers in the "Mosaic faith." However, what Jews as individuals may have gained by Emancipation, Jews as a group lost. By leaving the ghetto and attaining the status of citizens, the Western European Jews loosened the bounds of Jewish group identity which in many cases led to total assimilation or worse, expulsion, conversion, and extermination.

Quantitatively and qualitatively, the Nazi near-complete destruction of European Jewry represents the worst threat to Judaism's self-definition: a people made in the image of Torah, commanded by God to bring mankind ever closer to the prophetic ideal of the Fatherhood of God and the brotherhood of man. In the radical theology of Richard Rubenstein, the Nazi Third Reich (history) successfully overthrows a mature Jewish acceptance of covenant belief (theology). The evil that the Nazis unleashed against the Jewish people requires as a basic minimum that the Jews give up the notion that they are the Chosen People of a personal deity. Simply put, how can God permit the senseless slaughter of millions of Jewish victims, including 1 1/2 million children? Likewise shocking and tragic is the biblical-rabbinic belief that Nazi bestiality is a just compensation for collective Jewish sins. Equally absurd are Deutero-Isaiah's "Servant of the Lord" and Judah HaLevi's "Israel is the heart of mankind" themes which proclaim vicarious suffering by Israel for the sins of mankind. That is to say, the Jewish people's continuous suffering and misery at the hands of the nations in different climes of geography and shifting sands of history are not because of its sins, but because of its role in history as teacher and witness to God's law of justice, freedom, love, and peace. Rubenstein rejects these positions because a) they suggest that God is a powerless God and b) if not omnipotent, He enters into a pact with Hitlerism which sanctions the destruction of the six million.

Other harmony theodicies are presented and rejected. 1) The view that universal harmony exists now but we cannot recognize it due to our finite knowledge. Basic to this position is that everything that happened and is happening was/is part of a harmonious, cosmic order of things. Since we cannot fathom the total harmony of the universe, we therefore believe that certain events of history are inherently evil. In the total view of things, however, evil together with good are necessary components to the total harmony . Thus the miracle of the rise of the State of Israel is seen as a proper adjustment to the tragic loss incurred by the Holocaust. 2) Universal harmony does not presently exist but continual tragedies in the present will ensure its futuristic appearance. Variations of this theodicy theme are that evil exists to test our faith and challenge our freedom; and the victims of Hitler's war against the Jews are rewarded on earth by the posthumous citizenship granted to them in the State of Israel (act of Knesset, 1953) and in heaven by the bliss of the world to come. 3) The classic Jewish eschatological teaching that in the end of days, the messianic future, all known evils of mankind will be abolished.

Objections to the harmony theories are two-fold: a) Do the extremities of present distress ethically command a future harmony?; and b) can we morally believe and rationally accept that the Holocaust kingdom of enslavement, torture, pain, murder and death is necessary for eternal harmony? Also, pietists reject harmony theodicy because it questions the power and goodness of God. Could God plan His perfect kingdom on earth without exacting such a heavy price for the sake of His name? If God could not, then why call Him omnipotent? If God could but chose not — the Holocaust, for example — then why call Him good? Thus we have come full circle with the initial statement of Rubenstein's death of God theology, i.e., letting go of traditional Judaism's doctrine of God for a new symbol of God's reality conducive to the lessons learned from Auschwitz. Rubenstein's Godless Judaism is aptly put this way:

The religious symbol and the God to whom the religious symbol points were never more meaningful than they are today. It is no accident that the twentieth century is characterized by theological excitement and renewal. Our myths and rituals have been stripped of their historic covering. No man can seriously pretend that the literal meanings given to our traditions before our time retain much authority today. Happily, in losing some of the old meanings we have also lost some of the old fears.

God stands before us no longer as the final censor but as the final reality before which and in terms of which all partial realities are to be measured.

The last paradox is that in time of the death of God we have begun a voyage of discovery wherein we may, hopefully, find the true God.

[R. Rubenstein, *After Auschwitz* (Indianapolis: The Bobbs-Merrill Co., 1966), p. 241]

Option Two

Recognizes that the Holocaust differs not in kind from the other destructive events of Jewish history; meaning, Jewish faith in the covenantal God of history persists before, during and after the Holocaust.

The current Nobel Peace Laureate, Elie Wiesel reviewed the T.V. mini-series *Holocaust* presented on NBC television in April 1978, and wrote in the *New York Times* of April 16, 1978, "The witness feels here duty bound to declare: What you have seen on your screen is not what happened *there*. You may think you know how the victims lived and died, but you do not. Auschwitz cannot be explained nor can it be visualized. Whether culmination or aberration of history, the Holocaust transcends history. Everything about it inspires fear and leads to despair: the dead are in possession of a secret that we, the living, are neither worthy of nor capable of recovering."

The experience of the Holocaust is truly *sui generis*. Nothing can compare to the enactment of absolute human and historical evil that attacked the Jewish people and other minorities during the 1930s and 1940s. Wiesel suggests that all speaking about the Holocaust is thoroughly inadequate and sacrilegious to its millions of victims. Perhaps silence is the only proper posture.

In *The Oath*, Wiesel talks about Moshe, mad survivor of a pogrom, who has sworn never to tell of his ordeal. He is bound to silence as a testimony on behalf of all humanity to life against death. To scream about radical dehumanization raises the possibility that the world is not listening or does not care, which would be a victory for absolute evil. Within the Jewish tradition humanity is made in the image of God, and must imitate God. God's silence during centuries of Jewish pogroms and destruction may be interpreted as God's presence in suffering.

Yet one person's loyalty to the memory of the dead becomes another person's reason to go on living. This is the position taken by the famed Nazi hunter Simon Wiesenthal in the *Sunflower* (New York: Schocken Books, 1977). In a sensitive and provocative story, Wiesenthal tells of a Nazi soldier, a participant in the slaughter of innocents, terrified of dying with the burden of his guilt. He asks forgiveness from a concentration camp Jew, one who knows well the meaning of the Jewish moral millenia, when victim-survivor shakes hands and makes peace with the enslaver-destroyer. The Jew, for his part, listens with horror and feeling to the German's deathbed wish, and walks quietly out of his presence without giving absolution.

The author's moral dilemma now becomes the reader's as the latter is asked to confront the question, "What would I (you) have done?" A collection of 32 responses, from Jew and non-Jew alike, then follows, providing the reader with a situation which s/he cannot help but enter, analyze, and internalize. The result is a significant post-Auschwitz reality, echoing in part Elie Wiesel's mystical insistence that the Holocaust

> can still be experienced... even now. Any Jew born before, during or after the Holocaust must enter it again in order to take it upon himself. We all stood at Sinai... we all heard the *Anochi* — "I am the Lord... " If this is true then we are also linked to Auschwitz. Those who were not there can discover it now. How? I do not know. But I know that it is possible ... One does not speak about the beginning of creation and the end-time ... Today we know that all roads and all words lead to

the Holocaust. What it was we may never know; but we must proclaim, at least, that it was, that it is.

[Hunter and Hunted: Human History of the Holocaust, selected and edited by Gerd Korman. New York: Viking Press, 1973, p. 19]

The neo-mystical Hasidic strain of Elie Wiesel emphasizes that the Holocaust must be understood first and foremost as a unique Jewish experience; and the universal ramifications of the *Shoah* flow from its Jewish specificity. On the other hand, Simon Wiesenthal suggests that the parochial aspects of the Jewish Destruction be externalized in the objective world in such a manner to enable the Gentiles to join Jews in questioning, reflecting, and answering to the phenomenon of the Holocaust.

This brings us to the theocentric religious philosophy of Emil Fackenheim, who combines metaphysics and epistemology to satisfy two responses to the Holocaust, one practical, the other, theoretical. Starting with *Quest for Past and Future* (Boston: Beacon Press, 1970), continued in *God's Presence in History: Jewish Affirmations and Philosophical Reflections* (New York: Harper Torchbooks, 1970), and elaborated in *The Jewish Return into History: Reflections in the Age of Auschwitz and a New Jerusalem* (New York: Schocken Books, 1978), Fackenheim continually maintains that Jewish existence and world consciousness must be reconsidered after the destruction of the Holocaust and the rebirth of the State of Israel. He insists that every survivor of the Holocaust is gradually becoming a paradigm for the entire Jewish people. The State of Israel is collectively what the survivor is individually — testimony in behalf of all mankind to life against death, to sanity against madness, to Jewish self-affirmation against every form of flight from it, and loyalty to the God of the Sinaitic Covenant against all lapses into paganism. These paradigms confront the contemporary Jewish crisis wherein some Jews seek a universalism in which to lose their "Jewishness." Regarding the uniqueness of Jewish existence as a scandal amounts to a victory of Auschwitz over Israel.

"Auschwitz" is defined by Fackenheim as the extreme technological dehumanization which, to varying degrees, may in the end become the fate of us all. Nazism was simply the machine radically dehumanized, and its millions of victims, its waste products. Nazism was a murder camp: a nihilistic, demonic celebration of death; destruction was its animating principle. This was revealed during the last stages of the war when Nazis continued to transport Jews to death camps, choosing not to utilize the trains for immediate and necessary military operations. Hatred of Jews was a Nazi obsession and transcended the drive for self-preservation. Similarly, at the end, in the Berlin bunker, Hitler and Goebbels expressed demonic satisfaction that their downfall might doom not only the enemies but the "master race." The point is illustrated by Hitler's bunker-order to flood the subways of Berlin in an attempt to stop the Russian advance, though it was clear that thousands of Germans seeking shelter from air attacks would perish in the action. As Hitler had said in 1944 to his associate Walter Schellenberg:

> In this war there can be no compromise. There is only victory to extinction. In case the German nation should fall it will perish... Yes, in that case let it perish, let it croak; for the best will have fallen, and the rest should give way to those who are biologically stronger. In case the German nation falls, the end of Germany will be cruel. However, it will have deserved nothing better.

> [W. Jochmann and B. Nellesson, *Adolf Hitler: Personlichkeit-Ideologie-Taktik* (Paderborn, 1960), pp. 34-35; cited by E. Fackenheim, "Concerning Authentic and Unauthentic Responses to the Holocaust," in *Holocaust and Genocide Studies, An International Journal,* p. 118 (Vol. 1, Number 1, 1986)]

The mind shrinks from systematic murder which serves no purpose beyond itself, for it is ultimately unintelligible. Yet in Nazism this unintelligibility was real.

In addition to the murder machine, the Nazis played with the living, who were enslaved, prostituted, beaten, dismembered, experimented on, and subjected to all conceivable forms of dehumanization. An example cited by Fackenheim to illustrate the diabolical scenario of Nazism is the "two work permits." By this scheme able-bodied Jews were permitted to "live" and permit one member of the family to live-work; the others the Jew consigned to death. Certainly this was not an efficient plan for laborers ("able-bodied only" was not the rule) but reflected the satirical humor of the Nazis: to rob the Jew of his/her soul and make him/her forever guilty of the murder of all his/her family (mother, father, brother, sisters, children) save one.

Despite even this, the Jew rejected suicide, rejected the relief of insanity, preserved the tie with his/her God and remained a witness against darkness in an age of darkness, a witness whose like the world had not seen before. How else to explain the last and lasting testimony of many Jewish martyrs in the Nazi murder machine as they were led to the gas chambers and crematoria. They sang the 12th article of the Maimonidean Creed, belief in the messianic age to come, and by this, in contrast to a depraved world that failed them, proclaimed hope in an improved humanity as the divine goal of history.

Notwithstanding this heroism and humanism of the Jew, there is in the world today an identity crisis for many Jews who elect freedom from and not of Judaism. To surrender one's Judaism is a victory for Hitler. For a post-Holocaust Jew to act as though his Jewishness required justification is to allow for the possibility that none might be found. This is an act of betrayal, betrayal of the world as well as the Jewish people. Thus Fackenheim has suggested that though God was utterly silent, the Jews had heard a "commanding voice" come from Auschwitz, "The 614th Commandment": Jews must survive as Jews and under no circumstances must there be posthumous victories granted Hitler. If there is a Jewish hero today, it is s/he who confronts the demons of Auschwitz and defies them; the Jew who has defied equally anti-Semitism and self-hatred. It is the Jew at home in his/her own skin and at peace with his/her Jewish identity and destiny. It is the Jew who is whole, complete, *shalem*.

How is the Jew to aspire to and to acquire authenticity? Fackenheim's definitive statement is found in *To Mend the World: Foundations of Future Jewish Thought* (New York: Schocken Books 1982). The first part of the work explores the options in Jewish thought caused by modernity and reflected in the writings of Spinoza and Rosenzweig. According to Fackenheim, the holocaustal experience in history makes folly Spinoza's absolute of reason and Rosenzweig's Jewish antihistoricisms. Here, as found in earlier writings, he insistently argues that the Auschwitz experience cannot be compared to anything. One who minimalizes, universalizes, parochializes, assimilates, hyphenates, etc., Holocaust to any human experience is committing the unpardonable *pesha'*, ultimate rebellion against God and man. The uniqueness of Holocaust, the only example of absolute *novum*/evil in history, renders absurd all words, ideas, apologies, and actions derived therefrom. If rational thinking is rendered bankrupt in the post-Holocaust age, we give life and acts priority in the now Jewish existence. He posits that Jewish survival after Auschwitz cannot be regarded in mere physical terms. The individual and collective survival of Jews has become a religious commandment, which is seen and learned from the everday acts nurtured in the way of Torah (*tikkun*) in the death camps. The standard for millions of Jews trapped in Hitler's inferno — religious and secular alike — was not nihilism nor despair nor suicide but the sanctification of the deeds of everyday. The constant in the shifting sands of the Holocaust kingdom was the belief (for many) and the practice of Judaism to the extent possible under the most horrendous circumstances. It now challenges all Jews to act Jewishly, morally, ethically, and ritually.

In conclusion, it may be said that Fackenheim's lessons from the Holocaust are summarized in the divine imperative from the ashes, his often quoted 614th Commandment: no posthumous victories to Hitlerism; Jews must never forget the sacrifices and acts done by and to their holy martyrs; they must not despair of God, Torah, and Israel lest Judaism perish; and Judaism must be understood in its *own* self-hood, i.e., Jews are a kingdom of priests, and a holy nation (Exod 19:6), witnesses of God in the world (cf. Isaiah 43:10). Genuine Jewishness is living Jewishly, i.e., testifying against idolizing nature and paganism; it is to proclaim the transnatural God whose operative commandment is to mend the world (*tikkun 'olam*). [The phrase is associated with the 16th century kabbalist, Isaac Luria, but its original thought is biblical, cf. *na'aseh venishma'*, Exod 24:7]

Option Three

This option finds fault with Options One and Two, and charts its own course between the Death of God agnosticism of Richard Rubenstein and the existentialist thought of Elie Wiesel and Emil Fackenheim on the meaning of a post-Holocaust Jewish future. It asks of Rubenstein, if Holy Nothingness and Death are lord of us all and if man, responsible only to himself and his progeny, exists by his own resources (wit and animalistic instinct to survive as a group, people, race) then what constraints are there to distinguish between good and bad, murdered and murderer, victim and victimizer? To paraphrase Hannah Arendt's *Banality of Evil* thesis, if everyone, under particular historical conditions, is potentially guilty of murder then no one is actually guilty of this heinous crime or its facsimile. But there is something more important than survival, and that is preventing moral bankruptcy. When Auschwitz (survival at any cost) contends with Sinai (the Jewish moral standard) then Sinai must prevail. Cyanide succeeded because Sinai was removed from the thoughts and actions of man. In his *Morality and Eros* (New York: McGraw-Hill, 1970) and *The Cunning of History: The Holocaust and the American Future* (New York: Harper and Row, 1975), Rubenstein uses secular, moral imperatives to explain the symbolism of evil in the Western tradition, but this is not an effective response to the Holocaust, which saw Jews exterminated as Jews. Elie Wiesel's words are instructive:

> ... Listen to such *hutzpah*: first they make us suffer, and now they resent it when we acknowledge the suffering as ours... And why take away from the dead the only thing left to them — their Jewishness and their uniqueness? Don't they deserve at least that?

> (cited in K. Gorman, *loc. cit.*]

Recognition of this anger coupled with the lessons that we must not trivialize, minimize, compromise nor wrongly universalize the Holocaust are at the core of a theistic response (Option Two) to the Great Destruction. The Holocaust was unique. Its dead and maimed were not the victims of war and famine or politics in the normal sense. The Nazi bureaucratic murder machine claimed victims of all European nationalities, but Jews were the people for whom it was designed, the only people whose right to live was denied in principle. Thus Wiesel's above cited admonition and Fackenheim's suggested truism, the Holocaust claims another victim whenever a Jew doubts his Jewishness. Conversely, when a Jew lives up to Judaism's creeds and deeds, s/he defeats Hitlerism and carries out the legacy of the dead: "You are Jewish, your task is to remain Jewish" (Elie Wiesel's grandfather, Reb Dodye Feig's last charge to his grandson in Spring, 1944).

But the issue is more complicated than some theists are willing to admit. We want to make two observations. First, must we understand that the mandate for the present and future was forged in the crucible of the crematorium? No intelligent person can deny the heroism and the heroic acts of Jewish martyrs done in the shadow of Auschwitz; they serve as the exemplar of *Kiddush Ha-Shem*. But is this a healthy model for "sanctify Thy name in the presence of all men" (from the morning service)? Second, the holocaustal experience has shown and today's headlines verify that adherence to God's moral law can bring destruction and evil in its path. In September, 1986, two masked gunmen stormed into one of Istanbul's oldest synagogues (Neve Shalom Synagogue) during a Sabbath service and sprayed automatic weapon fire on the worshippers, killing 21 Jews and burning the bodies with gasoline before blowing themselves up. True, the evil deed of the murderers caused their own deaths, but how to explain the fright, suffering and death brought upon the victims?

Traditionally, an answer to this question may be cultivated from the biblical book of Job. The prologue to Job suggests a question: will the righteous Job, once deprived of the good things of life, abandon and curse his God? In 44 chapters of narrative and discussion, Job does not because he is righteous and his cry for justice is vindicated at the end. The author(s) of Job ask, if God is just and in control of life, if righteousness is rewarded and wrongdoing punished, then why does the righteous Job suffer horrendous misfortune? The traditional answers of Job's friends [Eliphaz: no man could achieve perfection and the punishment was a chastening for Job's own good; Bildad: suffering is rooted in human fallibility; Zophar: Job's challenging the justice of his suffering was akin to blasphemy; Elihu: God leads man to the brink of death only to rescue him so that man might forever be grateful in blessing God the redeemer] are inadequate and ultimately God declares them to be inaccurate (Job 42:7-8). Job's challenge is not to God but to popular theology. He stubbornly insists on his innocence, and so represents the refusal of Judaism to account for evil entirely as punishment for sins. Similarly, the trial and tribulations of millions and the spilled blood of innocent victims suggest that evil is unleashed by man, that it is not of God and, in the end, justice and righteousness will prevail.

The Jobian message that righteous man and righteous nation must in moments of dark despair live in unconditional trust with God is a central motif in the writings of contemporary Jewish theists. But the neo-Orthodox Jewish thinker, Irving Greenberg, insists that the biblical-rabbinic categories of redeeming faith are no longer valid due to the long history of Jewish pain, especially the quintessential expression of that pain, the Holocaust. After Auschwitz, he declares, we live not in ever-present faith but in "moments of faith, moments when Redeemer and vision of redemption are present, interspersed with times when the flames and smoke of the burning children blot out faith — though it flickers again" ["Cloud of Smoke, Pillar of Fire: Judaism, Christianity and Modernity after the Holocaust," in Eva Fleischner, editor, *Auschwitz: Beginning of a New Era? Reflections on the Holocaust*

(New York: Ktav, 1977, p.27)]. Greenberg's limited God theodicy argues that God is perhaps not all powerful as traditional theistic belief maintains, but He is limited in power.

How so? In the classical Jewish myth of origins, God is portrayed as an absolute, pure existence, unqualified and ineffable, by whose will the world was created. History, not cosmic phenomena, becomes the vehicle of the revelation of God's word to man. Man's dialogue with God began at creation, was ratified at Sinai, challenged at Auschwitz, and redeemed in the survival of Israel. The record of coming to grips with the dialogue in every age since Sinai and the emphasis on action rather than creed as the primary religious expression is Halachah, a pan-Judaic movement that subscribes to set systems of methodology and interpretation, whose insights, written and oral, are authoritative but never final in Jewish teaching and law. Greenberg's writings on religious problems are illustrative of the Halachic commitment to tradition through change in accordance with concessions of history. However, his chapters dealing with theodicean issues of faith precipitated by the Holocaust are more indebted to rabbinic midrash than rabbinic Halachah. Midrash means biblical inquiry; it is an attempt to explain the biblical text in as many ways as seemed possible to the inquiring mind of the Jewish sage. Thus midrash has a variety of interpretations and includes exegesis of Scriptures, sermons, and nonlegal discussions. The genius of midrash lies in its ethical and hermeneutical pronouncements peppered with philosophical wisdom and a vast amount of folk tradition. In summation, when Greenberg writes on holocaustal issues, he utilizes the traditional midrashic line of communication between God and Israel. This working principle is neither absolute nor relative but in a continuous, dynamic state of flux. His theology, therefore, is process theology, which by its very nature reveals a certain self-limitation, so chosen, on the part of an originally omnipotent God *(simsum)*.

Central to Greenberg's thinking on the Holocaust are his thoughts on the role of Israel's covenant and the nature of Israel's chosenness. In midrashic language, God and Israel enter into a partnership at Sinai; God promises protection for the Jews proportional to the Jews' promise of doing commandments *(na'aseh venishmna*, Exod 24:7). In the course of history both covenant partners reneged on their word: Israel collectively does not live up to its obligatory covenant, and God, in every generation, withdraws further and further from Jewish destiny. The cutting edge is the Holocaust, the murderous death of millions coupled with the horrific absence of God, which proclaims that a new age has begun: religionless Judaism. Greenberg holds that in the perspective of what the Holocaust presents, the self-definition of the Jew and his covenant with God must be totally revised, reevaluated and renegotiated. Greenberg is saying that the imposed covenant of Sinai is no longer valid after Auschwitz. How can it be otherwise? It has failed. Centuries of persecution have chipped away at its words and the flames of the Holocaust have obliterated its authoritative voice. Yet, in its place, a new covenant has arisen by virtue of the actions of survivors and other Jews who choose not to assimilate but to survive as a people. Jewish survival is the central tenet of the new voluntary covenant; all the rest, including performance of Jewish law, though important, is commentary.

The peculiar character of Greenberg's theology is his belief that God's original will for the Jews has been and remains operative. He is not willing to sacrifice the unity of Judaism any more than the unity of God Himself. But he acknowledges that the unity of Judaism is different from what one may have thought it to be. His maverick covenant theology emphasizes the transcendence of God so that the Jews, in some type of dialogical process with God/covenant, come into independence and maturity. This represents a beginning to reconstruct Jewish thought from the ashes of Auschwitz and to redirect meaningful Jewish living in a post-Auschwitz age. This plays havoc with the orthodoxy of many religious people who insist that their religious forms are equal to the ultimate reality and that the sacred tenets of Judaism, e.g., God gave an obligatory Torah to follow at Sinai, were, are, and will always be. Greenberg's orthodoxy is otherwise. He takes seriously the rabbinic suggestion that the Torah speaks in the language of man (TB Berachot 32B), and that Torah after Sinai is not in heaven (TB Bava Metzia 59A-B), and he reasons that an authentic religious person does not place his/her hope in religious language and symbols which represent the ultimate but in the ultimate itself. God is what He is; His plan for Israel is what it is. What is being altered by Greenberg is our understanding of God and His design as expressed in age-old sancta, dogma, doctrine, etc. Judaism's ultimate challenge is to survive, but the language of survival must reflect contemporary Jewish reality. Thus Voluntary Covenant and not Imposed Covenant since today's religionless Jew, according to Greenberg, lives Judaism either by being or in the process of becoming, and not by doing traditional beliefs.

Peoplehood and a contracting deity, parochialism and sheer existence as a Jew are consistent leitmotifs in the covenant theology of Irving Greenberg. But others say that today's Jewish survivalist is not concerned with creating methodologies in thinking about Judaism but rather in doing Judaism; in producing philosophies cut off from belief; is concerned disproportionately with emphasizing Jewish ethnicity over Jewish morality and ritual. One generation after the rebirth of the State of Israel and the Holocaust, s/he is asking searching questions of who God is, and what God wants, perhaps even needs of him/her as a Jew. S/he is finding meaningful answers in Jewish tradition, ethnicity, and in the performance of (obligatory) Halachah and mitzvah. S/he chooses to live Jewishly and not merely survive as a Jew. By returning home to Sinai, s/he exposes the secularism of today's religionless Jew as a deceptive disguise for a displaced commitment to Israel's covenant. Clearly, a new conservatism in modern Judaism prevails in rite and rights, *Zeitgeist* and timelessness, but it is forged in modern thought patterns of rationalism, democracy, pluralism, and humanism. Furthermore, Greenberg's process midrash relates directly to the Bible and offers existential observations *juxtaposed* to the text which at times are inconsistent with the accepted classical Jewish interpretations found in Midrash (collections of accepted rabbinical pronouncements intimately related to Scriptures), Talmud, or Codes. Classical Jewish faith affirms unhesitatingly the belief that God fulfills His promises (of redemption, for example) even though the overt evidence seems to indicate the opposite. Holocaust, therefore, is not the culmination of the eclipse of God but the supreme test of Israel's faith, thereby strengthening the faith by the heroic exercise of it. It is the celebration of the covenant at Sinai and not its demise.

Christian Response

Readers of F. Littell's *The Crucifixion of the Jews* (Harper and Row, 1975), A. Davies' *Antisemitism and the Foundations of Christianity* (Paulist, 1979), C. Thoma's *A Christian Theology of Judaism* (Paulist, 1980), E. Borowitz' *Contemporary Christologies: A Jewish Response* (Paulist, 1980), and R. Ruether's hard-hitting *Faith and Fratricide* (Seabury, 1974) will sense that there are four major emphases in a Christian response to the Holocaust. First, the need to expose the anti-Jewish bias of *contra-Judaeos* found at the crossroads of Christian preaching and teaching. By stressing the importance of the study of Judaism on its own terms, Christian scholars are able to assess correctly the positive value of Jewish cult, rite, and law on the nascent church and on the later history of Christianity. For example, the Pharisees, unjustly maligned in the New Testament and in the writings of the Church Fathers, have been misunderstood and damned by centuries of Christian laity and scholars. This image has only recently been corrected when George Foote Moore, Reinhold Niebuhr, Jules Isaac, James Parkes, and others exposed the church's prejudicial understanding of apocalyptic-Pharisaic-eschatological Rabbinic Judaism as bad theology and poor historical interpretation, which in turn led to the shameful "teaching of contempt" Christians have projected on the Jews for the past two millennia across all denominational barriers.

Second, whether or not there is a direct link between two thousand years of Christian supersession teaching and the Holocaust, Christian culpability in the near total destruction of European Jewry cannot be denied. The words of Franklin H. Littell are instructive and to the point:

> Certain traditional Christian teachings of alienation and hatred must be eliminated. More important and more difficult by far, some negative teachings deeply rooted in traditional religious and cultural antisemitism must be changed.

> Although Christian teaching carried a heavy overload of theological antisemitism, consent to mass murder of the Jews — let alone approval of it — was contrary to doctrinal statement, confessions of faith, and the ordination vows of the clergy. The trouble was that under pressure most of the clergy buckled, and the masses of the baptized simply ran with the murderous mob. Poorly trained and poorly led, they were unable to distinguish between Christian verities and Nazi slogans, between Christian spirituality and boundless Nazi enthusiasm *(Geistigkeit)*.

> The correction of bad teaching, therefore, must be paralleled by the recovery of a Christian discipline and style of life communicating credibility and worthy of the Name. The work of reconstruction has already begun a covenant fellowship, brotherhood movements, communities like *Nes Ammim* in Israel, seminary courses on the Holocaust and/or Christian/Jewish relations — and in such official proclamations as that of the Synod of the Protestant Church of the Rhineland (January, 1980).

Before the Third Reich, the German churches had largely accommodated to German values, German definitions and German ambitions. *Voelkische Kulturreligion* was far stronger in the parishes, both Protestant and Roman Catholic, than the law of Christ and the ecumenical Gospel. An important lesson of the Holocaust for Christians parallels a vital lesson for Jews: an easy assimilation to the predominant culture — whether *das deutsche Volkswesen* or "the American Way of Life" — is the path to spiritual and physical death.

[F. H. Littell, "Basic Lessons of the Holocaust" from National Institute on the Holocaust (N.I.H.) Notebook: November 1983, pp. 1-2]

We have quoted liberally from Littell's "Notes" in order to give the reader unfamiliar with his rhetoric a sense of his direction, peppery language, and strong condemnation of coreligionists who violated and violate the basic premises of Christianity's pristine origins. For Littell and other like-minded Christian theologians reflecting on the Holocaust, e.g., John T. Pawlikowski, Alice L. and A. Roy Eckardt, Robert McAfee Brown, *et. al.*, a proper Christian response to the catastrophe is a full and affirmative statement of Christian fraternity with the Jewish people.

Third, essays and books by Eugene Fisher, Krister Stendahl and Paul M. van Buren take seriously Jews as God's ongoing covenantal people whom Christians in their understanding of God's Word in Scriptures and tradition are morally bound to defend and support. Judaism and Christianity, the former seen as "the Chosen People" and the latter defined as "the Chosen Church," are viewed as counter-cultural; both, to the extent that the community is faithful to its divine calling, are swimming against the stream but knowing full well that their separate but equal efforts will one day help usher in a blissful age of peace and security for all mankind.

Fourth, the impressiveness of recent Christian expression of, on and with the Jewish people in the form of official pronouncements by world church bodies. For example, the recent Catholic publications, *Guidelines for Catholic-Jewish Relations* [Washington, D.C.,: Secretariat for Catholic-Jewish Relations, National Conference of Catholic Bishops, 1985] and *Notes on the Correct Way to Present Jews and Judaism in Preaching and Catechesis of the*

Roman Catholic Church, with a Note for the Preparation of the Document [Vatican City: Commission for Religious Relations with the Jews, 1985], distributed in this country by the United States Catholic Conference, are an important step forward to correct the "injustices directed against the Jews at any time from any source," and a significant contribution to ongoing Jewish-Christian dialogue. Inspired by the Second Vatican Council Declaration *Nostra Aetate* (1965) and subsequent official Catholic pronouncements on the Jewish people, the pamphlets' avowed purpose is to encourage the importance of Jewish sources (Scriptures, rabbinics, philosophy, mysticism, Zionism) for Christianity today as in the past. The Christian faithful is challenged to rediscover the Jewish roots of his/her faith, which is deep and far reaching, and to live the *imitatio Christi* without anti-Semitism. When relevant in Christian preaching and catechesis, Jewish understanding, belief and practice are to be presented without polemics, politics and paternalism. By encouraging lessons learned from the Holocaust and the reality of the State of Israel, the documents correct an ambivalent teaching about the Jews in *Nostra Aetate*, 4: "the Jews remain most dear to God because of their fathers" (suggesting past but not present validity) but "He does not repent of the gifts He makes nor of the calls He issues" (suggesting continual validity).

For many (Jews and Christians) the pamphlets will be met with mixed emotions: respect for the sincerity of the Conference and Commission to eliminate misrepresentation of the Jews (cursed; deicide; conversion) and "to strive to learn by what essential traits the Jews define themselves," but disappointment with denominationally oriented language, which reveals a marred knowledge of Judaism. To say, for example, the establishment of the State of Israel is not "in itself religious" is irritating. To apologize in the *Notes* for the continual use of the term *Old Testament* (" 'old' does not mean 'out of date' or 'outworn' ") and to report the "sad fact" that most Jews did/do not accept for themselves the salvific role of Jesus in history (but proclaim so for Christians, respecting th teaching of classical Christianity, which joins belief and salvation) is disturbing. Also controversial and seen as dangerous by many Jews is the *Guidelines* recognition and tacit support of interreligious marriages. Correction of these misgivings in future declarations will command respect from all who take seriously the interdependence of Judaism and Christianity.

III. The Written Assignment

Of the many aspects of the learning process, perhaps the most frustrating is the cross purpose of students and professors. The professor's lectures are for the most part not understood, and his/her intelligence is further insulted by the students' seeming anti-intellectualism. The professor blames his/her failure on his/her young charges. S/he vents dissatisfaction by "popping" quizzes, assigning busy work, asking trick questions on exams, and springing a host of other tricks which only his/her mind can issue. Students become apathetic, turn off, and consider class attendance a punishing jail sentence.

In reality, the problem grows out of the diversified roles played by the professor and the student. The professor sees him/herself as a knowledge dispenser, developing a new generation of scholars who share his/her philosophy and concerns, and are willing to spend infinite hours reading, researching, writing, and discussing the problems at hand. The average student does not embrace the scholarly way defined by the professor. S/he is a tradesman interested only in the bare essentials of the job: how, when, where, what is required of him/her to obtain his/her grade. S/he couldn't care less about schools of thought, philosophy, sociology, history, literary analysis, and theoretical abstractions; s/he is interested only in the here and now.

The nature of a college program, introductory classes in particular, is such that a professor does not trust his/her student and a student does not trust his/her professor. Students are regimented through a structured program which allots them little time to reflect, think, mature. No wonder passivity and inertia set in. To rectify this problem the professor could help his student understand the beauty of being a professional and not a mere worker. One of the ways in which this can be done is to change the nature of the Written Assignment. In place of hourly examinations, mid-terms, and finals, which often represent the scribbled jottings derived from a lecture hour, there can be the book review, article review, journal, and synthesizing project. The major pedagogical principle gained is that the students will learn better and appreciate more their understanding of the subject matter if they are actively involved in learning rather than being passively taught.

Book Review

There are two types of book reviews, "scholarly" and "popular."

A.   Scholarly Text

The review is brief and direct. About four double-spaced typewritten sheets in proper length. An essay style and not a question-and-answer format is suggested. The structure of the paper is constructed from the viewpoint of writing college quality work, using Kate L. Turabian's *A Manual for Writers of Term Papers* or the *MLA Style Sheet*.

The goals of the student's report are to demonstrate to the professor that s/he has read the book, has understood why it was written, and has related it consciously to the material presented in the lectures. In addition to writing on the main thesis of the book, the student discusses language and terminology used, the background presupposed in the reader, whether the material is presented in a predominantly explanatory or a predominantly argumentative form, etc. S/he is asked, finally, to discuss how the book affected his/her previous notions of the particular aspect or aspects of Holocaust with which it deals.

B.   Novel and Biography

An interesting way for a student to learn about Holocaust ideas, values, and history is through fiction and/or biography which shift the course curriculum from subject matter to activity, from subjects of study to experience. The reading of Holocaust novels and biographies is a Holocaust happening and is more popular than historical reading in fashioning meaningful, lasting ties to an awareness of Holocaust in Jewish and world history and culture. A good story provides a more vivid and intimate insight into life than does a textbook. A textbook must generalize but a story makes the subject matter more particular and personal. In addition, the novelist and/or biographer give a different dimension to what Holocaust and Final Solution mean than is found in the "heavy" findings of a theologian, historian, social scientist, etc.

An impressionistic essay is suitable for a novel or biography review. By "impressionistic" is meant: students' reactions, feelings about the book, how s/he experienced the book, any questions it may have raised in his/her mind to the central themes of the course, etc. The student may also approach the review by extracting those significant facts or observations related to aspects of Holocaust which the book purports to cover. Points to look for include: what can we learn from the author's life?; is his/her style distinctive?; age and type of Jew portrayed; historical background and implications of the story; changes in the religious life of the Jew caused by knowledge of the Final Solution; growing knowledge about the Holocaust and Jewish destiny in Europe, Israel, America, etc.; the Jewish minority in an overwhelming gentile environment; what message is there for the continuation of Jewish life, etc.

Article Review

An article review is short; approximate length is 2-3 pages. The review should contain (1) author, title of article, reference; (2) summary of main points of article; (3) statement of whether the article is empirical, analytical, or both.

A. If the article is empirical, what hypothesis does the article support? Can the empirical article be related to a more general statement?

B. If the article is analytical, describe the analysis. Does the analysis suggest hypotheses which could be tested?;

(4) the student's evaluation of the article.

Articles are selected from assigned articles or readings in the course outline or from relevant periodical literature on the subject matter.

Journal

The journal is intended to combine aspects of the formal essay with that of a diary. The entries are short exercises, 5 typewritten double-spaced pages are recommended, though there is no limitation on length. Thoughts associated with the lecture topics are written up as a journal entry and turned in during the class session at which the related topic is discussed. Thoughts and activities are many and varied, and provide an opportunity for the student to develop critical methodology and preserve or alter deep-seated commitments in his/her view of self, society, and history in light of the Holocaust.

Synthesizing Project

A synthesizing project permits a direct encounter of student with material and can serve as an option or alternative to a writing-only presentation. The depth, variety, nature, and breadth of the Holocaust are forcibly brought home if the student pursues his/her own special academic preference (e.g., art, music, religion, psychology, literature, sociology, etc.) in whatever media s/he deems most productive (short story, collage, audio-visual, etc.) in showing the relationship between these disciplines and some aspect of Holocaust Studies. If done properly, a synthesizing project can weave a thread of continuity into complex and diversified material, and make the course content more particular and personal. The project is clearly intended not only to synthesize the different motifs within the course but to provide a goal for the students from the very day it is appropriately introduced.

Role-Playing, Problem Solving

A writing exercise, old in years but recently discovered, designed to enhance a learning process is role-playing or problem solving. This method takes seriously the four sequential steps of learning: confrontation, analysis, interaction, and internalization.

Role-playing or problem solving offers a number of positive claims seldom found by other teaching strategies. It deals with real life situations and not theoretical abstractions; it enables the student to confront deep philosophical ideas in remarkable simplicity and convincing application; more cognitive avenues of knowledge are relied upon by this method than any other; students develop sensitivity and learn empathy when they interpret the different roles often in conflict one with another, of a problem solving exercise; finally, values, commitments, aspirations, etc., can be discovered or developed or changed when a student is engaged in ethical decision making and moral development, the twin pillars of a role-playing sequence.

Problem solving activities can be enacted in almost every phase of Holocaust Studies, from the Nazi-Jew-Church confrontation in the rise of the Third Reich to the different post-Auschwitz theologies and histories, from learning about the outlook and mentality of European Jewry in the inter-war years to understanding Israelis, 1948-present, and with all responses ever since Sinai to choose life and not death or stagnation.

[1]My views on what can and cannot be obtainable in teaching an initial class in Holocaust Studies are drawn from teaching experiences in a variety of educational settings: A one-day seminar, University of California at Riverside; adult education, University of Judaism; community college, Los Angeles Valley College; and a state university, University of Utah. In spring, 1988, I will be offering Holocaust and Zionism within a singular class setting at UCR.

[2]This section is a presentation of mind sets associated with Response topics 9, 10, and 11 (above). A part of its content is stimulated by Eugene B. Borowitz' fine chapter on "Confronting the Holocaust," in his *Choices in Modern Jewish Thought* (New York: Behrman House, 1983; pp. 185-217).

Chapter Three

Asking the Questions: Background and Recommendations for Holocaust Study

Richard Libowitz

The past decade has witnessed the dramatic growth of interest in the Holocaust (*Shoah*). Survivors — many of whom chose to remain silent for decades — now feel an urgency to tell their stories and have discovered audiences eager to hear them. Memorials to the "six million" have been raised in many communities; paintings, sculptures, musical compositions, and dances have been created and dedicated to the victims. Holocaust commemoration day, Yom HaShoah, is observed by an increasing number of Jews and Christians within their respective houses of worship and in joint public gatherings, while the topic of the Holocaust has become a commonplace agenda item for programs of interfaith conversation.

Nowhere has interest in the Holocaust grown more keenly than on American college campuses, where courses pertaining to the *Shoah* have come to be recognized as integral components of Jewish Studies programs to the extent that, on the undergraduate level, such classes are often the first to reach their enrollment maxima. That contemporary college students should now flock to these courses and programs, while taking their presence on campus for granted, is both a measure of the shortness of any collective student memory and a reflection of the radical flourishing of topics relevant to Jews and Judaism over the most recent two decades.

Background to Jewish Studies

For nearly twenty years following the end of World War II, the majority of American colleges and universities maintained an antipathy for Jews and an extremely truncated view of Judaism. A number of institutions continued the quota systems which limited the number of Jews within their faculties and student bodies and permitted social ghettoization through "restricted" fraternities, sororities, dining clubs, and other organizations.[1] Within the classroom, the only course offering remotely related to what is today called Jewish Studies was "Old Testament," in which the biblical text was usually presented as both the academic and theological precursor for "New Testament." Generally conducted by non-Jewish faculty, the former courses tended to evince either of two perspectives, each equally negative toward Judaism. The first, a faith perspective, saw the "Old Testament" (and Judaism generally) as a preparation for and prediction of Christianity; with the Church established, Israel had lost its *raison d'etre*. The second viewpoint, ostensibly representing the academic perspective and less overtly theological in nature, applied the tools of Higher Criticism, dissecting Judaism's forms, defining her documents, and explaining away her uniqueness in an apparently detached, impersonal manner.[2] Neither approach found inherent nor continued value in the Bible text itself, and the student was often left with the distinct impression that although Jews might yet survive, Judaism itself had ceased to possess a relevant existence by the year 70 C.E.

In the early 1960s, the anti-Jewish college and university quota systems began breaking down. The rapid expansion of many educational institutions seeking to respond to the demands of the "baby boom" generation (including the children of a significantly expanded Jewish middle class), and coincidental rise of liberalism as the predominant social and political attitude, established an atmosphere receptive to new admissions policies, as well as curricular experimentation and change. Jewish college students were not significantly visible as Jews in the first years of that decade; without emphasizing their distinctions, they tended to their studies, participated in broad-based social and political activities and, in growing numbers, sought to continue formal education beyond the Bachelor's degree. This pattern would soon change, however, as the later '60s ushered in a feeling of positive attitudes towards ethnicity. Even as, in one sense, the campus as melting pot was bringing together a variety of groups and shaping them in accord with the prevailing northwestern European (Christian) ethos, a number of those minority members were manifesting a new aggressive pride in their particular heritages. No groups exhibited this novel attitude more distinctly than Blacks and Jews, and it should not be surprising that within the subsequent development of ethnic study programs, Black and Jewish Studies enjoyed the greatest increases in interest, support and development.[3]   Black Studies received its impetus from the continuing struggle for civil rights in America; in a manner of speaking, the same may be said of Jewish Studies. In the spring of 1967, Dr. Martin Luther King, Jr. included the expression "Black is beautiful" in a public address. He was not the first individual to use the catch phrase, but King's statement placed an imprimatur of legitimacy on ethnic pride in distinctiveness for millions of American minority group members and their liberal mainstream sympathizers. In that brief era during which many Americans chose to display their political and/or social views on lapel buttons, the wearing of ethnic identification buttons became popular, proclaiming "Italian Power," "Polish Power," "Jewish Power," and "Black Power," among others. The cause of Jewish ethnocentrism was boosted immensely by the serendipitous fighting of the Six-Day War only a few weeks after the King statement. Israel's unexpected and swift triumph, coupled with the primal emotions stirred by the restoration of Old Jerusalem and the Temple Mount, provided a new positive sense of Jewish self-image and identification in the Diaspora. Otherwise assimilated undergraduates joined in the demand for courses cognizant of their heritage. As a result, Jewish Studies began its expansion beyond the narrow confines of rabbinical seminaries and a handful of (primarily public) universities with large Jewish student enrollments.

Generally speaking, contemporary multifaceted programs of Jewish Studies evolved from either of two sources. Many programs are rooted within religion-theology departments which had long been satisfied to confine investigation of Judaism to "World Religions" survey courses and classes in "Old Testament." The faculties of these departments were most often Gentile, although some institutions did engage Jewish instructors — usually local rabbis added to a staff on an adjunct basis — frequently through the B'nai B'rith Hillel Foundation or the Jewish Chautauqua Society. Those individuals' idiosyncratic inclusions of material pertaining to Jewish religion and/or history often provided students their only information about Jewish life and thought after the destruction of the Second Temple. The instructor notwithstanding, the majority of students in such courses tended to be Christians, many of whom viewed the materials solely in terms of the foundation of Christianity. Whatever their backgrounds, the students were likely to use non-Jewish Bible translations as well as interpretive academic texts which were also the products of Christian researchers; few Jewish scholars were writing textual studies or histories of the biblical period useful to general college audiences prior to the late 1960s. The initial expansion of Judaica courses in these programs often depended upon the efforts of one or two department members who agreed to depart from their usual teaching assignments.

The other general evolutionary pattern for Jewish Studies was interdisciplinary, developing a program from previously established courses and depending upon personnel within several departments such as history, sociology and political science. The strengths of this pattern include the ability to seek out and draw upon additional faculty members' expertise, enthusiasm and particular disciplinary viewpoints as well as the opportunity to attract students who for whatever reason might not be responsive to course offerings within one particular department. There are liabilities within this approach as well, however, as such programs may lack a central core or distinct intellectual focus, while being reliant upon continued departmental cooperation for existence. Once again, program growth frequently required individual faculty members to forego their standard teaching assignments, sometimes volunteering to present subjects beyond their academic specialties. In such instances, various permissions might need securing and more than one department's chairperson would have to be persuaded of the utility of this action.

In the rush to present new curricula, greater attention was given to rationales for course inclusion, rather than the development of ideology or methodology. Administrations may have been sympathetic and responsive to student interests but were unwilling, unable or limited in their ability to expand department staffs. As a result, the brunt of teaching "Jewish Studies" often fell upon junior faculty members whose task it was to create the variety of new classes, develop syllabi, raise funds for speakers or special materials, create "shopping lists" for library purchases, and locate spaces within departments and programs for their courses. At the same time, the continuing need to meet the broader expectations and obligations of individual departments, as well as the requirements pursuant to the attainment of tenure or (in the cases of those for whom tenure was not to be) the amassing of a publications record which would assist the securing of a next position, diverted energies and concentration upon the program(s). With few texts or past syllabi upon which to rely, the initial courses to emerge usually took the form of surveys in which breadth was given priority over depth, the instructors scratching the surface of multiple facets of Jewish civilization in the effort to introduce students to a range of fields, in some of which the instructors themselves may have been less than fully competent. With the inertia typical of many departments/curriculum committees and despite considerable progress within the field, including the development of Jewish Studies specialists, these first courses, once accepted, would resist replacement and remain listed within many an undergraduate catalogue. To provide a single example, one noted midwest liberal arts college continues to include among its offerings "Classical Judaism," a survey covering the period from the beginning of the Common Era to the French Revolution and proposing to examine Talmud, Midrash, Kabbalah, Philosophy, Hasidism, the wars with Rome, rise of Christianity and Islam, Dispersion, the Crusades, Inquisition and Expulsions, within the space of a ten-week quarter. Despite confessing to the endemic superficiality of these initial efforts, it must be noted that they have served a useful purpose, introducing students to the range of Jewish experience, providing a cursory view of the literature within the various realms and stimulating some individuals to seek more intensive study.

With the introductory course enrollments supporting their proponents' claims, Jewish Studies offerings began to expand, adding more narrowly focused classes and seminars. At this point, proposals began to appear for courses on the Holocaust, the rationales for which tending to emphasize that the unique nature of the event merited its study.[4]

While there have been exceptions, initial Holocaust courses have often maintained the pattern of the historical survey, tracing the chronology of events through one of the general Holocaust histories, such as Lucy Dawidowicz' *The War Against the Jews*, Raul Hilberg's *The Destruction of European Jewry*, or *The Holocaust*, by Nora Levin. These "big books" were supplemented by film, memoir, and increasingly, the testimony of survivors whose recent willingness to speak has been equalled by the demand for their presence. Although this approach was not unlike that of many previously successful history courses, it held difficulties for Holocaust studies, as will be discussed below.

By the late 1970s, Jewish Studies seemed to have surpassed many of its most optimistic proponents' prophecies of success. Course offerings and programs had developed on campuses throughout the country, libraries had made substantial increases in their holdings of both classical and *wissenschaftlich* Jewish materials, more and more schools were sending students to Israel for summer, semester, or one year programs of study, and faculties had been augmented by men and women whose newly minted Ph.D.s had been earned through application of traditional academic specializations to questions within the fields of Judaism. At a moment when it seemed approaching the brink of total success, a series of external factors combined to force a redirection in Jewish Studies. The decline in the traditional college age group, changes in career goals (leading students toward "marketable" subjects and away from the humanities), a less favorable image of Israel, and the financial retrenchment faced by many institutions led to a reevaluation of Jewish Studies courses, programs and emphases. Enrollment figures, always a concern to deans and registrars, assumed an increasing significance when weighing the fate of a course, a program or an untenured faculty member.

The growing popularity of Holocaust studies did not go unnoticed by those confronted by decreasing budget flexibility and demands that course offerings be justifiable on financial (i.e., registration figures) as well as intellectual grounds. In some instances, this has resulted in support for Holocaust courses and their subsequent scheduling without thorough consideration of purpose or methodology. On occasion, these mass-produced offerings have been assigned to instructors unprepared for the special demands such courses make.

Classroom Methodologies

For those to whom the Holocaust represents another example of "man's inhumanity to man" — albeit on a larger scale — the challenge of teaching students about the *Shoah* appears no different from that of any subject matter; courses follow the general rules and patterns of western pedagogy. Theories are offered, cases presented, outlines constructed into which data may be gathered and shaped. Through research papers, essays and periodic examinations, students are measured as to their absorption of the data. The end product of such normative efforts may be a standard tracing of patterns of destruction in a particular country, an analysis of German corporate complicity in genocide, or a collation of underground resistance movements. Cool, detached, impersonal, rigidly academic; in Buberian terms, the student/investigator and topic/event conform to the classic I-It relationship. This association, of the sort composing more than 95% of our contacts in life, is pragmatic, practical, necessary, and good. For the purpose of teaching about the Holocaust, however, it is insufficient.

The Holocaust is a unique event in human history; unlike geometry, its whole is far greater and infinitely more terrifying than the sum of its parts. Efforts to constrain knowledge within standard lines will conceal the uniqueness, effectively diminish student perception and lose sight of those lessons to which we are summoned. Confronted by data, students need only react with data and, ironically, may pile datum upon datum in avoidance of the event itself. Within a unit or course on Holocaust it is a mistake to establish student retention of a set of quantifiable data as the primary goal; the optimum for which we should strive is student realization of the human capacity for and achievement of evil. For the learning experience to assume the form of a revelatory event, students must be taken, in the words of Abba Kovner, to the edge of the abyss and made to look down.[5]

Holocaust courses have been developed which focus upon the history of the event, the theological questions which have confronted religious thinkers during and subsequent to it, the psychological effects upon survivors' children, and the literature which has arisen in the intervening years, including poetry, drama, short stories and novels as well as memoirs and other nonfiction writings. From a contextual perspective, it does not matter significantly if the subject is presented under the aegis of a department of religion, Jewish Studies, history, sociology, philosophy, psychology, or literature. The particular departmental shading will influence the literary selections through which the topic is approached and the perspective from which it is viewed; it may also affect enrollments due to ancillary student concerns such as departmental major or college distribution requirements, but that is a fact of academic life generally beyond one's control. In each instance, no matter what the particular nuance or slice of Holocaust material to be presented, the necessary initial task is a matter of consciousness raising, leading students to a realization of the enormity of the event itself (and the concomitant understanding that this course will be "different"). To this end, a massive assembling of data is in and of itself unnecessary and basically, unhelpful. Revelation is rarely achieved through the memorization of place names, dates or numbers; in the case of the Holocaust, those are the "trivial" details, included within Hannah Arendt's description of the "banality of evil," which will actually impede attainment of the educational desiderata.

Traditional pedagogical norms caution educators against subjective involvement with their materials; the Holocaust, on the contrary, demands entry into the event. The educational task begins not with the transmission of objective, quantified "facts" but rather with the preparation of students for a subjective meeting: the revelation of Holocaust, a confrontation which will frighten even as it may enlighten. Repelling while seducing, the intensity of Holocaust discovery may be likened to that relationship Buber named I-Thou. The emotional reactions which this revelation of evil may generate should not be mistaken as a substitute for hard knowledge but are the spirit transfiguring what might otherwise become just another set of statistics to be memorized and parroted on an examination or term paper. The difficulty, pain and risk inherent within this meeting transcend those to which students and faculty are accustomed; it is both easier and safer to submerge oneself in an objective accumulation of data through which one may become an adept in the jargon, even raising a reputation on the trivia of destruction. Moreover, the results of revelatory understanding are not readily converted to practical (communicable) forms. The inescapable dilemma is that even as one strives to attain the meta-level of understanding, one must return to the normative universe of discourse to express that understanding and share it with those who will follow.

Within unit or course, it is a mistake to compare the Holocaust to other acts of mass murder or genocide. As Elie Wiesel and others have warned, the comparison of tragedies achieves not positive purpose but ultimately will belittle each unique event, diminishing human catastrophe to an exercise in quantitative suffering. This is not to say that it would be inappropriate to include selections from Holocaust writings within a comparative literature course in conjunction with materials written by victims of the Armenian, Vietnamese or other atrocities. But the purpose of such a course would not be the teaching of the Holocaust, *per se.* In similar manner, comparative studies of survival strategies in crisis situations, the psychological effects upon survivors, or the sense of separateness felt by survivors' children would be entirely appropriate efforts; such projects have, in fact, been undertaken.[6]

A second strategy, equally erroneous, is the effort to universalize the Holocaust through broad statements and attitudes of the previously mentioned "man's inhumanity to man" variety. There are implications within the fact of the Holocaust which bear significance for all peoples, but while it is indisputable that many nations and peoples suffered tremendous casualties during the war, it must not be forgotten that the Nazi governmental policies of isolation, degradation and total extermination were directed against one particular people, the nation of Israel. At the same time, the recognition of the Holocaust as the particular calamity of the Jewish people should not be permitted to mislead either students or teachers into the reductionist trap that the Holocaust is therefore an exclusively Jewish concern. Those who arrive at this conclusion manifest, in essence, views identical to those of the bystanders of many nations — governments as well as individuals — who refused to involve themselves in a "Jewish" matter, a "German" problem or a "European" situation and retained their impassiveness to the appeals of refugees, "aliens" or "Jews" who remained barred from safe harbors. The fact that the vast majority of perpetrators of and bystanders to the Holocaust were baptised members in good standing of traditional Christian churches, none of whom has ever been formally rebuked by his or her particular denomination, suggests one of the primary non-Jewish challenges of Holocaust study demanding examination. Elie Wiesel has confronted the most disturbing facet of that realm with his reminder that "not every Christian was a killer, but every killer was a Christian." Franklin Littell, Roy Eckardt, Harry James Cargas, and others have constantly and eloquently offered correctives to the "Jewish problem" fallacy, presenting the Holocaust's implications for Christianity and Christians throughout the world.[7]

The pressures awaiting students only mirror those which faculty must face. The unique demands and inherent risks of teaching the Holocaust point to rejection of an instructor who merely instructs, in favor of the professor who will profess. To stand removed from the questions of the Holocaust implies an indifference rather than academic neutrality. While paradoxical to our traditional scholarly stance, one of the "lessons" which is incumbent upon us to impart is that indifference -- reaching at least to the extent of a popular unwillingness to risk involvement — was a singular factor abetting the Nazi policy of national extermination

Despite (or, in some cases, because of) the pressures of a new conservatism dominating the recent American political and popular ethos, many faculty members are reluctant to assume well-defined positions regarding controversial issue. The terror of tenure decisions, desire for promotion, grant funding, *et al*, may lead many to maintenance of postures that are conservative, respectable, and ultimately, safe. Proper study of the Holocaust demands removal of the usual safety nets, however. In the case of faculty, those risks must be considered long before the first person registers for the actual course, causing our own conscious choices to be more apparent and threatening than those which await our students.

A further confounding of traditional pedagogy comes with the realization that proper teaching of the Holocaust runs contrary to both inductive and deductive systems of reasoning, each of which presumes the existence and eventual discovery of answers to all questions. Standard academic thinking which, in simplistic terms, measures a faculty member's "bottom line" value in direct proportion to the ability to answer questions (be it within classes or through scholarly publications), is again found wanting. Within presentations about the Holocaust it is neither the primary obligation nor should it be the intent of the professor to provide answers; the revelation of which we have been speaking demands instead, as Franklin Littell has noted, discovery of the proper questions. The Holocaust raises fundamental and painful questions about God, Judaism and Christianity, the human species, Allied policies, and other subjects which may not have any answers, let alone "satisfactory" responses. The very lack of universally accepted answers underscores the questions' significance.

Student Responses and Problems

Experienced educators are aware that students do not always accept faculty opinions as to the importance of a particular point, issue or set of questions. The fact that a lecturer may place emphasis upon a specific issue will only reduce its relevance in some students' eyes. Applying the rabbinic principle of *kal v'homer* (that which applies in a simple instance is equally applicable in a complex case), this student neutralizing factor must be considered even within a Holocaust course. As some students may assume Holocaust rhetoric to be overblown and others wish to reduce the event's implications into an overstatement of evil, understatement will become one of the most effective tools for classroom presentations, particularly on the introductory level. By "understatement," what is meant is not only the eschewing of sweeping universal pronouncements but also a reduction of focus. Concentration upon single communities, families or individuals will provide more lasting lessons than studies of national and international policies. In that regard, Elie Wiesel's already classic memoir, *Night*, remains unsurpassed in terms of readability, content and effect.[8]   So, too, at the conclusion of an introductory course is Simon Wiesenthal's study *The Sunflower*, with its demand that the reader enter into the story and respond to the author's concluding question which pertains, ostensibly, to one person's actions toward another. Within film, the value of documentaries such as "Avenue of the Just," "The Courage to Care" or the recent work by Pierre Sauvage, "Weapons of the Spirit," is enhanced by their being based upon acts of unself-conscious bravery at the individual level.

Every age group has its educational strengths and weaknesses, but it may be argued that traditional college age students are ideally suited to pursue Holocaust study. Still young enough to regard learning as a habit, they have continued to hone their scholarly tools while advancing the levels of emotional and intellectual maturity beyond that which they possessed as high school students. Undergraduates also remain far more impressionable and idealistic than graduate students who have an unfortunate (if understandable) tendency to wrap themselves in a narrow world focused upon the dissertation. Undergraduates are, without question, more "teachable."

Their potential receptivity notwithstanding, most undergraduates have little real knowledge of the *Shoah*. Although Holocaust courses or units have begun to appear in a growing number of school districts, they remain the exception within high school curricula. Students may be expected to possess a vague familiarity with terms such as Nazi, Hitler and, perhaps, Auschwitz, but the concept of "six million" is just a phrase. By and large, the majority remain abysmally ignorant of the event itself and its significances.

As a first step in their study, students need a subjective sense of the Holocaust. For more than a decade, I have found success with a brief introductory unit, lasting no more than four class periods. Through selected readings, films and pointed discussions, a recognition of the Holocaust itself has been attained, preparing the way for more traditional studies, in greater depth.

Briefly summarized, session one consists of a lecture/discussion describing Germany at the close of World War I, including the fall of the Empire, rise of the Weimar Republic and its problems, development of the National Socialist Workers Party and its leader. The session concludes with an assignment, the reading of Wiesel's *Night,* to be completed for the next class. Students arrive for the second meeting anticipating a discussion of the reading assignment; instead, they view the French television documentary "Night and Fog," the original which, while rather sparsely subtitled, is superior to the dubbed-English version. The students are dismissed in silence at the film's conclusion, prohibited from any class discussion, and required to prepare a *subjective* analysis of that which had been read and seen. It is only during the third session, upon completion of the writing assignment, that emotional decompression is permitted. At that time, the class also begins to outline several of the sensitive questions which will arise throughout subsequent study, such as Allied policies concerning refugee immigration or the bombing of concentration camps, the role of the Roman Catholic Church and its pontiff in opposing Nazi policies, and the root sources of anti-Semitism. This initial questioning may extend to a fourth class meeting; thereafter, more data-laden sessions begin. At the unit's conclusion, in terms of that which may be measured quantitatively, students have become no better trained in *Shoah;* they have not learned dates, place names or numbers, no effort having been made to teach that material. Instead, they have been exposed to the enormity of the event itself, in hopes that such exposure will color not only future study but also future actions.

The emotional level raised in this unit cannot be maintained throughout an entire term or semester. As Buber noted, the epiphanous nature of I-Thou demands its brevity and a return to the normative I-It condition. Any sharing of the meta-level I-Thou experience must rely upon I-It descriptive language which may only hint at the nature of the experience. In like manner, responses to revelation return us to mundane life and terms; the exigencies of academe necessitate objective evaluation of each student's progress, based upon some sort of normative continuum. The challenge is to find a means of fostering student intensity without neglecting requisite academic standards or the means to make such evaluations.

Why does one study the Holocaust? What does one wish to know? Some students may cite a connection through family history — relatives having been in the concentration camps — while others are less able to define their attraction to the course.[9] It is generally safe to state that Christians may offer very different rationales from those of their Jewish classmates. In addition to carrying diverse agenda, Jewish and Christian students may also develop particular problems within the class; however, experience has shown that the most effective courses have contained a good "mix" of Jewish and non-Jewish students. Experience has also proven that the "mix" is enhanced when class size is kept below twenty; unfortunately, course popularity often demands expansion beyond that number, which may hinder the interactive process of class discussions.

Christian students, generally having little prior knowledge of the Holocaust and quickly rendered uncomfortable by their first new awareness of the topic, may fall silent in the presence of their Jewish colleagues, feeling what may be an unfamiliar sense of being "outsiders." Some of these students may hesitate to express an opinion in class, particularly should they wish to disagree with a statement from a Jewish source, uncertain of the propriety of their commenting. This situation is most likely to manifest itself following the viewing of documentary films or during any presentation by a concentration camp survivor. When the course focus is directed at root causes of anti-Semitism and the religious component is scrutinized, another set of problems can arise. Attributions of institutionalized anti-Semitism within Christianity may engender protests and denials from some students; in such cases, the most frequently noted defense tactic shifts the subject under examination from the institutional religion to those individual men and women whose claims to membership within the Church would appear disproven by their anti-Semitic (and thus anti-Christian) actions. Should either the professor or class presenter be Jewish, some students may fall back upon claims of bias and dismiss both arguments and evidences as nothing more than anti-Christian prejudice. The availability of recent works on the question of Christian anti-Semitism, written by scholars who are themselves confessing church members, can significantly forestall student protestations or accusations (both verbalized and tacit) of this variety.[10] Viewed in terms of credibility of witness, some Christian students will offer fewer protestations when the accusing voice uses the pronoun "we" rather than "you." Some Christian students may feel themselves under accusation by these charges, and their personal defenses may cause a significant rise in the temperature of classroom discussion.[11] Others, equally upset and unable to express or personal faith justifications, will withdraw into another type of silence; this need not create a classroom crisis, but one should be prepared to challenge students to speak at the very time at which some would prefer to remain mute.

The difficulties attending certain Jewish students within a Holocaust class arise from the spectrum's opposite pole; there are undergraduates who enter a course believing their Jewishness provides them with an expertise on suffering and a particular authority about the Holocaust. Left unchallenged, these attitudes would reduce a course to a Jewish sensitivity session; corrections are necessary. Allowing Jewish students to presume the *Shoah* is "their" subject reinforces the misconception that the Holocaust is only a Jewish matter; it can also create negative reactions among non-Jewish students who may feel that they have been enrolled on sufferance and encouraged to be passive by class members who may in fact suggest that the only proper role of the non-Jew in such a course is to listen. Similarly, some Jewish students may question the right or propriety of a non-Jew to direct a Holocaust study. Even today, some experienced non-Jewish teachers of the Holocaust, long respected for their knowledge by those within the field, feel it necessary to justify their efforts within a course's opening session. Jewish students must be disabused of these exclusivist assumptions while both groups are led to an awareness of the Holocaust's significance for Jews and Christians alike. The relevant questions may differ for each, but a genuine confrontation awaits them both.

Although exceptions will surely be found, student responses to Holocaust materials often arrange themselves within two broad categories, which also tend to divide along Jewish/non-Jewish lines. Within the first category, which may be labelled "particularist" and within which most Jewish students' reactions fall, there is a personal identification with the victims and a pronounced belief that a repetition of those events is not beyond the realm of possibility. The particularist response is well illustrated by the following student who, in 1982, wrote:

The first thing I feel is panic in my joints. . . What if I had to undress my little brother Harry, and lead him by the hand into the gas-chamber, and watch him perish before I die myself?

A second undergraduate added: "My biggest feeling is a fear that something like the Holocaust could happen again," while a third spoke against "the people who do become accustomed to the horrid pictures and for whom the only remaining emotion is, oh it was horrid, but it was so long ago, and it could never happen again." The second set of responses may be categorized "universalist" and tend to include expressions of sympathy for, rather than identification with, the victims and more sweeping declarations that such events must never be permitted to recur. Typical of these responses was the remark of a student in that same class, who wrote: "I find it so hard to believe that so many Germans would be so gullible as to follow Hitler, especially in the 20th century when people's ideas were becoming more liberal." Another student added: "I only hope nothing like this will ever, ever occur again."[12]

Final Recommendations

A course devoted to the Holocaust should be the most demanding class an undergraduate takes. The student must confront history and its contemporary questions or the course is a fraud; the student must wrestle with his/her own soul or the course is a failure. The latter demand is one which transcends normative academic obligations, leaving students vulnerable and in need of additional guidance and reassurance. Within so unique an atmosphere, the course leader must do more than explicate texts.

While many Holocaust resource materials carry themselves, as with any course, the instructor is both the foundation and its weakest link. Administrators and department chairpeople have demonstrated an eagerness to initiate such offerings within their schools' curricula.[13] In the haste to establish these courses, there have been instances in which the assignment of faculty has been less than optimal. Some have been encouraged to teach the Holocaust solely because they happen to be Jewish. That they may be totally unprepared for the special nature of the task has not always been a topic for consideration. Should a situation of this sort arise, an unusual role reversal becomes necessary, in which even those faculty who are proponents of Holocaust education must discourage the creation/implementation of courses until adequate preparation can occur. It is unfortunate that, with all the other difficulties inherent in Holocaust teaching, there is an additional obligation to protect the subject from those whose commitment tends to rise and fall with registration figures.

A final concern. One of the more unpleasant movements in recent years is the effort of neo-Nazi and other extremist groups in this country and abroad to deny that the Holocaust ever took place. The library publication, *Books in Print*, now includes a subheading "Myth" within its Holocaust listing under which is presented a growing bibliography of works of hate. Wrapped in the pseudo-respectability of titles such as the "Institute for Historical Review," these books and journals declare that the death camps were labor centers, the crematoria of Auschwitz were bakery ovens for bread and that any Jews who died in those places were merely unfortunate victims of illness in time of war. These materials are sent to academic and public libraries around the world and, with their slick production techniques, professional appearance and lack of cost, often find places on the shelves. Faculty must be dissuaded from including any of these works within their programs or courses, particularly under the rubric of "presenting both sides." The fact of the Holocaust and the anguish of its victims are not items for conjecture or debate; to legitimate these materials and to suffer their continuing presence within our libraries is to provide passive support for anti-Semitism in its latest guise. Individuals should check the periodical contents of their own institutions and, should these items appear, initiate the procedures necessary for their removal.[14] The proper teaching of the Holocaust is unlike other courses; when coming to that place, recognize that we stand upon sacred ground; neither we nor our students must lose our sense of awe.

---

[1]See, for example, Dan A. Oren, *Joining the Club: A History of Jews and Yale,* New Haven 1985.

[2]Solomon Schechter referred to this malignant scholarship as "Higher Anti-Semitism."

[3]It was also the period during which Women's Studies had its first stirrings on many campuses, the proponents of which understood themselves as a group separated from the mainstream of societal and political power.

[4]The first course providing an intensive examination of the Holocaust was offered at Southern Methodist University in 1959, under the direction of Franklin Littell.

[5]Kovner (b. 1918), now an Israeli poet and kibbutznik, was one of the leaders of the resistance in the Vilna ghetto. It was Kovner who warned that the Jews were being led to the death camps "like sheep to the slaughter."

[6]An "International Conference on the Holocaust and Genocide," meeting in Tel Aviv June 20-24, 1982, included among its many presentations "Trans-Generational Effects of Massive Psychic Traumatization: Psychological Characteristics of Children of Holocaust Survivors in Israel," "The Armenian Genocide and the Literary Imagination," and "Genocides, Survivors, and Religious Change."

[7]Among the texts raising the issue of specific Christian concerns with the Holocaust are Franklin Littell's *The Crucifixion of the Jews,* Rosemary Reuther's *Faith and Fratricide* and A. Roy Eckardt's *Jews and Christians.* Eckardt defines the problem by asking, in history's glare, if Christianity can be considered "morally credible."

[8] *The Diary of Anne Frank* is another familiar and effective first-person work, reflecting a different victim situation. Professor James Moore, of Valparaiso University, has concentrated upon Holocaust diaries as the medium for revelation, with success.

[9] Doubtless, a complete list of student rationales will include some which faculty members might not consider ideal or encouraging, such as convenience of scheduling or the sheer fascination of horror. This, too, is beyond our control.

[10] Littell's *Crucifixion of the Jews* is a particularly useful text for these purposes. As a Methodist minister, the author maintains a credibility of Christian witness which makes his charges far more difficult for Christian audiences to refute.

[11] One Christian student of German heritage wrote (1982): "What often scares me that I haven't realized until now is what I would have been like as a German then," echoing the questions of a classmate, who wondered "Would I have a been a passive watcher, involved, or a victim?" Reactions of this nature and their stimuli were challenged several years earlier.

> As a Christian I don't feel personally responsible... I don't think it's fair to put the blame on people for the Holocaust, make them feel personally responsible, just because they are related by blood or otherwise to people such as Nazi killers or because they are Christians, regardless of the fact that all the actual "killers were Christian." I resented that when it came up in class.

[12] Student responses recorded at Carleton College, May 1982. Black students may comprise a third response group, manifesting elements of both "particularist" and "universalist" reactions. Many black students have paralleled Jewish suffering with the black experience in America and found chords of common understanding. Most recently, the inclusion of students who were refugees from Southeast Asia has added another complementing component to discussions.

[13] In some otherwise temperate and conservative colleges, a new course on Holocaust has been paired with a traditional offering in "Old Testament" and the combination publicized as the institution's program in "Jewish Studies."

[14] Lists of these newer anti-Semitic organizations, the names and pseudonyms of their authors and publication titles may be secured from the Anti-Defamation League of B'nai B'rith or any of the regional Holocaust centers in the country.

Chapter Four

Teaching the Holocaust in Israel:
The Dilemma as a Disturbing Reality and
Pedagogical Concept

Arye Carmon

A. The Dilemma as a Disturbing Reality —
the History of Teaching the Holocaust in Israel

The methods of teaching the Holocaust in Israel,[1] as well as its stated educational goals, have been closely connected with the complex role this unique human phenomenon plays in the Israeli collective consciousness.[2] The Holocaust presents an unsolvable dilemma which is exceedingly incomprehensible for any single human mind. In Israel this universal reality has been interwoven with a highly emotional climate pertaining to the Holocaust; a climate that stems both from the vast number of Holocaust survivors as well as the wedding of the role of this phenomenon in the Israeli collective consciousness to the implications of the ongoing political conflict which continuously underscores the ethos of "survival." The problematics posed by this dilemma will guide the discussion in this chapter; we will analyse its role as a disturbing reality which reinforces the various traits of relating to the Holocaust and its possible role as a pedagogical concept.

The difficulties of coping with the Holocaust educationally, then, have been closely connected with three major factors. First, the problems posed by the magnitude of the phenomenon. Second, the dilemma created by the tension between incomprehensibility and the role of the phenomenon in Israeli collective consciousness. And third, the difficulties inherent in any attempt at incorporating the Holocaust within any curricular framework.

The first of these three is a permanent, ongoing factor. It reflects the incomprehensibility of the depth of evil and magnitude of murder which the Holocaust represents. The second is of a more contemporary nature and relates directly to the cultural climate associated with the historical circumstances of Israeli society. The third results from the link between school and society in Israel, as well as from the inherent structure of any curriculum.

The prominent mode in the average Israeli's behavioral pattern toward the Holocaust could be described as an ongoing attempt at dissociation; that is, a dissociation both from the perpetrator and the victim. This mode reflects more than anything else the problematics of relating to the Holocaust in Israel. Dissociation from the perpetrator has been characterized by escape from the evident reality that Auschwitz, "a factory of death," was built by central-European human beings in the 20th century. This escapism has been expressed by relating to the Nazis as 'animals' and to the death camps as 'another planet'.[3] Any attempt to draw analogies to events connected with the Nazi era has been condemned or dismissed.

Dissociation from the victim has been more complex and is discussed below. Here it suffices to say that these Jews, described as "sheep who went to the slaughter," have been perceived as the antithesis of the self image that has been inculcated into Israeli collective consciousness. As a result of this dual dissociation, a macabre symmetry evolved in the attitude of the Israeli to the victim and the perpetrator. This indirect desire to separate from both parties has posed enormous difficulties for educators attempting to develop a value-judgmental approach to dealing with the Holocaust. It has led to a split between "us" and "them"; the latter are either "animals" or "our" (the "new Jews' ") antithesis. The split from the victim has been of special significance in Israel because it arose indirectly in conjunction with a conscious ideological decision to reject the "old Jew." This was a product of the Zionist premise of "negating the *Galut*" (exile or Diaspora way of life).[4] For the founding fathers of Zionism this negation, this denial of any link with Jewish history, was aimed at strengthening the future orientation of the Zionist movement; as such it should be seen as a necessary part of the Zionist revolution. Yet, for the founding fathers the past against which they rebelled was an organic part of their substance and would always remain so. The generations born and raised in Israel were brought up without any direct link with their Jewish past. All images of that past would, therefore, be stereotypical and artificial.

The founding fathers' generation, the generation of the Zionist revolution, sought to shape the "new Jew" as the opposite of the "old" or *"Galut* Jew" by making forceful use of the educational system. This severing of ties with the past was perceived as a necessary step in the founding of the new state. The consequence of that severance was that the sons' generation was brought up and educated on tomorrow's values only, without any knowledge of their heritage. They condemned their past, as their fathers had taught them, but unlike the latter they did so without knowing what they were condemning.

Generally speaking, the sons' generation perceived themselves largely as their fathers expected them to: as proud, handsome Sabras (Israeli born), masculine, healthy, naive and honest. They realized the Zionist dream by doing whatever work had to be done, especially by taking up arms. It was during this generation's finest hour, before and immediately after 1948 (the year of Independence), when it was forced into a very profound and cruel encounter with the epitome of the *"Galut* Jew"*: the Holocaust survivor. He arrived in Israel illegally, beaten and broken by the Nazis, and represented the precise antithesis of the "New Jew," the product of the Zionist revolution. This dichotomy between the Sabra and the refugee immigrant provided one of the more tragic dimensions for the complex attitude of Israelis toward Jewish history at large. For both the fathers' and the sons' generation, but principally for the former, the magnitude of the painful mental confusion caused by this encounter cannot be overestimated. The symbols and myths that it presented in apposition to the traditional Zionist outlook and the misleading disjunction between Holocaust and rebirth that resulted from that apposition are but two of the more prominent indications of the enormous role that the Holocaust has had in shaping Israeli collective consciousness.[5] In retrospect, it appears that a disturbing conjunction evolved between the incomprehensible magnitude of evil of the Nazis and the victims, who conscientiously were presented as an ideological object to be dissociated from. This conjunction may explain the duality of guilt and shame that has portrayed mourning in Israel.[6]

The Holocaust became a mandatory subject in Israeli schools in April, 1979. From a historical perspective it is clear that an entire generation had to pass before the transition from "Knowing about the Holocaust" to "Being aware of its implications" could occur.[7] This transition from knowledge to awareness (two words that in Hebrew stem from the same root: *"Yadoa"*) was an essential prerequisite to the decision of the Ministry of Education to introduce the Holocaust as a mandatory study in the Israeli curriculum. There is historical evidence that Israelis knew about the Holocaust as early as 1942, and they certainly knew in a profound way with the termination of World War Two and the arrival of Holocaust survivors. It was not before the 1970s, however, that the subject was related to in a comprehensive manner.

The development of the Holocaust as an educational issue in Israel can be divided into four phases. The first phase began in the second part of the 1940s and lasted until the Eichmann trial, 1961. It was marked by an almost complete absence of the subject from the curriculum.

The following table surveys the appearance of the theme, quantitatively,[8] in history textbooks, 1943-1983:

Year	Author	Title	No.Pages
1943	Hazan	Toldot Yisrael VeHa'Amim	1
1948	Spivak/Avidor	Am Yisrael BeArtzo Ubanechar	1
1954	Sela	Kitzur Toldot Am Yisrael	1
1954	Riger	Toldot Yisrael BaZman HeHadash	12
1958	Katan	Toldot HaYehudim MeMilhemet Ha'olam I Ad Yamanu	5
1960	Caner/Ophir	Kitzur Toldot Yisrael	2
1961	Ziv/Tory	Divrey HaYamim	3
1962	Katz/Hershko	Yisrael VeHa'Amim	5
1964	Ahia/Harpaz	Toldot Am Yisrael	8
1966	Ziv/Etinger	Divrey HaYamim	21
1969	Kirshenbaum	Toldot Am Yisrael BeDoreinu	12
1970	Shmueli	Toldot Ameinu BaZeman HeHadash	13
1975	Avivi/Persky	Toldot Yisrael	22
1975	Carmon/Oron	Hiunuit Yehudit BaShoah	booklet

Year	Author	Title	No.Pages
1977	Shatzker, et al	Antishemiut VeShoah	book
1980	A. Carmon	HaShoah	2 vols
1983	Gutman/Shatzker	HaShoah UMashmauta	book

During the first phase, the Holocaust emerged as an educational theme only on occasions, the most prominent of which was '*Yom HaShoah Ve-Ha Gevura*' (Holocaust and Heroism Memorial Day), in the spring of each year. This absence from the normal curriculum, and the nature of its annual treatment, are symptoms of the general attitude towards the Holocaust which prevailed in Israel. This attitude was compounded of guilt and shame, attempting to separate between "us" — the new Israeli Jews, and "them" — the "*Galut*" (Diaspora) Jews. At the same time, however, it overemphasized the few examples of active resistance during the Holocaust (the general Holocaust memorial day is set annually to commemorate the Warsaw Ghetto Uprising). The overemphasis on active resistance was coupled, in the 1950s and 1960s, with an obsessive search for further examples of such resistance.[9] This duality in attitude toward the Holocaust, that of guilt and shame, stemmed from an overall negative attitude toward the *Galut* which has been a major facet in the Israeli collective consciousness predating the Holocaust. The stereotyped images with which this phenomenon was related reinforced preconceived notions of what *Galut* Jewry was like. The resounding silence of survivors during that period, the use of derogatory terms (e.g., "mussel-man," "soap") and the emphasis on "our pride" in those who resisted, usually represented as Zionists, were some of the characteristics of this attitude toward the Holocaust. From the perspective of three decades later, it appears that the "intensive defense against guilt, shame and anxiety" debilitated the mourning of the loss.[10]

The capture and trial of Eichmann in 1961 marked the beginning of a second phase, forcing Israelis to take a fresh look at the Holocaust and its survivors. The testimonies of those who "did not resist" and "went like sheep to the slaughter" breached the dam of silence and planted the seeds of a new attitude towards both the victims and the perpetrators, although another decade had to pass before those seeds bore meaningful fruit. The Eichmann trial brought forth extensive testimony which raised questions and forced a change in the homogeneous picture of the six million victims that had prevailed until then.[11]

This trial provided a powerful arena from which the until then unknown terrifying realities were disclosed; by doing so, it legitimized discussion of the Holocaust.[12]

It would not be accurate to talk about a complete transformation of the Israeli collective consciousness in the trial's aftermath, but there was a transition to an attitude of ambivalence, which was a precursor of the third phase. This transformation can be seen in the Israeli reaction to two books which appeared in the 1960s: Hanna Arendt's *Eichmann in Jerusalem*, and Raul Hilberg's *The Destruction of European Jewry*.[13] While the two books are written in different styles, both attempt to explain the presumed passivity of Hitler's Jewish victims. The furious Israeli reaction, led by academics, to what was seen as Arendt's and Hilberg's simplified and unresearched generalizations, seems paradoxical.

In retrospect, it appears that the generalizations found in these two books were typical of the mood of the 1950s. Had the books been published a decade earlier, Israeli reaction would indeed likely have been different. The angry reaction of Israelis in the period following the Eichmann trial reflected the new ambivalence, the midway point between dissociation and acceptance.

The period between 1961 and the beginning of the 1970s saw the introduction of the unsystematic teaching of the Holocaust in the Israeli school system. The then newly-formed Curriculum Center of the Ministry of Education (in the early 1960s) included, for the first time, a syllabus for the teaching of the Holocaust in its general history curriculum guide.[14] The teaching of the Holocaust in this period, however, was marked by the teachers' apologetic manner which stemmed from the still-prevailing need to explain why those caught up in the Holocaust were not perceived as heroes and had not resisted.[15] The growing number of hours devoted to the teaching of the Holocaust, unsystematic as it was, on the one hand, and the teachers' apologetic manner, on the other, reflected the ambiguity in the educational arena in the second phase.

The Six-Day War and the Yom Kippur War precipitated the change to the third phase. These two conflicts introduced significant changes in the way Israelis perceived their own role in Jewish History.[16] Seeds were planted that would allow a change from the traditional Israeli view of separation from the main continuum of Jewish history, a view in which the *"Galut"* was something to be negated rather than related to. Since the middle of the 1970s, Jewish history textbooks in Israel have dealt with this subject in a more evenhanded manner. More importantly, a new approach to Jewish behavior during the Holocaust emerged. The main feature of this approach was the growing emphasis on Jewish *'Amida'* (stand). This approach implied that the Jewish response to the Nazis was basically active rather than passive and that the various ways in which Jews coped with Nazi decrees, collectively and individually, reflected both physical and spiritual resistance.[17] Illustrations of this change in attitude can be seen in, among other things, the academic conference held in Yad Va'Shem in 1977 on various aspects of the *Judenrate* (Jewish Councils), an event that would have been impossible in the 1960s; and in the removal of the word *"Gevura'"*(Heroism) from the name of Holocaust Memorial Day.[18] Another development which became significant during this third phase was the introduction of different modes of relating to Jewish life in the Diaspora. Pogroms, persecutions and a handful of negative images pertaining to Jewish life in the Diaspora were no longer the exclusive manner of portraying Diaspora Jewish life in school textbooks.[19] The most prominent expression of the change, however, was the inclusion of this approach in newly developed curricular units; first for informal educational activities[20] and then in two curricular programs devoted exclusively to the Holocaust.[21]

The modification of the role of the Holocaust in the Israeli collective consciousness could have continued in the direction described above, but it did not. As asserted, the role of the Holocaust in the Israeli collective consciousness has gone hand-in-hand with the events that determined Israel's life. In other words, it is impossible to separate the developments of attitudes toward the Holocaust from the developments of a society shaped through major conflicts in the social, cultural and political arenas. From a current perspective the implications of both are imprinted in the Israeli ethos of survival.

The origins of this ethos lie in the constant threat to *"Hisardut"* (Hebrew — bare physical existence) which has existed since the founding of the State. Broadly speaking, this ethos affected a major shift in the modes of Israel's socio-cultural orientation. To provide one example, the pre-State era's strong orientation toward the future, connected with the symbol of the pioneer, has been transformed into an orientation toward the "Here and now." The main feature of this ethos, nonetheless, is its lack; a lack of ongoing effort to provide meaning and purpose to existence. At the same time this ethos has thrived on accumulated anxieties and the constant need to invest energies, physical as well as intellectual, to maintain physical existence. The shift in orientation is reflected in the literature of third generation Israelis, who did not participate in the War of Independence. This literature reveals a sincere disappointment with the focus on the "Here and Now"; on the almost exclusive concentration on the problems of the present rather than looking toward a better future. To paraphrase Robert Kennedy's words — they look at things as they are and ask "why?", rather than dream of things as they might be and ask "why not?". This emphasis on the present is a dominant feature of the ethos of survival.

The link between the Holocaust and the ethos of survival is expressed by the phrase "From Holocaust to rebirth." This concept, which has attained the function of a principal symbol, underlines the centrality of the physical lesson of the Holocaust. Within circumstances in which survival is indeed a major facet, a number of factors have transformed "From Holocaust to rebirth" into a symbol:

1. The fact that very little time passed between the end of the Holocaust and the birth of the State of Israel and the difficulty of coping with the implications of two such events simultaneously. Either of the two events alone would have generated a trauma in the soul of any society. Their concurrence created an even greater difficulty, particularly because the two events were diametrically opposed to one another: On the one hand, humiliation, murder, death, and destruction, and on the other, birth and creation; annihilation vs. renewal. The idea of "From Holocaust to rebirth," simplified and morally impoverished as it is, might have been virtually the only solution to an impossible dilemma; a last and only resort in dealing with helplessness.

2. The fact that the generation which had to deal with the two events was the same generation which ideologically denied its past. This generation, nevertheless, had to come to terms with and find compensation for the tragedy of the Holocaust. The concept of "From Holocaust to rebirth" provided a comfortable consolation.

3. The fact that the forty years since the two events occurred have been marked by virtually continuous threats to the physical existence of the State of Israel. Against this background of all-too-frequent wars, the contradiction between the two events seemed to lessen and death became a common factor to both. The fact that only a week separates Holocaust Memorial Day from the memorial day for those who have fallen in battle, further affects the perception of the two opposing modes of death in the collective consciousness. The centrality of death has played a debilitating role because it focuses attention on the past rather than on the future, and because it

fosters pessimism rather than optimism. Death becomes a sort of filter in the observation of past events, and prevents the drawing of rational lessons from them. Thus both the deaths of the Holocaust ("sheep to the slaughter") and those of the War of Independence ("in their deaths they ordered our lives"), reinforce the ethos of survival.

B. The Dilemma as a Pedagogical Concept

In 1976 the first attempt was made to develop a comprehensive approach to teaching the Holocaust. It attempted to deal with what were described as the "presuppositions of the problematic role of the Holocaust in the schools."[22] It was asserted that "any student who approaches the phenomenon of the Holocaust must confront the barrier between himself and the phenomenon; a barrier which existing programs do not resolve."[23] The development of this program, entitled "The Teaching of the Holocaust as Education Toward Values," followed a comprehensive survey in a wide variety of high schools in Israel. This survey was an attempt to clarify the attitudes of both teachers and students towards the teaching of the subject. The major guideline of the program stemmed both from the results of the survey and the presuppositions mentioned above. The program was "meant to focus on the student in his search for meaning and import of his life as a human being, as a Jew and an Israeli... The principles, aims, contents, and methods are all meant to derive from and serve the intellectual needs of the student as an individual who is both searching for his identity and reflecting on his role and function in society."[24] This was a deliberate and radical departure from the typical method of teaching in Israeli schools. Rather than teaching the subject matter, in this case the Holocaust, to the students, an attempt was made to teach the students about the lessons of the Holocaust with reference to their own lives.

In the first stage of development an attempt was made to establish ideal educational objectives as well as the best means of achieving them, including the contents of the texts which would be used. In retrospect, it is clear that this attempt to ignore the curricular reality until the ideal program could be completed was rather naive. This curricular reality, it should be noted, consisted not only of existing Holocaust units but also of the prevailing teaching strategies. These, coupled with the enormous role the Holocaust played in the Israeli collective consciousness, effected the tremendous vulnerability of Israeli schools toward novelties in pedagogic approaches toward the Holocaust.

Shifting the emphasis from teaching the Holocaust to teaching the student was meant to achieve two separate educational objectives, one pertaining to the universal dimension and the other to the Jewish dimension. The former attempted to guide students to relate to the perpetrators as human beings who committed excessive crimes and as such ought to be judged. It was stressed that the Nazis were on the same continuum as the students, only at the furthest pole of that continuum. The educational message was two-fold: First, as human beings, the students themselves had the potential to deteriorate in the direction of that pole. Second, that this fact provides each human being with the means of arriving at a value judgment of the perpetrator.

The central question guiding the preparation of both the detailed educational objectives and, later, the specific contents of the course, was not whether it could happen again, but rather, how to foster personal responsibility in order to prevent a potential sliding on that human continuum toward such a recurrence. Students were not expected to identify the warning signals of the deterioration of any particular society, but to grope, in a responsible way, with the human tendencies at the beginning of that continuum of evil. More specifically, the program was not intended to trace the origins of Nazism but to develop in the students a personal awareness of the dangers of stereotyping, prejudice, blind obedience to authority, and ethnocentrism; to enable the students to grope with the ambiguities, uncertainties and questions that the study of the Holocaust always leaves.

On the Jewish dimension, focusing on the student was meant to provide a significant contribution to collectiveness. It was stressed that attitudes of individual Jews, as well as of Jewish communities during the Holocaust, were the opposite of what Israelis perceived them to be. Rather than going "like sheep to the slaughter," it was emphasized that, in the most extreme circumstances, the Jewish moral code was demonstrated in profound ways. In the unique circumstances into which they were forced, the Jews' actions exemplified the values that have always been central to their faith, namely, the primary responsibility of the individual to the community (in Hebrew: *Arevut Hadadit*).

Two examples will, perhaps, clarify these objectives and the methods used to achieve them. One important unit in the universal dimension was entitled "The Socialization of a German Adolescent in Nazi Germany." This unit was comprised of authentic texts from schoolbooks used in Nazi Germany on subjects ranging from Geography and History through Biology and Racial Studies as well as documents regarding the activities of the Hitler-Youth (Hitlerjugend). Hence, students were encouraged to compare their environment to that of their peers in Nazi Germany. This caused most students to ponder the thin line that separates the legitimate from the illegitimate use of force; the desirable fostering of national pride from the reprehensible practice of stereotyping and discrimination against others. Further, students began considering the personal responsibilities involved in living in a democracy as opposed to being relieved of that responsibility in a totalitarian environment.

Similarly, a central unit on the Jewish dimension presented three examples of moral dilemmas faced by Jews during the Holocaust. First were those of the *Judenrate* who, as part of the Nazis' malicious program, unwittingly formed part of the machinery of destruction and had to face severe moral dilemmas in executing the Nazis' policies in various ghettos; second, that of the active resistance, who, contrary to the myth engendered in Israel, knew that their efforts would not bear any military fruit and who, therefore, faced a number of communal and individual dilemmas; third, the dilemmas faced by those individuals, groups and families who were forced to act in ways repugnant to their own religious and other values.

This program represented a radical departure from the accepted Israeli attitude toward the Holocaust. It was meant to create empathy, albeit for very different ends, with both the victim and the perpetrator, whereas the predominant behavior had been one of dissociation from both. Empathy with the perpetrator was meant, first and above all, to foster ability to make meaningful moral judgments. Students were placed in a role analogous to that of a judge confronting a criminal before him. Empathy with the victim, on the other hand, was meant to provide tools with which to appreciate the severity of his conditions and to evaluate our inability to answer a fundamental moral question: "How would I have behaved under such circumstances?" It was designed to engender humility instead of the typical arrogance and, beyond that, to provide a springboard to instill major identity traits that could be drawn from the events of the Holocaust. Moral inquiry, then, was the central trait of the entire program. Generally speaking, this exercise in moral inquiry was intended to enable the student to identify and distinguish on his cognitive map evil and justice; crime and the human response to it.

This program was never used in a large number of Israeli schools. As a matter of fact, only a few schools adopted it in its entirety while in many others teachers selectively used documents from its unique collection. The major objection to this educational approach was directed toward the program's universal dimension. It is now possible to assume that the Israeli educational establishment of the 1970s was not yet ready to accept the universalistic messages that the program contained. One of the critics argued, for example, that, while the program helped eliminate the stereotypic notion of "sheep to the slaughter," it also "blurred the Zionist lessons which other programs emphasized."[25] The Zionist lesson to which this author referred was, of course, that of "never again."

Similarly, it is not atypical that when those critics discuss the positive aspects of the program they do so using phrases, such as "The author offers a new equation of shame and honor in which the Germans, the supposed victors, were actually defeated in the struggle for the human image, while the humiliated and defeated Jews appear to be the real victor..."[26] In the early 1980s the point of departure for the evaluation of Holocaust programs is still rather emotional, even ethnocentric: the images — of the Jew and the Nazi-German — are the central factor; it is not yet the critical thinking of the student.

C. Social Reality, Collective Consciousness and the Dilemma as a Pedagogical Guideline.

On the threshold of a new century, the teaching of the Holocaust in Israel has arrived at a crossroad. The pace of events appears to force an adjustment of the Israeli collective consciousness to changes engendered by social realities. While the features that have characterized this consciousness in the past several decades are still salient, events such as the Lebanon War, the election of a member of the Knesset on the basis of a racist platform and mounting socio-cultural tensions (e.g. between religious and non-religious Jews), have clearly left their marks. For instance, the Ministry of Education declared that in the years 1986/7 the Israeli educational system will focus on the teaching of democratic values, and allocated funds for it. This has clearly been a response to the social reality in Israel.

From the perspective of the role of the Holocaust, an intrinsic part of that social reality is the realization that a new era is around the corner — a post-survivors era. More than the external traits of reality, this notion may affect the role of the Holocaust in the Israeli collective consciousness. It appears that the impact of the trauma, effected and transmitted until now by the survivors' generation, is being reproduced and reshaped by a second generation; a second generation of survivors, a second generation of Israeli-born. And thus the ground seems to be ripe for a transition whereby the dominant role of the idea from "Holocaust to rebirth" could be replaced by the acceptance of an alternate concept — orphanhood. This hypothesis rests on the assumption that changes in the social realities, extrinsic as well as intrinsic, may generate a transformation of the previously dominant tendency of dissociation from the past. As we distance ourselves from the cauldron of the Holocaust, the past may acquire its customary function in the process of shaping the traits of identity. And from the perspective of the Holocaust as a distinct event, it may pave the way for less emotionally charged modes of commemorating it.

The concept of "orphanhood" is particularly applicable to a large portion of the current body of Israeli teachers. They have been called "a generation without grandparents." Particularly for those born in the 1940s, "orphanhood" as a concept has a number of components. Firstly, a recognition of a deficiency; the lack of an organic link to the continuum of Jewish history. This recognition is the necessary condition to vanquish that denial, which, during the first decades after the Holocaust, was tightly linked to the dissociation from the shared Jewish history in the *Galut* (Exile). This recognition, then, is a necessary condition for substantiating the Holocaust as a meaningful event which can crystallize both the present and the future in the Israeli collective identity. Secondly, the concept of orphanhood establishes a rather rational and restrained interaction with the Holocaust and allows it to be perceived as a watershed in the continuity of Jewish history in general and in the biography of the second generation in particular. Thirdly, while the concept of "rebirth" helped compensate destruction and loss, the acceptance of "orphanhood" denotes maturating from the need to rationalize. And, as our concern is pedagogy, this maturity may contain the key for a rational and constructive observation of a reality in which survival, with its shallowness and void, dominates.

The acceptance of the concept of "orphanhood" may mean, then, the ability to confront the moral consequences of what otherwise has been an unbearable psychological experience. In other words, it allows resensitization, the beginning of the elimination of "psychic numbing."[27] From another perspective, this acceptance entails a meaningful perception of history in which the dimension of time constitutes an autonomous cognitive map on the individual's identity level. According to this perception, man is responsible for his destiny and history, and they are his own creation. The past is interpreted according to prevalent norms and as the sum-total of events. It is a projection that stems from a personal perception of the universe. At the same time the past treasures the assembled totality of that cultural code which affects the individual's affinity to his society and defines the mode of his participation in it. The past is perceived as it should be, different from the present.

A rational understanding of each individual's past on the historical continuum to which he belongs furnishes an appreciation of the function of the analogy; that is, an analogy to human or social experiences. That continuum on which the individual is located is always part of the wider human continuum on which every human experience may be a legitimate object for analogy; not an analogy for analogy's sake but rather for the application of meaningful lessons. To phrase it in more concrete terms, the major question to which any Holocaust curriculum should provide a meaningful answer is "what is the relevance of the Holocaust for the adolescent student within a given time and circumstances?"

"In youth, the life history intersects with history; here individuals are confirmed in their identities and societies regenerated in their life style. Historical processes have already entered the individual's core of childhood. Past history survives in the ideal and evil prototypes... To enter history, each generation of youth must find an identity consonant with its own childhood and consonant with an ideological promise in the perceptible historical process. But in youth the tables of childhood dependence begin slowly to turn: no longer is it merely for the old to teach the young the meaning of life. It is the young who, by their responses and actions, tell the old whether life as represented to them has some vital promise, and it is the young who carry in them the power to confirm those who confirm them, to renew and regenerate, to disavow what is rotten, to reform and rebel."[28]

The major application of the aforementioned analysis and argument is quite conspicuous. Commemoration in general, and particularly regarding the

Holocaust, must not be static; the remembrance of the past is of significance only when it is meaningfully connected with the realities of the present. When pedagogy is related to and concerned with the evaluation of existing social realities, its principles, indeed, are of an innovative character.

---

[1]Surveys on methods of teaching the Holocaust in Israel, have recently been completed in two accounts, (both in Hebrew): Ruth Firer, The Agents of Zionist Education, "Afik", (Haifa) 1985; Nili Keren, "The Impact of Public Opinion Shapers and Historical Research on the Development of Holocaust Teaching in High Schools and non-Formal Settings in Israel," an unpublished dissertation for a Doctoral degree, Hebrew University, 1985.

[2]Nili Keren has dealt with some aspects of this issue. *ibid.*

[3]First discussed in Arye Carmon, "Teaching the Holocaust as a Means of Fostering Values," *Curriculum Inquiry,* 9:3 (1979) pp. 209-228.

[4]For broad discussion of this issue, see A. B. Yehoshua, *Between Right and Right,* Doubleday (Garden City, N.Y.) 1981; and Amos Elon, *The Israelis: Founders and Sons,* Weidenfeld and Nicolson (London), 1971. About this issue and education, Arye Carmon "Education in Israel — Issues and Problems" (Hebrew and German), in W. Ackerman, A. Carmon, D. Zucker (eds.), *Education in Evolving Society,* Van Leer Institute (Jerusalem) 1985.

[5]Arye Carmon, *The Need for a Dialogue — A Third Generation Zionist Approach to the Relationship between Israeli and non-Israeli Jewry,* La Semana and the Moshe Sharet Institute, (Jerusalem) 1983.

[6]For some theoretical remarks about this specific issue see: Robert Jay Lifton, Preface to Alexander and Margarete Mitscherlich, *The Inability to Mourn* Grove Press (New York) 1965.

[7]See Arye Carmon, "Holocaust Teaching in Israel," *Shoah* (Fall/Winter, 1982/83) pp. 22-25.

[8]For further quantitative analysis, see: R. Firer, *op.cit.*

[9]See, for example, Shaul Ash, "In the Major Themes in the Teaching of the Holocaust and Heroism" (Hebrew), in: *Igeret La'Madrich,* 1961

[10]Lifton in: Mitscherlich, *op. cit.* p. viii.

[11]See: Arye Bauminger, "The Impact of the Eichmann Trial on Israeli Youth," (Hebrew), in: *Yediot Yad Va'Shem*, 28 1962.

[12]Gideon Hausner, *The Jerusalem Trial,* 1980, provides a comprehensive survey of the trial.

[13]Raul Hilberg, *The Destruction of European Jewry*, Quadrangle Books (New York) 1961; Hanna Arendt, *Eichmann in Jerusalem: A Report on the Banality of Evil,* Viking Compass, 1965.

[14]The Ministry of Education and Culture, *History in Senior High Schools,* (Hebrew) The Curriculum Wing, 1967.

[15]Chaim Shatzker, "Ba'ayot Didaktiot Be'Horaat Ha'Shoah," *Yedion,* No. 2, (The Israeli Historical Association) 1962; "Megamot Be'Horaat Ha'Shoah Be'Beit Ha'Sefer Ha'Yisraeli," *Moreshet* 26, 1978.

[16]See: Yehuda Bauer, "Le'Ahar Yom Ha'Kippurim Tav Shin Lamed Dalet" *Moreshet* 17, 1974.

[17]See: Sarah Guri, "An Evaluation of Cognitive and Affective Changes Among Youth, Pertaining to the Holocaust, Following the Teaching of a Curriculum Based on an Adaptation of a Jewish Community" an unpublished dissertation for a Master's degree, Tel Aviv University, 1978.

[18]For further illustrations of the change, see: "HaShoah Be'Mehkar U'Behorah," *Siah La'Moreh Le'Historia,* The Shazar Center (Jerusalem) 1979; *Mekomah Shel Ha'Universita Be'Horaat Ha'Shoah Ba'Hinuch Ha'Al-Yesody,* Haifa University (1977).

[19]Firer, *op. cit.,* pp. 92-103.

[20]A. Carmon and Y. Oron, *Hiuniut Yehudit Ba'Shoah,* Israeli Ministry of Education, 1975.

[21]Arye Carmon, *Ha'Shoah,* 2 volumes, Maalot (Ministry of Education) 1980; Israel Gutman and Chaim Shatzker, *Ha'Shoah U'Mashmauta,* Mercaz Shazar, (Jerusalem) 1983.

[22]Arye Carmon, "Teaching the Holocaust as Education Toward Values: Proposal for a Research Project," unpublished manuscript. Ben Gurion University 1976.

[23]*ibid.*

[24]"The Teaching of the Holocaust as Education Toward Values — the Setting." Unpublished pamphlet, the Van Leer Jerusalem Foundation, 1977.

[25]Firer, *op. cit.,* p. 90.

[26]*ibid.*

[27]Mitscherlich, *op. cit.,* pp. IX and 67-69.

[28]Erik Erickson, "Youth, Identity and Fidelity," *Daedalus* 91, No. 1 (Winter 1962): 5-28.

Chapter Five

Resistance and Submission: Teaching About Responses to Oppression*

Ruth Zerner

The Buchenwald survivor and noted psychiatrist Bruno Bettelheim has admitted that after his concentration camp release, he aspired "to return to the same person" he had been before. Not until years later did he realize that he could never be the same again. He had been changed by the camp experience, unforgettable in its "utter degradation and sheer misery."[1]

The same may be said by those of us who teach courses related to twentieth-century oppression, particularly the Holocaust and responses to it, including the resistance movements of World War II. One may rationalize, claiming that the Holocaust is just another topic in the academic fruit salad of intriguing courses on campus. As in other courses, professors apply social science methods or deal in varieties and complexities of causation to explain the historical developments associated with that cataclysm. Scholars still debate whether the Holocaust itself was unique. Whatever the outcome of that academic debate, I am convinced that the *teaching* of the Holocaust *is* a unique classroom experience. As a teacher, I have been changed and am being changed, as I guide and share with students in journeys through the grim realities of what Elie Wiesel has called the Kingdom of Night.

For me a unique catalyst for personal and professional growth has been the opportunity to meet with survivors of the Holocaust in classrooms, conference centers, and archives in New York City. I live in a special place in special times — following whirlwinds of human destruction that scattered the living remnants of the Nazi orgy of death throughout the world, many to our shores and to our city. Time has since provided distance and new strength for these survivors to speak and to write their tales and reflections. The students in my Holocaust course invariably testify to the powerful impact that such personal sharings by the survivors arouse. After a lively classroom presentation and encounter between two Polish-Jewish survivors (one of whom had been a small child and the other a teenager during the Holocaust), a young student in my class concluded: "This was better than any program I've ever seen on television!"

Survivors who have come to terms with their own experiences of terror and who attempt to communicate them with sensitivity and insight can reveal the ultimate realities of modern oppression in ways that contrived, second-hand, vicarious thrills of many popular television programs can never approximate. The world, not a television screen, became their cage and prison. They can never regain the luxury of innocence. The survivors are condemned to know — to know how fragile the balance between constructive forces and destructive determinants in modern, technological, bureaucratic societies; to know how seemingly irreconcilable extremes can coexist in the same individual: desire for life support and drives to annihilate. Holocaust survivors have experienced not just the sadism of many of their corrupted keepers, but also what Hannah Arendt has termed "the banality of evil"[2] — as embodied in technocrats, bureaucrats, businessmen, railroad officials, engineers, including those who never looked upon the end results of their directives of death and slavery. These ordinary citizen-servants of the state have been aptly termed by one vigorous Holocaust survivor, Simon Wiesenthal, as "murderers of the desk."[3]

Along with several of my students, I heard Simon Wiesenthal use this phrase in a lecture at a Manhattan synagogue. While teaching German history, Holocaust, a seminar on "Resistance and Submission in Nazi Europe" at Lehman College in the Bronx, I have developed a series of Manhattan field trips to places such as the Leo Baeck Institute (German-Jewish archives), the YIVO Institute on East European Jewry, special Holocaust art exhibits, as well as meetings of the Annual Scholars' Conference on the Church Struggle and the Holocaust. Visits to my classes by survivors as well as diplomats are also a regular part of my course scheduling.

Recent preoccupation with Holocaust studies has stimulated a broadening of my sensitivities in teaching and a widening of my curricular interests. The highly charged emotional responses that Holocaust materials engender need several outlets. For some students it is helpful to record their reactions systematically in a journal or a diary. In fact, as I began working with these materials I found it valuable to start keeping a journal myself. Here is one of the entries I penned at the conclusion of a 1977 seminar on "Resistance and Submission in Nazi Europe":

> This seminar forced us to reflect on the basics, the essentials of human experiences; we touched on the deepest human emotions. It is a course which deals with the *whole* person, compelling students and instructor to integrate many avenues to learning — emotional, aesthetic, psychic, spiritual, as well as intellectual. This is a new kind of teaching for me — with great humanizing possibilities.

Since that time I have shaped several new courses that emerge as increasingly interdisciplinary, rather than strictly historical: "Responses to Dehumanization: The Nazi Experience," "Survivorship," and "Human Rights and Films." As I move beyond the field of political and diplomatic history in which I was trained, I find myself less hesitant in dealing with religious history, theology, and sensitive subjects connected with edge of life experiences. By acknowledging my own background at the start of every course, I try to reflect the honesty in self-confrontation which many survivors exhibit, at the same time inviting students to share freely in this process. As a Lutheran Christian whose parents emigrated from Germany in 1929, I grew up in New York City during the Second World War — in a neighborhood flooded with German-Jewish refugees. My German-Jewish playmates sometimes showed me photographs of relatives who had perished in German ovens. Although I had been born in America, I could not help wondering how such horrors had been possible in the land of my parents' birth. That was the start of an intellectual journey that has now given me the opportunity to probe the edges and boundaries of life and death, those grotesque extensions of everyday evils that became the hell of Auschwitz. Not many of my colleagues envy me this exploration.

Yet many scholarly pursuits are highly personal, and it is precisely such personal quests that answer the deepest needs. I must be ready daily to encounter my own pains, if I am to guide students through their emotional turmoils as they respond to the Holocaust. Sometimes students cry in class or come to me privately, complaining of sleeplessness or nightmares due to the course materials. For some, recording their dreams and reactions in a diary may provide a form of relief. I also discuss in class the dreams recorded in the 1930s by Charlotte Beradt, whose book *The Third Reich of Dreams* shows how the oppression and tyranny of that regime extended even into the dream life of ordinary Germans. A housewife, for example, would dream that the Dutch oven suddenly began talking, repeating all the anti-Nazi comments that had been made in the room.[4] Oddly enough, those students with histories of deep psychic disturbance are often the least likely to be emotionally upset by the course materials. I suppose that once you have experienced hell in one form, you recognize it for what it is the next time you encounter it. Therefore, the psychic impact is lessened. It is also possible to re-evaluate one's own suffering in the perspective of Holocaust agony and abandonment.

My students' comments and journal entries reveal that the two most successful methods of motivation are art forms; films and fiction. Both in its literary and graphic expressions, art impresses as the most challenging and creative frontier for communicating the innovative insights of our century. In the eighteenth century it was philosophy, and in the nineteenth century — history. Although I am committed and trained as an historian, I recognize that the key to understanding this century's changes lies in its art, with film being one of the most powerful new forms of artistic achievement and communication.

The Nazi film *Triumph of the Will* provides unforgettable images of the Nuremberg party rallies, speech-making, marching, singing, which fulfilled deep psychic needs for many Germans who felt that after World War I their nation had provided neither psychic fulfillment nor adequate economic and political fulfillment. The significance of these rallies has been capsulized by Henry Kissinger, in a review he wrote in 1968:

> ... the emotional orgies of which the Nuremberg party rallies were an integral part also reflected a yearning for belief and a need to belong that transcended the tactical.

> There is a danger that modern mass society starves the individual emotionally. Among the careful calculations of the bureaucratic state there is often no residue for commitment. But when all the normal avenues of commitment are closed, the need to belong may break forth in elementary ways. It is no accident that in the beginning the Nazi party was especially

attractive to students, the very group which has felt
increasingly unfulfilled by modern society.

Fortunately, the Nuremberg party rallies belong to the
past. Still we should read about them not as historic relics
but as a warnings of what may happen if society neglects the
inner being or if man loses faith in his future.[5]

Just as one of our most famous intellectuals acknowledges the dangers of
emotional impoverishment, so we as teachers should consider the importance of
encouraging emotional developments and insights in our classes. Films may be
the most powerful medium of such affective education. The movie *Night and
Fog*, Renais' evocation of Auschwitz then and now, invariably moves my
student audiences. Its effects are so intense that I normally never lead a
discussion immediately following this film; I usually wait until the next class
meeting.

Elie Wiesel's novel *Night*, a small volume of distilled power, stands out for
the majority of students as the most memorable concentration camp account. As
a fictionalized version of Wiesel's Auschwitz experiences, it usually has more
impact than straightforward documentaries or memoirs. For those teachers who
do not have the advantages I have — access to survivors living in this
metropolitan area, it is, of course, essential that they also assign the many
written memoir accounts that are becoming increasingly available in paperback
form.

But very few can draw on the added bonus I have experienced as an instructor
in the New York area; I regularly encounter the children of survivors in my
class. Besides listening thoughtfully to survivors, we can learn much from their
children. In my seminar on Resistance and Submission, a son of Auschwitz
survivors taught me to broaden and to rethink my definition of resistance. He
explained that for years he had asked himself why his parents had not revolted in
Auschwitz; and then as he read Wiesel's works and struggled to understand the
camp experience, he realized that in such extreme, controlled situations "to live,
to wish to survive, is to resist." Rather than simply categorizing survivors
(heroes, resistance fighters, or "sheep") and freezing definitions, we need fluidity
of explanations as we attempt to re-create that past and apply its lessons today.

The emotional abyss between ourselves and Holocaust survivors diminishes as we begin to comprehend the subtleties of submission, which is sometimes a strategic maneuver to conceal resistance of mind and spirit. Such submission is, of course, to be distinguished from the kind of joyful submission with which many Germans responded to Nazism, including anti-Semitism, and its demands. The victims of Nazi oppression, however, are especially entitled to our most sophisticated, subtle analyses, maintaining sensitivity to the complexities of motivation, as well as the realities of the historical setting. One concentration camp survivor told me that he was particularly pleased by the success and honor attained by Elie Wiesel, because it shows that the "sheep" also are to be respected, not just the martyred resistance fighters.

Among other lessons that camp survivors have taught me is the efficacy of those internal reservoirs of aesthetic and spiritual strength, which we can draw upon in crises. To have a sense of something transcendent, beyond ourselves, *can* support us in responding to crisis situations, as can the memory of a deep human love. In addition, survivors often have a sense of proportion about life, knowing what values have ultimate priority; trivialities need not overwhelm, when one knows that life itself is *the* great gift. The intensity of their earlier experiences has left many Holocaust survivors with hypersensitivity to psychic states, an awareness not unrelated to that of the artist or mental patient. In their borderline, life and death experiences, many of them learned to "see" people, to see those with evil intent, no matter how masked, as well as the purer natures. Among the Holocaust victims, during the Nazi era there was not a solidarity of response, but among the survivors there is a solidarity of suffering remembered and of desire to avert a repetition.

For some prophetic thinkers in America a concentration camp or prison has become the central metaphor for modern life and society; such writers note that many Americans feel trapped or imprisoned, if not by the violence in cities, then by the overconfidence of experts, who may value efficiency, progress, and productivity more than human life. In 1973 the American Christian thinker, critic, and lawyer William Stringfellow maintained that "the social ethic of Nazism... more and more prevails in specific American versions — not literally identical to the particulars of Nazism, but nonetheless having the same moral identity as Nazism — which can be symbolized and summarized in three words: war, racism, genocide."[6] Warning of "totalitarian tendencies" and of "the idolatry of death"[7] in America, Stringfellow in *An Ethic for Christians and Other Aliens in a Strange Land* focuses on the model of the anti-Nazi Resistance:

If, with the cessation of the Second World War, the anti-Nazi Resistance can be said to have come to an end, the resistance to the power of death did not then cease, nor did the necessity of that resistance then diminish. That resistance goes on wherever human beings truly esteem the gift of their own humanity.[8]

With the Bible as his source, Stringfellow finds the central ethical issue to be: "how can a person act humanly now?"[9] He draws strength from the anti-Nazi resistance movement, because he perceives that under Nazi tyranny "resistance became the only human way to live."[10]

One can approach this resistance movement as a study in group activity or on the basis of individual biographies. In my research I prefer the microscopic, biographical approach to the macroscopic study of larger social and political patterns and groupings. This is not to deny the necessity of corporate structures and group support then and now; in fact, I think that the existence of numerous, diverse voluntary groups in a society retards potential technological totalitarianism and attempts at atomization of a society by a tyrant. But I still prefer to focus on individual models in the classroom and in my research.

I am convinced that a resister, like a Christian, is one who has met one. Dietrich Bonhoeffer, the German Lutheran pastor-theologian, became involved in the anti-Hitler plot through the invitation of his brother-in-law, an official of the German counter-intelligence. Moreover, I suspect from my continuing studies of Bonhoeffer's life and work that the qualities of a potential activist-resister were shaped early in his life. Strong women in his family trained and supported the young men and women who became the core of a civilian resistance circle in Berlin (including Bonhoeffer's sister, brother and brothers-in-law). Dietrich's mother, a licensed teacher, did not allow her children to attend the German public schools during the first four years of their education; she taught them at home. One of the family sayings was that Germans had their backs broken twice in the course of their lives: first at school and then during their military service.[11] Thus the Bonhoeffers resisted societal pressures and potential oppression well before the Nazi regime began. In addition, Paula Bonhoeffer inspired in her children concern for the weaker person and sensitivity to the plight of the oppressed and less fortunate around them. In 1933 Dietrich's grandmother defied a cordon of Nazi SA men in order to shop in Jewish stores, despite the Nazi boycott.[12] Thus the Bonhoeffers of Berlin opposed the Nazis from the start and attracted others to their circle. With Dietrich's father, a leading German psychiatrist, they were in many ways a conventional, upper middle class family in the center of German social and academic life — but they genuinely cared about those on the edges of society (as evidenced by Dietrich's pastoral work with young people in Berlin slums and in the Harlem ghetto in New York). Dietrich Bonhoeffer did not trivialize enormous evil. Yet he had the capacity of discerning the roots of great evil in bureaucratic banalities and petty tyrannies.[13]

Personally I prefer resistance that is life-affirming, rather than self-consciously courting death. Yet I recognize how crises and pain can make seductive the escape into death rather than into life. Even while resisting the demonic powers of death, as a last resort, resisters may find violence necessary, as did those who, like Bonhoeffer, plotted to assassinate Hitler. In the case of Simone Weil, that brilliant and perplexing personality, her attempt to identify so completely with her fellow French resisters impelled her to starve to death in England. Balance and moderation in life were not her goals. While my research leads me to focus on such fascinating and often contradictory personalities, my teaching usually results in a greater sense of balance. I invite to my classes survivors who outwardly submitted, as well as the resistance fighters; I examine German resisters who were, above all, men and women of conscience, as well as Germans who succumbed to the Nazi system. Thus I hope to challenge simplistic stereotypes, including the Jewish "sheep" and the "cold-blooded" Germans.

For me models mean more than sermons or lectures. The American comedian and film director Woody Allen expressed a similar sentiment, when he spoke of his concern about how he would cope with crises like a concentration camp (for him the metaphor for life): "I worry that I tend to moralize, as opposed to being moral."[14] Luminous lives like those of Bonhoeffer, Weil, and the current Pope John Paul II, who as a member of the Polish underground assisted Jews in the Nazi era, may challenge young people to resist contemporary oppression. I am moved by those who for their faith or intellectual freedom today face confrontations of life and death dimensions. The English journalist Trevor Beeson sensitively and subtly sketched such dilemmas in his book *Discretion and Valour: Religious Conditions in Russia and Eastern Europe* (1974). Particularly relevant is his portrait of one of Dietrich Bonhoeffer's pupils, Bishop Albrecht Shönherr of the East German Evangelical Church:

a sophisticated theologian, a trusted leader and of independent mind, able to compromise in non-essentials but fully able to stand up to the pressures of a State seeking to impose an atheist ideology. Men such as Shönherr will not be trapped into mindless opposition or spineless approbation. Their 'Yes' and their 'No' will always be qualified. Which means living with tension. None of the leaders, whatever his reactions, will allow the Church to be pushed into a narrow religiosity, which is of course what the State would like. Social concern, with all its agonies, is now fully accepted.[15]

On February 21, 1944, more than a year before his execution by the Nazis, Schönherr's seminary teacher, Dietrich Bonhoeffer outlined in one of his prison letters the ingredients in that mixture of discretion and valour with which many individuals, like Schönherr, in the postwar years decided how to face oppression:

I've often wondered here where we are to draw the line between necessary resistance to 'fate,' and equally necessary submission... It's therefore impossible to define the boundary between resistance and submission on abstract principles; but both of them must exist, and both must be practised. Faith demands this elasticity of behaviour. Only so can we stand our ground in each situation as it arises, and turn it to gain.[16]

Just as Bonhoeffer balanced strategies of resistance and submission within Nazi society, so teachers who focus on responses to modern oppression recreate the past most effectively by balancing their presentations of victims' experiences of suffering in the Holocaust with accounts of actions by individual bystanders (either supporting, undermining, or displaying indifference towards victims) and by the organized anti-Nazi resistance movement. A refreshing perspective on courage, ethics, and resistance in France during the Nazi occupation may be found in Philip Hallie's book: *Lest Innocent Blood Be Shed* (1979). In addition to this story of Pastor André Trocmé's family and village, teachers may refer students to several biographies of the Swedish diplomat Raoul Wallenberg, who saved thousands of Hungarian Jews from deportation to Nazi concentration camps.

However, to communicate the tales of anti-Nazi resisters or of supportive bystanders, there are no fictional works or films as potent and dramatic as Holocaust films and writings. The distilled power of Elie Wiesel's novel *Night* rockets its readers to the "planet" Auschwitz. *Shoah,* Claude Lanzmann's film, makes oral history, based on interviews with Holocaust survivors, an unforgettable art. Yet even the lengthy, masterful film *Shoah* does not dwell sufficiently on the inner, spiritual resistance that buoyed certain Holocaust victims. This omission was pointed out to me by a Jewish woman who had survived Auschwitz; she discussed with me her disappointment over the film's failure to present spiritual resistance among prisoners (while we were attending a Conference on the German Church Struggle and the Holocaust held in Chicago). Moreover, *Shoah* does not focus on the memories of female survivors. For example, two Jewish women who suvived Auschwitz, recorded their memories of imprisonment, and who teach us to celebrate life in spite of or in face of death are: Livia E. Bitton Jackson *(Elli: Coming of Age in the Holocaust,* 1980) and Isabella Leitner *(Fragments of Isabella,* 1978). The master teacher in *Fragments of Isabella* is Isabella's mother, who in the cattle car hurtling toward Auschwitz admonishes her children:

> Stay alive, my darlings — all six of you. Out there, when it's all over, a world is waiting for you to give it all I gave you. Despite what you see here — and you are all young and impressionable — believe me, there is humanity out there, there is dignity... I want you to live for the very life that is yours. And wherever I'll be, in some mysterious way, my love will overcome my death and will keep you alive. I love you.[17]

Isabella's concluding message echoes her mother's vision:

> I want to tell my mother that I kept her faith, that I lived because she wanted me to, that the strength she imbued me

with is not for sale,that the God in man is worth living for, and I will make sure that I hand that down to those who come after me... And children will someday plant flowers in Auschwitz, where the sun couldn't crack through the smoke of burning flesh. Mother, I will keep you alive.[18]

It is a broken world. But these fragments which Isabella Leitner, her mother, and many survivors, Jewish and Christian, victims and resisters, have collected and shared can transform our "beseeching" of the past into a quest for wholeness of life.

This paper, recently revised, was originally delivered at an International Colloquium on "Religious Responsibility and Human Rights: Lessons from the Holocaust — Directions for Today," sponsored by The National Conference of Christians and Jews and The International Council of Christians and Jews, in New York City on June 14, 1979. Copyright by Ruth Zerner.

[1] Bruno Bettelheim in a conversation with Dick Cavett, on "The Dick Cavett Show," broadcast on television, Channel 13, New York City, May 17, 1979.

[2] Hannah Arendt, *Eichmann in Jerusalem: A Report on the Banality of Evil* (New York: Viking, 1963).

[3] Simon Wiesenthal in a presentation at The Metropolitan Synagogue of New York, New York City, October 26, 1973.

[4] Charlotte Beradt, *The Third Reich of Dreams,* translated from the German by Adriane Gottwald (Chicago: Quadrangle Books, 1966), p. 45.

[5] Henry Kissinger, "The Need to Belong," a review of Hamilton T. Burden, *The Nuremberg Party Rallies: 1923-39,* in The Book Review Section, *The New York Times,* March 17, 1968.

[6]William Stringfellow, *An Ethic for Christians and other Aliens in a Strange Land* (Waco, Texas; Word Books, 1973), p. 125.

[7]*Ibid.,* pp. 117, 125.

[8]*Ibid.,* p. 126.

[9]*Ibid.,* p. 56.

[10]*Ibid.,* p. 119.

[11]Eberhard Bethge, *Dietrich Bonhoeffer: Theologe, Christ, Zeitgenosse* (Munich: Christian Kaiser Verlag, 1967), pp. 38-39.

[12]*Ibid.,* p. 31.

[13]Renate and Eberhard Bethge, eds. *Fragmente aus Tegel: Drama und Roman,* by Dietrich Bonhoeffer (Munich: Christian Kaiser Verlag, 1978), p. 17.

[14]Interview with Woody Allen, *Time,* April 30, 1979, p. 69.

[15]Trevor Beeson, *Discretion and Valour: Religious Conditions in Russia and Eastern Europe* (Glasgow: Collins, 1974), p. 172.

[16]Dietrich Bonhoeffer, *Letters and Papers from Prison: The Enlarged Edition,* ed. by Eberhard Bethge (New York: Macmillan, 1953, 1967, 1971), pp. 217-218.

[17]Isabella Leitner, *Fragments of Isabella* (New York: Dell, 1978), pp. 28-29.

[18]*Ibid.,* pp. 102-103.

Part II

Teaching Others

Chapter Six

What Can Anyone Do?

John K. Roth

In the spring of 1942, SS officer Ernst Biberstein went east. He had already been involved in deporting Jews to killing centers, but his new assignment would take him from an administrative post into the field to relieve an officer in *Einsatzgruppe C*. One of four Nazi squadrons charged with eliminating Jews behind the lines of the German advance into Russia, *Einsatzgruppe C* policed the Ukraine. Among its credits was the murder of more than 33,000 Jews at Babi Yar the previous September, a task accomplished in only two days. Biberstein missed Babi Yar, but he did nothing to diminish the record of his unit once he assumed command. It was unnecessary to deport thousands of Jews because Biberstein and his men worked efficiently. This Nazi, however, was not bloodthirsty. No evidence shows that he actively sought to lead a crew of killers or that he relished the operations carried out by those under his command. His is only one example within a spectrum of activity that included not only direct participation in murder but also the many sorts of complicity required to make a process of destruction happen. And yet when we ask "What can anyone do?" and direct that question toward the Holocaust, Biberstein's case makes us wonder. It does so because, prior to his joining the SS in 1936, Biberstein had been a Protestant pastor.

As Biberstein moved from killing by administrative decision to killing by ordering executioners to fire machine guns, a young German soldier reached Munich, following orders that transferred him to the university there for training as a medic. Earlier, his letter alluded to events that had shaken him to the core. "I can't begin to give you the details," he wrote, "it is simply unthinkable that such things exist... The war here in the East leads to things so terrible I would never have thought them possible."[1] Willi Graf referred not to combat against Russian troops but to slaughter by the *Einsatzgruppen*.

In Munich two of Graf's closest friends were Hans and Sophie Scholl, both in their early twenties. Motivated by an understanding of Christianity and a love for Germany that were at odds with Hitler's, the Scholls were determined to do more than ask haplessly, "What can we do?" With Hans in charge, their public dissent began. Although they possessed abundant courage, ingenuity, and high ideals, their power was scant. Nonetheless, along with their philosophy professor, Kurt Huber, 51, and fellow students Alex Schmorell, Christoph Probst, and Willi Graf, leaflets from their resistance movement, "The White Rose," attacked Nazism.

German resistance to Hitler remained scattered. It did not land many telling blows, as the Scholls' effort seems to demonstrate. Their group operated for less than a year, its output restricted to several thousand copies of seven different flyers. The war and the death camps churned on for more than two years after the White Rose was crushed.

The results seem paltry, but a second glance is in order. The war was still in Hitler's favor when the students' protest began in 1942. By the time the Scholls were caught, that tide had turned at Stalingrad. The White Rose could assume no credit for this reversal, but the Nazis did take its activity seriously, all the more so as Hitler's war plans began to collapse. Nazi justice proceeded quickly. On 22 February 1943, only four days after their arrest, the Scholls and Christoph Probst stood trial. Eight hours later they were beheaded. Again the question "What can anyone do?" comes to mind. Sophie Scholl's testimony, documented by the court that convicted her, was that "somebody had to make a start."[2]

The lives of Ernst Biberstein and Hans and Sophie Scholl unfolded in the midst of modernized economic systems, technological capabilities, and political structures that have produced abundant blessings but also surplus people, unique forms of human domination, and unprecedented quantities of mass murder. As the Holocaust exemplified, the modern political state may not flinch from putting its apparatus of destruction into action. If a ruling elite still retains control over this overwhelming power, the more ordinary man or woman seems to fall impotently before it.

The truth about the Holocaust cannot be taught unless one communicates the fact that twentieth-century states may progressively squeeze the individual into obedience devoid of dissent. As students become aware of this reality, however, they are tempted to put the Holocaust into a deterministic framework.

What happened seems inescapable, and individual responsibility recedes. Such an outlook is as dangerous as it is easy, for it is the stuff of which indifference is made. The truth about the Holocaust cannot be taught unless indifference is resisted, and thus the importance of meditating on what individuals could and could not — can and cannot — do. From time to time, courageous resistance did save lives and prevented the Nazis from doing their worst. Many Jews resisted. Some Gentiles did, too, including a few deep within the German system itself. If Jewish losses did not exceed two-thirds of European Jewry and one-third of the Jewish people worldwide, the credit does not belong entirely to Allied military might. Persons acting as individuals or within small groups made their contributions as well.

The immensity of the Holocaust becomes too impersonal and more inevitable than it really was if one overlooks the fact that individuals made the decisions and obeyed the orders that destroyed millions. To drive home that lesson is one of the most important tasks for those who teach about the Holocaust. By exploring, moreover, what people did and could have done to thwart the destruction process, we may be able to forge responses to the question "What can anyone do?" that are hopeful and realistic at once. Consider, therefore, the question put to an imprisoned Franz Stangl, formerly commandant of Sobibor and Treblinka, on 27 June 1971 by the journalist Gitta Sereny. "Do you think," she asked near the end of a long series of interviews, "that that time in Poland taught you anything?"[3] To be more specific, it is crucial to ask: Could Franz Stangl have left the path that took him to Treblinka where he occupied a middle-management position requiring him to see that others carried out the murderous responsibilities handed to him? And if he could have done so, would it have made any difference if he had?

Simon Wiesenthal, the famed Nazi-hunter, was once quoted as saying that "if I had done nothing else in life but to get this evil man Stangl, then I would not have lived in vain."[4] At the time, Stangl was on trial in Düsseldorf, Germany, having been extradited from Brazil where on 28 February 1967 he was arrested in Brooklin, one of the better residential areas of Sao Paulo. Although Stangl had never flaunted his past, neither was he in hiding. In 1945 American authorities knew about his activity at Treblinka, but Stangl fled to Rome. Assisted by clergy in the Vatican, he obtained a Red Cross passport — it reversed his name to Paul F. Stangl — and then travelled to Damascus, following a route used before and since by his SS peers. Before long he sent for his wife and children, who traveled under their own names and told the Austrian police of their destination. In 1954 the Stangls openly entered Brazil, registering at the Austrian consulate in Sao Paulo. Eventually employed by Volkswagen, Stangl had made a new beginning.

Although the surprise was less that Stangl had been found than that he had ever been lost, his court appearance brought the darkness of his past to light. On 22 December 1970 he was sentenced by a West German court to life imprisonment. Early in April of the next year, Gitta Sereny met him for the first time. This meeting occurred because Sereny, who had covered Stangl's trial, became convinced that he was "an individual of some intelligence" and that "things had happened to and inside him which had happened to hardly anyone else, ever."[5] Stangl used the initial interview to rebut accusations made against him, but Sereny was after something more, "some new truth which would contribute to the understanding of things that had never yet been understood."[6] She encouraged Stangl to provide it, promising "to write down exactly what he said, whatever it would be, and that I would try — my own feelings notwithstanding — to understand without prejudice."[7]

After deliberating, Stangl agreed. In fits and starts the layers of his life unfolded in the seventy hours of conversation held in April and June 1971. First published in the *Daily Telegraph Magazine*, these dialogues were later elaborated into book form. In addition to keeping her promise to Stangl, Sereny provides an account more valuable than Rudolf Hoess's autobiographical description of his career as the commandant of Auschwitz.[8] For Sereny went on to interview Stangl's family, many of his associates, and other Holocaust authorities in compiling her narrative. Even after all of the cross-checking, elements of the Stangl story remain open to conjecture but Sereny's work has the advantage of multiple dimensions missing in Hoess's confession.

Born in 1908 in the small Austrian town of Altmünster, Stangl claimed that he was "scared to death" of his father, a former soldier, who died of malnutrition when his son was eight.[9] Leaving school at fifteen to become an apprentice weaver, he was good at the work and soon supervised others. Music and sailing were his diversions. Looking back, Stangl called these years "my happiest time." In the Austria of the 1930s, however, the young man saw that a lack of higher education would prevent him from further promotions in the textile field. Police work attracted him as an alternative, particularly since it might enable him to assist in checking the turbulence that economic depression had brought to his country. He passed the required entrance examination in 1931 and was notified to report to the Linz barracks for training. Upon announcing his departure, Stangl learned that his textile employer had been planning to send him to Vienna for additional schooling. When Sereny asked whether he still could have seized that opportunity, Stangl responded that his boss "didn't ask me."[10]

Stangl's account frequently reveals his passivity, a sense of being conscripted into circumstances beyond his control. A case in point is his early affiliation with the Nazis. It remains unclear whether Stangl was an illegal Nazi in Austria prior to the *Anschluss* (March 1938), but he offered the following story. As a young police officer he was decorated for meritorious service, including special recognition for seizing a Nazi arms cache shortly after Engelbert Dollfuss, the Austrian chancellor, was assassinated in July 1934. That achievement would plague Stangl, but the immediate result was his posting to Wels as a political investigator "to ferret out anti-government activities."[11] Stangl, now married, claims to have had no Nazi sympathies at this time, but by 1938 his situation had changed. Shortly after the *Anschluss* the National Socialists purged the Austrian police. Among the first victims were three of Stangl's colleagues who had received the same decoration that had come to him for his earlier raid against the Nazis. Out of fear, Stangl told Sereny, he arranged for a friend to enter his name on a list that would certify his having been a Nazi party member for the previous two years.

According to Stangl, the die was cast: "It wasn't a matter of choosing to stay or not stay in our profession. What it had already become, so quickly, was a question of survival."[12] Thus, Stangl remained in police work after his branch was absorbed into the Gestapo in January 1939. Over his wife's objections, he also signed the standard statement that both identified him as a *Gottgläubiger*, a believer in God, but severed his ties with the Roman Catholic Church. The next decisive step on the path to Treblinka came in November 1940 when Stangl was ordered to Berlin.

These orders, signed by Himmler, transferred Stangl to the General Foundation for Institutional Care *(Gemeinnützige Stiftung für Heil und Anstaltspflege)*. This foundation, one unit in the larger network code-named T-4 because its headquarters were at Tiergartenstrasse 4, helped to administer T-4's program of "mercy-killing" for the mentally and physically handicapped in Germany and Austria. Stangl was to be a leading security officer in this secret operation. He reports that the assignment was presented to him as choice, though prudence ruled out the alternatives. Thus, when Stangl returned to

Austria, his new post was a euthanasia center not far from Linz, Schloss Hartheim, which later on would kill Jews from the concentration camp nearby at Mauthausen.

The activities of T-4 were under Hitler's personal control. Moreover, the euthanasia project, utilizing carbon monoxide gas, had the blessing of influential German scientists and physicians. It lasted many months and claimed some 100,000 lives. Public protest led by prominent German Christians helped stall this death machine in August 1941, but by then the project's goals were virtually achieved. The euthanasia program was probably not consciously devised as a training ground for staff to carry out the Final Solution, but it cannot be sheer coincidence that personnel from Schloss Hartheim and other centers regrouped in Poland to officiate at the death camps. In February 1942, for example, T-4 offered Franz Stangl a new choice: either report back to Linz, where he would be subject to a superior whom he feared, or take a position in the east near Lublin. This "either-or" was no accident either. The Berlin officials were confident that Stangl would choose Poland, and he did. Soon after arrival, he learned that his commanding office, SS General Odilo Globocnik, "intended confiding to me the construction of a camp called Sobibor."[13]

   Nazi objectives called for much of western Poland to be incorporated into the Reich. Jews from that area would be deported to the Polish interior, an area referred to as the *Generalgouvernement*, where they would be ghettoized with countless other Jews from this region and eventually exterminated. In the *Generalgouvernement*, Globocnik, assisted by Christian Wirth and a team of T-4's euthanasia experts under Wirth's direction, had overall command of "Operation Reinhard," named for its mastermind, Reinhard Heydrich, who had been assassinated in the spring of 1942 by Czech patriots.

The "pure" death camps opened by Globocnik in the *Generalgouvernement* during 1942 — Belzec (March), Sobibor (May), and Treblinka (July) — were in administrative channels that led directly to Hitler's chancellery. In contrast, Auschwitz and Majdanek, the latter also in this zone, remained under authority of the Main Office of Economic Administration (WVHA) because they were labor installations as well. Himmler often sought to intensify the zeal of his underlings through competition, and thus he had given Hoess sole charge of Auschwitz. Rivalry ensued, but if Globocnik, Wirth, and their associates finished second to Hoess as architects of mass death, they certainly were not failures. Before Belzec, Sobibor, and Treblinka were shut down less than two years later, they destroyed nearly two million Jews and thousands of Gypsies, children making up one-third of the total. Sereny reports that the survivors of these camps — "work Jews" who had to help run them — numbered under one hundred.

Stangl claims not to have known at first the purpose of his construction project at Sobibor, but ignorance vanished when he was taken to Belzec to witness the first large-scale extermination with permanent chambers using exhaust gas. He learned that Sobibor would do likewise and that he would be in charge. Back at Sobibor, Stangl discussed the options with a friend: "We agreed that what they were doing was a crime. We considered deserting — we discussed it for a long time. But how? Where could we go? What about our families?"[14] Stangl applied for a transfer. He got no reply, but in June he did receive a letter from his wife. She wrote that his superiors were arranging for her to bring the Stangl children to Poland for a visit.

Sobibor opened in May 1942 and operated for two months before equipment malfunctions halted exterminations until October. Meanwhile the Stangl family arrived, lodging at an estate about three miles from the camp. Heretofore Franz had kept Theresa Stangl in the dark about the particulars of his work at Schloss Hartheim and in Poland. Now she learned the truth about Sobibor from one of her husband's subordinates. Apparently the possibility of an open confrontation that might lead to Theresa's rejection of him was more than Stangl could risk. He not only told her that he had no direct responsibility for any killing but also arranged a speedy departure for his family. By the time they were back home in Austria, Franz had been transferred to Treblinka.

Franciszek Zabecki, one of the persons interviewed by Gitta Sereny, was a member of the Polish underground. As traffic supervisor at the Treblinka railway station, he tracked German military movements and also became "the only trained observer to be on the spot throughout the whole existence of Treblinka camp."[15] Zabecki counted the extermination transports, recording the figures marked on each car. "The number of people killed in Treblinka was 1,200,000," he testifies, "and there is no doubt about it whatever."[16]

Dr. Irmfried Eberl, formerly in charge of a euthanasia center at Bernburg near Hannover, was the builder and first commandant of Treblinka. His administration had been wanting in Globocnik's eyes, and thus Stangl replaced him. Describing his arrival there as an entry into Dante's Inferno, Stangl rationalized that his major assignment was to care for the riches left behind by those on their way to the gas. "There were enormous — fantastic — sums involved and everybody wanted a piece of it, and everybody wanted control."[17] Indeed, Stangl argued, the main reason for the extermination of the Jews was that the Nazis were after their money. At least one Jewish survivor, Alexander Donat, does not disagree completely. He credits Stangl with being "sober enough to realize that behind the smoke-screen of Nazi propaganda and racist mystique there was no sacred mission but only naked greed."[18] In any case, Stangl tried to convince himself that his involvement was limited to handling Treblinka's windfall. Actually he headed the entire extermination process, which destroyed five to six thousand Jews per day. The system worked, says Stangl, "and because it worked, it was irreversible." With unintended irony, he reiterates that his work was "a matter of survival — always of survival." "One did become used to it," he adds.[19]

Stangl made "improvements" at Treblinka, among them a fake railroad station to deceive the arriving victims. It was unveiled at Christmas 1942. Meanwhile Stangl was in Austria on furlough. He obtained such leaves every three or four months, but relationships with his wife were strained throughout his time at Treblinka. The gassing and burning continued under Stangl's administration during the first half of 1943. However, on August 2, a Monday, which usually was a light working day because transports were less frequently loaded on Sundays, Treblinka's death machine temporarily jammed when a long-planned revolt broke out among the Jewish workers. Although the camp was set ablaze, the gas chambers remained intact. Transports from Bialystok would still end there, the last one arriving on August 19. Thereafter the camp itself was liquidated, disguised with plantings and a small farm "built from the bricks of the dismantled gas chambers."[20] Stangl was reassigned to Trieste.

That same Christmas of 1942, Stangl had become fully assimilated in the SS, and at the war's end his SS uniform led to his arrest by Americans in an Austrian village on the Attersee. Two years later, as Austrian officials investigated Schloss Hartheim's euthanasia campaign, Stangl came to their attention. They requested jurisdiction, which was granted. Interned in an "open" prison at Linz, Stangl walked away as the Hartheim trial proceeded. Twenty years passed before he was brought to justice.

In conversation with Gitta Sereny, Stangl never stopped implying that he was himself a victim of the Holocaust. He reckoned that he was caught in a web from which he could not escape. And yet his excuses were less than ironclad, even in his own eyes. Responding to Sereny's question, "Do you think that tha time in Poland taught you anything?", Stangl's final words included these: "Yes, that everything human has its origin in human weakness."[21] Not twenty-four hours later, Franz Stangl died of heart failure.

Could anything have strengthened Stangl's heart enough to divert him from the course he took? That issue climaxes *Into That Darkness*, and at this point, surprisingly, not Franz but Theresa Stangl takes center stage. In October 1971, Gitta Sereny ended her last conversation with Frau Stangl by inquiring:

> Would you tell me,... what do you think would have happened
> if at any time you had faced your husband with an absolute
> choice; if you had said to him: "Here it is; I know it's terribly
> dangerous, but either you get out of this terrible thing, or else
> the children and I will leave you." What I would like to
> know... is: If you had confronted him with these alternatives,
> which do you think he would have chosen?

Theresa Stangl contemplated that painful question for a long time. At last she expressed the belief that given the choice — Treblinka or his wife — her husband "would in the final analysis have chosen me."[22]

The next day Sereny received a note from Frau Stangl qualifying her previous statement. Franz Stangl, wrote his wife, "would never have destroyed himself or the family."[23] Sereny, however, believes that the first appraisal contains the greater truth, no matter how difficult it may have been for Frau Stangl to accept it. If Gitta Sereny is correct, the web of responsibility, and of human frailty, too, spreads out. Yet one also must ask a second question: would resistance really have made any difference? Franz Stangl, for one, had his doubts. Quizzed about what might have happened if he had refused his orders, Stangl replied: "If I had sacrificed myself, if I had made public what I felt, and had died... it would have made no difference. Not an iota. It would all have gone on just the same, as if it and I had never happened." Sereny accepted the answer but pressed on to ask whether such action might at least have given courage to others. "Not even that," insisted Stangl. "It would have caused a tiny ripple, for a fraction of an instant — that's all."[24]

Such testimony cannot be discounted. Fear and insecurity are never easily dislodged, and even if every SS man had shared Stangl's professed ambivalence about the Final Solution, an isolated defection from the ranks would hardly have

...ı process. Those truths, however, detract nothing from ...e stressed as well. First, Sobibor and Treblinka testify that ...owever realistic, does not deserve to be the last word. Second, ...ıps, as Theresa Stangl helps to show, also signify that such ...closer to self-fulfillment whenever people, especially those nearest anu ...to each other, fail to help one another oppose the weakness that enables ı..e powers that be to consign defenseless victims to misery and death. Third, had more individuals done for each other what was very much within their power, namely, to call each other to account for their actions, the Holocaust need not have gone on just the same. We are and must be responsible for each other as well as for ourselves. We must be born again as men and women blessed with the capacity to confront each other and care for each other here and now. If those points are obvious, they are anything but trivial. Not to underscore them is to create a silence in which personal responsibility can be too easily shirked and in which helpless people can be too easily found redundant and killed.

Gitta Sereny's encounters with Franz Stangl drove home to her "the fatal interdependence of all human actions."[25] If those actions are to forestall progress that culminates tragically in a paralyzing doom, Theresa Stangl must be taken no less seriously than her husband, his superiors, and their obedient underlings. To discern what she and other individuals, ordinary ones like ourselves, could and could not do, including the ways in which her voice dissolves sanguine illusions about the costs of resistance, is a vital lesson to learn from that time in Poland.

On 9 October 1974, some three years after Franz Stangl's heart finally failed in a German prison, advanced hardening of the arteries felled a person who played a Holocaust role quite different from the Treblinka commandant's. Black-marketeer and *bon vivant*, Oskar Schindler had a "life-of-the-party" style that frequently made him an unfaithful husband.[26] By some moral conventions, Stangl was a better man than this tall, blond Czech-German who pursued his fortune in the Polish city of Krakow in 1939. Before the war, Schindler joined the Sudeten German Party. Wearing its swastika lapel pin proved good for business. Hence, this industrial speculator followed the *Wehrmacht's* invasion into Poland and took over an expropriated enamelware factory. Soon he realized handsome returns by using Jewish labor, which cost him practically nothing — at first. That qualification, however, spells the difference between Schindler's remaining a pleasure-seeking profiteer and his becoming an individual whose personal initiative saved more than a thousand Jews from annihilation.

The tyranny that followed Hitler's seizure of Bohemia and Moravia in March 1939 both surprised and disillusioned Schindler but not completely. Indeed, Schindler would go on to lend his services to Admiral Wilhelm Canaris' *Abwehr* (the foreign and counterintelligence department of the German High Command). What changed Schindler's mind decisively was the violence he witnessed as special squads recruited from Heydrich's *Sicherheitsdienst* began to attack Krakow's Jews. Insofar as those tactics targeted productive laborers, Schindler found them utterly counterproductive to the war effort. More than that, this wasting of human life struck him as profoundly morally wrong. Deciding that he could intercede from within the German system itself, Schindler negotiated a daring series of bargains. If the initial purpose was to keep healthy the labor needed to sustain his factory's productivity, before the war's end his obsession become more fundamental. He was determined that the hundreds of workers in his care would survive and have a future.

Schindler kept a list. It contained the names of some 1,300 men and women who came to call themselves *Schindlerjuden*. As liberation approached in the spring of 1945, Schindler promised he would "continue doing everything I can for you until five minutes past midnight."[27] His promise was as good as his word had been for years. During that time in Poland, when his Jewish workers had been forced to live in a slave labor camp under the sadistic Amon Goeth, Schindler spent a fortune in bribes to set up his own subcamp haven at the factory. With the dedicated help of his wife, Emily, that practice continued when Oskar had to relocate his factory in Czechoslovakia as the Red Army advanced. Schindler's efforts even plucked from Auschwitz some of those whose names were written in his list of life.

With the war's end, Oskar and Emily Schindler were refugees. They had lost everything, except that they were not forgotten. Under the leadership of Leopold and Mila Pfefferberg, the *Schindlerjuden* rallied to help him when their own recovery permitted. Among many other kindnesses , they saw that Schindler's last wish, a Jerusalem burial, was granted. Today in Jerusalem a tree at Yad Vashem, the Israeli memorial to the Holocaust, grows in honor of Oskar Schindler. It testifies that he took to heart the Talmudic verse he heard in Krakow in 1939 from Yitzhak Stern, a Jewish accountant: "He who saves the life of one man saves the entire world." Even now, however, the *Schindlerjuden* do not know exactly why Oskar Schindler performed his life-saving missions.

Although the Jewish philosopher, Jean Améry, was not on Schindler's list, he did survive Auschwitz. Decades after his release from Bergen-Belsen, he observed that "the expectation of help, the certainty of help, is indeed one of the fundamental experiences of human beings."[28] But the gravest loss produced by the Holocaust, he went on to suggest, was that it radically undermined that "element of trust in the world,... the certainty that by reason of written or unwritten social contracts the other person will spare me — more precisely stated, that he will respect my physical, and with it also my metaphysical, being."[29] Hoping to revive at least some of the trust that Améry lost, there are social scientists who are trying to determine why people like Schindler helped the defenseless while so many others did not.[30] Just as it is clear that very few of the rescuers regard themselves as moral heroes, it may be that an "altruistic personality" will emerge from these Holocaust studies. Whatever we can learn on that score is important. As another Jewish survivor, Pierre Sauvage, aptly puts the point:

> If we do not learn how it is possible to act well even under the most trying circumstances, we will increasingly doubt our ability to act well even under less trying ones. If we remember solely the horror of the Holocaust, we will pass on no perspective from which meaningfully to confront and learn from that very horror. If we remember solely the horror of the Holocaust, it is we who will bear the responsibility for having created the most dangerous alibi of all: that it was beyond man's capacity to know and care. If Jews do not learn that the whole world did not stand idly by while we were slaughtered, we will undermine our ability to develop the friendships and alliances that we need and deserve. If Christians do not learn that even then there were practicing Christians, they will be deprived of inspiring and essential examples of the nature and requirements of their faith. If the hard and fast evidence of the possibility of good on earth is allowed to slip through our fingers and turn into dust, then future generations will have only dust to build on. If hope is allowed to seem an unrealistic response to the world, if we don't work towards developing confidence in our spiritual resources, we will be responsible for producing in our time a world devoid of humanity, literally.[31]

"What can anyone do?" If we neither deny our century's wounds nor submit meekly to the Holocaust scars that deface humankind, perhaps we can have more than dust to build on. The mending of the earth and the healing of trust depend on the determination to resist the world's horror with undeceived lucidity. Few have done as well on that score as the winner of the 1986 Nobel Prize for Peace, Holocaust survivor Elie Wiesel. Speaking of the Holocaust, Wiesel says, "I'm afraid that the horror of that period is so dark, people are incapable of understanding, incapable of listening."[32] And yet Wiesel's work, including his thirty books, testifies that he does not despair. Hatred, indifference, even history itself, may do their worst, but that outcome does not deserve to be the final word. Such themes permeate Wiesel's writings. In his recent novel, *The Fifth Son*, which he dedicates to his son, Elisha, "and all the other children of survivors," those themes take on nuances of special significance for all students and teachers who try to listen and understand more than forty years after Auschwitz.

The story introduces us to Wolfgang Berger, but that is not his name. He should be dead; yet he lives. This man, who is actually Richard Lander, dwells in Reshastadt, a German town. His real home, the place where he became the *Angel*, is farther east. Its name has been Davarowsk as long as anyone can remember. But Davarowsk is not the same place now that it was before. No place is. Nor is any person, whether they know it or not. *The Fifth Son* shows as much by exploring "an ontological Event" that cannot be reduced to a word: the Holocaust.[33]

Ariel is the fifth son. But who is Ariel? That question makes him wonder. It makes him suffer, too, and not least because the dilemma drives him toward Reshastadt where he intends to be "the bearer of a message." Although Richard Lander is "not aware of either message or messenger," the *Angel* must reverse his customary role and receive both.[34] Whether either reaches him remains unclear. Still, no reader of this novel is likely to be unmoved by Ariel's testimony.

"Was it dawn or dusk? The town of Reshastadt appears crouched and unreal under a steady slow drizzle...Here is the station. In my confusion, I did not know whether I had just arrived or was preparing to leave again. Was I awake?"[35] Linked stylistically to the work of Borges, Camus, and Kafka, this book creates intense personal encounters. Past, present, and future collide within them as the characters interrogate appearance and reality to see what sense life makes during and after the Final Solution. The resulting art — complex and simple at once — transmutes despair into determination by converting revenge into renewal.

At the outset, the author reminds us of the Torah tradition that refers to "four sons: one who is wise and one who is contrary; one who is simple and one who does not even know how to ask a question."[36] But here Wiesel writes to, for, and about the fifth son. This son is different — not because he lacks qualities the others possess but because he is not there. Death explains the absence, and yet it does not because death explains nothing. Besides, even if it has everything to do with death, the fifth son's absence is not a matter of death alone.

The fifth son is Ariel. In a dual sense, he is both dead and alive, for Ariel is not one son but two. The Ariel born in 1949, who seeks and then bears his message by narrating Wiesel's story, is today a professor "in a small university in Connecticut."[37] Raised in New York, a college student during the sixties, he has experienced the tumult of America during the years of Vietnam. Lisa, his girl friend, initiates him. Sex, drugs, politics, love — they share them all. But just as "Lisa has left me," though at thirty-five he misses her, so Ariel is shaped less by the American Dream than by the Kingdom of Night he never knew in Davarowsk.[38]

Ariel has a brother. That fact was long unknown to him because his brother is also Ariel, the fifth son. If such facts are puzzling, puzzlement only begins to tell the tale. For there is much more to the relationship between Ariel and his brother than questions about a name might suggest. In the case of either of the Ariels, for example, it is an issue whether one or the other is truly the elder or the younger brother.

Though he is eleven years older, the professor's brother will be six forever. That was his age when the *Angel* and his SS cohort hunted Ariel down and took his life in Davarowsk. His Jewish parents, Rachel and Reuven Tamiroff, tried their best for him, although the best was not to be in Davarowsk. Ghettoized with the other Jews, Reuven led the Jewish Council there. He did so fairly, with dignity, and he paid the price. Once he learned the fully murderous intent of Richard Lander and the Nazis, Tamiroff resigned his post and told the ghetto what he knew. The *Angel* allowed Reuven to live but took the lives of six members of the Council and then readied the entire ghetto for deportation to the gas.

The Tamiroffs had to board the death train. Before doing so, they took two other steps. First, Reuven met with Simha Zeligson, Tolka Friedman, and Rabbi Aharon-Asher. He invited them together to share secretly an avenging oath: " 'Whoever among us shall survive this ordeal swears on his honor and on the sanctity of our memory to do all that he can to kill the killer, even at the cost of his life.' "[39] All save the Rabbi agreed. Second, Rachel and Reuven located "some good honest people" who would hide Ariel from the killers.[40] Then they left him behind. Eventually Reuven learned that Lander, too, took an oath and kept it. Later he also must contend with the realization that his own resolution to kill was no match for the Nazi's.

Lander knew the Tamiroffs too well. When he spied them boarding the train without Ariel, he disbelieved their story that the child had died from ghetto disease. Keeping his word to Rachel and Reuven, the *Angel* found the boy. His vengeance was "terrible and cruel, people spoke of it in all the ghettos near and far." Since learning of it, Ariel's New York brother "cannot tolerate hot milk."[41]

Learning of it — that is what obsesses the American Ariel, the fifth Jewish son who is alive but not there because he is the child of Holocaust survivors whose Ariel did not survive Davarowsk. If Rachel and Reuven endured, reunited, and crossed the ocean, they could not make the new beginnings for which America is famous. Burdened by a past too heavy, they wanted new life, even gave Ariel a second birth to affirm it, and yet they found that a second Ariel might double their sadness more than their joy. For what identity could they give him, and what identity did they give him by naming him Ariel?

No one is better equipped then Elie Wiesel to probe such issues. The two Ariels, their father, and the encounters they have — all are encompassed by his own experience. In the words of Ariel, who in this case seems to speak for Wiesel himself, "I have said 'I' in their stead. Alternately, I have been one or the other."[42] Surviving the extinction of his own childhood in Auschwitz, Wiesel found his way to New York and then to marriage and fatherhood. This book is wrung from his soul. Together they give voice to the silence that threatens to dominate when a life suffers more than anybody's should. Elie Wiesel lives. So does Ariel. And so must *The Fifth Son*, because the tale has to be told. Even Reuven Tamiroff knows as much, although the second Ariel cannot fully extract the story from him until his mother is gone and he discovers the letters that his father has written to the Ariel who is not there. In the discovery, those letters become his as well, and they lead the New York Ariel to strike up a correspondence of his own with the brother in Davarowsk.

Ariel's letters to Ariel are also prompted by discovery of another kind. Part of Reuven Tamiroff's melancholy derives from the conviction that he and Simha Zeligson made good their attempt to assassinate Richard Lander in 1946. For years they meet weekly to study and debate, seeking to determine in retrospect whether their action was indeed just. Their inquiry does little to assuage the guilt whose persistence troubles them in more ways than one. Ariel's discovery goes further. It comes to include the knowledge that the *Angel* lives, prosperous and happy, as Wolfgang Berger, the Reshastadt businessman.

The business Richard Lander started must not remain unfinished. So Ariel Tamiroff, his appointment made with death, heads for Germany to encounter the Herr Direktor. Ariel reaches the station where he must change trains for Reshastadt. It is Graustadt, that gray city where one "can buy anything: a woman for the morning, insurance with a suicide clause or a lifetime ticket on the German Railroad System."[43]

What happened in Graustadt and not long after is not for an article to say. Nor may it be for Elie Wiesel to determine completely. No one but Ariel is Ariel. And yet that is not where we should leave *The Fifth Son*, for the message that Ariel bears in the novel is that he did not kill. The reason he did not, moreover, has everything to do with Ariel's being Jewish, with his being the fifth son, with his being human.

How does that work? Wiesel gives us hints: Ariel, for example receives advice from his neighbor and friend, Rebbe Zvi-Hersh, who says, " 'To punish a guilty man, to punish him with death, means linking yourself to him forever: is that what you wish?' "[44] In this case, however, the question is just as important as the traditional counsel that precedes it. If "yes" is not the best answer, "no" does not follow without pain. For anyone who cares, as Ariel's "sad summing up" implies, the truth is that a life lived after Auschwitz cannot be one's alone but instead will be permeated by "the memory of the living and the dreams of the dead."[45]

That fact may account for the name Elie Wiesel bestowed on the two fifth sons. Ariel is a biblical name. It appears more than once in Scripture, and its meanings are diverse. The name can mean "lion of God" and also "light of God," which could explain why a later tradition thought of Ariel as an angel altogether different from the *Angel*. Unfortunately, a darker side haunts the name as well. In Isaiah's prophecy the following words can be found: "Yet I will distress Ariel, and there shall be moaning and lamentation, and she shall be to me like an Ariel" (Isa. 29:2). The first Ariel signifies Jerusalem; the second suggests that Ariel will become like an altar, a scene of holocaust. But the oracle sees more. In time, "the nations that fight against Ariel" will themselves be quelled by "the flame of a devouring fire" (Isa. 29:5-8). Perhaps that is true — or will be — but having met the *Angel*, Ariel Tamiroff remembers an old saying: "The Lord may wish to chastise, that is His prerogative; but it is mine to refuse to be His whip."[46] For both his brother's sake and his own, Ariel, whose American life has also been a scene of Holocaust, will identify with his people, with Jerusalem even though he chooses to live in the Diaspora, and thereby with the well-being of humankind. Thus, he seems most like his namesake in another part of scripture.

The biblical book of Ezra only mentions Ariel. His name is nonetheless important and vital. For Ariel is called a "leading" man (Ezra 8:16). His leadership urges remembrance and return from exile. It means to respond to devastation and sadness by acts of restoration that rebuild Jerusalem and mend the world. Masterfully recounting the history of the Holocaust and its aftermath, *The Fifth Son* leads the same way. It is therefore fitting that Eliezer is also among Ezra's "leading men." His namesake, the author of this book, nurtures us all to respond to the question "What can anyone do?" by becoming like Ariel — lions, if not angels, of light.

---

[1] Cited by Richard Hanser, *A Noble Treason: The Revolt of the Munich Students Against Hitler* (New York: G. P. Putnam's Sons, 1979), pp. 152-53. See also Annette E. Dumbach and Jud Newborn, *Shattering the German Night: The Story of the White Rose* (Boston: Little, Brown and Company, 1986).

[2] Hanser, *A Noble Treason*, p. 274.

[3] Gitta Sereny, *Into That Darkness: An Examination of Conscience* (New York: Vintage Books, 1983), p. 363.

[4] Ibid., p. 351.

[5]Ibid., pp. 13, 33.

[6]Ibid., p. 23.

[7]Ibid., pp. 23-24.

[8]See Rudolf Hoess, *Commandant of Auschwitz: The Autobiography of Rudolf Hoess*, trans. Constantine Fitzgibbon (London: Pan Books, 1974).

[9]Sereny, *Into That Darkness*, p. 25.

[10]Ibid., pp. 27, 28.

[11]Ibid., p. 29.

[12]Ibid., p. 35.

[13]Ibid., p. 103.

[14]Ibid., p. 113.

[15]Ibid., p. 149.

[16]Ibid., p. 250.

[17]Ibid., p. 162.

[18]Alexander Donat, ed., *The Death Camp Treblinka: A Documentary* (New York: Holocaust Library, 1979), p. 14. Donat's book, which features eyewitness accounts by survivors of Treblinka, is a valuable complement to Sereny's work. See also Claude Lanzmann, *Shoah: An Oral History of the Holocaust* (New York: Pantheon Books, 1985), which is the complete text from Lanzmann's epic film about the Holocaust.

[19]Sereny, *Into That Darkness,* pp. 202, 164, 200.

[20]Ibid., p. 249.

[21]Ibid., p. 363.

22Ibid., pp. 361-62.

23Ibid., p. 362.

24Ibid., pp. 231-32.

25Ibid., p. 15.

26For more detail on Oskar Schindler, see Thomas Keneally, *Schindler's List* (New York: Penguin Books, 1983). The title of this account is apt, for in addition to referring to Schindler's record about his Jewish workers, the German world "list" means cunning. Schindler possessed it abundantly and for good ends. Another remarkable story — that of Hermann "Fritz" Graebe — is told by Douglas K. Huneke, *The Moses of Rovno* (New York: Dodd, Mead & Company, 1985). Graebe, the only German citizen who volunteered to testify against the Nazis at Nuremberg, was a structural engineer during World War II. Assigned to the Ukraine by the Railroad Administration of the Third Reich, he was horrified by the murder of nearly 1,500 Jewish men by Nazi killing squads. His response was to build a rescue network that protected hundreds of Jews. At the war's end, he used his own train to bring scores of them across Allied lines to freedom.

27Keneally, *Schindler's List*, p. 371.

28Jean Améry, *At the Mind's Limits: Contemplations by a Survivor on Auschwitz and Its Realities,* trans. Sidney Rosenfeld and Stella P. Rosenfeld (New York: Schocken Books, 1986), p. 28. Born in Austria as Hans Maier in 1912, Améry fled Nazism by going to Belgium in 1938. There he later joined the resistance. Captured by the Nazis in 1943, he was tortured and sent to a series of concentration camps. He took his own life in 1978, but not before writing a series of remarkable essays about his Holocaust experiences. See also his *Radical Humanism: Selected Essays,* ed. and trans. Sidney Rosenfeld and Stella P. Rosenfeld (Bloomington: Indiana University Press, 1984).

29Améry, *At the Mind's Limits*, p. 28.

30Perhaps the most ambitious and promising work of this kind— incomplete at the time of this writing — is the Study of the Altruistic Personality Project, which is headed by Samuel P. Oliner. This sociologist is a Holocaust survivor who was hidden by Polish Catholics during World War II. His important autobiography, *Restless Memories: Recollections of the Holocaust Years* (Berkeley: Judah L. Magness Museum, 1986), tells that story. Oliner has interviewed hundreds of rescuers and survivors to clarify the factors and motivations that led people to save Jewish lives during the Nazi era. The findings of his study are scheduled for publication in 1988 under the title *The Altruistic Personality: Rescuers of Jews in Nazi Europe.* Although exceptions to them exist, among Oliner's most important discoveries are the following: (1) Rescuers, women and men alike, came from different social classes and diverse occupations.   (2) They had learned and deeply internalized values such as helpfulness, responsibility, fairness, justice, compassion, and friendship.   (3) They had friends in groups outside of their own family circles or immediate communities.   (4) They had high levels of self-confidence and self-esteem and were not afraid to take calculated risks.   (5) They knew what was happening around them, and, in addition, benefited from a supportive emotional network — their rescue efforts met with approval from family members or others who could be trusted.   Oliner believes that, if he were in trouble and could identify persons with these qualities, his chances of receiving assistance would be excellent.

[31]Pierre Sauvage was born during the Holocaust in the French village of Le Chambon, where many Jews were hidden and saved. A distinguished filmmaker, he has produced *Weapons of the Spirit,* a documentary about that place. He also heads "The Friend of Le Chambon," an organization that honors those who saved Jews during the Holocaust. His words are quoted by permission.

[32]Cited by Richard Zoglin, "Lives of Spirit and Dedication," *Time,* 27 Oct. 1986, p. 66.

[33]Elie Wiesel, *The Fifth Son,* trans. Marion Wiesel (New York: Summit Books, 1985), p. 208.

[34]Ibid., p. 13.

[35]Ibid.

[36]Ibid., p. 9.

[37]Ibid., p. 218.

[38]Ibid., p. 217.

[39]Ibid., p. 155.

[40]Ibid., p. 184.

[41]Ibid., p. 185.

[42]Ibid., p. 219.

[43]Ibid., p. 200.

[44]Ibid., p. 190.

[45]Ibid., p. 220.

[46]Ibid., p. 213.

Chapter Seven

Teaching About the Holocaust: Theory and Method for Non-Jewish Audiences

Hubert Locke

Introduction

It has long been axiomatic that the lessons of the Holocaust are as important to non-Jews as they are to those who were its intended victims. Holocaust education, with few notable exceptions, nevertheless continues to be predominantly a Jewish interest conducted primarily for Jewish audiences. This commitment on the part of Jewish citizens everywhere is eminently understandable; the lack of attention to the Holocaust and its meaning by non-Jews is equally tragic.

The tragedy is heightened by the increasing knowledge of complicity on the part of the Western world in the virtual destruction of European Jewry. For over a decade, Arthur Morse's *While Six Million Died*[1] stood virtually alone as an indictment of American silence and inaction in the face of the unfolding Nazi horror. More recently, David Wyman's *The Abandonment of the Jews*[2] together with other studies have begun to document the extent to which key officials and leaders of the Allied governments did virtually nothing to thwart the Nazi policies and machinery of death, until it was too late. While much more awaits to be learned, there are lessons of sufficient significance to warrant major attention to the Holocaust by the non-Jewish world, as much for insight on the Western tradition of liberal, humanistic democracy and its monumental failure to comprehend and respond to the greatest human horror of the twentieth century as for gaining an understanding of the fate of European Jewry during World War II.

The "bystander" in the title of this essay, therefore, points principally to the attitudes roles and behavior of individuals, organizations, groups and governments outside of Nazi-occupied Europe who had some knowledge of what was taking place with respect to the fate of the European Jewish populace, and who did little or nothing in response. By extension, it encompasses everyone, even if unaware at the time, who now knows the tragedy that took place. In essence, all of humankind living in the post-World War II era are by-standers in the sense that we, even if non-participant observers of the record of the Holocaust, confront the question of how we shall respond to its implications for the future.

"Theory and method," on the other hand, are academic terms which frequently promise more than they can deliver. By "theory" is simply meant the conceptual framework within which we seek to identify the major issues, questions or perspectives relevant to the role of the by-stander and the Holocaust experience. This, it should be noted, is a much more modest undertaking than that envisioned by social scientists in their use of the term and for whom rationality, testability and predictability are essential components of theory. While a rationale for focusing the efforts of Holocaust education on non-Jewish audiences has been suggested and will be examined further, attempts to introduce elements of empirical validation and prediction are not a part of this undertaking.[3] "Method," likewise, is used to permit the introduction of examples and effective approaches for educators and others to reach non-Jewish audiences; it is not intended to suggest any systematic procedures for such efforts.

Theory

According to a survey conducted by the Roper Organization for the American Jewish Committee, four out of ten Americans no longer want to hear anything about the Holocaust and think the Jewish community should concern itself with other topics.[4] Why have those of us who consider this event to be a watershed in human experience failed to produce a more sensitive and humane public response than these statistics suggest? It is possible that contemporary concerns with the continuing crisis in the Middle East, the knowledge of other genocidal acts in modern Turkey, Cambodia, Nigeria and elsewhere, or the continuing concern for oil supplies and the predominantly Arab monopoly over this important natural resource have served to eclipse the memory of and concern for what happened to Europe's Jewish populace during the Hitler era? Or should we take comfort in the fact that sixty percent of the American people — six out of ten Americans — apparently believe that the Holocaust continues to be an important issue?

The first set of explanations are all possibilities — given the short and fragile nature of human memory especially concerning matters that are painful to recount and for which we may feel no personal responsibility, and the tragic tendency of we moderns to shape our values and priorities by our more immediate self-interests. The latter reaction, consoling as it might be, is an unwarranted presumption. Instead, we might take the problem posed by the AJC study as an opportunity to reexamine our past efforts in Holocaust education and as an incentive to search for new approaches to this continuing task. One such approach is suggested by asking whether there are contemporary issues, problems, or concerns being expressed in our society that can be related, in an authentic and relevant manner, to the Holocaust experience.

Both theory and method are anticipated in this question. Theoretically, it posits that an appropriate or, at the least, alternative framework within which to view Holocaust education for non-Jewish audiences may be one which focuses, initially, not on the Holocaust as an historical event but on issues and problems of current interest and debate that can be illumined by the Holocaust experience. Methodologically, it suggests that beginning in our own era, with our own cultural and societal dilemmas, and working back to those of a half-century ago in another cultural/political situation may offer a more effective approach.

Put briefly, what are the issues of deep moral significance, the current problems and tensions of our society, or the dilemmas of a democratic polity that occupy, or ought to, the minds of American citizens in our time? A partial list would include issues of corruption in government or, stated more positively, that of professional integrity in the public service, the tensions between ideologies of the left and the right in American politics, and the curious mixture of religion and politics in American life. The list would extend to encompass the growing debates over militarism and national security, the perceived breakdown in the moral fabric of our society, and the rise of extremist groups — political and religious — across the nation. For many Americans, the list should also take into consideration fundamental questions of social justice and equality as they are either addressed or ignored in contemporary American society.

Each of these issues, problems and dilemmas has its parallels in the history of the German Third Reich and the Holocaust. Volumes have been written which make clear the parallels to any discerning reader. The pedagogical challenge is that of searching for ways to link authentically and effectively contemporary concerns and issues with the insights which can be derived from one of history's most traumatic experiences in the recent past.

If such a task is undertaken, it must be approached with care and caution. Historians, by the very nature of their craft, are basically adverse to the quest for historical "parallels" and "linkages," in spite of Santayana's oft-quoted dictum that those who do not learn from history are condemned to repeat it. Santayana, however, was a philosopher, not an historian; however much we may be persuaded by the compelling wisdom of his observation, historians would insist that all human events have their uniqueness, that compiling the record of those events is both a process of collection and reflection, that the latter inevitably brings a personal perspective and judgment to bear upon events and their meaning[5], and that the discovery of historical parallels, therefore, may be much more a function of personal predilection than of an accurate reading of the historical record.

This scholarly caution, however, is a warning against superficiality; it is not an invitation to impotency and non-discernment. In the face of the compelling and urgent questions of our time, it would be a dereliction of the highest order were we not to search for light from the past in order to illumine our present predicaments and choices. The Holocaust, more than any other experience of recent memory, presents the story of a tragic past against which we can weigh and measure our present, as well as seek a more decent and humane future. But to begin with the present and to ask what kind of future we seek can be viewed as a way of initiating an inquiry that leads back to the past which may capture the attention and interest of persons who are inclined to view history, including the Holocaust, as best left to the historians.

This approach also commends itself in relation to an unfortunate concern which periodically emerges about teaching the Holocaust in both Jewish and non-Jewish circles. On occasion, expressions ranging from mild curiosity to considerable resentment are heard within the Jewish community over the involvement of non-Jews in what is considered a Jewish event and experience. The concern has to do with how and even whether persons who are not Jewish can ever hope to fathom — not to mention authentically interpret — what was a calamity which uniquely focused on Jewish people as its victims. How does one fully understand the plight of the victim, it is asked, if one is not among its potential number? Can one hope to speak concerning or on behalf of those who were the targets of the Holocaust if one did not potentially share in their fate?

Among segments of the non-Jewish community, this same concern expresses itself in reverse. The Holocaust is seen as a tragic but uniquely Jewish experience, so much so that attempts to deal with it are best left to Jews. Whether as a sincere effort to avoid offense or a less meritorious desire to avoid involvement, this stance acknowledges the dimensions of the horror but denies the responsibility of others than those who have a direct relationship, to be particularly concerned with it.

Both concerns are unfortunate because both underestimate or ignore the role of the bystander. As much as we need to grasp the perspective of those who were actual and potential victims of the Holocaust, we need, to an even greater extent, to wrestle with the minds and deeds of its perpetrators. Although that examination will never be complete, we need as much to try and fathom the posture of those who stood by while the Holocaust occurred — both within and outside Nazi Germany — who might have made a difference. Finally, we need to understand the painful potential that resides in all of us to be bystanders in the face of human tragedy.

There is a third reason that teaching the Holocaust to non-Jewish audiences by means of an analysis of contemporary issues and problems is important. There is a pronounced tendency in many contemporary circles to treat any potential large-scale disaster as a holocaust — from unanticipated consequences of gene-splitting research to the mounting crisis in South Africa and the ever-present threat of nuclear conflagration — commercial or military. Such an undiscerning use of the term tends to extend its application to any phenomenon one dreads or finds distasteful. It does not permit the identification and isolation of those events in human experience in which willful efforts of persons and governments, based on raw racial antipathy, are directed toward the extermination of an entire racial or ethnic populace (i.e., genocide). It especially fails to discern the unique feature of the one genocidal experience in which such an effort was carried out to a degree unrivalled in history.

By working back from the present, we are enabled to engage in discussion and the learning process those whose interests center on contemporary issues which merit consideration, but also issues whose underlying moral, political or technological principles and features can be linked to and illumined by the experience of the Holocaust. By focusing on the place of the by-stander in current events in which choices and decisions are required, we can relate contemporary indifference and apathy to that of a half-century ago and its consequences. By moving from present concerns to a past experience, we can demonstrate the tragic human capacity to repeat previous mistakes of apathy and indifference in the face of issues that call for moral choice and personal responsibility.

In all of this, however, there remains an ultimate caution. Properly examined and considered, the Holocaust serves as a measuring-rod against which we can weigh the human propensity for that which is evil and barbaric. At the same time, the Holocaust must not be exploited as a convenient historical cloak within which to wrap every concern or horror that potentially presents itself to the human imagination. Working from present moral questions to the Holocaust as a sign post in the past is not to be taken as a device or excuse for elevating every current issue to the moral scope or dimension of this past event. To do so, as Franklin Littell has always warned, is to risk trivializing the Holocaust; it may also invest greater moral weight and moment in present events than circumstances warrant. Human history has had nothing to date, to compare with the horror of the systematic extermination of six million men, women and children exclusively because of their putative racial identity. The principal task of Holocaust education is to make that fact sufficiently clear, discreet, and concrete that it never occurs again.

Method

A.   Scholars Conference on the German Church Struggle and the Holocaust.

In 1970, Franklin H. Littell, a Methodist minister and university professor who is widely revered as the dean of Christian Holocaust studies in the United States, established the first of an annual series of Scholars Conferences on the Church Struggle and the Holocaust.[6] The combination of inquiries on a then little-known dimension of German history during the Third Reich with that of the destruction of European Jewry was a deliberate and carefully considered decision. It was designed to examine critical historical, theological and political questions regarding the role and response of the German churches during the Third Reich and to link this examination with one of the major questions that arises from such an inquiry: why did the German churches, as one of the very few institutions in German society to offer a modicum of dissent and resistance to Nazi ideology and, by implication, to the Nazi State, remain so painfully silent regarding the plight of Germany's Jewish citizens in the critical years of 1933-39 and that of Jews throughout German occupied Europe after 1941?

The annual Scholars Conferences, in one respect, were a precursor of the approach to Holocaust education that begins not with the Holocaust itself but with events, issues and circumstances which then lead inexorably to the Holocaust. The Scholars Conferences admittedly did not begin with current history but rather a segment of the history of the Holocaust period; the intensive examination of that segment of German history, however, and its concern with questions regarding the theological, institutional, and political developments within the German churches has raised, inevitably, the fundamental moral question of the churches *vis a vis* the Jewish populace. To study the history of the German churches, therefore, is to come unavoidably to the history of the Holocaust and to all of the basic issues which Holocaust education seeks to raise and address.

Over the fifteen years that the Scholars Conferences have been convened, it has been a matter of considerable interest to note the character and process of their intellectual evolution. They began in a period in which Conway's *The Nazi Persecution of the Churches*, published two years prior, and Cochrane's *The Church's Confession Under Hitler* (1962) were the only major sources available to English readers concerning the history of the Church Struggle.[7] Subsequently, in an impressive number of journal articles and several other major volumes, the contours of German church history from 1931-45 are now well in place and many of its details have come into clearer focus.[8] As scholars have gained a greater degree of comfort with the mastery of the history of the German church experience, they have become more willing to note, in their analyses, its parallels with and implications for problems and issues of our generation. For a group primarily composed of historians and theologians, the Scholars Conferences have worked appropriately from a specific past to the present. It is to be hoped that the engagement of other disciplines from the social sciences which, with few outstanding exceptions, have largely avoided inquiries on the Holocaust might advance and enhance the effort to proceed from contemporary questions and concerns to that watershed event in the modern era against which our present and the future ought to be assessed.

It is also of importance to note a parallel development in Germany itself where, briefly stated, the German churches moved from a general acknowledgment of their failure to stand more firmly against the Third Reich (The Stuttgart Declaration of 1945) but which made no mention of anti-Semitism or the Holocaust, to the Declaration on Renovating the Relationship between Christians and Jews, issued by the Synod of the Rhineland Church in 1980. The latter is as clear a "recognition of Christian co-responsibility and guilt for the Holocaust" as one could wish; in the intervening period between the Stuttgart and Rhineland Declarations, much effort to uncover and lay bare the church's history during the Third Reich led to the painful recognition of the church's virtual silence concerning the fate of the Jews.

In an ironic sense, while American theologians and church leaders were still idolizing Bonhoeffer and Niemöller, their German peers and counterparts were moving beyond the appropriate recognition of these two courageous examples of dissent and resistance to the larger questions of general guilt and complicity. It is quite likely that any serious and careful examination of our nation's recent past or its present circumstances also would lead to questions and issues which the history of the Holocaust would greatly illumine.

B.   The International Symposium of Scholars and Church Leaders
     (The Barmen Symposium)

The annual meeting of the Scholars Conference was convened in Seattle in 1984 as part of an international symposium to commemorate the fiftieth anniversary of the Barmen Synod and its Declaration. Attended by over six hundred participants, including two revered delegates to the Barmen Synod, the symposium was both a culmination of fifteen years of scholarly exchange and a major turning point in deliberations on the twin themes of Church Struggle and Holocaust.

In reading the symposium addresses, it is striking to note the extent to which the major speakers looked both retrospectively and prospectively, the degree to which the Holocaust has become a *terminus a quo* and *terminus ad quem* — a major point of reference for assessing the significance, achievements, and failures of the Church Struggle as well as a framework or moral plumb-line against which to measure issues and challenges of our present era. Speaker after speaker found occasion to raise the spectre of nuclear warfare or the unfolding crisis in South Africa, not as events that represent potential new "holocausts" but rather as moral questions demanding response, as major lessons to be learned from the world's silence almost a half-century ago when the slaughter of Europe's Jewish populace was taking place.

It is in this way that the role of the by-stander is being identified and related to the Holocaust and our own time.

C. The Raoul Wallenberg Seminars on Professional Ethics and The Public Service

The foregoing "case-studies" reflect a method of teaching about the Holocaust to non-Jewish audiences that has its primary application to one institution and its constituency — the churches. In an entirely different setting, this method has been used in addressing contemporary issues of personal integrity and professional ethics for careerists in the public service.

In 1981, the William O. Douglas Institute, a Seattle-based educational and research organization which has had a long-term commitment to Holocaust education and a small role in both the Scholars Conferences and the Barmen Symposium, established the first in a series of seminars in tribute to Raoul Wallenberg. The seminars are designed to explore, with small groups of public service professionals in a specific field (e.g., law enforcement, education, public health, et. al.) current issues, problems, and dilemmas that involve questions of ethics and ethical standards in the professional field. In the wake of Watergate and in the light of continuous revelations regarding shoddy or corrupt ethical practices in the public realm the importance of the seminar topic speaks for itself.

Each seminar opens, however, with an examination of the life and career of Raoul Wallenberg and, principally, with his efforts from June, 1944 to January, 1945 on behalf of Hungary's Jewish populace. Wallenberg is presented as a public servant, one actually working on behalf of the U.S. government and its War Refugee Board, who confronted a problem of monumental proportions and a professional dilemma of profound ethical dimensions and consequences. Wallenberg is put forth as a symbol of the question of professional ethics against which the seminar participants then proceed to raise the ethical concerns of their own profession and to weigh the merits and implications of their responses.

To date, seminars have been held with public school teachers and police officers. For each professional group, the consideration of Wallenberg's career serves to surface dimensions of the issue of professional ethics that do not normally arise in the course of discussions of this topic in a contemporary context — issues of bureaucratic inertia, of the willingness of and capacity of individuals to go against the stream of professional conventionality and propriety, and the fundamental question of the ends toward which one's professional efforts are directed — questions of justice and basic human decency. Viewed in the framework of the Holocaust, it is a way for every profession to ask of itself whether it wishes to be a by-stander to the compelling moral quandaries of our age or a participant in their alleviation.

Implication

Theory and method have their utility primarily as ways of organizing our thoughts about and approaches to difficult questions. But the theory we construct as a framework for analysis and the method we employ in efforts to transmit the meaning or significance of what we understand to be central or relevant about the matter under inquiry, have certain implications for scholarship and its application.

The framework and method proposed as an approach to teaching about the Holocaust to non-Jewish audiences also carry implications and consequences. It places an especial, pedagogical burden on educators who might choose to adopt this approach.

It requires, in the first instance, a solid immersion in the history and literature of the Holocaust, not only so that one can identify relevant linkages between present situations and this past experience but also to insure that one avoids the pitfall of superficiality or, even more basic, of inauthenticity in seeking to illumine current questions and issues by reference to this past experience. It does not do justice to the Holocaust simply to view or relate it as one more example of "man's inhumanity to man," of the evils of totalitarian regimes or of the pervasiveness of racism in the modern world. The Holocaust at one level — a very obvious one, in fact — expresses each of these intractable themes; unless one is prepared, however, to detail and discuss the ways in which the Holocaust was, to date, a unique expression of these problems, how such an experience came about in a nation prized for its intellectual achievements in science, philosophy, theology and music, the ways in which the institutions of German society at best acquiesced and, at worst, abetted this occurrence, and the dynamics of economic life and political processes which reinforced its acceptance, one should not attempt to relate the Holocaust to anything — past, present, or future.

As a second consideration, this approach acknowledges and addresses directly the need for non-Jewish citizens to come to terms with the roles of perpetrators and bystanders in the Holocaust experience, as having an importance for inquiry, analysis and understanding as great as that regarding its victims. After almost a half-century, we are beginning to get contributions to the literature which examines the history, behavior and responses on the part of specific segments of the German professional communities during the Third Reich; Beyerchen's *Scientists Under Hitler*, a study of German physicists, and Ericksen's *Theologians Under Hitler* are two recent and well-received examples.[9] Detailed attention to the fate of the Jewish populace in Nazi-occupied Europe will continue to be a major part of Holocaust studies. But an overwhelming preoccupation with its victims without attention to those who caused it to happen or who stood by while it unfolded, provides too easy a rationale for we who are not numbered among its potential casualties to dismiss the Holocaust as a "Jewish issue" or to relegate its lessons to consideration by others than ourselves.

This consideration has its obvious implications not only for teaching but also for the new avenues of scholarly research that need to be mapped and explored. There is still a paucity of literature about the history and responses of other institutions and professional groups during the Nazi era: universities and their faculties, the medical profession, public school teachers, lawyers, judges, et. al. English readers have available to them descriptions of geographic communities and their reactions to the advent of National Socialism, as in William S. Allen's *The Nazi Seizure of Power* [10] and there are intriguing vignettes of individuals such as Kurt Gerstein, found mainly as brief treatments in other larger works, which offer us a glimpse of the professional and personal dilemmas, triumphs or tragedies of Third Reich citizens. We have little of the scope of Gordon Zahn's sensitive and compelling treatment of Franz Jaggerstatter[11], Kramarz's study of Claus von Stauffenberg, the chief of the German Army's Intelligence operation who was one of the architect's of the 20 July 1944 plot against Hitler's life[12], the growing literature on Raoul Wallenberg, or the voluminous materials available on Dietrich Bonhoeffer to aid our understanding of how the professions and individuals in their ordinary, everyday roles and responsibilities, aided and abetted — or tried to thwart — the aims and designs of the Nazi State.

We especially need detailed analyses of the German civil service and of those who, with the professional efficiency for which the German bureaucracy is renowned, implemented the vast and intricate machinery of death which ended in the killing camps of eastern Europe. An elaborate process of planning, design, and operational effectiveness lay behind the rounding up and transport of millions of Jewish citizens to Auschwitz, Treblinka and the other camps; it was the work of government architects, engineers, and other civil servants who worked in bureaus of transportation, ministries of health, and offices concerned with industry, labor, communications and defense. An essential and crucial question involves trying to fathom how such persons went about the routinized tasks of sending six million people to their deaths.

Finally, understanding of the role and conduct of the business and industrial sector is of major importance. Arthur Schweitzer's *Big Business in the Third Reich* is one of the early studies in this area; its treatment of anti-Semitism within the German business community is shockingly sparse and the complicity of such firms as I.G. Farben in the operation of the death camps goes unnoticed.[13] Thanks to the work of the late Joseph Borkin we have a clearer picture of this relationship as it is reflected in the history of I. G. Farben[14] but the full record of the German business community is still incomplete.

Holocaust research, like Holocaust education, is a task that should command the attention of non-Jewish as well as Jewish scholars. Focusing inquiries, by non-Jewish scholars, on the roles of perpetrators and implementors of the Holocaust, and on by-standers to its occurrence, also suggests an apportionment of the research task that is intellectually defensible and would greatly extend the direction in which recent investigations have begun to move.

Summary

The current world scene presents a set of problems and issues for nation-states to address and resolve that are as troublesome as they are complex. It is striking to note, on reflection, how many of the major world issues engage, in some sense, concerns of world Jewry. Soviet treatment of dissidents and policy toward emigration, U.S. policy toward the Middle East, the latter as the most prominent, long-term political tinder-box out of which a super-power conflict might erupt, the world's precarious economic dependence on oil and the pivotal role of the Middle East in its supply, the current worldwide preoccupation with South Africa and the virtually singular stance that Israel has taken regarding relations with its government — these and other world issues have a particular nexus with the interest of Jewish people everywhere.

To note this nexus is not to provide an unwitting justification for those who speak pejoratively of a Jewish influence in world affairs or who seek other excuses to express a covert anti-

Semitism. Its intent is precisely the opposite: to propose what may be the ultimate rationale for attention by non-Jews to the meaning and significance of the Holocaust. For while no experience — even that of the Holocaust — can serve to explain or defend every stance or position of Jewish people regarding major issues of our era, it nevertheless remains true that non-Jews who have not confronted the tragedy that befell world Jewry under the German Third Reich will not begin to understand the sentiments of contemporary Jewry on a wide range of world issues.

The issues of our time, as in every age, are those on which we may choose to be participants in, or bystanders to, their resolution. If a key to world peace lies in a better understanding of the hopes and fears of various nations, their peoples, and the particular histories that have shaped their experiences, the effort to grasp the meaning of the Holocaust and its implications for the world's present and future, is one of the imperatives of our age.

---

[1]Morse, Arthur, *While Six Million Died* (New York: Random House, 1967).

[2]Wyman, David, *The Abandonment of the Jews* (New York: Pantheon 'Books, 1984).

[3]See Merton, Robert K., *Social Theory and Social Structure* (New York: The Free Press, 1957, pp. 96-97) for a discussion of the concept and function of theory in the social sciences.

[4]Reported in *The Christian Century* (Vol. 103, No. 1, Jan. 1-8, 1986, p. 10). The poll also found that "a majority of Americans expressing an opinion on the subject

would like the United States to halt efforts to locate Nazi war criminals." The American Jewish Committee's Director of Research, Milton Himmelfarb, observed "there would appear to be a widespread desire to invoke a kind of statute of limitations on being reminded of the Holocaust" (ibid.).

[5]See Carr, Edward Hallett, *What Is History* (New York: Vintage Books, 1961). This work, originally given as the Trevelyan Lectures at Cambridge, devotes its first chapter to an exposition of the theme that "history consists essentially in seeing the past through the eyes of the present and its problems." Carr quotes R. G. Collingwood's well-known dictum, "... history is the reenactment in the historian's mind of the thought whose history he is studying."

[6]The volume of addresses given at this conference were published by F. H. Littell and H. G. Locke (eds.), *The Church Struggle and the Holocaust* (Detroit: Wayne State University Press, 1974).

[7]Conway, John S., *The Nazi Persecution of the Churches* (New York: Basic Books, 1968); Cochrane, Arthur C. *The Church's Confession Under Hitler* (Philadelphia: Westminster Press, 1962). These works remain indispensable sources for students and scholars of the Church Struggle.

[8]See, for example, Ernst C. Helmrich's *The German Churches Under Hitler* (Detroit: Wayne State University Press, 1979) and, for a post-war analysis, Frederic Spotts, *The Churches and Politics in Germany* (Middletown, Ct.: Wesleyan University Press, 1973).

[9]Beyerchen, Alan D., *Scientists Under Hitler* (New Haven: Yale University Press, 1977); Ericksen, Robert P., *Theologians Under Hitler* (New Haven: Yale University Press, 1985).

[10]Allen, William S., *The Nazi Seizure of Power* (Chicago: Quadrangle Books, 1965).

[11]Zahn, Gordon, I*n Solitary Witness* (Boston: Beacon Press, 1964).

[12]Kramarz, Joachim, *Stauffenberg* (New York: The Macmillan Co., 1967).

[13]Schweitzer, Arthur, *Big Business in the Third Reich* (Bloomington, IN.: Indiana University Press, 1977).

[14]Borkin, Joseph, *The Crime and Punishment of I. G. Farben* (New York: The Free Press, 1978).

Chapter Eight

Teaching About the Rescuers of Jews

Lawrence Baron

Until recently, most Holocaust courses have devoted either insufficient or no attention to the topic of Gentile rescuers of Jews. Instead, they understandably have focused on the more typical Gentile responses to the plight of the Jews in Nazi-dominated Europe — namely, participation and collaboration in the persecution of the Jews, indifference to Jewish suffering, or passivity exacted by German intimidation.[1] Insofar as these courses have treated the subject of Jewish rescue, they usually have approached it through narratives about famous rescuers or national rescue operations. Such coverage neglected the sort of analysis of psychological and sociological reasons for individual behavior that is customary when studying the executioners, victims, and bystanders of the "Final Solution." This omission reflected the previous lack of scholarly research about the motivations of those who saved Jews during the Holocaust.

Over the past decade, there have been a number of notable attempts to fill this gap in our knowledge.[2] As the findings from these pioneering studies of rescuers become available to the public, Holocaust educators need to familiarize themselves with the new literature and incorporate its insights into their treatment of this subject. Rather than just cite instances of how Jews were helped, teachers now must try to explain how the backgrounds, traits, and values of the rescuers contributed to their dangerous decision to aid Jews. Seen from this perspective, the rescuers emerge as decent human beings acting upon feelings and principles that in any setting other than the Holocaust would sound rather ordinary. For students, this perception may make the rescuers more realistic role models of ethical behavior than the idealized images of rescuers presented in conventional Holocaust courses.

To assist teachers in revising their units on rescuers along these lines, I first will discuss the limitations of three approaches which are commonly employed when dealing with this topic. Then I will briefly review the major theories currently being advanced about what factors prompted people to jeopardize themselves and their families to shield Jews from the Nazis. Finally, I will suggest techniques for integrating these theories into classroom lessons about rescuers.

Teachers often assign *The Diary of Anne Frank* to include something about the rescue of Jews within their Holocaust courses. To be sure, it is a moving account of Anne's introspective maturation while hiding from the Germans with her family. As such, it gently pays homage to every Jewish youngster whose childhood and life were lost in the Holocaust. Yet this strength is also its greatest weakness: it is about Anne and not her rescuers. Although Anne mentions them frequently in the book, the reader never learns exactly who they were or why they sheltered the Franks. Indeed, Anne invented names for her helpers to keep their identities from being discovered by the Nazis and to protect their privacy in case her diary ever would be published. Yad Vashem's postwar interview with Victor Kugler (alias Mr. Kraler) and the recently released memoirs of Miep Gies (alias Miep Van Santen) reveal how much was not known previously about the motivations of Anne's guardians, the extent of their rescue and resistance activities, and the punishments some of them endured for concealing the Franks and other Jewish friends in the "Secret Annex[3]."

Another method of exposing students to the exploits of the "Righteous Gentiles" is by chronicling the remarkable story of Raoul Wallenberg. Wallenberg has been justifiably honored for organizing the rescue of as many as 100,000 Jews in Budapest in 1944. Yet the circumstances under which he operated differed markedly from those encountered by most rescuers. After all, Sweden had appointed him as a special envoy to Hungary specifically to mount a Jewish relief program sponsored by the American War Refugee Board. Taking full advantage of his diplomatic status and outside funding, Wallenberg issued bogus Swedish "protective passports" to endangered Jews, rented apartment buildings to serve as Jewish sanctuaries, whisked Jews off German transports, and solicited the support of other neutral embassies and the Catholic Church for similar rescue work.[4] Although this endeavor was a collective effort, there is a tendency to attribute it entirely to Wallenberg who looms like a superman in our historical imagination. Mere mortals, especially high school and college students, stand in awe of his almost mythical feats of courage and cunning, but probably do not find them particularly relevant to their own lives. The subliminal message conveyed by presenting Wallenberg as *the* archetypal rescuer may be that helping Jews was beyond the capacity of the average person. It also may perpetuate the traditional concept of individual heroism which had been rendered largely obsolete by the enormous power wielded by modern totalitarian states.[5]

When rescue is examined at the national rather than the personal level, the example of Denmark is usually cited. Faced with the imminent arrest and deportation of the Jews there in October of 1943, the Danes shepherded 95% of them by boat to safety in Sweden. Although this was a unique and impressive response to the threat of Nazi genocide, teachers must be wary about generalizing from the Danish experience to the situation faced by the citizens in other countries under German control. Germany initally treated Denmark leniently and permitted the Danish government to continue to function. When the Nazis reversed this policy in 1943, several factors favored the mass rescue of the Jews: the shortage of SS manpower, Germany's military setbacks elsewhere, advance warnings about the planned deportations, the willingness of nearby Sweden to receive Jewish refugees, the limited size of the Jewish community and its concentration in Copenhagen, and the anger of the Danes towards Germany's recent imposition of a state of emergency.[6]

The case of Denmark illustrates how crucial it is to view the phenomenon of rescue from a comparitive national perspective. The overall extent and success of Jewish rescue in countries defeated by or allied with the Third Reich depended primarily on the nature and degree of German control or influence there and secondarily on the local civil heritage. For example, teachers tend to ascribe the fate of the Jews in Denmark to that nation's historical commitment to democracy and religious tolerance. Despite the fact that the Netherlands had equally strong traditions in this regard, 80% of the Dutch Jews perished in the Holocaust. The critical difference stemmed from the determination and power of the SS occupation regime in Holland to gradually disenfranchise, impoverish, and isolate the Dutch Jews before deporting the majority of them in 1942 and 1943.[7]

Teachers should place the rescuers within their specific historical contexts so that their students can appreciate the differing objective obstacles rescuers confronted in each country. To do so, they might want to consult Helen Fein's useful model of variables that affected a nation's Jewish victimization and rescue rates. These include the "intensity of German control," the amount of autonomy retained by the native government, the degree of prewar local anti-Semitism, the response of indigenous elites to Nazi persecution of the Jews, and the proximity of potential havens where Jews could flee.[8]

Just as the aforementioned variables determined the national parameters of rescue, more immediate situational factors could deter or promote an individual's involvement in rescue work. A tradition of positive Jewish-Christian relations in certain cities like Amersterdam and Berlin enhanced the prospects of Jewish rescue there.[9]   The local concentration of ethnic, political, or religious subcultures whose ideals and interests were antithetical to those of Nazism could serve as the basis for an effective Jewish rescue network. The familiarity, leadership, solidarity, and shared values of such groups provided a reassuring framework for members who otherwise might be too intimidated to resist the Germans alone. The mobilization of the Huguenot enclave of Le Chambon in behalf of the Jews attests to the viability of this type of communal rescue effort.[10] Sometimes participation in underground movements against the German occupation entailed saving Jewish fugitives or engendered the formation of specialized Jewish rescue rings like *Zegota* in Poland. Resistance membership made the daunting task of aiding Jews seem more feasible by giving rescuers access to additional food rations, counterfeit documents, and intelligence about impending police raids.[11]

Douglas Huneke has hypothesized that an assessment of personal resources and skills possibly influenced the rescuers' decision to help Jews. Having a convenient place to hide somebody at home, the ability to build one, or sufficient income to sustain fugitives initially may have made rescuers feel capable of concealing Jews for protracted periods. Residents of rural areas where Nazi surveillance was light may have had less anxiety about being caught than their urban counterparts who, conversely, may have enjoyed more anonymity. Rescuers who were peasants had the advantage of producing the food they fed their Jewish wards rather than running the risk of arousing suspicions by procuring larger quantities of food with forged or stolen ration coupons. Individuals who could control their emotions, act normally, and lie credibly when conversing with neighbors or answering quesions posed by German officials perhaps originally possessed more confidence in their dramatic and psychological competency to engage in clandestine activities than most people had.[12]

Of course, the above national, local, and personal circumstances constituted only preliminary considerations which rescuers kept in mind when evaluating their chances of successfully saving Jews. These factors, however, do not adequately account for the motivations behind their decisions to help Jews. Recent analyses of the autobiographies, interviews, and written depositions of rescuers point to the following key sources for their altruistic behavior: their relationship toward the Jews they rescued and the affective traits and basic values they derived from their upbringing as children and experiences as adults.

Rescuers often acted out of a sense of affection, loyalty, or obligation to Jews they previously knew. Their personal bonds with Jews had been forged in earlier business relationships, friendships, intermarriages, and political, professional, and social associations. Samuel Oliner has suggested that people are also more likely to help others who are culturally similar to themselves than strangers or foreigners.[13] The incidence of both of these types of rescue appears to be directly correlated to the degree of integration Jews had achieved in their host societies since this usually fostered Jewish acculturation, increased the number of Jewish-Gentile contacts, and discredited traditional negative stereotypes of Jews.[14]

In the first psychological study of Christians who saved Jews during the Holocaust, Perry London found that one category of rescuers consisted of socially marginal people whose own experience of insecurity and ostracism predisposed them to side with others who were persecuted.[15] Nechama Tec has discovered the same characteristic among many of the Polish rescuers she has investigated, but has argued that the significance of this finding is not limited to the fact that outsiders perceived the suffering of the Jews as analogous to their own memories of exclusion and maltreatment. "Those who are on the periphery of their community," she contends, "are not strongly controlled by it" which, in turn, increases their sense of freedom, independence, and strength. In her opinion, these related qualities enabled such rescuers to befriend Jews and overcome the virulent anti-Semitism which was prevalent in Poland then.[16] My own study of Dutch rescuers indicates that marginality may be a less significant factor in rescuers from countries where positive attitudes towards Jews represented the consensus of prewar public opinion.[17]

Other researchers have traced the roots of rescuing behavior to the parenting rescuers received as children. On the basis of her sessions with a number of "Righteous Gentiles," psychotherapist Frances Grossman observes that most of them had communicative and nonauthoritarian fathers and warm and affectionate mothers and that both parents established warm and trusting relationships with their offspring. She maintains that the manner in which the rescuers were raised endowed them with a keen sense of personal responsibility, empathy towards others, and the independence and confidence to follow their consciences and feelings despite the possible consequences for doing so.[18] Expanding on the unpublished research of Stanley Coopersmith, Oliner also notes that many rescuers "felt loved and secure" as children and links their upbringing to the high levels of compassion, confidence, mental stability, moral integrity, self-esteem, and tolerance exhibited by them.[19]

Childhood socialization also plays an important role in the theory advanced by Eva Fogelman and Valerie Lewis Wiener. They report that the motivations of one group of rescuers were "mainly emotional." These people became emotionally upset and involved when they personally witnessed or heard about the persecution of the Jews. Their intense feelings of indignation, protectiveness, and sympathy compelled them to care for the downtrodden Jews they encountered. To Fogelman and Wiener, it is not a coincidence that this group consisted mostly of women. Citing Carol Gilligan's theory of female moral development, they view this as a logical outcome of the traditional socialization of girls and women to be emotive, empathetic, and nurturing.[20] Similarly, in his first essay on rescuers of Jews, historian Philip Friedman postulated that women may have been more sensitive than men to the ordeal of the Jews, especially of Jewish children, and more likely to help them because women were "more easily moved by their emotions and thought less of the consequences."[21]

It has long been obvious that many rescuers reacted to the agony of the Jews as an expression of their political principles or religious beliefs. Nevertheless, the question remained why many more people who professed a commitment to the same ideologies or faiths did not respond accordingly to the extermination of the Jews. London's initial finding that these rescuers strongly identified with and emulated parental or other significant role models of moral conduct provided a partial answer to this question. Such parents or adults consistently practiced what they preached and involved their children in humanitarian or political activities from an early age on. The children correspondingly internalized the activism and values of their parents. Defending those who were victims of injustice or succoring the needy became a lifelong habit to such people. Most subsequent research has confirmed this analysis.[22] Nechama Tec cautions that rescuers independently could develop a value system which guided their daily behavior, but agrees that helping others was so ingrained in the personalities of the rescuers that offering refuge to helpless Jews "followed automatically without much conscious thought." This also explains the humility of most rescuers who frankly do not consider their actions extraordinary because their consciences would not have permitted them to have done otherwise.[23]

Finally, certain political and religious outlooks were more prone to inspire their adherents to join Jewish rescue efforts. Although many devout Christians simply felt they were fulfilling the Golden Rule, others derived their sense of responsibility for the fate of the Jews from the philo-Semitic theological tendencies of denominations like Dutch Calvinism or Seventh Day Adventism.[24] The doctrines of Catholic and Protestant churches often mirrored the civic values of their surrounding societies. Hence, the Lutheran Church of Denmark vehemently condemned and resisted the Nazi assault on the Jews; whereas only a minority of the pastors from the German Lutheran churches did so. Though the Pope failed to issue an explicit denunciation of the deportation and slaughter of European Jewry, the Catholic clergy provided moral leadership for their parishioners in combatting Nazi genocide in countries like Belgium, Italy, and the Netherlands.[25] Partisans of secular ideologies like liberalism, socialism, or communism were more inclined to view German oppression of the Jews as an intolerable affront to their own notions of civil liberties, equality, and internationalism. This conviction often was strengthened by the disproportionate affiliation of Jews with these movements.[26] Shocked and shamed by Nazi excesses against the Jews, even traditional Christian or nationalistic anti-Semites sometimes came to the rescue of their former enemies.[27]

The approach which teachers use to introduce these theories about rescuers to their students will naturally vary depending on the academic level of the class, the time allotted to the subject of Jewish rescue within the Holocaust course or unit, and the available resource materials. If both time and resources are scarce, an easy way to deal with this topic is to have students view a movie like *The Avenue of the Just* or *The Courage to Care* or read a book like Peter Hellman's *Avenue of the Righteous* or Philip Friedman's *Their Brothers' Keeper*. Each of these works exposes them to the stories of many different rescuers.[28] For the purposes of discussion, however, students should be asked to make a list of the various motives given by these rescuers for their actions and to trace the course of events which led them to save Jews. As the discussion progresses, certain recurring themes will emerge. Once this happens, the conversation should turn to student speculations about what sort of experiences and personalities the rescuers must have had to have responded to the persecution of the Jews in the way they did. The discussion can be concluded by asking the class if they see anything in the examples of these rescuers which could be applied to their own lives. The drawback of this approach is that the above books and films deal only superficially with the backgrounds and mentality of the rescuers. Consequently, students probably will detect only the most obvious reasons why rescuers helped Jews.

To delve deeper into this subject requires more work and time on the part of both the teacher and the students. The teacher might present a lecture outlining the major hypotheses of the existing research on rescuers. Then the entire class or a smaller number of students could be assigned to read books like Miep Gies' *Anne Frank Remembered*, Philip Hallie's *Lest Innocent Blood Be Shed*, Douglas Huneke's *The Moses of Rovno*, or Thomas Keneally's *Schindler's List*, which are more extensive and probing in their depictions of rescuers than the works mentioned in the previous paragraph.[29] One or several class periods should be set aside for students to report on whether any of the theories covered in lecture apply to the rescuers they have read about. These can be formal presentations or role plays where the students pretend they are particular rescuers explaining what caused them to aid Jews. The reports will reveal radically different types of rescuer backgrounds, motivations, and personalities. If your students are fairly bright, you might forego the introductory lecture and see what sort of analytical insights into the rescuers they can develop on their own in preliminary discussions, the individual reports, and the final synthesis of the findings of the reports as a whole.

The recent research about rescuers helps us understand how people retained their decency in the most trying of times. Forthcoming publications promise to broaden our knowledge of how to cultivate an abiding concern for the welfare of others in future generations.[30] Whatever approach is taken in conveying this information, students should become aware of the decision making processes, past experiences, personality traits, and values of the rescuers. The goal of this exercise is to reduce the rescuers to their human dimensions and thereby enable students to realize that they are plausible and relevant role models of moral activism. The rescuers tried to fight Nazi tyranny by affirming life through caring and compassion. Alternatives to Rambo figures who right wrongs through violence are sorely needed today. Anne Frank clearly recognized what distinguished the people who hid her from those who engaged in more conventional forms of resistance when she wrote, "Although others may show heroism in the war or against the Germans, our helpers display heroism in their cheerfulness and affection."[31] With benefactors like that, is it any wonder that Anne still could believe "that people are really good at heart"?

---

[1]For a discussion of possible reasons why there previously had been so little research about the rescuers, see Lawrence Baron, "Restoring Faith in Humankind," *Sh'ma,* XIV:276 (September 7, 1984), pp. 124-128.

[2]For surveys of the psycho-social and historical research in this field, see Samuel P. Oliner, "The Need to Recognize the Heroes of the Nazi Era," *The Reconstructionist,* XLVIII:4 (June 1982), pp. 7-14 and Lawrence Baron, "The Holocaust and Human Decency: A Review of Research on the Rescue of Jews in Nazi Occupied Europe," *Humboldt Journal of Social Relations,* XIII:I/2 (Fall/Winter & Spring/Summer, 1985/1986), pp. 237-251.

[3]The Reminiscences of Victor Kugler — the "Mr. Kraler" of Anne Frank's Diary, as told to Eda Schapiro," *Yad Vashem Studies,* XIII (1979), pp. 353-385; Miep Gies with Alison Leslie Gold, *Anne Frank Remembered: The Story of theWoman Who Helped to Hide the Frank Family* (New York: Simon and Schuster, 1987).

[4]Per Anger, *With Raoul Wallenberg in Budapest,* Trans. David Mel Paul and Margarita Paul (New York: Holocaust Library, 1981); John Bierman, *Righteous Gentile* (New York: Viking Press, 1981); Eleanore Lester, *Wallenberg: The Man in the Iron Web* (Englewood Cliffs: Prentice-Hall, 1982); Kati Marton, *Wallenberg* (New York: Random House, 1982); Harvey Rosenfeld, *Raoul Wallenberg: Angel of Rescue* (Buffalo: Prometheus Books, 1982); Frederick E. Werbell and Thurston Clark, *Lost Hero: The Mystery of Raoul Wallenberg* (New York; McGraw Hill, 1982).

[5]See Terrence Des Pres, *The Survivor: An Anatomy of Life in the Death Camps* (New York: Oxford University Press, 1976), pp. 5-25.

[6]Harold Flender, *Rescue in Denmark* (New York: Simon and Schuster, 1963); Leni Yahil, *The Rescue of Danish Jewry* (Philadelphia: Jewish Publication Society, 1969).

[7]Leni Yahil, "Methods of Persecution: A Comparison of the 'Final Solution' in Holland and Denmark," *Scripta Hierosolymitana,* XXIII (1972), pp. 279-300; Henry L. Mason, "Testing Human Bonds Within Nations: Jews in the Occupied Netherlands," *Political Science Quarterly,* IC: 2 (Summer, 1984), pp. 315-343; Jacob Presser, *The Destruction of the Dutch Jews,* Trans. Arnold Pomerans

(New York, Dutton, 1969); Werner Warmbrunn, *The Dutch Under German Occupation* (Stanford: Stanford University Press, 1963).

[8]Helen Fein, *Accounting for Genocide: National Responses and Jewish Victimization During the Holocaust* (New York: Free Press, 1979), pp. 31-92. For an account that eschews the usage of a general model to focus on the unique conditions of the Holocaust in Western European countries, see Michael R. Marrus and Robert O. Paxton, "The Nazis and the Jews in Occupied Western Europe," *Journal of Modern History,* LIV: (December 1982), pp. 687-714. Monographs on the history of the Holocaust in countries where the majority of the Jews survived also reveal what national factors contributed to this phenomenon. For example, see Frederick Barry Chary, *The Bulgarian Jews and the Final Solution, 1940-1944* (Pittsburgh: University of Pittsburgh Press, 1972); Michael R. Marrus and Robert O. Paxton, *Vichy France and the Jews* (New York: Basic Books, 1981); Susan Zuccotti, *The Italians and the Holocaust: Persecution, Rescue, and Survival* (New York: Basic Books, 1987); Eds. Yisrael Gutman and Efraim Zuroff, *Rescue Attempts During the Holocaust: Proceedings of the Second Yad Vashem International Historical Conference* (Jerusalem: Yad Vashem, 1977).

[9]Leonard Gross, *The Last Jews in Berlin* (New York: Simon and Schuster, 1982). Compare the experience of Jews in Berlin to that of their small town counterparts as depicted in Frances Henry, *Victims and Neighbors: A Small Town in Nazi Germany Remembered* (South Hadley; Bergin and Garvey, 1984).

[10]Douglas K. Huneke, "A Study of Christians Who Rescued Jews During the Nazi Era," *Humboldt Journal of Social Relations,* IX:1 ('Fall/Winter, 1981/1982), pp. 144-145. Huneke's article is based on his unpublished study *In the Darkness... Glimpses of Light* (Report to the Oregon Committee for the Humanities: September 1980). Also see Philip Hallie, *Lest Innocent Blood be Shed: The Story of the Village of Le Chambon and How Goodness Happened There* (New York: Harper and Row, 1980).

[11]Joseph Kermish, "The Activities of the Council for Aid to Jews ('Zegota') in Occupied Poland." in *Rescue Attempts During the Holocaust,* pp. 367-398; Louis De Jong, "Help to People in Hiding," *Delta,* VIII:1 ("Spring 1965), pp. 37-79.

[12]Huneke, "A Study of Christians," pp. 147-148. Also see Douglas K. Huneke, "The Lessons of Herman Graebe's Life: The Origins of the Moral Person," *Humboldt Journal of Social Relations,* XIII:1/2 (Fall/Winter & Spring/Summer, 1985/1986), pp. 320-332.

[13]Samuel P. Oliner, "The Unsung Heroes in Nazi Occupied Europe: The Antidote to Evil," *Nationalities Papers,* XII:1 (Spring 1984), pp. 134-135.

[14]Lawrence Baron, "The Dynamics of Decency: Dutch Rescuers of Jews During the Holocaust" (Frank P.Piskor Faculty Lecure: St.Lawrence University, May 2, 1985), pp. 7-8.

[15]Perry London, "The Rescuers: Motivational Hypotheses About Christians Who Saved Jews from the Nazis," in Eds. J. Macaulay and L. Berkowitz, *Altruism and Helping Behavior: Social Psychological Studies of Some Antecedents and Consequences* (New York: Academic Press, 1970), pp. 247-248.

[16]Nechama Tec, *When Light Pierced the Darkness: Christian Rescue of Jews in Nazi-Occupied Poland* (New York: Oxford University Press, 1986), pp. 152-154, 188-189.

[17]Baron, "The Dynamics of Decency," pp. 8-9.

[18]Frances G. Grossman, "A Psychological Study of Gentiles Who Saved the Lives of Jews During the Holocaust," in Ed. Israel W. Charny, *Toward the Understanding and Prevention of Genocide* (Boulder: Westview, 1984), pp. 202-216.

[19]Oliner, "The Unsung Heroes," pp. 134-136; Oliner, "The Need to Recognize," pp. 9-12.

[20]Eva Fogelman and Valerie Lewis Wiener, "The Few, the Brave, the Noble," *Psychology Today*, XIX: (August 1985), pp. 61-65; Carol Gilligan, *In a Different Voice: Psychological Theory and Women's Development* (Cambridge, MA: Harvard University Press, 1982).

[21]Philip Friedman, "Righteous Gentiles in the Nazi Era," in Ed. Ada June Friedman, *Roads to Extinction: Essays on the Holocaust* (Philadelphia: Jewish Publication Society, 1980), pp. 411-414.

[22]London, pp. 245-248; Oliner, "The Need to Recognize," pp. 9-12.

[23]Tec, pp. 188-190.

[24]Baron, "The Dynamics of Decency," pp. 11-13; Pieter De Jong, "Responses of the Churches in the Netherlands to the Nazi Occupation," in Ed. Michael I. Ryan, *Human Responses to the Holocaust: Perpetrators and Victims, Bystanders and Resisters* (New York: Edwin Mellen, 1981), pp. 121-143; David R. Blumenthal, "Religious Jews and Christians in the Holocaust," in Ed. David R. Blumenthal, *Emory Studies on the Holocaust: An Interfaith Inquiry* (Atlanta: Emory

University, 1985), pp. 84-88. For examples of Seventh Day Adventist rescuers, see Herbert Ford, *Flee the Captor* (Nashville: Southern Publishing Association, 1966) and Frida Michelson, *I Survived Rumbuli,* Trans. Wolf Goodman (New York, Holocaust Library, 1979).

[25]Fein, pp. 93-120.

[26]Baron, "The Dynamics of Decency," p. 13. For an account of left-wing support of Jewish resistance and rescue, see Anny Latour, *The Jewish Resistance in France (1940-1944),* Trans. Irene R. Ilton (New York: Holocaust Library, 1981).

[27]Tec, pp. 99-109.

[28]See the "Filmography and Bibliography" (September 1984) prepared by the United States Holocaust Memorial Council for its 1984 "Faith in Humankind" conference. There is also a companion volume to *The Courage to Care* movie, Eds. Carol Rittner and Sondra Myers, *The Courage to Care: Rescuers of Jews During the Holocaust* (New York: New York University Press, 1986). Peter Hellman, *Avenue of the Righteous* (New York: Athenaeum, 1980); Philip Friedman, *Their Brothers' Keepers* (New York: Crown, 1957).

[29]Douglas K. Huneke, *The Moses of Rovno* (New York: Dodd, Mead, and Co., 1985); Thomas Keneally, *Schindler's List* (New York: Simon and Schuster, 1982); Luitgard N. Wundheiler, "Oskar Schindler's Moral Development During the Holocaust," *Humboldt Journal of Social Relations,* XIII: 1.2 (1986), pp. 333-356.

[30]The first volume on the findings from the extensive interviews of rescuers conducted by Samuel Oliner's Altruistic Personality Project will be published soon by The Free Press. Scholars such as Jacob Boas, Eva Fleischner, and Andre Stein are also working on studies of rescuers. For suggestions on how to integrate ethics into school curricula, see Pearl M. Oliner, "Legitimating and Implementing Prosocial Education," *Humboldt Journal of Social Relations,* XIII:1/2 (1986), pp. 389-408.

[31]Anne Frank, *The Diary of a Young Girl,* Trans. B. M. Mooyaart (New York: Doubleday, 1952).

Chapter Nine

Crossing the Experience Barrier: Teaching the Holocaust to Christian Students

James F. Moore

Teaching any student about the Holocaust creates a gap that is finally impossible to bridge. In fact, Elie Wiesel warns us that this gap ought not to be bridged for the bridge leads us directly into a horror that even the victims ought not to have experienced.[1] What do we gain for our generation if we seek to lead them through the experience of Auschwitz? To seek to do this in the name of education is nothing less than the most horrible of jokes. The teacher of the Holocaust must, therefore, be resigned with a breach in experience that cannot be healed, indeed, must not be healed; but then why teach about the Holocaust?

Despite our recognition that a real encounter with Auschwitz is beyond any of us, we teach about the Holocaust in order to recreate a story that transforms the experience of the student into an encounter with the "evidence" of the Holocaust. We intend to confront our students with the moral and theological challenges that the bare fact of Auschwitz presents to us. Thus, teaching about the Holocaust engages the teacher in the task of shaping a picture with the semblance of the "Holocaust experience" but clearly with the intent of telling the story of Auschwitz from the perspective of one who is, who must be, morally outraged. This moral rage is a beginning point on the way to meaningful action which is perhaps the prime goal of teaching courses on the Holocaust. Obviously, how we shape the story in order to reach the goal, bridging the gap between modern complacency and meaningful action, is of fundamental significance.

Those of us who teach Christian students about the Holocaust face another gap as well. Though difficult to believe, our Christian students are also isolated (most almost entirely) from Jews, Jewish life, Jewish thought, Jewish history, and the Jewish spirit. Thus, teaching about the Holocaust to Christian students means teaching about Judaism as well. The gap that Christian students must cross in simple understanding of the Jews who suffered and died at Auschwitz and other Nazi camps makes the other gap of experience even wider for these students. Naturally, we must ask why teach Christian students about the Holocaust? We do so with the assumption that Christian students must come to realize that the Holocaust is both their concern and their tragedy, that Jews are brothers and sisters, that Jewish loss is their loss and the questions Jews struggle with are vital and to be taken seriously.

This essay seeks to uncover the basic factors that are involved in teaching the Holocaust to Christian students by taking as a central motif this notion (image) of crossing barriers. In laying out the picture of such a course, we suggest that a particular device — the study of and use of the journal — can be a most effective way of leading students across the two seemingly impenetrable barriers. Therefore, the thesis of this paper is that any course on the Holocaust, and most especially a course designed for Christian students, must move beyond academic engagement with the material toward personal encounter. That is, courses on the Holocaust must involve some measure of experiential learning like the journal.

Telling the Story

Elie Wiesel urges all of us to tell stories.[2] Surely Wiesel knows as we do that the telling the stories of Auschwitz means a complex of different possibilities and combinations. Each story bears the mark of the storyteller that comes not only from the particular viewpoint of that person but also of the purposes for telling the story. Is the story intended to justify, defend, exhort, condemn, exonerate? Each story shapes the events of the Holocaust in a particular direction aimed at creating a different vision in the hearer. Some stories focus on good, others on evil, while still others dare not decide that there was good or evil, or, more to the point, that we can so easily tell the difference. If we are to tell stories, ourselves, we must hear stories and that becomes a major task of a course on the Holocaust.

Pure history bears a story of sorts. That is, mere confrontation with facts as they can be reconstructed will tell a story for each student who hears those facts, or sees those facts. Still, there is no entirely pure history. Each assemblage of facts is already a shaping of the history into a particular story. We dare not miss this inescapable fact that looms over the whole of the Holocaust, that humans can distort facts to suit their own purposes. Shaping the story for students must bear this message completely aside from the efforts we make to present the "evidence."[3] Telling the story of Auschwitz in order to help the student to realize the Nazi corruption of history is a difficult and a slow task that is only partially effective.

Usually teachers of the Holocaust find that this task is best served by confronting the student with a variety of different media and perspectives. Only the sorting out process of reading different accounts relating the picture of the same (or supposedly the same) evidence will bring the student to the realization of how fragile our conception of the "truth" is.[4] If our conception of the truth is fragile, then surely the process of leading the student to make judgments about the truth will be arduous and frustrating. Most students in our Holocaust courses find this frustration the most difficult hurdle to overcome.

One way to meet the challenge of this frustration is to expose the student to as much first-hand material as possible. A particularly useful tool is the diary or journal of Holocaust victims. These very personal materials provide a feel for the experience that texts of interpretation could never convey. Aside from the obvious advantage of reading a witness to the events, these journals lead the student into an experience of reflection rarely duplicated with any other classroom exercise. Holocaust journals shape the student's learning experience in three significant ways. First, the journal is open-ended meaning that to come to terms with the journal the student must forego immediate inclinations to provide answers, interpretations, conclusions. Second, the journals generally convey models (individuals) of personal courage and religious faithfulness. Whatever a student's personal convictions, no student can completely ignore the impact of these witnesses to human goodness. Third, the journal often conveys a picture of intensified struggle over central life issues. Of course, many materials raise questions of life-importance, but the journal's existential setting intensifies these questions. This intensification is an important way for the student to gauge the radical nature of the evil and suffering of the Holocaust.

Open-ended Meaning

The journal approach to teaching is a new experience for many students, differing markedly from reading an historical account about an event. Though the data may be the same, the perspective is different — the journal is written from within the experience by an identifiable person *experiencing* the events he or she is writing about. In other words, the reader must come to terms with the "author" in a quite different way than with any other kinds of literature. The author is in many ways the subject matter of the journal and attempting to make judgments about persons is much more difficult and less definite than making judgments about historical facts.

The journal format is closer to the nature of a novel than an historical document. That is, the reader is as much concerned about the characters as about the events of the story. Thus in reading a journal, the students will be asking questions about what shapes the author's values, hopes, lifestyle, and ability to make independent decisions. Naturally the Holocaust makes this probing even more essential since those very things are what the *Shoah* calls into question.

A notable example of such a journal is Etty Hillesum's *An Interrupted Life*.[5] This diary of a Dutch university student has been particularly useful for my classes on the Holocaust since the author is relatively close to the ages of my students. However, nearly all aspects of Etty's value system, goals and aspirations, personal lifestyle, and particular decisions open up puzzles for our students that require piecing together before any assessment of the whole can be made. Our students must, in short, struggle with every turn in the text.

This story differs from the novel, however, in concerning itself with real people and events that can be documented by other sorts of records. The "realness" of the journal story has an immediate impact. We as readers know that Etty's death is imminent even though that knowledge is only vaguely apparent to Etty in the early part of her journal. We the readers know the terrible fate that awaits, can do nothing at this point to change those events, yet are fully aware that Etty really experienced all of this.

The "realness" of the story lends another important dimension to the student's learning experience. We cannot impose arbitrarily the conclusion we know is coming. Etty's story is filled with occasions of possible escape. Most students, having grown to care for Etty, are frustrated by these roads not taken. Many ask, why didn't Etty try to escape? The very nature of the journal finally forces the reader to see possible meaning beyond the mere need to escape. The nature of Etty's journal forces the student to see that, for Etty, meaning is taken as open-ended awaiting God's action as the ultimate meaning of any event. For example:

"I shall allow the chain of this day to unwind link by link, I shall not intervene but shall simply have faith. 'I shall let you make your own decisions, O God.'"[6]

Of course, this open-endedness of meaning is something imbedded in both Jewish and Christian faith in ways similar to that expressed here by Etty. The necessity to trust God rather than one's experience and wisdom is part of the mutual commitment between God and his people. Etty so often is reminded that after centuries of others committing horrendous crimes against the Jewish people, they still trusted in the ultimate wisdom of God rather than in the immediate appearances of life. In the midst of suffering and struggle, that simple trust, surprisingly, is often the easiest path.

For the student attempting to make sense of a larger whole than Etty could have conceived, such patient trust is more difficult. The threat is different than that to Etty, both physically and spiritually much less. Yet, the emotional turmoil blinds most students even to the resources of their own faith or makes them settle all too easily for pat solutions. Trust even while engaging in the struggle, such as that exemplified by Etty and countless others who told of their daily experience of the Holocaust, is extraordinarily difficult for the student. Truth and its importance for faith is often overbearing. Most think that answer must come immediately.

Dealing with religious impatience is a strange irony when teaching about the Holocaust. The events of the Holocaust are so deeply challenging in their evil that most students cannot manage the resulting frustration of lacking adequate responses. Yet telling the story of the Holocaust requires the context of uncertainty, the kind of uncertainty finally brought home with full clarity in the Holocaust journals. Not only is the open-endedness of the journal an important lesson in terms of learning patience about assigning meaning to the events studied. Allowing the event to be opened up as an event of persons and not objective facts is, in addition, an essential ingredient in the effort to cross experience barriers.

Meeting Persons In the Events

The journal format is by far the most effective tool for bringing the students into contact with the personal level of the Holocaust. Other resources are clearly important as a means for introducing the student to the personal level. Films and/or video-tapes can give students a sense of the larger scope that can only be accomplished by visual means.[7]   Historical texts are important objective resources to help students to be firmly planted in the reality of the event.[8] Other types of accounts and recollections are an important corollary to the use of journals since they also confront students with persons and personal experience.[9] The journal, however, not only presents persons but places them into the setting of their experience; this fact is soon made real for most students.

This effort to confront students with the personal dimension is especially important for Christian students since, as noted, such students have a second experience barrier to cross when dealing with the Holocaust. These students must also learn to relate to Jews as persons (some students being so isolated that they have never met Jews). Of course Christian students can be sensitized to the human dimension as quickly as anyone. Our students are morally outraged by the event almost immediately. They will, however, never be able to ask the penetrating questions or confront the lingering religious doubts contributing to the context of the Holocaust unless they are led to cross this experience barrier separating them from the lived-world of Jews. For this reason, the experience of suffering is likely to be different for Christians and Jews (in spite of what we might do). Nevertheless, leading students across this barrier can result in some students beginning to appreciate the world from a different perspective and perhaps coming to realize the *validity* of that perspective.

Etty Hillesum's journal works well since the student is forced to come to terms with a perspective shaped not only by Jewish tradition and life but also by the culture of pre-World War II Western Europe (specifically that of Holland). Add to this the world of a female university student and the effort is already posed for the student even before the necessity to come to terms with Etty's religious perspective. The student is challenged to deal with Etty on an individual level, not with stereotypes; and this initial effort leads the student to deal with Etty's religious perspective also on an individual level rather than with stereotypes. In fact, Etty is likely to break down most stereotypes of Jews, making any effort to understand her on those terms fruitless. Naturally, the world of Etty Hillesum must be balanced with the experiences of Eastern

European Jews who were by far the majority of victims of the Holocaust. Any number of journal formats are available to us now;[10] as well as other materials that relate eyewitness accounts.[11] Eliezer Berkovits, for example, presents a variety of concerns in a short space that provides a full perspective on how the particular view of the Jew confronted the atrocity of the death camps. However, Berkovits presents a view which is an apologetic for traditional theodicy, just as much an individual perspective as that of Etty Hillesum even as it is strikingly different from that of Hillesum.

The objective of this personal confrontation is three-fold. The first level is subtle but important; we hope that students will begin to think of the Holocaust not just from general perspectives but will begin to struggle with *their own response*. Secondly, we want the students to realize the variety of views encompassed within the larger framework of Judaism. Realizing that individual persons faced the horrors of Auschwitz may be self-evident; but actually letting that fact register helps the Christian student to realize the individual nature of each person's response. Each person must be judged on their own terms and not by preconceived evaluations or expectations. Finally, the personal dimension creates for our students the only "true" stream of hope arising out of the Holocaust. For the most part, our students are greatly impressed by the courage of the Jewish victims of the Holocaust.

This impression carries benefits beyond simply the personalization of the events. Our students not only find hope in the courageous acts of the Jews but also are challenged by Jewish faithfulness. Students are led to ask now with complete seriousness, "What is there in the faith and life-perspective of these Jews that could give them such fortitude and faithfulness?" Having begun to experience this "Jewish world" of the Holocaust victim, the student is led to realize the validity of the Jewish perspective portrayed through these lives. Even more, our students for the first time really confront the question, "Why have Christians been so ready to persecute Jews simply because they were Jews?" The combination of these two questions now brought to the level of personal experience is both a stinging reality for our students and a necessary component on the road to creating a personal response after Auschwitz.

Facing Life Questions

Approaching the Holocaust through the use of journals automatically focusses attention on life questions. Nevertheless, the teacher must be cautious in leading students to these questions since the setting of the Holocaust makes both the questions and the response different than what any of us experience in at least three ways.

First, those we study experienced an extra ordinary situation that is unique in many ways. That Jews had little or no choice about the direction of their lives during those years made a response to life questions wholly a matter of personal fortitude and values. Students must be led to see that their situation could never approximate the urgency experienced by an Elie Wiesel or an Etty Hillesum.

Second the evil that confronted these people is like none that we have faced.[12] Thus, the shape of questions that for us seem abstract, or facilely answered, had a stark reality that will be difficult even for the most sensitive to understand. Can we possibly understand the meaning of survival or the importance of a single Sabbath observance as these victims came to understand them? Undoubtedly we will only barely sense the significance of these matters.

Third, in almost every sense the individuals we study, together with their reflections in journals, represent a world that is now gone, not only in the physical loss of people, homes and lifestyle, but also in spiritual and emotional richness. The task of understanding requires literally an effort to reconstruct a world or worlds that have no parallel in our experience. Christian students who did not have the benefit of growing up in a Jewish family have fewer resources for appreciating and reconstructing that world.

Nevertheless, the responses of these various courageous people do become a reservoir of wisdom for us not primarily in understanding the hell of Auschwitz but rather in understanding our humanity, its possibilities and its fallibilities. The task of searching is, thus, a task of discovering ourselves, both the great potential for good and the fearful potential for evil. Students who are led through the journals of the Holocaust are led to see not so much answers as the necessity for caution in our efforts to create easy answers.

Christian students usually find this aspect of the study of the Holocaust the most threatening but also the most rewarding. It is the most threatening because they must come face to face with the real possibilities for evil latent in their own beliefs and the way that they have come to answer some of the most challenging of life's questions. Yet, it is the most rewarding since they are usually led to view their own beliefs in such a way that they gain a real even if cautious hope that acceptance and cooperation might be possible in their future.

Naturally, particular individuals like Elie Wiesel, Eliezer Berkovits, Anne Frank, or Etty Hillesum can become resources for some hope not in their own answers to these life questions (how shall I live and what must I do?) but in their courageous example. The situation of the Holocaust is so extraordinary that actual responses to challenges by various persons at Auschwitz or other death camps could not be translated to our lives. On the other hand, the courageous attitude of the victims can model the kind of response available for us, that is, a faithfulness in the face of evil.

The Use of the Personal Journal

Because the impact of the study of the Holocaust requires a personal response and involvement unlike other classes, I have devised an assignment for my students that is intended to maximize the lesson learned from exposure to Holocaust journals and diaries. Each student is asked to keep a personal journal during the course of the semester with the intention of encouraging students to record their daily response to this exposure. The point of this exercise has taken shape through the various offerings of the course.

First the journal format allows escape from the tendency most students have to respond (at least in their minds and in their writing) only through their intellect. They are encouraged to write in whatever form is appropriate at the time of each entry (e.g., poetry, sketches, dialogue). Students discover soon enough that the events of the Holocaust cannot be understood or even approached simply through the intellect. Daily journal entries bring this fact to the fore that much sooner.

Second, the task of responding to the experience of the class on a regular, even daily, basis enables the students to see their own growth toward greater appreciation of the extent of the Holocaust and of the "faith" of the victims. In addition, the journal records for the instructor this pattern of growth as a check on a student's response to the course. In some cases the journal provides greater positive feedback on progress toward course objectives especially in courses like those on the Holocaust already filled with emotional experiences and laden with uncertainty. The feedback may also give clues about particular difficulties for some students that might require special attention.

Finally, if the journal entries are carefully directed, the results will confront students with their own views, even prejudices, making it even less likely that students will escape the fact that our views often parallel those of Christians before, during and after the Holocaust. Despite protestations, students can hardly avoid the evidence; they have crossed over an experience barrier of great importance especially if our intention in teaching about the Holocaust is to raise awareness so as to avoid as much as possible a re-occurrence.

An additional advantage of this exercise is that students are led to record their day-to-day experience at the same time that they read the day-to-day records of the journal writers of the Holocaust. Since the journal became an important way to combat the terror of the *Shoah*, the experience of writing a journal in this class draws students closer to the meaning of that fact. Naturally some students learn more from this assignment than others, but nearly all find the journal an invaluable component of the Holocaust course.

Crossing Experience Barriers

We began our discussion of the use of journals in teaching a course on the Holocaust by claiming that teaching Christian students requires crossing experience barriers. The barriers we confront in these courses are nearly impenetrable particularly in the short space of a semester. Nevertheless, any effort to link the experience of the student with that of the victims of the Holocaust or to expand the experience of the student by leading them into the world of the Holocaust victim can begin this necessary ongoing task of increased openness and respect for others, particularly an openness by Christian students to Jews in their own experience.

The use of the journal also leads the student to cross over a barrier of astonishment at the evil of the Holocaust in order to see possible positive response even by those victimized by these events. This discovery not only enables students to take heart through discovering the experiences, the courage and faith of others, but also radically changes some of their views about the viability and strength of Jewish life and faith. For Christian students, this is a barrier that once crossed can never again be erected. Christian students are radically changed by the course on the Holocaust, not primarily by the enormity of the evil perpetrated but by the extraordinary witness of Jewish people in the midst of that evil.

Preparation for a New World

It is dangerous for anyone to claim too much for a single course. Courses on the Holocaust are not guarantees against religious or political fanaticism or moral intolerance. Students are impressionable but not completely so; the changes they experience cannot completely alter years of religious and moral training that, in some cases, might be opposed to the evidence that they discover through the course. Thus, the study and writing of journals can never be seen as the only necessary elements of such a course and courses on the Holocaust are only a small component of what is needed to extend awareness and moral sensitivity.

However, insofar as courses on the Holocaust do make an impression in an increased awareness, they do so by breaking through experience barriers that seem almost impossible to cross. The use of journals is founded upon that presumption that has been further illustrated in this essay. For Christian students, an objective aimed at crossing experience barriers is absolutely essential.

Taking heed once again from Elie Wiesel, however, we are led to add this final word. The story of the Holocaust is not our story; thus the stories of the victims of the Holocaust cannot be our story. Instead we must learn to tell our story perhaps aided by the witness of Etty Hillesum or Anne Frank. We must learn to shape a story for our time now forever affected by our experience of the events of the Holocaust. My hope is that the task of reading and writing journals can help my students to be readied for that work.

---

[1] Elie Wiesel, "Art and Culture After the Holocaust" *Auschwitz: Beginning of an Era?* ed., Eva Fleischner (New York: KTAV, 1977), p. 403.

[2] Ibid., Wiesel, p. 415.

[3]One resource that bridges the two tasks well, especially for Christian students, is: Harry James Cargas, *A Christian Response to the Holocaust* (Denver: Stonehenge Books, 1981).

[4]Irving Greenberg, "Cloud of Smoke, Pillar of Fire," *Auschwitz: Beginning of a New Era?* ed., Eva Fleischner (New York: KTAV, 1977), pp. 7-55.

[5]Etty Hillesum, *An Interrupted Life* (New York: Washington Square Press, 1981).

[6]Ibid., Hillesum, p. 203.

[7]Among the growing bibliography of films are *Night and Fog, Genocide* and *Shoah.*

[8]Naturally, great care is needed in leading students to historical sources. Two good resources are: Raul Hilberg, *The Destruction of the European Jews* (New York: Harper and Row, 1961), and Nora Levin, *The Holocaust* (New York: Schocken, 1973).

[9]Any number of these recollections are useful, such as:

Eliezer Berkovits, *With God in Hell* (New York: Sanhedrin Press, 1979).

Alexander Donat, *The Holocaust Kingdom* (New York: The Holocaust Library, 1978).

Primo Levi, *Survival in Aushwitz* (New York: Collier, 1969).

Elie Wiesel, *Night* (New York: Bantam, 1960).

[10]E.g., Emmanuel Ringelblum, *Notes from the Warsaw Ghetto* (New York: Bantam, 1960).

[11]Ibid., Berkovits.

[12]The argument for the uniqueness of the Holocaust is not shared by all. It is made with some force in:

Emil Fackenheim, *God's Presence in History* (New York: Harper and Row, 1970).

Also, cf.:

A. Roy Eckardt and Alice Eckardt, *Long Night's Journey into Day* (Detroit: Wayne State University Press, 1982).

Part III

Literature and Arts

Chapter Ten

Memory and Meaning: The Holocaust in Second Generation Literature

Alan L. Berger

Reflecting on the meaning and purpose of memory after Auschwitz , Elie Wiesel observed that memories must be made into offerings.[1] Consequently, for Wiesel and the generation of witnessing authors, writing frequently assumed the dimensions of prayer. These "prayers" were sometimes for, and sometimes in spite of, God and His covenant. Seeking to restore a moral universe, many survivors wrote meditations on the human condition which utilized memory as a weapon in the ceaseless struggle to banish unyielding evil and overcome the outrage of oblivion. Holocaust literature written by witnesses thus emerged as an audacious and complex concept whose purpose encompassed a multiplicity of meanings; literary, metaphysical, psychological, and theological. The situation becomes more complicated, however, as time distances us from the *Shoah* while claiming ever more of its primary witnesses.

As Holocaust literature enters a second generation, the relationship between memory and meaning is at once increasingly tenuous and more important to articulate. On the one hand, reverberations of holocaustal loss and unrestrained evil continue to affect those who may legitimately be viewed as the *Shoah's* secondary and even tertiary victims. At the same time, however, the Holocaust itself is subject to increasing manipulation both within and outside the Jewish community; scholars warn against overemphasizing its role in the Jewish historical experience, literary distortions of the catastrophe abound, and an ugly revisionism has appeared which either trivializes or completely denies the Event.

Second generation Holocaust literature reraises in an acute manner the problem of transmitting meaning from generation to generation, a central and ancient concern of Judaism. *Pirke Avot,* for example, reports that "Moses received Torah from Sinai and delivered it to Joshua, and Joshua to the Elders, and the Elders to the Prophets, and the Prophets delivered it to the men of the Great Synagogue." Centuries later, the hasidic movement employed a four-generation model which revealed both the necessity and the possibility of communicating the sacred. The Besht would solve spiritual problems by going to a certain place in the woods, meditating, and lighting a fire. His successor, the Maggid of Mezhirech, was unable to light the fire, but knew the place and the proper meditation. This proved sufficient. Rabbi Moshe Leib of Sassov, the third generation figure, only knew the sacred place, but this was enough. Israel of Rishin, Moshe Leib's successor, could only recall the tale. But that was all that was necessary. The point here is not that the efficacy was diminished, although surely diminishment there was. Crucial to this story is the necessity of remembering and telling the tale.[2] Second generation Holocaust literature is an attempt to voice the legacy of the tragedy.

This literature thus shoulders a pedagogical as well as an ontological burden. Yosef Yerushalmi asserts, for example, that novelists and not historians are defining the Holocaust's image by offering what he terms a new metahistorical myth[3] for encountering the *Shoah's* multilayered implications. Such literature emerges as a vital and frequently overlooked resource for comprehending the Holocaust's continuing impact. In what follows, I define second generation literature and note its concerns, examine selected contemporary English language examples of memories' struggle for meaning, and point to the emergence of a trend toward parody and distortion of legitimate motifs. I conclude by offering a meditation on the pedagogical role of such literature.

Second Generation Literature Defined

Second generation literature of the Holocaust is a slowly-emerging multidimensional genre consisting of novels short stories, plays, poetry, essays and biographies about survivor parents, journalistic accounts, and most recently, comic strips.[4] International in scope, still lacking canonical status, and of uneven literary quality, literature of the second generation seeks to preserve parental memory while coming to its own terms with holocaustal loss. It is not composed of first-hand accounts. Indeed, as Lawrence Langer has observed, "With the exception of the narratives buried in the vicinity of the gas chambers, all accounts are filtered through memory and imagination... ."[5] Second generation literature, for its part, tends to focus on the aftermath rather than on the storm itself. Collectively, this literature underscores the painfully human dimension of a catastrophe of biblical proportion.

Authors of this literature may be seen as comprising three links in a chain of memory. There are, first of all, child survivors; those who were born in Europe under Nazi domination between 1939 and 1945. The second link is formed by survivors' children; those born after the war, either in European Displaced Persons camps, or after the survivors reached their eventual destinations. Heirs of an evil they did not personally experience, survivors' children embody both the despair and the hope of post-Holocaust Judaism. Menachem Rosensaft, born in the shadow of Bergen Belsen in 1948 and currently Chairman of the International Network of Children of Jewish Holocaust Survivors, refers to his peers as the first and the last generation: "the first to be born after the Holocaust and the last to have a direct link with that... Jewish existence that was so brutally annihilated."[6] Implicit in Rosensaft's observation is the belief that children of survivors are a bridging generation whose creative work is of inestimable importance for Jewish and human continuity.

The third and largest link is composed of nonwitnessing writers who, nonetheless, live and write in the shadow of the Holocaust, focusing literary attention on children or grandchildren of survivors. These writers comprise a group whom the literary critic Alvin Rosenfeld describes as those "who were never there but know more than the outlines of the place."[7] Transmitting the Holocaust as an "orienting event" is, like the retelling of the Exodus, a task of serious writers of literature. If, as Yehuda Bauer argues — correctly in my view — the "crucial problem is how to anchor the Holocaust in the historical consciousness of the generations that follow it,"[8] then these three groups of authors will play a decisive role in shaping what and who is remembered as well as how that memory is placed within the Jewish ritual tradition. Memory is thus as much about the present as the past. Bauer's observation bears far more than historiographical significance.

Concerns of Second Generation Literature

Many questions arise concerning the content of second generation literature of the Holocaust. Such queries can be examined under three headings: literary, psychological, and theological. Literarily, one must enquire into the relationship between memory and imagination. For Cynthia Ozick the generation of post-Auschwitz Jewry stands in a "shockingly new relation to Jewish history."[9] Amplifying her statement, Ozick writes:

> We, and all the generations to follow, are and will continue to be into eternity, witness-generations to Jewish loss.[10]

Ozick's view is significant because she underscores that what has been lost is not only the Jewish past, but also a "major share of the Jewish future." Both the "intellect of a people in its prime" and the "treasure of a people in its potential" were exterminated. "We will," observes Ozick, "never be in possession of the novels Anne Frank did not live to write."[11] Consequently, for Ozick, nothing less than Jewish memory itself is threatened with extinction. Genocide is prelude to narrative extinction.

Other literary tasks include defining the precise pedagogical role of second generation literature. What is the relationship between genre and meaning? Is it possible, for example, to confront the meaningless deaths of millions through utilization of a comic book such as *Maus?* Does the appearance of this work mark a new form of Holocaust novel? Are there guidelines for determining authentic from spurious forms of second generation literature?

Psychologically important issues are also raised. What, for example, are the dimensions of survivor parent-child relationships? What images of survivors emerge in second generation literature? The concept of vengeance appears, but is frequently transformed into a quest for justice or a telling of holocaustal tales. Children of survivors often attempt to imagine their parents' reactions to the Holocaust's fading from public memory as well as issues such as intermarriage and assimilation. There is as well the entire problem of the relationship of the *Shoah* to Jewish identity.

Theological questions concern the covenantal obligation of nonwitnesses. How, for example, can one account for the increasingly ambiguous nature of the divine-human relationship? How are traditional Jewish rituals modified to incorporate Holocaust remembrance? Are Jewish-Christian relations viewed as either viable or desirable after Auschwitz? What is the nature of the relationship between Jewish particularism and the Holocaust's universal implications for the generations which come after?

Selected Contemporary Examples

Amidst the growing examples of second generation literature, I focus on six novelists; three are children of survivors, two who have written on the second or third generation, and one who is himself a survivor. Geographically, their works were written in Australia, Canada, and the United States. In five of the examples the intertwining of literary, psychological, and theological concerns is revealed through the dynamic of parent-child relationships. The memories of the survivor generation become the legacy of its offspring and others whose lives have been altered by the dreadfulness of the *Shoah*.

America

American second generation Holocaust literature constitutes a type of psychohistory of survivors and their children. Utilizing a variety of ritual settings, each of the following works shares the view that the Holocaust was decisive for the survivor's Jewishness and his decision to raise Jewish offspring. Children of survivors, for their part each view their identity as singling them out, transforming their consciousness, and endowing them with a mission to speak of the Holocaust.

Hugh Nissenson's short story, "The Law" (1963) is a pioneering literary effort which recognized both the relationship of the Holocaust to Jewish identity and the continuing impact of the Holocaust on children of survivors.[12] Detailing the Bar Mitzvah preparation of Daniel Levy, the tale provides a capsule history of the Holocaust as told by the boy's father, Willi Levy, a pre-war assimilationist who had later survived Bergen-Belsen. Daniel is mesmerized by Willi's tales of survival which included overcoming Nazi brutality, Christian anti-Semitism, and the unprecedented situation of the victims whose very birth was a death sentence. Daniel receives two types of instruction; traditional - he studies his haftarah portion - and contemporary - he listens to his father's Holocaust stories. The boy's Jewish identity is shaped by the *Shoah* no less than by the Bible.

Nissenson, an American-born nonwitness, correctly portrays the genocide of the Jews as a massive trauma, yet the story reveals certain positive legacies. For example, while Willi was indifferent to Judaism before the war, his post-Holocaust insistence that Daniel become a Bar Mitzvah reveals an aspect of Emil Fackenheim's contention that Jewish existence is itself a mystery, in the religious sense of the word, encompassing both believers and non-believers. Willi's position is a literary anticipation of Fackenheim's "Commanding Voice of Auschwitz" which, speaking from amidst the chaos of destruction, compels

Jews to remain Jewish. Daniel, for his part, is both son of and disciple to his father. Nissenson portrays the ineffable nature of holocaustal suffering in juxtaposition with the survivors' need to testify. Willi's testimony, written in German, has not been, and can never be, translated. Yet Daniel, much in the hasidic tradition, will continue to tell his father's tale.

Nearly two decades elapsed before the appearance of novels and short stories written by or specifically about survivors' children. In America, novels such as Robert Greenfield's *Temple* (1982)[13] Thomas Friedmann's *Damaged Goods* (1984)[14], Elie Wiesel's *The Fifth Son* (1985)[15], and short stories by Rebecca Goldstein, "the legacy of raizel kaidish: a story" (1985), and Marjorie Sandor's "The Gittel" (1986) attest to the continuing ripples of evil and pain which emanate from the *Shoah*. Also in the late seventies and early eighties the Canadian writer Abraham Boyarsky wrote short stories and a novel, *Shreiber* (1981),[16] reflecting his perceptions as a child of Holocaust survivors. In Australia, Serge Liberman, son of survivors, has written two collections of short stories, *On Firmer Shores* (1981)[17] and *A Universe of Clowns* (1983)[18] which contain important sources for understanding the relationship of the Holocaust to Jewish identity.

Focusing first on the American novels, one notes that their authors represent three different relationships to the Holocaust: Greenfield is an American nonwitness, Friedmann the son of Holocaust survivors, and Wiesel is himself a survivor. Each of the novels is set in the political and social turbulence of 1960s America, and each centers on graduate students as sons or grandson of survivors. Implicitly, each author invites the reader to contrast the outer turmoil of America with the inner turmoil experienced by their identity-seeking characters. Differing from Nissenson's portrayal, the children in these stories are older and attain a greater measure of individual thought and feeling. Greenfield tells the story of Paulie Bindel, a disaffected graduate student, whose grandfather is a survivor. A mystery both to his divorced parents and Paulie, his grandfather Mendel always leads *kaddish* (the prayer for the dead) in temple. Paulie's search for identity and Mendel's need for a disciple lead to the formation of an unarticulated but strong bond between the two.

Greenfield connects the *Shoah* and contemporary Judaism through the *tashlich* ritual. *Tashlich,* the symbolic casting away of sins during the New Year ritual, forms the novel's opening scene in America. Mendel recalls the gruesome and brutal murder of his crippled friend, Schissel, during a clandestine *tashlich* ceremony in the death camp. Suffering a stroke, Mendel remembers the hunger, corruption, cruelty, and deprivation of the Nazi annihilation camps. His stroke-induced trance yields, as well, an indictment of assimilationist Jews. Vienna, where he had lived prior to the Nazi onslaught, was populated by Jews whose highest aspiration was to mimic the Gentiles. Jewish piety is embodied by the untutored and deformed Schissel who is shunned and scorned by his fellow Jews. Greenfield's attack on the smugness and naivete of European assimilationists is similar to the point of view of the Israeli survivor and novelist Aharon Appelfeld.

Theologically, Mendel is portrayed as undergoing several stages in his covenant orientation. He had lost faith in God earlier when he fought in the army. In the death camps, he never said *Kaddish* because "God the Father has apparently chosen to abandon the faithful." Greenfield, in fact, has Mendel echoing Wiesel's position, in *Night,* that "life itself is an endless *kaddish,* for the living as well as the dead." After Schissel's murder, however, Mendel risks his life by reciting the *kaddish* daily, both morning and evening.

Despite his intentions, there are problems with Greenfield's novel. Although implying that survivors are being heard, if not by the second, then by the third generation, the grandson rarely speaks to his grandfather. Greenfield's characters do not wrestle with the covenantal issues raised by the *Shoah.* There is, for example, little in the way of reflection about the meaning of history, the purpose of chosenness, and the post-Holocaust obligations of God and man. Paulie, the character closest to the survivor, is himself described at novel's end as a survivor, like his father and his father before him. This dilution of the meaning of survivor does no justice to the victims, nor does it help educate those who come after. Perhaps the most curious feature of *Temple* is the lack of tales about the Holocaust. Mendel, the survivor, remembers but does not tell. Paulie, his grandson, sees but does not hear. There is no *Sh'ma Yisrael* prayer here and neither public witness by the survivor nor articulation of the second or third generation's covenant obligations.

Friedmann and Wiesel have written far more feeling and knowledgeable works about the second generation. Friedmann tells of the complexity of survivor parent-child relationships while detailing how the *Shoah* has become part of the fabric of existence for its secondary victims. His story concerns the attempt of Yaakov, an Orthodox Jew who in America is called Jason, to avoid the draft while coming to terms with his father's traditional Judaism. Jason's relationship to the tradition is ambivalent. He describes himself as "semi-observant, semi-rebellious." Friedmann's work is rich in detail and suggests much concerning Orthodox Jewish expression in America. His romance with a Jewish, but non-Orthodox woman, reveals the enormous cleavages existing within American Jewish expression.

Specifically concerning the Holocaust, *Damaged Goods* provides an unrivaled novelistic look at the continuing psychological impact which the *Shoah* has on parent-child relations. Jason's father is a remote figure who relates to his son only in terms of ritual rather than filial love. The father speaks to his son about survival. Member of a forced labor gang during the Holocaust, he contends that those who survived were the ones who, like Orthodox ritual itself, paid attention to details. Neither the physically strong nor the "wiseguys" were able to endure the ordeals. Jason's mother, on the other hand, is portrayed as a warm and caring woman. Survivor of a death camp, she offers her own lesson to the son. She is convinced that her survival was due to the fact that she rubbed beets on her face to give it color, thereby convincing the Nazis that she was healthy enough to live another day.

Friedmann's novel makes it possible to understand in a personal way the human dimension of holocaustal loss. Jason is, for example, an only child, but the second son. His father had lost his first family during the Holocaust. Jason discovers the existence of an older half-brother indirectly when, we read, "Father told me I need not say the blessing for the first born the morning before Passover" (P.72). This method of indirection is frequently noted in psychiatric literature as one way survivor parents communicate their Holocaust history.[19] Other insights are given concerning the psychic life of survivors' children. Jason's friends are, to cite one example, also children of survivors. They, like their parents, exhibit a great variety of orientations to the covenant tradition. Dov is studying to be a rabbi and is authorally shipped to Israel. Jonesey is pampered and sexually licentious, having little or no regard for Jewish ritual life. Jason, not knowing what really happened to his parents during the Holocaust, imagines events. Desperately attempting to learn, and therefore remember, Jason tells the reader:

> I overhear incomplete pieces of conversation, try to match the
> jagged ends to stories Jonesey occasionally requests from his father,
> fill spaces with books taken from an unlocked yet clearly off-limits

glass cabinet. Among them all, I have constructed perfectly clear visions (p.73).

Jason is, however, a victim no less than a possessor of memory. The abiguity of memory for the second generation is expressed in Jason's musing to his American-born lover.

> If only we could forget, if only the baggage on the back and the fear in the heart and the numbers on the arm weren't along to remind us of the past (p.178).

Although describing himself as "the ultimate bystander," Jason's status as a child of survivors is, like the covenantal burden itself, unshakable. He observes and absorbs survivor rituals (food is regarded with near sanctity) and survivor dreams. His mother, who disappears midway through the novel and is presumed drowned, shares with Jason her dream of an enormous flood which would smother the fires of the death camp ovens. These and other incidents are manifestations of what Robert Jay Lifton has called the "death imprint" which is passed from survivors to offspring.[20] Taking the Holocaust into his own being, like Nissenson's Daniel and unlike Greenfield's Paulie, Jason is transformed into a witness.

In terms of ritual, Jason recalls that his parents commemorated the Holocaust dead in the weeks after Passover, a time which tradition ascribes to the counting of the *Omer*. Historically, *Omer* recalls the grave threat to Jewish continuity which resulted from the Bar Kokhba rebellion. In Jason's home candles are lit:

> ...in memory of the concentration camp deaths, particularly the uncharted, hectic cremation during the final days. (pp. 29-30).

The symbolism of the novel's title is significant and deserves attention. Damaged goods can refer to those items, animals, or people unsuitable for ritual use. It may signify individuals who have been corrupted by nonorthodox or secular lifestyles. Idiomatically, the term refers to a divorced person. Damaged goods may also be understood, however, as referring both to survivor parents, who have been damaged by their Holocaust experience, and to the entire post-Holocaust *Kl'lal Yisrael.*

The Fifth Son is a highly symbolic novel in which Wiesel articulates theological guidelines for the second generation.[21] Moving beyond the four sons of the traditional Passover Seder, Wiesel's new *Haggadah* introduces a fifth son meant to symbolize American Judaism in general and the second generation in particular. It is not accidental that Wiesel dedicated this novel to his own son and to all children of survivors. The novel's twin foci are a concern for theodicy and the relationship between survivors and their children. *The Fifth Son,* unlike *Damaged Goods,* stresses the covenantal rather than the psychological turmoil of post-Holocaust American Judaism.

In brief, the plot concerns the assumption of his murdered brother's name and identity by the American-born Ariel, both of whose parents are survivors. Wiesel has, for the first time in his literary career, attempted to imagine what a nonwitness would feel about the Holocaust. He has Ariel claim:

> I suffer from an Event I have not even experienced. A feeling of void: from a past that has made History tremble I have retained only words. War, for me, is my mother's closed face. War, for me, is my father's weariness (pp.192-193).

A panoply of second generation themes appear in the novel: vengeance against Nazi murderers, the covenantal struggle of faith and doubt, the vast gulf separating survivors and their children and both of them from nonwitnesses, the necessity of the second generation's immersing itself in reading about the Holocaust, and the transforming effect of survivors' tales. Wiesel's position regarding this latter point is well stated by Ariel, who contends that survivors' tales "fuel his imagination."

A brief comparison of Wiesel and Friedmann reveals certain similarities as well as some significant differences. In both novels, the son has a dead half-brother. Each author underscores the singularity of survivors and their children. A remote father and an absent mother are also shared features. The differences are those which exist between a survivor and the second generation. Wiesel's Ariel, for example, hears fuller versions of Holocaust tales, whereas Friedmann's Jason knows only fragments. The crucial distinction, however, resides in the relationship between memory and imagination. Friedmann has only limited access to his parents' memory. Wiesel, convinced that Holocaust tales transform their listeners, boldly has the son of the survivor assume his father's memory. Both authors portray parents who maintain the Jewish tradition, have children - itself an act which must be viewed as a celebration of life (*kiddush ha- hayyim*), and raise their children Jewishly.

Wiesel's focus on the second generation is noteworthy for a variety of reasons. It represents a dramatic change from the author's earlier view of survivors' children as presented in *The Oath* (1973). Wiesel told an interviewer that the young man in *The Oath:*

> ... is a special person - he is the son of a survivor. ... He arouses our pity because he doesn't even have the consolation of being a witness. He represents all my students and all the young people who are so perplexed today.[22]

More recently, however, and speaking specifically to children of survivors, Wiesel emphasized that in his view the witnesses and their children have "become partners."[23]

Wiesel now views the task of the second generation as keeping the survivors' tale alive - "and sacred."[24]

In the second place, it underscores the contention that Wiesel has written a theological manifesto for children of survivors whose task he views in messianic terms. Eschewing both despair and nihilism, Wiesel's newest "prayer" is that this generation will embrace the stance of messianic waiting. *The Fifth Son* is also a tacit statement acknowledging that the survivors are dying and that the message of the Holocaust and the struggle of survivors and their children against evil is in danger of being abandoned, ignored, or trivialized. "Memory," Wiesel has one of his characters observe, "is our real kingdom."[25] Finally, in portraying Ariel as a professor, Wiesel emphasizes the pedagogical role that children of survivors must play if society at large is to learn from the Jewish catastrophe..

The four American authors, despite their varying backgrounds, share a literary strategy which serves to heighten the Holocaust's importance for the American Jewish Community. There is significant interchange between survivor memory and second generation imagination, thereby linking the past to the present and extending both into the future. Each novelist is, moreover, concerned with the Jewish family as the context for learning about the *Shoah*. Interestingly, all refrain from portraying any evidence of post-Holocaust Jewish-Christian encounter, emphasizing instead contemporary Judaism's post-Auschwitz struggle between faith and doubt.

Canada and Australia

The Canadian and Australian literature represent a significant variation on the survivor parent-child relationship by describing either the physical destruction of the Jewish family or its dissolution through intermarriage. Stress is placed on the isolation of survivors and the inability of their message to transform their listeners. Events in the outside, non-Jewish world play a much larger role than in the American examples, thereby diffusing the pedagogic task of children of survivors.

Boyarsky's novel *Shreiber* reverses the theme of *The Fifth Son* by showing a child of a survivor imagining himself a survivor and vengeance seeker.[26] Boyarsky tells the tale of Menachem Shreiber, a physician who had fought with the partisans in Poland. Shreiber's own parents, wife, and sons were murdered in the Holocaust. Returning to post-war Poland, Shreiber seeks the killer of his brother, treats the survivors in Byalestok, administers to a group of child survivors, and witnesses the struggle among Zionist, Polish Nationalist, and Communist Jews. Two Christian women testify on his behalf at a political trial staged by the Communists.

Most important, however, are the encounters between Shreiber and the mystical Zalmen, his pre-war tutor. Shreiber, who prior to the Holocaust had abandoned his secular ways to become a *ba'al t'shuvah*, is now unable to believe; a literary embodiment of Richard Rubenstein's "Death of God" position. Zalmen, on the other hand, continues to seek traditional responses to the catastrophe, despite having lost his wife and child. Combining talmudic, mystical and philosophical sources, Zalmen typifies the stance of Eliezer Berkovits in *Faith After the Holocaust* (1973). The novel's denouement occurs when Zalmen involves himself in an act of murder in order to free Shreiber from prison, thereby acknowledging the necessity of power in the post-Holocaust world.

Boyarsky's use of a survivor's voice and point of view lends authenticity to the novel. Depicting Shreiber as a man whose past and future have been murdered underscores the Holocaust's devastation of Jewish existence. There are, however, certain hopeful indications. Shreiber unofficially "adopts" Rachmiel, one of the survivor children. Israel is portrayed as a beacon of Jewish hope, the place to which these children are sent. Shreiber is also finally able to achieve a limited transcendence over his feelings of survivor guilt. There is as well the significance of the title itself. Shreiber, as his name reveals, is a writer who faithfully records and transmits the Jewish experience. The novel also reveals the ambiguity of Jewish-Christian relations both during and after the war. Jewish survivors observe the Passover Seder, but utilize that time to examine God's apparent abandonment of His people, thus heightening the sense of post-Holocaust theological upheaval.

Serge Liberman, an Australian Jew who was born in Russia in 1942, treats the survivor parent-child theme from a somewhat different perspective. His second generation characters attempt to imagine the reactions of their survivor parents to the child's leaving the faith and to the Holocaust being ignored by the public. Two short stories "Drifting" (1981) and "Words" (1983), explore the growing isolation of survivors from society and from their children. "Drifting" tells the story of Isaac, a survivor who initially views the Holocaust as having killed God, and survival itself as meaningless, and Bernard, his son. The father is a quasi-intellectual who lectures occasionally to his peers. Upon recovering from a serious illness, he declares, "I have been spared twice and for that I can only be grateful" (p.70) . Bernard, at college, drifts away from Judaism - torn between reading Elie Wiesel or Bertrand Russell he chooses the latter, and lives with Rosemary, a non-Jewish woman.

The tale reveals two types of drifting: the father, abandoning his earlier rejection of Judaism, drifts toward or embraces the faith. The son, however, grows increasingly estranged from the tradition and ends by marrying Rosemary. Isaac twice queries Bernard, Is this what I survived for? The first query is occasioned by Isaac's discovery that Bernard is living with Rosemary and the second occurs when his son comes to temple to tell Isaac that he is a grandfather.

Liberman's Bernard realizes that an unbridgeable gulf separates his world of reason from the madness his father had lived through. He spends much time looking at the numbers on his father's arm, and attributes an unattainable authenticity to survivors, observing of his father:

> ...if any man had the right to believe or the privilege to doubt, it was he, ... who had suffered that madness, and not myself who, nurtured in the security of unbeleaguered theory, had learnt of life from mere dabbling in books (p. 75).

Bernard, rejected by his parents, and rejecting Judaism, feels a void that cannot and will not be filled.

"Words" is a short story which imagines survivor anger and dismay over the second generation's rejection of the Holocaust. Shraga Sztayer is criticized by his anger and dismay over the second generation's rejection of the Holocaust. Shraga Sztayer is criticized by his daughter Rita for always writing poetry about "...the war, the camps, the gas chambers, always the black side of life" (p.78). Shraga counters by reminding his daughter that his past is also her own and the Jewish people's history. Rita's husband compounds Shraga's pain by claiming that Shraga's generation is obsessed with Auschwitz. Finally Shraga's publisher tells the survivor that the public is fickle and while his poetry is beautiful:

> A poet who wants to leave his mark must adapt and respond to change, and progress in the same direction as society around him (p. 85).

Liberman captures the singularity of survivors in Shraga's exclamation:

> Exhausted themes! ... I lost a wife and child in Auschwitz. There is only one true theme for the Jew of today. Auschwitz and survival. In our time, the rest is commentary. (p. 85).

The survivor knows that the Holocaust represents absolute evil, and that it must be recognized and dealt with as such. In Shraga's words, "Can any man, of any generation, now ignore it?" (p.82). The Holocaust is for its survivors an epoch making event. For society at large, Liberman's tale suggests, it is merely one topic among many.

"Words" cleverly attempts to resolve the dilemma of generational distance by drawing a parallel between the situation of father and daughter. Shraga is depicted as depending on his daughter in a twofold manner; he wishes to borrow money from her and, more importantly, he wants his memories, in the manner of Wiesel's survivors, to "fuel her imagination." Arriving at his daughter's home to ask for a loan, Shraga discovers that she and her husband have just had distressing medical news. They are unable to have children because Rita is sterile. In a voice full of anguish, Rita asks her father if he knows what it means to be sterile. Embracing her, Shraga says "my child. Oh God, my God, how well I understand" (p.90). Despite the somewhat contrived nature of this conclusion, Liberman has succeeded in demonstrating both the necessity and difficulty of confronting the Holocaust.

A Note on Distortion

In an insightful essay, Cynthia Ozick warns that the Holocaust has already become dangerously literary.[27] I take this to mean that literature has a special moral obligation when confronting the Holocaust. The nature of this obligation requires a recognition that the Holocaust is not a literary theme but, as Rosenfeld observes, a "major turning point in history and the history of consciousness."[28] There are abundant examples of literary distortion of the Holocaust, both in America and abroad. The cultural and philosophical bases of these distortions have been discussed with precision and insight by Saul Friedländer in *Reflections on Nazism: An Essay on Kitsch and Death.* [29] Here I offer one American example which underscores the difference between serious writings by and about the second generation and those works in which the topic has become "dangerously literary." I refer to Frederick Busch's *Invisible Mending,* winner of the 1984 National Jewish Book award for fiction. Set, like the works of Greenfield, Friedmann, and Wiesel, in Sixties America, the novel ostensibly deals with a Nazi-hunting daughter of a survivor and her Jewishly informed but cynical friend. After going to extreme lengths to spy on a blind man they think a Nazi war criminal, Rhona and Zimmer discover that the man is actually a Jewish Holocaust survivor. The rest of the book deals with Zimmer's failing interfaith marriage.

Several points are worthy of note. *Invisible Mending* is a Holocaust spoof which trivializes the *Shoah* and views evil in a humorous way. It is conceptually flawed in portraying survivors who think constantly about death. The issue for survivors is not death, but the dead. Memory and not morbidity is what distinguishes Holocaust authenticity. Busch's work can be seen in fact as a reaction against the entire genre of second generation Holocaust literature, much as William Styron's *Sophie's Choice* was a reaction to the entire genre of Holocaust literature.[30] Busch has ignored, however, what the authors examined above all realize. The Holocaust is not a genre issue. It is the ultimate encounter with evil. That *Invisible Mending* was awarded a literary prize only serves to emphasize the widespread phenomenon of culture's tendency to diffuse and distort the nature of evil.

The Pedagogical Role of Second Generation Literature: A Meditation

Studying and teaching about the Holocaust through literature is an indispensable mode of approaching the unapproachable. Second generation Holocaust literature, for its part, combines pedagogic and salvific values. Such literature, at its best, reveals what Wiesel terms an "example for the world of how to deal with evil and the memory of evil."[31] But this literature, as we have seen, teaches by indirection. It is not so much about the Holocaust as it is about the moral and religious meanings of survival. Its stories are not the original act. Nevertheless, this literature is a metahistory which expresses particular pain while hoping to sensitize its readers to the experience of others. There is as well the point that second generation literature becomes, as it were, the memory of those born after World War II.

Collectively, the literature we examined, which is only a very partial sampling, portrays the diversity of Jewish fate under the Nazis; labor camps, hiding, fighting with partisans, and death camps. One sees as well great variety among the second generation itself concerning its relationship to the tradition. Some are raised as Orthodox Jews, some as secularists, and some intermarry. All, however, share an identity as children of Holocaust survivors. There is as well a portrayal of the struggle between faith and doubt among the post-Auschwitz generation. Yet, the very fact that survivors married and had children may in itself be viewed as an act having messianic overtones. The father in Wiesel's novel reports that failing to have children would be tantamount to "handing over another victory to the enemy."

Second generation Holocaust literature appears also to challenge views which contend either that too much attention is paid to the Holocaust or that the *Shoah* serves in effect to deflect American Jewry from its vital task of seeking an authentic identity.[32] Children of survivors are bearers of their parents' tales, communicated in both verbal and nonverbal modes. These children marry other Jews, or non-Jews, and thereby continue the legacy and the memory. Their message is passed to ever-widening circles of nonwitnesses.

Memory thus emerges as being concerned only partly with the past. It has as much to do with the present and how one lives one's life in the future.[33] Memory is a reminder of how to remain human under conditions of incomparable oppression, and it underscores the vulnerability of the human condition. Second generation Holocaust fiction preserves memory of the

Holocaust past while providing a window on the contemporary struggle against the deep and abiding nature of evil. Collectively, this literature becomes part of the ripple effect of the destruction of the Jews. Its message about the humanizing role of memory, however, integrates family survival and a world historical event, and may yet prove of universal value for a a complex and perilous world.

---

[1] Elie Wiesel. Interview on ABC in reaction to Bitburg, 5 May 1985.

[2] Yehuda Bauer employs this hasidic tale in order to emphasize the uniqueness of the survivors' experience. See Bauer's insightful study *The Holocaust in Historical Perspective* (Seattle: University of Washington Press, 1978), pp. 44-45. The example applies with equal force, however, to the entire enterprise of second generation literature.

[3] Yosef Hayim Yerushalmi. *Zakhor: Jewish History and Jewish Memory* (Seattle: University of Washington Press, 1982), p. 98.

[4] The list expands considerably when one includes films, mostly documentaries, made by the second generation.

[5] Lawrence Langer. *Versions of Survival: The Holocaust and the Human Spirit* (Albanay: SUNY Press, 1982), p. 191-192.

[6] Menachem Rosensaft. "Reflections of a Child of Holocaust Survivors," *Midstream* 27:9 (November 1981), page 31.

[7] Alvin Rosenfeld. *A Double Dying: Reflections on Holocaust Literature* (Bloomington: Indiana University Press, 1980), p. 19.

[8] Bauer, *Op. cit.,* p. 45.

[9] Cynthia Ozick. "Notes Toward Finding The Right Question," *Forum On the Jewish People, Zionism, and Israel* 35 (Spring/Summer, 1979), p. 47.

[10] *Ibid.*

[11] *Ibid.*

[12]For a detailed analysis of "The Law" and Nissenson's role as a writer of Holocaust fiction see Alan L. Berger *Crisis and Covenant: The Holocaust in American Jewish Fiction* (Albany: SUNY Press, 1985), pp. 59-65, and 137-144.

[13]Robert Greenfield. *Temple* (New York: Summit Books, 1982).

[14]Thomas Friedmann. *Damaged Goods* (New York: The Permanent Press, 1984). Text citations are from this edition.

[15]Elie Wiesel. *The Fifth Son* Translated by Marion Wiesel (New York: Summit Books, 1985). Citations are from this edition.

[16]Abraham Boyarsky. *Schreiber* (Ontario, Canada: General Publishing Co. Limited, 1981).

[17]Serge Liberman. *On Firmer Shores* (Fitzroy, Australia: Globe Press Pty Ltd, 1981). Page citations are in the text.

[18]Serge Liberman. *A Universe of Clowns* (Brisbane, Australia; Phoenix Publications, 1984). Page citations are in the text.

[19]The literature here is extensive. Useful studies include Jack Nusan Porter "Is There a Survivor's Syndrome? Psychological and Socio-Political Implications," *Journal of Psychology and Judaism* 6, 1 (Fall/Winter, 1981), pp. 33-52; Robert Prince *The Legacy of the Holocaust: Psychohistorical Themes in the Second Generation* (Ann Arbor, Michigan: UMI Research Press, 1985); and Lucy Y. Steinitz and David M. Szony (Editors) *Living After the Holocaust: Reflections by Children of Survivors in America* (New York: Bloch Publishing Company, 1979).

[20]For an application of Lifton's theory to Jewish Holocaust survivors see Alan L. Berger "Holocaust Survivors and Children in *Anya* and *Mr. Sammler's Planet*", *Modern Language Studies* XVI, 1 (Winter, 1986), pp. 81-87.

[21]I have analyzed *The Fifth Son* and its relationship to covenant Judaism in *Crisis and Covenant*, pp. 68-79.

[22]Lily Edelman, "A Conversation with Elie Wiesel," *Responses to Elie Wiesel* edited by H. J. Cargas (New York: Persea Books, 1978), pp. 17-18.

[23]Irving Abrahamson (editor). *Against Silence: The Voice and Vision of Elie Wiesel* (New York: Holocaust Library, 1985) volume III, p. 314.

24 *Ibid.,* p. 321.

25Elie Wiesel. *A Jew Today,* translated by Marion Wiesel (New York: Vintage, 1979), p. 85.

26The theme of vengeance is prominent in Boyarsky's work. His 1978 short story "The Birthday Party" portrays a child of survivors' sixth birthday party held in a displaced persons camp. Surrounded by survivors, all of whom had lost children, the boy's father tells his son, "You are now the guardian of our memories! You are the avenger of the dead!" The father then tells his son that when the boy grows up he should return to this "wretched land" as a pilot and bomb the cities... "indiscriminately, day after day, until they are as flat and as deserted as our *shtetl."* The story appears in Boyarsky's collection *A Pyramid of Time* (Ontario, Canada: The Porcupine's Quill, 1978). Citations are from page 14.

27Cynthia Ozick. "The Uses of Legend: Elie Wiesel as "Tsaddik," *Congress Bi-Weekly* June 9, 1969, p. 19.

28Rosenfeld. *A Double Dying,* p. 10.

29Saul Friedländer. *Reflections on Nazism* (New York: Harper and Row, 1984).

30I am grateful to Professor Thomas Friedmann for initial discussions on this matter.

31Abrahamson, *Against Silence,* vol. 1, p. 164.

32Proponents of the first view include Rabbi Harold Schulweis and Professor Michael Wyschogrod. Professor Jacob Neusner is the best known advocate of the second position. For a critique of these views see my essay "Holocaust and History: A Theological Reflection," *Journal of Ecumenical Studies* 25:2 (Spring, 1988).

33For an insightful discussion of how memory of the Holocaust influences the present, and future, of nations see Michael Berenbaum "The Nativization of the Holocaust," *Judaism* 35, 4 (Fall, 1986), pp. 447-457.

Chapter Eleven

"The Almost Meeting"[1]:
The Quest for the Holocaust in
Canadian Jewish Fiction

Rachel Feldhay Brenner

The study of Holocaust preoccupation in the work of North American Jewish writers is of special educational value. The assessment of the Holocaust as a formative component of post-war Jewish consciousness defies the process of abstraction of the geographically as well as historically distant event. Furthermore, the exploration of the traumatic effects of the European tragedy elucidates, to some extent, the conflicted sense of ethnic identity of the North American Jew. Thus, for the North American student of the Holocaust, investigation of post-Holocaust literature is an important reminder of the tragic loss of heritage. At the same time, the study of Holocaust consciousness illuminates the relevance of this loss in terms of Jewish interaction with the world in the post-war reality.

Representation of the unspeakable horror of the Holocaust posits a complex problem for the writer-outsider as well as the writer-survivor. In effect, the outsider's search for literary strategies to convey consciousness of the Holocaust is closely related to the predicament of the survivor who is reluctant to tell the story. For the outsider, the survivor's testimony and tale have been essential sources of knowledge. The writer's deep sense of identification with the victims of Nazi bestiality is then transmitted in his or her own work. Yet, it is the writer-survivor who constantly raises questions as to the validity and merit of the literary representation of the experience. Awareness of the reader's presence and response seems to underscore the survivor's doubts and misgivings. It is, therefore, pertinent to study the outsider's work in view of the survivor's tormented response to literary representation of the Holocaust.

The writer who survived the catastrophe is torn between a necessity to tell the tale and the realization of his or her inadequacy of means to communicate the experience. Aharon Appelfeld observes that "the unspeakable is a secret. You can only surround it. You cannot speak about it.[2]" Elie Wiesel disclaims the very existence of the proper language to convey the truth: "The moment it is said, it isn't: the moment it is offered, it is withdrawn.[3]" The survivor, despite the eventual decision to write, considers the undertaking doomed to failure: an account of the experience seeks, by definition, to present an inexplicable act of genocide in a form comprehensible to the reader. The necessity to shape the event as an artistic construct results in loss of authenticity. The desire to remain silent is rooted in the conviction that representation of the Holocaust has become, in fact, a misrepresentation of the dead, and that silence is the only safeguard of truth.

Some literary critics have subscribed to the notion of the inadequacy of art to relate the horror. T. W. Adorno's claim "After Auschwitz, no poetry"[4] was taken up by critics such as Reinhard Baugmart who finds that Holocaust literature "by removing some of the horror, commits a grave injustice against the victims," and Michael Wyschogrod who submits that "any attempt to transform the holocaust into art demeans the holocaust, and must result in poor art."[5] George Steiner concurs with Adorno in his dictum that "the world of Auschwitz lies outside speech as it lies outside reason."[6]

Other critics, however, assert the legitimacy of Holocaust literature; assuming the perspective of the reader-outsider, they express the absolute need for literary testimony. Alvin H. Rosenfeld sees the Holocaust "as a testament of our times.[7]" Lawrence Langer maintains that "the challenge to the literary imagination is to find a way of making this fundamental truth [the existence of Dachau and Auschwitz] accessible to the emotions of the reader.[8]" Similar considerations of the relationship that the Holocaust writer creates with the reader emerges in Sidra Ezrahi's study. Ezrahi emphasizes the function of Holocaust literature to turn the reader into "a 'collaborative' witness to the events"[9], that is, a vicarious participant in the drama of the Holocaust.

The issue of the reader's implied presence and involvement foregrounds the survivor's emotional conflict. In his essay "Why I Write," Wiesel talks about the necessity to write in order "not to go mad"[10] and about the constant struggle against silence to remain sane. The act of telling becomes part of a healing process which exacts its own price; to preserve sanity the survivor must detach himself from his experience and share it with the world. On the one hand, the presence of the outside world is indispensable for the story to be told; on the other hand, the consciousness of writing for others signals the beginning of separation as it drives the wedge of objectivity between the survivor and his or her experience. The tale seeks the reader's attention, yet the very act of addressing the reader detracts from the uniqueness of the survivor's past.

Hence, the survivor faces a paradoxical situation: if the nature of the experience, "defies words, language, imagination, knowledge"[11], then the very attempt to find appropriate words, images, and literary structure to impart the truth neutralizes and distorts the original experience. In the form of a story, the experience becomes history, anchored in time and past circumstances. The literary form sets the event in a comprehensible context, drawing the reader closer to the event but, at the same time, subverting the writer's desire to retain an experience whose horror, as remembered, escapes the notions of time and space. Ironically, the attempt to concretize the Holocaust for others universalizes it in terms of the writer and, therefore, abstracts the survivor's painful intimacy with the experience.

From a literary perspective, the survivor's emotional predicament vis-á-vis an experience captured in the text illustrates the notion of the subjectivity of discourse. While the writer may think that through the act of writing he or she determines the meaning of the text, in fact, the transmission of the text to the reader neutralizes the writer's control over that text. It is the reader of the text who gains considerable authority over its meaning. There is an irrevocable split between the writing and interpretation of text. The interpretation actually amounts to recreation of the work, as Anthony Easthope sees it: "... however much a poem claims to be the property of a speaker represented in it, the poem finally belongs to the reader producing it in a reading.[12]" The reader, as an active collaborator and participant, affirms the subjectivity of the discourse by shaping it in his or her own image. The consciousness of forsaking, so to speak, one's truth at the mercy of the reader's subjective interpretation accounts for the survivor's predilection for silence.

The North American Jewish writer draws upon the survivor's story. In a sense, then, treatment of the Holocaust in post-war literature does, indeed, manifest the reader's consciousness of the event shaped by the subjective act of reading and, subsequently, represented in the subjective act of writing. Consciousness of the Holocaust in American (United States) literature became manifest as late as the early nineteen seventies with the publication of Saul Bellow's *Mr. Sammler's Planet* (1970).[13]   Canadian literature, however, presents a much earlier preoccupation with the Holocaust. A. M. Klein, for instance, published *The Hitleriad*, a long satirical poem about the Nazi leadership, in 1944. Fiction produced by prominent Canadian writers manifests the need to come to terms with the forbidding consciousness of the tragedy. This paper examines treatment of the Holocaust in three significant novels: Henry Kreisel's *The Rich Man* (1948), A. M. Klein's *The Second Scroll* (1951), and Mordecai Richler's *St. Urbain's Horseman* (1970), which present an interesting pattern in the fabric of North American response to the European tragedy.

While some United States writing — for instance Bellow's *Mr. Sammler's Planet*, Roth's *Eli the Fanatic*, and in a sense, *The Ghost Writer* — transplants the survivor to the American continent, the three Canadian novels confront the reality of the Holocaust on the opposite shore of the Atlantic. The recurring motif of the protagonist's search for a lost relative in Europe reveals the emotional need to "meet" history. The recurring failure of such undertaking signals the inability of the writer-outsider to venture into the actual sphere of the Holocaust experience. It seems that the horror that emanates from the survivor's text prohibits fictional penetration into the universe of the Holocaust. Dismayed by the intensity of the experience, these novelists can view the tragedy only through an intermediating metaphor of the quest for the irrevocably lost heritage.

In a 1980 interview, Henry Kreisel spoke openly about his inability to recreate the reality of the concentration camp experience in fiction. Kreisel lived in Vienna until 1938 and knew the forboding atmosphere of the approaching disaster much more acutely than any other Canadian writer. Yet, he found it impossible to write about the direct experience of the Holocaust. Kreisel admitted that he was planning a novel about the Holocaust experience in the early 1950s, but had to give it up because "I felt I was inventing things as I went on... *the theme still haunts me*, it didn't go away. *I was just not close enough*, and other people who had been there were coming out with memoirs and personal accounts... how could I compete"[14] (Italics added.)

The survivor's tale, despite its author's apprehension of improper understanding, teaches an important lesson: its authenticity defies powers of imagination and, consequently, outlines the limitations of the writer-outsider. The survivor may feel that words and images distort and weaken his truth;

nonetheless, the impact of the tale is powerful enough to dissuade the outsider from adopting the voice of the Holocaust victim.

The complex issue of interrelationships between the Holocaust event and the writer's perspective thus reemerges. Like the survivor, the outsider faces the alternative of silence, yet, as Kreisel asserts, "the theme still haunts" him and he must speak. Unlike the survivor, however, who perceives the literary medium as a distancing factor, the outsider sees the narrative as a means to explore the distance that separates him from the fate of his European brethren.

Kreisel's first novel, *The Rich Man,* is also the first novel to raise the issue of the European tragedy in Canadian consciousness. Published in 1948, the novel presents the outsider's preoccupation with the Holocaust, while anticipating the patterns of literary response to the event in Canadian literature.

The protagonist, a Toronto Jew, visits his native city, Vienna, in 1935. In pre-Anschluss Vienna, Jacob Grossman is exposed to the threat of imminent war and impending Nazi hostilities against Jews. Unable to help his suffering family, Jacob returns to Toronto consumed by guilt and shame.

The manipulation of space through the journey metaphor reduces the geographical distance and reestablishes the protagonist's physical contact with his European family. Paradoxically, the physical closeness of the Canadian brings forth is actual remoteness from the circumstances that have been forced upon his relatives. Seemingly, Jacob becomes involved in his family's increasingly difficult situation. In fact, the reader is never allowed to forget that the Canadian Jew has an option to withdraw into the safety of his territory at any time. The legal status of the North American Jew invalidates the attempt to share Austrian Jews' sense of entrapment and despair.

In one episode depicting the crossing of the German border, Kreisel outlines the fundamental disparity between the Jewish victims and their Canadian visitor. The abstract knowledge of the Nazi threat becomes a frightening reality when the Toronto Jew is transferred to Germany. Jacob "saw the strange and ominous insignia on [the storm-guard officer's] cap — two crossed-bones and a leering death's head. He had once read newspaper accounts of this, but now saw it with his own eyes" (p. 43).[15] For a moment, Jacob feels trapped, weak and helpless at the mercy of threatening authorities. The terror is tangibly close; the danger is about to engulf the appalled traveller. However, the Canadian passport "he held out... with a slightly trembling hand without waiting to be asked for" (p.

42) subverts the seriousness of the moment. "Kanader," Jacob identifies himself and the word dispels the threat; the incident becomes a bad memory, a story he tells his family. Yet, for the family, trapped in Nazi Europe, the menace has become a reality. Albert, Jacob's brother-in-law, points out the hardship of "all the hundreds and thousands who must travel unprotected, hunted from place to place, like wild animals" (p. 64). Albert's response outlines the tremendous distance between the two Jews despite their physical proximity. Jacob's Canadian passport assumes the dimensions of an impenetrable shield that protects its owner wherever he goes. The absence of the document signifies isolation, suffering, and degradation. In the reality of 1935, the passport differentiates between the free and the oppressed, those who will live and those who will not.

The Rich Man depicts a world governed by brutal power and blind fortune; it is a world where the gift of life and the sentence of death are meted out at random, personal fate is determined by the tyranny of political and historical circumstances beyond the individual's control. Still, against the backdrop of hopelessness and premonition of doom the novel explores an inner world of spiritual strength and humanism. Kreisel considers himself an outsider whose vision cannot reach the Holocaust itself; he can, however, envisage the courageous stature and conduct of the entrapped people at the time when they could see very clearly the terrible writing on the wall. In this sense, the Canadian protagonist becomes the witness of Jewish courage and fortitude before the increasingly foreboding reality. Returning to Toronto, Jacob carries a legacy of Jewish pride and dignity maintained in the face of inescapable disaster.

In the atmosphere of growing despair and hopelessness, Shaendl, Jacob's sister, fends off the dehumanizing effects of oppression and poverty; under duress, she demonstrates love and unshaken devotion towards her family. A long tradition of loyalty and togetherness unifies the family, and the sense of mutual responsibility intensifies in times of need. Thus, the whole family rallies behind Shaendl — everybody, except Jacob. Jacob's confession that he is not the rich man he has pretended to be sets him apart from his family. He shatters the hope to relieve Shaendl's financial burden but, even more significantly, his conduct demonstrates qualities of obtuseness and selfishness that dissociate him from the moral value system that keeps the family together. Jacob remains the outsider because he cannot meet his family's standards and expectations. His older sister's ironic statement, "You go back to your great country... we will look after Shaendl" (p. 193), enhances the moral disparity between Jacob and his family. The new country, she seems to imply, big and free as it is, has impressed upon Jacob an identity that his European family is neither willing nor able to accept. The deceitful role of a rich man that Jacob has chosen to play for his poverty-stricken family manifests his self-indulgence combined with crass insensitivity. His lack of moral fibre estranges him from his family.

This harsh perception of the North American Jew is especially poignant in the political reality of the 1930s. Jacob's failure to help resolve the family crisis adumbrates the ineffectuality of the North American Jewish community regarding the situation in Europe. Jacob's missed opportunity to alleviate his kin's suffering spells out the victim's complete isolation in face of the rising horror. His shameful departure from Vienna foreshadows the pervasive consciousness of moral failure and emotional impotence of North American Jewry vis-á-vis the annihilated European community.

Jacob's departure from Vienna marks the end of the pre-war interaction between the North American Jew and the European community; the subsequent annihilation of Jacob's closest relatives precludes any possibility of mending the disrupted family bonds. With their disappearance in concentration camps, Jacob will be left to cope with the ensuing sense of "unfinished business" and irrevocable loss.

By the time of the novel's publication in 1948, Kreisel's reader has been informed of the tragedy of European Jewry. Conscious of the tragic sequel to Kreisel's story, he or she reads how Jacob returns to Canada, horrified and bewildered by the omens of an impending disaster, enraged by his own helplessness and impotence. In his or her subjective consideration of the novel, the reader is bound to recognize the protagonist's emotional predicament as his or her own. In the post-Holocaust reality, Jacob's vivid regret at having shirked his brotherly duty brings forth the unrelieved guilt of all those who passively watched the destruction from the safety of the North American continent. Kreisel's novel, then, initiates a self-searching process; subjective reading of *The Rich Man* becomes self-reading in that it reveals the extent to which the loss of the European community has affected the sense of well-being of the North American Jew. In that respect, Jacob's failure engenders the impulse to compensate for the loss. His return to North America creates the need for yet another journey across the Atlantic in search of severed links and inner peace.

A. M. Klein, whose work greatly influences Kreisel's writing[16], responded warmly to *The Rich Man*.[17] Practically a native Canadian, Klein recognized the need to relieve the burden of guilt and restore an image of potency for North American Jewry. Like Kreisel's fictional character, Klein sensed his own inability to act in defense of his people. In a novel he never completed, Klein openly acknowledges his predicament. Of particular interest is his account of a dream in which he watches his father "beard, humility and all" tortured by the Nazis who "hung [him] by his feet" and "dipped his head... into a barrel of human dung." Klein recalls that upon awakening "I was frightened at the passive role I seemed to have played in the dream. To horror, there was added a sense of guilt.[18]

Like Kreisel, Klein was unable to complete his novel about direct experience of the Holocaust. Nonetheless, this unpublished account of his nightmare characterizes the Holocaust's tremendous impact on the North American psyches. The Holocaust has bereft the North American Jew of his or her European family and heritage; it has also elicited feelings of powerlessness and fear. Thus, even the safely distant North American Jew has become a Holocaust casualty in that the tragedy not only destroyed national roots and parentage, but also inflicted severe emotional injury.

Klein's consciousness of the searing effects of the European tragedy emerges in his poem "Meditation Upon Survival" (1947).[19] The poem's powerful imagery which invokes physical suffering and death of the Holocaust victim refers, in fact, to the tormented North American Jew who "continues to live, though mortally" wishing "for the centigrade furnace and the cyanide flood." The tragic loss of heritage has reduced the "spared one" to a lifeless object, "a curio; the atavism of some old coin's fact... the last point of diminished race." In a sense, Klein approaches the nightmare of the Holocaust through a dramatic presentation of its devastating consequences with regard to the future of Jewish survival.

The intensity of this lament reflects the depth of Klein's personal anguish and despair. At the same time, his profound insight and sensitivity made him recognize the necessity of healing the North American Jew's scathed self-image. It seems that Klein's integrity as a Jew and his boundless dedication to Jewish survival motivated him to convey a powerful vision of national rebirth before his withdrawal into silence.[20] *The Second Scroll* (1951), Klein's last work and only novel, reconfirms the providential aspect of Jewish History. Indeed, the analogous structure of the novel whose five chapters are named after the Five Books of Moses counteracts the sense of arbitrariness and alienation engendered by consciousness of recent history. The representation of the birth of the Jewish State as a reenactment of the biblical story of Exodus places the Holocaust event within the spectrum of Jewish tradition. Such perception of the Holocaust as a path of suffering and oppression leading to redemption aims at an explication of the Holocaust as "Chevlei Mashiah" — the world-wide agony which tradition claims will precede the coming of Messiah.

Klein's contemporary version of the original scroll suggests meaningful historical patterns which unify rather than divide the dispersed segments of the Jewish people. His exegesis of the history of Jewish suffering envisages the Holocaust as a component in the divine scheme of Jewish return to the land of Israel.

In *The Second Scroll*, Klein seems to be taking on the Miltonic mission to "justify the ways of God to men.[21]" In a sense, the novel resumes the journey initiated in *The Rich Man* and redirects it toward a hopeful denouement: the ties with European Jewry, so brutally severed by the tragedy of the Holocaust, are triumphantly restored with the birth of the Jewish State. The mourner's Magnificat that the Canadian-born nephew recites at the grave of his uncle, a Holocaust survivor, reconfirms the continuity of Jewish faith and family tradition. On the symbolic level, Klein's nameless narrator is the prototype of the North American Jew. His odyssey in the footsteps of Melech Davidson, the emblem of the Messiah, holds a promise of redemption for all Jewish people.

Based on Klein's own journey to Europe, North Africa, and Israel in 1949, *The Second Scroll* is partly autobiographical. As such, it reflects Klein's strong wish for renewal of contact with the European heritage. The first person narration of the persistent quest for a surviving European relative implies the author's need to claim his share of the spiritual legacy of his people. As the intensity of the search for uncle Melech seems to indicate, the future participation of the North American Jew in the continuum of Jewish history is predicated upon successful reestablishment of the severed links with the past. An encounter between the survivor and the outsider is necessary to restore this bond.

"Quest is all," says one of the characters in Kreisel's short story significantly entitled "The Almost Meeting."[22] The nephew's hopeful quest for his surviving uncle in *The Second Scroll* inverts the process that mercilessly and irrevocably distanced Jacob from his closest relatives in *The Rich Man*. The circumstances of such a miraculous "almost meeting" defy the mundane. It is in the context of the eschatological vision or return to Zion that the distant outsider may reestablish contact with his lost heritage. In Klein's perspective, the monumental events of the establishment of the Jewish State, the rebirth of the Hebrew language, and the Ingathering of Exiles transcend the split between those who experienced the Holocaust and those who did not. Interestingly, Klein addresses the same issues that underlie Kreisel's view fo the North American position vis-á-vis the Holocaust. His repeated attempts to downplay the significance of geographical and historical distance imply awareness of the psychologically crippling sense of guilt experienced by the North American Jew.

In *The Rich Man,* Canadian citizenship spelled absolute security for the Canadian Jew. In the reality of The Second Scroll, a Canadian passport no longer provides protection. Whereas Kreisel's protagonist safely crossed borders controlled by the Nazis, Klein's narrator becomes the victim of terrorism in Rome, his passport is treated with contempt and his nationality is ridiculed.[23]

It appears that in the post-war world a Jew is no longer sheltered by his Canadian status. As portrayed in Klein's novel, however, he is not a powerless individual either. The decisiveness and self-confidence manifest in the nephew's attitude towards Uncle Melech offset the passivity and helplessness displayed by Kreisel's protagonist regarding his Viennese family. Unlike Jacob, Melech's nephew acts promptly from a sense of responsibility and gratitude. Upon receiving Melech's letter, the narrator realizes that his uncle "might be in need and I might be of help" (p. 40)[24] and immediately sets out on a journey to rescue his long suffering relative. Furthermore, the survivor's consistent reaffirmation of national unity seems to deflate the notion of irrevocable separation that marks the conclusion of *The Rich Man.* The geographical distance that guarantees Jacob's survival seems of no consequence to Uncle Melech who identifies the Holocaust as a tragedy of all Jewish people. In a letter to his Canadian nephew, Uncle Melech points out their common fate claiming that "we were all in that burning world, even you who were separated from it by the Atlantic — that futile bucket." (p. 30)

Thus, the journey across the ocean indicates growing closeness between the North American Jew and the Holocaust victim. At the same time, however, the diminishing distance between outsider and survivor marks an increasing remoteness from the event itself. As a metaphor, the journey charts the process of national regeneration in the wake of disaster. The same metaphor, however, also outlines a route that circumvents the tragedy: the journey takes place in the post-Holocaust reality and, although it concludes with a promise of renewed bonding of the disjoined communities, a direct encounter between the North American Jew and the Holocaust victim never occurs. The complete truth of Jewish suffering in the Holocaust eludes the outsider forever. Paradoxically, reconstruction is possible only when the consciousness of the destruction is suppressed: Klein's fiction does not deal with the guilt that surfaces in the nightmare of his father's torture; neither does it evoke the sense of obliterated national vitality depicted in the poem "Meditation Upon Survival." In a sense, the metaphor of the journey displaces the Holocaust's unutterable horror and fear with a sweeping vision of spiritual and physical rebirth.

Hillis Miller's definition of the metaphor and its psychological function seems applicable to Klein's metaphoric treatment of the Holocaust. Miller submits that "there is no language except figurative, that is, improper, language for the movements of the soul." Since human beings became ashamed of their sexuality, "the literal, naked language has been impossible, shameful." Metaphors "present the unpresentable"; they replace diction that has become taboo.[25]

Miller's observation thus proposes that all language, in fact, is metaphor, a screen which conceals the speaker's suppressed fears and inhibitions. Since language cannot mirror reality, it is not descriptive but reflexive: it reflects subjective and mutable states of mind. The act of renaming "forbidden" objects manifests a consciousness unable to confront inhibiting phenomena. All text is metaphoric because it disguises and, at the same time, reveals the idiosyncrasies of the individual who has shaped it. Consequently, the manipulation of the metaphor signals the writer's fear to uncover emotional nakedness. In fact, the epigraph in *The Second Scroll* communicates Klein's awareness of the metaphoric concealment that language produces: he quotes Milton's criticism of scholars who argue that the original text of the Talmud lacks modesty and offer to "clothe" it through changes of words.[26]

It seems that the all-important objective of national and universal rebirth determined Klein's choice of metaphor in his novel.[27] To offset incapacitating fixation on the past, Klein discusses consciousness of the tragedy in the context of a redemptive journey. This approach implies persistent belief in the eventual victory of universal morality and justice over human proclivity to evil. Once before, a literary strategy marked Klein's humanist stance. In *The Hitleriad* Klein indicts Hitler and his henchmen. While the content of the poem raises the issue of revenge and justice, its form, the eighteenth century heroic epic modelled on Milton's *Paradise Lost*,[28] invokes the long history of civilization and culture as a buttress against man's lapse to barbarity.

Klein's strong faith in humanism emerges in his journalistic writing as well. In his editorial "The Mystery of the Mislaid Conscience" (1942), he turns to the free nations with a strong moral exhortation to act for European Jews in the name of democracy and liberty.[29] In 1946, with the war over he pleads with the "European conscience, the Christian conscience" to "make amends": to the Jewish people and exercise the sense of justice and morality by declaring Palestine the Jewish Homeland.[30]

The ideal of universal humanism thus informs Klein's vision of the post-Holocaust Jewish future. *The Second Scroll* presents a symbol of rebirth not only of the Jewish people, but also of the enlightened world. The metaphor of the intercontinental journey underscores Jewish universalism. Naim Kattan, in his analysis of the novel, demonstrates how "Klein parcourant le monde, circulant entre l'Aise, l'Afrique, l'Europe, et l'Amérique, retrouve le Juif dans son integralité, son humanisme universel."[31] Similarly, Miriam Waddington, in her important study of Klein, asserts the significance of the journey in *The Second Scroll* as a rediscovery of the "humanist resolution which combines devotion to God with an equal devotion to man."[32]

Affirmation of humanism underscores the novel's metaphoric treatment of the Holocaust. The displacement of horror is effected through particular "placement" or contextuality of the survivor's experience which precludes hopelessness and despair. The text does not evade the horror altogether. In a letter to his nephew, the survivor tells in great detail about his experience: he describes the atrocities committed in the Jewish community of Kamenets, dwells on the horrible death of the helpless victims, denounces the brutality and sadism of the Nazi persecutors. Yet, despite the horrifying content of the story, its context shapes a metaphoric screen which deflects the full implications of that which has happened. The Holocaust experience is essential but not central in Melech's letter; it functions as a rationale for Uncle's as-yet-unfinished journey to safety and freedom, and marks one of the stages of his turbulent progression toward the discovery of the *raison d'être* for Jewish survival in today's world. The Holocaust experience takes the form of an episode inserted between the account of Melech's disenchantment with communist ideology and his vision of the Israel "Navy of Redemption" returning the survivors to their Homeland.

Significantly, the letter is written in a DP camp where the writer feels "like one that dreamed" (p. 31) and constantly praises the Lord for his miraculous rescue. The conjunction of the Holocaust with the hope of new beginnings constructs a powerful metaphor which attenuates and displaces the horror.

The effect of displacement is further enhanced in that the survivor's letter is transmitted by a fictional mediator, Melech's Canadian nephew, cast also as the first person narrator. The narrator thus transmits the letter to the reader of the novel in the context of his own story; consequently, the letter reaches the reader in conjunction with the nephew's subjective perception of Melech's experience. Clearly, the contextuality of Melech's letter which highlights faith and hope rather than grief and mourning affects his nephew's point of view. The hopeful mode of the narrator's journey re-enacts his mentor's progressive vision of redemption. His enthusiastic endorsement of Melech's perspective affects in turn the reader's own reaction of the story. Hence, in a subtle way, the reaction of the narrator invites the reader to espouse faith in the ultimate victory of morality and justice even in the aftermath of the Holocaust.

Twenty years later, Mordecai Richler's satiric portrayal of his protagonist's aborted journey in *St. Urbain's Horseman* (1971) refutes the hopeful vision of the post-Holocaust world propagated in *The Second Scroll*. Richler's satiric writing has earned him a great deal of deprecatory criticism. Many of his Jewish readers perceive him as a writer who has mispresented the Jewish way of life to society at large,[33] while some literary critics consider him a rather superficial humorist who has failed to present a clearly defined moral stance.[34]

It would appear that Richler has often been misread; certainly, his consistent preoccupation with the Holocaust and its refractions in the post-war world has rarely been noticed. Yet, in his journalistic as well as fictional work Richler invokes the spectre of the Holocaust both as a Jew and a liberal humanist. In an article discussing the position of the Jewish individual in post-war Canada, for instance, Richler is unequivocal about lingering memories and association of racial persecution in his country. He admits: "I've never been sent to a concentration camp. But no Gentile is expected to give thanks to the government that does not intern him. So why should it be expected of me?"[35] In his essay "The Holocaust and After," Richler states clearly that "the holocaust... is at the very core of most serious Jewish writing since the war." Stressing the moral duty of the outsider to gain insight into the experience of the survivor, Richler claims that "Wiesel's personal account of survival at

Buchenwald, *Night,...* should be obligatory reading..." At the same time, he criticizes harshly writers, film-producers and public personalities who trivialize the Holocaust and abuse the memory of the six-million murdered Jews to promote their self-interests.[36]

The theme of the Holocaust informs Richler's fictional writing; the loss of European heritage is represented in his work as a formative aspect of North American Jewish consciousness.[37] The desire to "meet" history seems most pronounced in *St. Urbain's Horseman* where Jake Hersh, the protagonist, feels compelled to undertake the quest. Jake was growing up in Montreal at the time of the Holocaust. Despite the remoteness of the event, he has become increasingly obsessed with the tragedy of his people. Yet, he refuses to adopt the rebirth of the Jewish State as a sign of restitution of universal justice and order. On the contrary, Jake's growing sense of alienation and self-dissatisfaction stems from consciousness of an unavenged act of ultimate injustice. In this respect, Jake's recognition of his own passivity regarding his people's suffering evokes Jacob Grossman's helplessness vis-á-vis his European family. The unheeded cry of the Holocaust victim in *The Rich Man* reverberates in *St. Urbain's Horseman,* haunting the post-Holocaust generation.

In terms of structure and theme, Richler's work appears to re-enact the patterns of *The Second Scroll:* the search for a family member who relates directly to Jewish suffering informs the plot in both novels. Both protagonists' persistent quests communicate the desire to restore faith in universal justice, as well as the need to redefine the position of the North American outsider. Presented through Richler's ironic lenses, however, the search does not signal a regenerative process but, rather, an unhealthy obsession. Jake's eagerness to meet Cousin Joey, the heroic avenger of the Holocaust, does not bring forth a sense of strong family ties; on the contrary, it sets him apart from closest relatives and friends. In fact, Jake's excessive loyalty to the Horseman brings about a scandalous court case which costs him his reputation and damages his career. Furthermore, the elusiveness of the avenger exposes the absurdity of faith in justice in the post-Holocaust world. Richler's ironic treatment of the quest undermines the vision of the world's forthcoming moral rehabilitation. In terms of the metaphoric construct in both novels, Richler's subversion of the journey motif removes the metaphoric veil that displaces the reality of the Holocaust in Klein's fiction.

In contrast with Klein's progression towards harmonious unity, Richler's irony reveals the deepening fragmentation and discord within the Jewish people. For Jake's parental generation, "the holocaust was when they prospered on the black market." (p. 81.)[38] Years later, they hypocritically adopt the hopeful view of Jewish history and subscribe to the notion of universal order "where God watched over all, doing his sums. Where everything fit. Even the holocaust which, after all, had yielded the State of Israel." (p. 370) Laura Groening defines the moralist stance in Richler's satiric view of society. She maintains that "a recurrent theme in Richler's fiction is our society's ability to defuse history... by trivializing its significance... We must not forget, Richler cries throughout *St. Urbain's Horseman*, we must never trivialize."[39] Understanding the Holocaust as a preordained act of justice dissolves the sense of guilt, allows the rationalization of passivity, extends the distance from the horror. Richler's satiric exposure of trivialized perception of justice contradicts Klein's vision of the Jewish State as a revelation of divine Providence.

Even Jake's indignant reaction against his community's double standards cannot redeem the vision of the post-Holocaust rebirth of national unity. Jake strongly believes that violent retribution meted out to surviving Nazi tormentors will redress injustice and restore a sense of potency, belonging, and well-being to the Jewish individual. Like Klein's narrator, whose search for his spiritual mentor takes him to the Jewish State, Jake tries to locate his idol, the avenging Horseman, in Israel. Whereas the nephew's journey ends in an emotional reconfirmation of Jewish unity, Jake's visit to Israel becomes a totally discouraging and alienating experience. Neither the nephew, nor Jake meets his elusive relative. However, Melech leaves his nephew a posthumous message of hope that he has found in the restored Jewish Homeland. Joey, in total contradiction to Melech, found Israel as a complacent and indifferent about the Holocaust as the rest of the world. Jake discovers that the Horseman left Israel contemptuous for and disgusted with its attitude which amounted in his opinion to an act of betrayal. In contrast with Klein, Richler clearly rejects Israel as the symbol of Jewish spiritual regeneration.

The protagonist's increasing realization of the cynicism and hypocrisy that typify the Jewish response to the European tragedy results in gradual transference of the Holocaust issue into the world of fantasy. Eventually, the quest for justice filters into the sphere of dream and loses even a semblance of reality. The vicarious witness of the Holocaust becomes the vicarious follower of a phantom avenger. The obsessive preoccupation with the horror at the dream level reveals the tremendous emotional impact of the tragedy on North American Jewish consciousness. At the same time, removal of the encounter with horror to the realm of the unconscious signals a state of emotional paralysis which precludes both direct realization of the tragedy and the forceful reaction that such realization should entail.

Of the three novels, *St. Urbain's Horseman* is furthest removed from the actual event of the Holocaust. Yet, through the particular manipulation of the metaphor, Richler's protagonist practically relives the horror of the Holocaust experience. The motif of revenge denudes rather than covers up the "shameful" impotence of the North American Jew: the fantasy of revenge exposes the wish to compensate for helplessness and passivity. Like Jacob Grossman in *The Rich Man,* Jake Hersh experiences consuming guilt provoked by inability to act in defense of the helpless. His sense of guilt and impotence produces an extreme degree of identification with the victim; in his imagination, Jake becomes a Holocaust victim witnessing his family's brutal murder. The roles have reversed: the North American Jew who seeks to avenge the Holocaust becomes ironically the object of a brutal Nazi quest

> Then, in Jake's Jewish nightmare, they come. Into his house. The extermination officers seeking out the Jew vermin. Ben is seized by the legs like a chicken and heaved out of the window, his brains spilling to the terrace. Molly is raised in the air... to be flung against the brick fireplace. Sammy is dispatched with a pistol. (p. 67)

This horrible fantasy is almost identical to Klein's account of his dream in which he passively watches his father tortured by the Nazis. Klein, however, recognizing the immediate need of national regeneration, refrained from naming the unnameable," and the only experience of the Holocaust in his fiction is related to and integrated into the metaphoric context of rebirth and redemption. Richler attempts to penetrate the metaphoric screen and "present the unpresentable." Like Kreisel, he finds it impossible to traverse the distance that separates outsider from victim. Richler's representation of the horror demonstrates that, like Kreisel, he cannot approach the experience except through the survivor's account. Indeed, Jake's Holocaust fantasy actually rehearses the authentic accounts of survivors. His fantasy is presented in the context of Holocaust documentation: Jake's imagination is triggered by testimonies from Auschwitz and photographs from the Jewish ghetto during the war. (p. 66-67)

In his essay *"St. Urbain's Horseman:* the Novel as a Witness," Thomas E. Tausky maintains that "in St. Urbain's Horseman, Richler is faithful to his conviction that unadorned fact is the appropriate means for conveying the horror of the Holocaust." The recurring fragment of investigation: "Mengele cannot have been there all the time." "In my opinion, always. Night and day." (pp. 67, 163, 254, 353), Tausky notes, "is the actual testimony of one Arie Fuks, as reported by Bernd Naumann, at the Auschwitz trial."[40] The testimony reverberates in Jake's consciousness, impressing the horror and yet, at the same time, circumscribing the inapproachable boundaries of the survivor's experience. Use of the actual transcription of the testimony in fiction signals the ultimate failure of poetic imagination to appropriate the experience.

Methodological solutions to the problem of the literary representation of the Holocaust in the three Canadian novels do not encroach upon the sacredness of the survivor's suffering. The story of the experience, inadequate as it may seem to survivors such as Wiesel and Appelbaum, surpasses the realms of human imagination and, therefore, cannot be recreated through simulation; neither can the very act of telling separate the survivors from their tale — their truth will stay with them forever. It is the profound impact of this truth that affects the consciousness and, consequently, the subjective discourse of the writer-outsider.

The "meeting" with the Holocaust never takes place; history cannot be undone. But, after all, "quest is all" in that the process of searching for the past indicates the wish to gain insight into the present. Attempts to rediscover history are essential to exploration of the Jewish psyche in the aftermath of the Holocaust; the exposure of guilt, impotence, and fear constitute the beginning of the healing process. Failure to complete the journey signals that yet another journey has to follow — a quest that will lead the outsider towards inner reconciliation with the past and restoration of potency and pride. The fateful decision of the survivor to break the silence and tell the tale has committed the North American Jew to a search for self-definition in the post-Holocaust world.

---

[1]The title of Henry Kreisel's short story "The Almost Meeting" tells about his unsuccessful attempts to meet A. M. Klein. In the story, the elusive character identified as Klein leaves the protagonist a message: "Quest is all."

[2]Aharon Appelfeld in an interview with Stephen Lewis in *Art and Agony: the Holocaust Theme in Literature, Sculpture and Film*, ed. Stephen Lewis (Toronto: CBC Enterprises), p. 16.

[3]Elie Wiesel in an interview with Stephen Lewis in *Art and Agony*, p. 155.

[4]Cited by Lawrence Langer, *The Holocaust and the Literary Imagination* (New Haven: Yale Univ. Press, 1975), p. 19.

[5]Reinhard Baugmart and Michael Wyschogrod quoted in *Confronting the Holocaust: the Impact of Elie Wiesel*, eds. Alvin H. Rosenfeld and Irving Greenberg (Bloomington: Indiana Univ. Press, 1978), p. 3.

[6]George Steiner quoted in Langer, *The Holocaust and the Literary Imagination*, p. 15. Yet Steiner himself has overturned his earlier advocacy of silence in his controversial novel *The Portage to San Cristobal of A. H.* For further discussion of this point see Alan L. Berger *Crisis and Covenant: the Holocaust in American Jewish Fiction* (Albany: State University of New York Press, 1985), p. 30.

[7]see Rosenfeld and Greenberg, eds., *Confronting the Holocaust*, p. 5.

[8]see Langer, p. xii.

[9]Sidra de Koven Ezrahi, *By Words Alone: the Holocaust in Literature* (Chicago: Univ. of Chicago Press, 1978), p. 200.

[10]see Elie Wiesel in *Confronting the Holocaust*, p. 200.

[11]see Elie Wiesel in *Art and Agony*, p. 154.

[12]Anthony Easthope, *Poetry as Discourse* (London: Methuen, 1983), p. 47.

[13]see Ezrahi, *By Words Alone*, pp. 177-8. Bellow's *Mr. Sammler's Planet* was published in 1970, twenty-five years after the Holocaust. Ezrahi's comment: "That quarter-centry measures a gradual shift in the engagement as well as the familiarity of the American-Jewish writer with the fate of the Jews in Europe." In his "The Holocaust in American Jewish Fiction: A Slow Awakening" Edward Alexander talks about earlier American writings which touched upon the theme of the Holocaust. He mentions Malamud's story "The Lady of the Lake" (1958) and Edward Wallen's *The Pawnbroker* (1962) He finds, however, that this literature does not deal with the specific issue of Jewish suffering, but rather uses it to sustain its "universalist-humanist delusion" by discovering analogies between

Jewish suffering and that of whatever oppressed and allegedly oppressed group... *The Resonance of Dust: Essays on Holocaust Literature and Jewish State* (Columbus: Ohio State University Press, 1979), p. 125, 127.

[14]Henry Kreisel in an interview with Mervin Butovsky on Nov. 6, 1980, in *Another Country: Writings by and about Henry Kreisel,* ed. Shirley Neuman (Edmonton: NeWest Press, 1985), p. 199.

[15]All the quotations from Kenry Kreisel's *The Rich Man* are taken from the McClelland and Stewart edition, 1971.

[16]On numerous occasions, Kreisel attests to the importance of Klein's model in his writing. See *Another Country,* pp. 127, 129.

[17]In his letter to Sharon Drache, Kreisel says: "Both Frank Scott and Art Smith had told me on separate occasions that Klein had read *The Rich Man* and has been moved by it." *Another Country,* p. 152.

[18]see Usher Caplan, *Like One that Dreamed: A Portrait of A. M. Klein* (Toronto: McGraw-Hill Ryerson, 1982), p. 110.

[19]A. M. Klein, "Meditation Upon Survival" in *Collected Poems of A. M. Klein,* ed. Miriam Waddington (Toronto: McGraw-Hill Ryerson, 1974), pp. 288-9.

[20]Klein's emotional breakdown in 1954 put an end to his literary career.

[21]John Milton, *Paradise Lost* (New York: Reinhart, 1951), p. 6.

[22]see note 1.

[23]see Mordecai Richler, "It was Fun to Be Poor in Paris," *Maclean's,* 6 May 1961, p. 49. Incidentally, the uselessness of the Canadian passport in face of anti-Jewish sentiments is evident in Mordecai Richler's latest novel, *Joshua Then and Now* (1980). Joshua, a Canadian citizen, finds out that his identity provides no immunity when he encounters an ex-Nazi officer on the Spanish island of Ibiza. With the support of Franco's fascist authorities, the German accuses Joshua of espionage and makes him flee the island. This central episode of Joshua's humiliation is based on Richler's own youthful experience on the island.

[24]All the quotations from A. M. Klein's *The Second Scroll* are taken from the McClelland and Stewart Edition, 1969,

[25]J. Hillis Miller, " 'Herself Against Herself': The Clarification of Clara Middleton" in *Representations of Women in Fiction,* ed. Carolyn G. Heilbrun and Margaret R. Higonnet (Baltimore: the Johns Hopkins University Press, 1983), pp. 108-9, 115.

[26]The epigraph to *The Second Scroll* reads: ... "And ask a Talmudist what ails the modesty of his marginal Keri that Moses and all the prophets cannot persuade him to pronounce the textual Chetiv. John Milton."

[27]Klein's choice of metaphor offers an insight into the problematics of Holocaust literature. Literary representation of the Holocaust raises the moral issue of approaching evil through artistic devices. Alvin Rosenfeld, for instance, discusses the exploitation of the Holocaust which has turned the Nazi "aspect of terror... into sexual and political fantasies, religious allegories, pseudohistories, science fictions." See *Imagining Hitler* (Bloomington: Indiana Univ. Press, 1985), p. xiv. Klein's approach seems to offset the evasion of the unspeakable which "clothes" it in diversive and distorted imagery. He counteracts the obliteration of the terror of suffering by focusing on the triumphant return of the victim as a redeemer.

[28]see Rota Herzberg Lister, "Out of Silence: Canadian Testaments," *The Canadian Forum,* Nov. 1985, p. 31.

[29]see M. W. Steinberg and Usher Caplan, eds., *A. M. Klein: Beyond Sambation: Selected Essays and Editorials 1928-1955* (Toronto: Univ. of Toronto Press, 1982), pp. 155-6.

[30]*Beyond Sambation,* p. 275.

[31]Naïm Kattan, "A. M. Klein: Modernité et Loyauté," *Journal of Canadian Studies,* vol. 19, No. 2 (Sept. 1984), p. 26.

[32]Miriam Waddington, *A. M. Klein* (Vancouver: The Copp Clark publishing, 1970), p. 99.

[33]see, for instance, Frank Rasky's recent unfavorable comparison of Richler to Bellow. Rasky writes that "Richler comes closest to Bellow in contemporary mordant Jewish wit." At the same time the critic qualifies that "Bellow is markedly different from Richler in the sense that he is a brillian comic writer who has a heart as well as a head." *(The Canadian Jewish News,* Aug. 13, 1987, p. 9)

[34]see, for instance, Kery McSweeney, "Mordecai Richler (1931-   )," in *Canadian Writers and Their Works: Essays on Form, Context, and Development,* ed.

Robert Lecker, Jack David, and Ellen Quiglie, Fiction Series, vol. 6 (Toronto: ECW, 1985), pp. 129-74.

[35]Mordecai Richler, "We Jews Are Almost As Bad As the Gentiles," *Maclean's,* Oct. 22, 1960, p. 82.

[36]Mordecai Richler, "Holocaust and After," *Shovelling Trouble* (Toronto: McClelland and Stewart, 1972), pp. 87-93.

[37]see my doctoral dissertation "The Formative Influence of the Holocaust in the Writings of Mordecai Richler," Toronto, York University, 1986.

[38]All quotations from Mordecai Richler's *St. Urbain's Horseman* are taken from the Bantam Books edition, 1972.

[39]Laura Groening, "The Jew in History: a Comparative Study of Mordecai Richler and Bernard Malamud," in *Perspectives on Mordecai Richler,* ed. Michael Darling (Toronto: ECW, 1986), p. 66.

[40]Thomas E. Tausky, *"St. Urbain's Horseman:* The Novel as Witness," in *Perspectives on Mordecai Richler,* ed. Michael Darling (Toronto: ECW, 1986), pp. 76, 78.

Chapter Twelve

Ka-Tzetnik's Literary Portrayal of Holocaust Experience

A Study of "Kochav Ha'efer" *(Star of Ashes)* as a Model for Analysis of Holocaust Literature

Moshe Pelli

Critics of literature have long hesitated to discuss literary works on the Holocaust on their literary merits, as a special genre now referred to as literature of atrocity, or Holocaust literature. While sporadic reviews appeared in connecton with the publication of books on the Holocaust, more serious discussions on the literary evaluation of such works have been a recent phenomenon.

In the previous decade, there appeared book-long works on the literature of the Holocaust. Irving Halperin published *Messengers from the Dead* (1970)[1] which contains, among other things, a discussion of Elie Wiesel's works. A more sophisticated literary discussion and a more impressive treatment of the literature of atrocity as a special form of literature was offered by Lawrence Langer in his *The Holocaust and the Literary Imagination* (1975). Although the book contains a discussion of Elie Wiesel's writings, analysis of Judaic themes and allusions to biblical and post-biblical Jewish literature are not the strong points of this book.[2]

More recently, there was a surge of literary discussion on Holocaust literature. Edward Alexander published his *The Resonance of Dust* (1979), which examines a Holocaust diary (by Moshe Flinker), Jewish and Hebrew poetry (by Nelly Sachs and Abba Kovner), and Hebrew prose by Yehuda Amichai, Hanoch Bartov, Haim Gouri, and others.[3] Two significant contributions to the field were published by Sidra Dekoven Ezrahi, *By Words Alone* (1979), and by Alvin Rosenfeld, *A Double Dying* (1980).[4]

In 1984, two books were published which attempt to review the responses to catastrophe in Hebrew and Jewish literature. David Roskies examined "Responses to Catastrophe in Modern Jewish Culture," from the early liturgy to contemporary Yiddish literature, in his *Against the Apocalypse*.[5] Alan Mintz, too, probed "Responses to Catastrophe in Hebrew Literature," from Lamentations to Midrash, from medieval literature to contemporary Hebrew letters, in *Hurban: Responses to Catastrophe in Hebrew Literature*. Mintz studied such Hebrew poets and prose writers as Uri Zvi Greenberg, Aharon Appelfeld, Hanoch Bartov, Haim Gouri, and Yehuda Amichai.[6]

Observers of this field note the abundance of books, in addition to numerous articles, on Elie Wiesel many years before he received the Nobel Peace Prize. Among these many works, it is worthwhile mentioning, in the context of studies on Holocaust literature, the collection of essays entitled *Confronting the Holocaust: The Impact of Elie Wiesel* (1978), and Ellen Fine's *Legacy of Night, The Literary Universe of Elie Wiesel*, among others.[7]

Concurrently, a number of critics concentrated on the Holocaust theme as found in American Jewish fiction (Alan Berger; Arthur Cohen), in women's literature (Marlene L. Heinemann), and in art (Stephen Lewis).[8]

The limited discussion of Holocaust literature written in Hebrew is, however, quite noticeable. Apart from several chapters or articles written by such critics as Robert Alter, Gershon Shaked, and Leon Yudkin, very little has been published in English during the 1960s and 1970s on the Holocaust as portrayed in modern Hebrew letters.[9]

The 1980s have witnessed a significant increase of published books on the theme of the Holocaust in modern Hebrew literature with Murray J. Kohn's volume on Hebrew poetry, *The Voice of My Blood Cries Out* (1979), and Alan J. Yuter's *The Holocaust in Hebrew Literature* (1983). Yuter examines Katzetnik briefly, but does not analyze the book under study here. The most recent work is a selection of Israeli fiction, *Facing the Holocaust*, with an introduction by Gila Ramras-Rauch and an afterword by Gershon Shaked.[10]

It is, however, curious to note that even in Israel very little has been published on the literary aspects of Holocaust literature, the exception being reviews of Aharon Appelfeld's prose, although several anthologies of texts and analysis have been published in the last few years.[11] While many aspects of the literary study and critical analysis about non-Hebraic works do indeed pertain to works originally written in Hebrew, there are some unique features in Hebrew literature which merit the attention of any student of the literary expression of the Holocaust experience.

In the present article, I will examine one such work by a Hebrew and Yiddish writer, Yehiel Dinur, better known as Ka-tzetnik. He is considered one of the major spokesmen of the survivors. I hope that the ensuing analysis will contribute to a better understanding of the unique nature of Holocaust literature, and may serve as a model for similar probes of literary works on the Holocaust experience. Under the pen name of Ka-tzetnik, he has published widely on the universe of the Holocaust, and many of his works have been translated and are thus readily available.

Yehiel Dinur is remembered by many for his dramatic testimony at the Eichmann trial in Jerusalem in 1961, on which occasion he fainted overcome by his emotions and memories. Undoubtedly, both his emotions and memories are the foundation of his work. Yet his own definition of his literary endeavor may be of interest. He said, "I do not consider myself as an author writing literature. It is chronicles [that I write] out of the planet Auschwitz."[12] Some accepted this statement at face value. In 1972, an Israeli reviewer cited his early encounter with Ka-tzetnik's writings as a teenager and his shock of learning about the Holocaust. Yet, a few years later, that reviewer approached Ka-tzetnik's books more critically and concluded that "Ka-tzetnik's books are not literature."[13] Since this short review of two or three columns is rather limited in scope, it seems to me that Ka-tzetnik deserves more serious attention. To this end, I will examine one of his most impressive works, a small volume which has the English title *Star Eternal*. It was originally published in Hebrew in 1960; the English translation appeared in 1971. It is a story of the Holocaust experience in Auschwitz, with a prologue and an epilogue both having the same locale, the narrator's city of Metropoli. The book ends with an editorial statement of great emotional impact on reparation, which, regardless of significance, seems to have been artificially attached to the book.

The structure of the story as such, having a prologue and an epilogue, is intended to achieve the "before and after" effect — that is, before the Holocaust and after this most horrendous event in history. The story unfolds in the autumn of 1939, a few days before the war, and ends immediately after the war. In between the two dates, the narrator relates his experience at the "other planet," Auschwitz. He uses many parallels in the prologue and the epilogue, such as the clock, the Hall of Justice, and the statue of the Goddess of Justice. Indeed, these parallels become symbols which epitomize the Holocaust experience. The clock showing the same time before and after the Holocaust evokes the notion that time stood still. Thus, one may deduce that either the Holocaust was unique in the history of mankind, or that nothing has really changed after the Holocaust. Also, Justice is blindfolded like its symbol, the goddess of Justice. Similarly, the sun's light appears to shine before and after the war. The similarity, indeed the parallel, carries a terrifying message to the reader: He who returns from the other planet, Auschwitz, realizes, much to his horror, that "Here, nothing has changed."[14] It is the most agonizing conclusion that the author shares with the reader at the end of his depiction of the Holocaust reality, that nothing has changed after Auschwitz. The Hall of Justice has not changed; the goddess of Justice is still blindfolded — an obvious ironic allusion to the miscarriage of justice, and the hands of the clock continue to show the same time as before, as if nothing has happened between 1939 and 1945.

Although these symbols are not presented with a high degree of literary sophistication or subtlety, their impact on the reader is significant. One concludes that Ka-tzetnik is at his best when he does not editorialize on aspects of the Holocaust as in the subject of reparations. He is most effective when he lets his reader experience the "before and after" effect and reach his own conclusion.

The structure of the book is based on scenes, more often than not loosely connected to one another: forced labor, transport of the old and the young, and the last transport to Auschwitz. Subsequently, there are a number of chapters devoted to the actual experience of the Holocaust in Auschwitz. The chapters follow a rough course of a day, beginning most appropriately at night — the night of Auschwitz — and ending at the evening roll call. They concentrate on such scenes as entering Auschwitz, the bath house, block curfew, cruelties, prayers, and food. This experience ends in the last parade to the crematorium, at which occasion theological questions pertaining to God's attitude towards His people are raised. This chapter ends in a note of hope about some Jewish continuity in Israel. Liberation is thereafter thrust upon the narrator and the reader as an act of *deus ex machina,* an unexpected salvation.

Upon examining this little book, the critical reader endeavors to look for Ka-tzetnik's unique way of depicting the Holocaust reality as he experienced it. His style is not the sort which would attract a sophisticated reader, for it is rather austere, containing little imagery. Nevertheless, it is this very language — brief, laconic, almost impoverished — that is most appropriate for Ka-tzetnik's subject matter. His language lends itself to abrupt changes, jerks and twists, resembling epileptic seizures. It is as though the author was struggling with words and their ability to translate the reality of atrocity into the medium of verbal expression. His struggle is discerned in the abundance of exclamation points, generally considered a weak literary device. The statement, "Words are no more" (p. 41), used in the context of Auschwitz, typifies the author's perception of post-Auschwitz language as well. This attitude towards language appears to be in concert with Steiner's view: "The world of Auschwitz lies outside speech as it lies outside reason."[15] Aware of the limitation of language, the author resorts to the bare linguistic minimum. For example:

"Earth.

"Fifteen men dig one pit in the earth.[...]

"They dig" (p. 17).

Typically, the structure of the individual sentence follows the pattern established in the paragraphs and the chapters. As depicted by Ka-tzetnik in the very structure of the book, the Holocaust experience is structurally fragmented; events and time do not flow, they just occur without any logical sequence or order whatsoever. Thus, there is an artistic attempt to present reality as distorted, lacking its normal components of time and space. There is no movement in time, in the normal sense, as there is no development of character, which is essential to any novel. The reader is made to experience the suspended time and space of the Holocaust reality. In spite of the apparent austerity in style, Ka-tzetnik does employ a variety of literary devices intended to enhance his message. The most effective of these devices is the second-person narrative pervading most of the book. The opening line reads: "Behind you, in the spacious show-window [...]" (p. 11).

Through the employment of the second-person voice — you! — Ka-tzetnik attempts in a most effective way to relate the experience of the Holocaust *directly* to the reader. The direct and constant reference to "You!" does have a cumulative effect. It makes the reader not only a direct witness to the Holocaust experience, but indeed it forces him to experience that reality. The reader is unable to stay outside of this experience as he reads about "You" — being himself! He must become involved. He is there in Auschwitz, together with the author, or the narrator. At times the narrator will not only invite the reader into the scene, but will indicate that the reader — whom he has designated as "you" — precedes him. On the way to Auschwitz, the narrator tells his reader: "I now follow in your step" (p. 37). This subtle change in the roles played by the narrator and reader forces the reader to be completely involved in the story.

In a similar vein, the reader is made to witness the atrocities as they occur: "The cane rises: Everybody watch now — magic! Nothing up my sleeve! Take a good look! Here before you is a life. Right? In the twinkling of an eye you'll see —" [...] "See for yourselves" [...] (p. 68). "Here in front of you lies a life" (p. 69).

This technique compels the reader to emerge from his normal role as a passive outsider and relate to the events described, thus getting close to becoming a temporary insider. In Langer's words, "The reader is temporarily an insider and permanently an outsider."[16]

This concept of the reader *being there* tends to shatter the reader's security and his ostensible awareness that it is definitely a story told of past events. Thus, the employment of second-person voice places the reader in that very same predicament as though the literary convention of storytelling no longer shields him, or at least in the frame of mind that in effect leads him to conclude: *"You could have been there."* And it is extremely frightening.[17]

Furthermore, by employing the pronoun "you," the author shrewdly establishes an unusual rapport between the speaker-narrator and the addressed person, who turns out to be an Everyman figure. Thus, the narrative achieves a point which extends beyond the mere telling of a story. For it is in effect a loaded message, a call for humanity at large to experience the Holocaust and thus become a survivor.

Related to this technique is another which employs the present tense in the narrative. Events are described in the book under the illusion of a continuous present tense. As a result, scenes seem to occur in the reader's presence, right *now* and *here*. Combined with the second person narrative, this technique intensifies the literary reality of the Holocaust, as it compels the reader to experience the catastrophe in a literary way. The reality of the *Shoah* (Holocaust) is thus brought closer to home, while the reader experiences the possibility of his own person going through the catastrophe of the *Shoah* as a temporary insider, and as a result he may consider himself permanently a survivor.

Significantly, the present tense stops abruptly at a major turning point in the story, and the narrative is suddenly presented in past tense. It occurs as the end draws near and the inmates are thrown into isolation blocks to await their final transport to the crematorium. It is as though life stopped for these inmates as well as for the reader. They are deemed dead while yet being alive; they are already in the realm of the past tense. The narrator explains this ironic phenomenon as follows: "Here there's no longer anyone to fear. Here you're already free of the rules that govern the normal blocks of Auschwitz" (p. 103). Death seems to bring an end to the reality of the Holocaust.

It is at this point that the narrator allows himself a dialogue, a feature omitted almost completely from the total text.[18] The dialogue centers on the theological questions of the Holocaust and presents a note of hope for the doomed inmates and for Judaism. It is hoped — the dialogue stresses — that elsewhere, namely, in Israel, life goes on — in spite of the horrendous attempt to eradicate Jews and Jewish life in Europe.

It is important to note that while one does understand the necessity for such a "transcendental" reasoning about the meaning of the *Shoah*, it looks somewhat artificial in the way it is presented by the narrator. Ostensibly, it is a post-Holocaust concept that justifies the existence of Israel as a haven for Jews who might face future annihilation. While one is hesitant to set standards on what is authentic and what is not in the context of literary work on the Jewish catastrophe, one is indeed permitted to get cues from the author himself elsewhere in the story. Based on comparison, we may conclude that this rationalization about the Holocaust — namely, that life should go on elsewhere, as presented by Ka-tzetnik — is less effective than other segments of the book which depict the actual experience of the Holocaust. A more subtle way of introducing this notion — which is by itself significant — would have been much more convincing. It should be mentioned that what appears to be an accepted historical theory (that is, the close connection between the Holocaust and the establishment of the State of Israel) — formulated after the Holocaust — may, in the context of relating an authentic Holocaust experience, look like an anachronistically "planted" rationalization. It is exemplified in the following quotation:

" 'Rabbi of Shilev,' Ferber asks, 'for whose sake does Jacob wrestle with the Angel, if his children did not cross the river but stayed here in the blackness of the night?' "

The Rabbi answers:

" 'From the very blackness of this night Jacob will bring forth the name 'Israel.' Before that, the morning star will not rise.'

"Light of full understanding flashed within Ferber: his brothers, there, in the Land of Israel! Revelation bared itself to him. For a split second only" (p. 108).

Nevertheless, this chapter, entitled "The Last Argument," is not without its message and significance. For the first time, some of the Jewish inmates are identified by name. Previously, a total dehumanization and lack of identity prevailed in the book, a technique intended to present a mimetic aspect of concentration camp existence. As the rest of the people are demanding "The ration!!!" (p. 104), Ferber, the faithful, is engaged in matters which transcend the immediate time and place. He discusses the meaning of the destruction with the rabbi. While drawing heavily on the biblical paradigm of Jacob's struggle with the angel, the revelation, let it be noted, is no longer perceived to be in the domain of the divine. The emergence of Israel is totally engulfed by the secular — namely, it is the national continuity of the people in the land of Israel (p. 108). It looks as though it is divorced from divine providence. Importantly, the religious authority of the Jewish people, the rabbi, is made to become the carrier of this secular revelation of the *Sho'ah* experience.

Upon liberation, the Ka-Tzet, the concentration camp inmate, arrives at his own conclusion on the whereabouts of the divine: "God abandoned this earth; Devil, too, turned his back on it" (p. 110). It is not the death of God concept which is promulgated here by Ka-tzetnik. Rather, it is an idea of abandonment by all supernatural powers. Even the Devil, supreme representation of evil, would not have any part in the atrocities of the *Sho'ah*.

In spite of the secular and somewhat realistic setting of "The Last Argument," the author resorts to a mystical and enigmatic ending as a catharsis. As the end draws near, Ferber feels redeemed: "Roundabout him all was distillate, pure. No longer did he feel himself in his own skeleton. At that moment he was utterly oblivious of his body's existence. The Rabbi's eyes were like two open gates. He entered in unto them" (p. 108). Death is delineated as having not only the power of personal salvation, but as possessing some inexplicable mystical powers of uniting the individual with his national and historical past. Indeed, it is a very subtle way of attempting to give some meaning to the meaningless, illogical, and savage annihilation of the Jews. It brings to bear the historical dimension of the Holocaust, relating this calamity to the tragic fate of the Jewish people throughout its bloody history.

Some of Ka-tzetnik's other techniques are very effective as well. In an attempt to recreate the reality of the Holocaust for the reader, the narrator abolishes at times the borderline between the real and the unreal, between the physical and the metaphysical. He directs a question to 'Life': "Life! Life! Who are you?" (p. 69). More overwhelming, perhaps, is the personification of death as an entity, a concrete essence, in the Holocaust experience.

Death is so ingrained in reality that it characterizes the act of living more than does life itself. In this distorted reality, as conceptualized by Ka-tzetnik, death could be physically felt and spoken to: "Death prowls around you" (p. 20); "Death has eased his stranglehold" (p. 36); "Death holds your life between his hands" (p. 40); "Death, your master, is now taking you to his abode" (p. 40). This literary device of referring to death as an omnipresent entity — not merely as a literary personification — enhances the feeling of its immediacy and omnipotent presence.

In this device, it is the indirect reference to the essence of the Holocaust that makes a lasting impression. It is the overall tone of paradox that registers with the reader as one of the most dominant features of the Jewish catastrophe. Through an understanding of the centrality of paradox in the Holocaust, the reader is given a unique insight into the experience of atrocity where death has paradoxically become a symbol for life. The paradox abounds: "'As long as your hands keep digging [your grave] — you live.... .

"'Dig and stay alive!'" (p. 23).

Or:

The old people marching to their death know that "their going spells life for those left behind in the ghetto" (p. 29).

Ka-tzetnik's particular style of portraying the Holocaust experience is best demonstrated in the second chapter, entitled "The Men of Metropoli." It depicts the first encounter with death as a group of Jews is ordered to dig a pit which is nothing else but a mass grave. Significantly, chapter subtitles in the original Hebrew version of the book are designated as phases in a numerical order, each chapter representing a phase in the Holocaust. The reader is impressed by the fact that phase one — the digging of the pit — occurs without any preparation. The omission of a detailed background being quite outstanding, it is indeed the author's way of representing the Holocaust as a sudden, illogical, senseless event. The literary components are so structured as to reflect a general concept of the historical Holocaust, namely, the fact that most Jews were totally unprepared to confront the situation.

Reality as presented by the narrator is selective; it is narrowed down to the elements, to the essentials of existence. Thus, the first word in this chapter is "earth." The sentence, too, is stripped to its bare essential, to the subject. The lack of verbs here, as well as in many other sentences throughout the book, signifies the passivity of reality: "Naked march into the night" (p. 39); "Backs. Backs and eyes —" (p. 49); "A cataract of yellow, dried bones" (p. 71); "Rows. Naked rows" (p. 90). The tendency to deprive the scene of any unnecessary description — adjectives being a rarity in the book — helps in stripping reality as well. Similarly, human experience as depicted by the narrator is limited to the essentials: food, rollcall, curfew, cruel punishment, prayer, and death.

The tone employed here, as elsewhere, is ironic. The ground — "earth" — is the private property of a Jewish family; as it turns out, the pit dug in the earth epitomizes, at the outset, the common fate of the Jews in the Holocaust. The scenes depict the atrocity of extermination, showing the sadism, inhumaneness, the dishonesty of the Germans incorporated with their alleged cultural traits, namely, cleanliness, orderliness, mechanical performance of duty, and accuracy of reporting the results of their hideous acts. The atrocity is performed in broad daylight, as the sun shines unashamedly. The narrator enacts a symbolic struggle between the atrocity and the sun's shining: "With every thrust of your spade — you bury the sun in the earth. But with every shovelful of sod tossed away, the sun floats up once more — brighter than ever" (p. 17). For the citizens of Metropoli are silent witnesses to the atrocity carried out in broad daylight.

The narrator chooses the sun to function as a leitmotif, relating the prologue to the epilogue, and serving as a cementing bond between the prologue, the pre-Holocaust situation and the beginning of the war in chapter one. Subsequently, chapters two, three and four, depicting the transports of the old and the young, and later of all the inhabitants of the ghetto, have both day and night scenes in them. The sun is playing the same role as before. As the scene shifts to Auschwitz, night reigns supreme. It is cited as "Midnight silence of Auschwitz" (p. 39) or "Night-of-Auschwitz" (p. 52).

The sun reappears in the Auschwitz reality as "the naked skull of the sun" (p. 80), more than ever reflecting the state of the inmates at the concentration camp. The sun is portrayed in its setting, indeed, the sunset of humanity, as "the bottom strands of the barbed-wire dykes bathe in a pool of blood" (p. 80). "A day dies in Auschwitz" (p. 80). The transitory chapter on the narrator's city of Metropoli also presents this notion as "a city sunk into the bottom of a luminous sea" (p. 23), namely, a civilization in decline; a modern-day Atlantis. Only once more would the sun appear in all its glory and brightness; it happens, ironically, as the end draws near, in line to the crematorium. "It's bright out. Brilliant light. Suddenly you see a sky" (p. 91). The English translation loses the religious subtleties inherent in the original Hebrew text. For the author is using the *Zohar* — brilliance — in the context of *Shamayim* — sky — thus alluding to the memorial prayer, *El Male Rahamim*.[19] The sun foreshadows their departure — and their demise... . Concurrently, this brightness, *Zohar* in Hebrew, carries with it a transcendental revelation. The narrator expounds: "Until this moment nobody knew that in Auschwitz there is sky" (Hebrew: *Shamayim*, meaning also heavens; p. 91).[20] And he goes on saying: "Only now, at final rollcall, it has disclosed itself to the eye. At the very last moment" (p. 91). Ironically, heavens reveal their existence in line to the crematorium... .

This heavenly body is employed as a powerful metaphor at the concluding scenes of liberation. The Ka-tzet summarizes the total image of the sun as symbol of the Holocaust and his experience at the concentration camp: "the eclipse of this world's sun [...] the eclipse of his life's sun" (p. 115).

The dominant figure of the sun is replaced by the equally forceful image of the stars in the dominion of night as the "Night-of-Auschwitz" (p. 52) prevails. As conceptualized by the narrator, the stars, like the sun, reflect the mundane, down-to-earth reality in all its gruesomeness: "Over your head vaults a star-sprinkled sky, and before your eyes a smokestack thrusts skyward. Thick, fatty smoke gushes out. Sparks beyond count. Sparks scatter and flash across the starry sky, mingle with the stars, and you cannot tell whose light is the brighter" (p. 40). Smoke, too, is a symbol of the Holocaust here and elsewhere in the literature. Its color is blue (p. 94) as is the color of the Ka-Tzet number on the narrator's forearm (p. 118), which — we are told — resembles a blue river of Jewish experience during the Holocaust (p. 119). The author's metaphor of the river may allude to the well-known episode told in *The Ethics of the Fathers* of Hillel's walking by a river. Seeing a skull [of a highway robber] floating on it, he said: "For drowning others thou wast drowned." Of course, this phrase evokes the notion of retribution. Other Hebrew writers, such as Yehuda Amichai, so intensified this saying that it has become a major concept of the Holocaust experience.[21]

In the context of stars and sparks, one should note another significant literary device employed in Ka-tzetnik's writings. It is especially discernible through his use of the Hebrew language in the original work. The narrator designates those stars and sparks, as described in the above scene, to serve as a leitmotif throughout the book, charged with meaningful biblical allusions. In so doing, the author adds historical and religious depths to the meaning and the significance of the *Shoah* in the history of the Jewish people. The depiction of the stars ostensibly refers to the biblical covenant between God and Abraham as follows: "And He brought him forth abroad, and said: 'Look now toward heaven and count the stars, if thou be able to count them;' and He said unto him: 'So shall thy seed be' " (Genesis, 15:5). The author portrays the reality of the Holocaust where the numberless smoke sparks replace the promised numberless stars, which symbolize the eternity of the Hebrew people. Ironically and quite painfully, these sparks represent the actual doom of the Jewish people in the Holocaust. As "Sparks slip out of the smokestack" — "Stars vanish" (p. 41). These two phenomena of the Holocaust are directly connected to the disappearance of "human language" (p. 41), as previously mentioned.

The Star which appears in the original title of the book and was given the English rendering of *Star Eternal* is an erroneous representation of the original *Kochav Ha'efer*, namely, *Star of Ash(es)*, a title which is more meaningful. For it is the author's intention to enhance the symbol of the ashes as a major concept of the Holocaust not only as part of the concentration camp experience (which is also used by other writers),[22] but indeed as a dominant feature of the post-Holocaust experience. Liberated after the war, the Ka-Tzet faces the crematorium — and his past, and he says:

"No one inside, no one outside. All are here now — in the mound of ash.

"'Dear ones! My darlings! This is the liberation! —'

"He flung himself upon them. Took them in his arms. Held them tight. He was lying on the mound, his arms deep, deep in ash" (p. 112).

This mound of ash becomes a biblical archetypal guide, which is intended "to point out his way" (p. 112). The use of the Hebrew phrase *Lanhoto hadarech* (to point out his way) in the original Hebrew edition is a direct borrowing from the biblical reference to the divine guidance: "And the Lord went before them by day in a pillar of cloud to lead them the way" (Exodus, 13:21).

To the survivor, the divine guidance is replaced by the memory of those exterminated in the concentration camps. He says: "— I vow on you[r] ash embraced in my arms, to be a voice unto you" (p. 113). Similar vows appear in other writings on the Holocaust. One remembers Elie Wiesel's similar utterances in *Night:* "Never shall I forget."[23]

Other biblical allusions abound in his writing and are related to Ka-tzetnik's conceptualization of the *Shoah*. While not referred to directly, yet existing in the backdrop as a subconscious phenomenon, the biblical covenant with the Hebrew people emerges through a variety of biblical allusions in their caustic contradiction. As previously seen, stars — the symbol of the covenant — become ashes in the Holocaust. This major concept of the Jewish catastrophe, as presented from an historically meaningful point of view, is enhanced by a similar expression which becomes the title of a chapter. It is "Covenant Between the Crumbs," a parody of the Covenant Between the Pieces (Genesis ch. 15), which contains both doom and a promised salvation. It is related to the promise of land and people to Abraham. Yet in the context of the Holocaust, the ironic covenant is one of separation between the lover and his beloved, with nothing to hope for except the token expression of love. Under the circumstances, one notes the disappearance of the stars: "See! There are no stars twinkling above our heads. They are stray sparks from the crematorium chimney..." (p. 89). The star of ashes emerges as the most impressive symbol of the Holocaust.

Ka-tzetnik's style tends to be repetitious; thus it adds some poetic touch to the book. It looks as though the English edition, unlike the original Hebrew, was trying to capitalize on the poetic qualities of the book by having the text printed in uneven lines. By so doing, the editors of the English edition ostensibly ignored Adorno's well-known statement: "To write poetry after Auschwitz is barbaric."[24]

More importantly, the continuous repetition seems to reflect the monotony of life... or rather, the monotony of death in the Holocaust experience. The monotonous rhythm reflects the narrator's struggle in an attempt to recapture events, situations, scenes, and places in order to make them look authentic. A repetitive phrase would be used a few times in a given chapter. For example, the phrase "Isolation Block" is repeated three times (pp. 102-103), or "Eyes" some five times (pp. 50-52).

This device of repetition becomes, at times, a very sophisticated way by which Ka-tzetnik conceptualizes and presents reality. Note the following examples:

"Backs.

"Backs and eyes —" (p. 49);

or:

"Rows.

"Naked rows.

"Naked yellow skeletons" (p. 90).

Through this use of repetition, the narrator presents a linear perception of reality, somewhat limited in scope, depth, and breadth. Field of vision, too, is narrow. Ability to grasp simultaneous or complex components is curtailed. It is a tired outlook, primitive in nature, which concentrates on the bare essentials as does the actual Holocaust experience itself.

Perception and portrayal of people are also linear and limited. The narrator refers to people by citing only parts of their bodies: eyes, legs, backs, and necks. There is no concept of the person as an individual or as a personality, but as a member of a group identified only by that body part which the group has in common. It is a very powerful way of delineating the experience of the *Shoah*. In a more subtle way, it is a cruel and sardonic, yet authentic, a foreshadowing of the tragic fate of these people in the Holocaust. Viewers who saw a moving documentary film as *Night and Fog* will never forget the visual trauma and emotional impact of such scenes as the piles of skulls or hair displayed in a macabre, satanic way. (Ka-tzetnik uses such scenes in the final chapter on reparations.) They utterly distort reality as we know it and introduce us into the reality of *l' univers concentrationnaire* (the reality of the concentration camp). It is a reality of a shopkeeper of human organs and life whose terrifying magnitude defies human imagination. It is, as Langer puts it, the disfiguration of empirical reality.[25]

While Ka-tzetnik's book on the Holocaust does have its limitations and shortcomings, it is nevertheless very impressive for the general reader, for the Jewish reader, and for the student of the literary expression of the Holocaust. To the latter, this book serves as a fascinating study — if one is permitted to use this improper term — of the art of atrocity. Ka-tzetnik struggles with his own conceptualization of the Holocaust, and he perceives it and portrays it as only an author writing in Hebrew can.

---

[1]Irving Halperin, *Messengers from the Dead* (Philadelphia, 1970).

[2]Lawrence L. Langer, *The Holocaust and the Literary Imagination* (New Haven, 1975). Langer followed his work in related subjects in his book *The Age of Atrocity* (Boston, 1978) on the theme of death in modern literature. He continued his Holocaust literature pursuit with *Versions of Survival* [,] *The Holocaust and the Human Spirit* (Albany, 1982).

Several articles published in the 1970s reviewed Langer's work, and are indicative of some research and criticism under study; they are: Edward Alexander, "The Holocaust in American Jewish Fiction: A Slow Awakening," *Judaism,* XXV (No. 3, Summer 1976), pp. 320-330; Norma Rosen, "The Holocaust and the American Jewish Novelist," *Midstream,* XX (No. 8, October 1974), pp. 54-62; David Stern, "Imagining the Holocaust," *Commentary,* Vol. 62 (No. 1, July 1976), pp. 46-51.

[3]Edward Alexander, *The Resonance of Dust* (Columbus, 1979).

[4]Sidra Dekoven Ezrahi, *By Word Alone* (Chicago, 1979); Alvin H. Rosenfeld, *A Double Dying: Reflections on Holocaust Literature* (Bloomington, 1980). See also Rosenfeld's *Imagining Hitler* (Bloomington, 1985).

[5]David G. Roskies, *Against the Apocalypse* [,] *Responses to Catastrophe in Modern Jewish Culture* (Cambridge, 1984).

[6]Alan L. Mintz, *Hurban: Responses to Catastrophe in Hebrew Literature* (New York, 1984).

[7]Alvin H. Rosenfeld & Irving Greenberg, ed., *Confronting the Holocaust: The Impact of Elie Wiesel* (Bloomington, 1978); Ellen Fine, *Legacy of Night, The Literary Universe of Elie Wiesel* (Albany, 1982).

[8]Alan L. Berger, *Crisis and Covenant: The Holocaust in American Jewish Fiction* (Albany, 1985); see also Edward Alexander's article cited in note 2 above; Arthur Allen Cohen, *The American Imagination After the War: Notes on the Novel, Jews and Hope* (Syracuse, 1981); Marlene E. Heinemann, *Gender and and Destiny: Women Writers on the Holocaust* (Westport, 1986); Stephen Lewis, *Art Out of Agony, The Holocaust Theme in Literature, Sculpture and Film* (Montreal & New York, 1984), which contains a conversation with Aharon Appelfeld.

[9]Robert Alter, *After the Tradition* (New York, 1960); Gershon Shaked, "Childhood Lost, Studies in the Holocaust Themes in Contemporary Israel Fiction," *Literature East and West,* XIV (No. 1, March 1970), pp. 90-108; Leon I. Yudkin, *Escape into Siege* (London & Boston, 1974). See also Alexander's book cited in note 3 above.

[10]Murray J. Kohn, *The Voice of My Blood Cries Out* (New York, 1979); Alan J. Yuter, *The Holocaust in Hebrew Literature, From Genocide to Rebirth* (Port Washington, N.Y., 1983), which has chapters on Ka-tzetnik, Kaniuk, Kovner, Greenberg, Pagis, Carmi, Appelfeld, Ben-Amotz, Amichai, Bartov, Oz, Shenhar, Hazaz, and Agnon; Gila Ramras-Rauch & Joseph Michman-Melkman, ed., *Facing the Holocaust* [:] *Selected Israeli Fiction,* with an introduction by G. Ramras-Rauch and afterword by Gershon Shaked (Philadelphia, 1985). See also Mintz's book cited in note 6 above.

[11]Some of them are: Natan Gross, Itamar Yaoz-Kest & Rina Klinov, ed., *Hasho'ah Bashirah Ha'ivrit* [Holocaust in Hebrew Poetry], with an introduction by Hillel Barzel (Tel Aviv, 1974) [Hebrew]; Shammai Golan, ed., *Hasho'ah, Pirkei 'Edut Vesifrut* [The Holocaust: Eye Witness and Literary Accounts] (Tel Aviv, 1976) [Hebrew].

[12]Golan, *Hasho'ah, Pirkei 'Edut Vesifrut,* p. 177.

[13]"K. Tzetnik," *Keshet,* XV (No. 1, Fall 1972), pp. 188-189, by H. B. [Hebrew]. A more favorable review by another Israeli critic appears in Mordechai Ovadyahu,

Besa'ar Uvidemamah [In Storm and Silence] (Tel Aviv, 1976), pp. 82-90 [Hebrew].

[14]Ka-tzetnik 135633, *Star Eternal* (New York, 1971), p. 119.

[15]George Steiner, *Language and Silence* (New York, 1967), p. 123.

[16]Langer, *The Holocaust and the Literary Imagination*, p. 3.

[17]Compare, for example, Steiner's statement, "I am a kind of survivor," in *Language and Silence*, p. 145, originally published in *Commentary*, Vol. 39 (No. 2, February 1965), p. 32.

[18]The intentional omission of dialogue in order to depict an uncivilized state of humanity is a device used also in *The Painted Bird*. See Jerzy Kosinski, *The Painted Bird* (Boston, 1972), and his *Notes of the Author on The Painted Bird* (New York, 1967), p. 16. *Cf.* Langer, *The Holocaust and the Literary Imagination*, p. 168.

[19]The Memorial Prayer reads: *"El male rahamim... kezohar haraki'a mazhrim,"* having *zohar* (brilliance) and *raki'a* (sky) in the same sentence.

[20]Hebrew edition: *Kochav Ha'efer* [Star of Ashes] (Tel Aviv, 1966), p. 84.

[21]Yehuda Amichai uses this allusion in his novel *Not of This Time, Not of This Place* (1968).

[22]Elie Wiesel, *Night* (New York, 1969), p. 44.

[23]*Ibid.*

[24]Theodor W. Adorno, *Noten zur Literatur, Gesammelte Schriften*, II (Frankfurt A/M, 1974), s. 422: *"Nach Auschwitz noch Lyric zu schreiben, sei barbarisch."* Adorno's statement, quoted abundantly in the literature, has been discussed, disputed, and refuted since.

[25]Langer, *The Holocaust and the Literary Imagination*, pp. 2-3.

Chapter Thirteen

Experimental Drama and the Holocaust: The Work of the Jewish-German Dance Theatre and Its Application to theTeaching of the Holocaust

Björn Krondorfer

Elie Wiesel's struggle to find expression for the years he spent in death camps is paradigmatic. Tormented by the insight that ultimately no word can capture the pain, Wiesel asks himself how survivors — how anybody — can write literature about the Holocaust. It took him ten years after his liberation before he was able to tell his story of survival in *Night*. Ever since, Wiesel has been torn between silence and the need to be witness. Although Wiesel has created an immense body of literary work and mastered the art of storytelling, he says that "there is no such thing as Holocaust literature... The very term is a contradiction."[1] Still, everyone who does not want to be "an accomplice to the enemy," Wiesel continues, has to tell the stories of victims, "tales of solitude and despair, tales of silence and defiance."[2]

To listen to and learn from Holocaust survivors is important. Their stories can be characterized as a literature of testimony.[3] They call for people willing to listen and more importantly, to remember. Each generation has to find its own expression of this remembrance. Postwar generations have to look for their own particular means to approach, shape, and pass on their knowledge and memory of the Holocaust. The arts, I think, have a special responsibility for this task. The simple literary form of a survivor's story is often the most helpful way to deal with the unprecedented terror of Germany's genocidal program. Contemporary and future art take up this legacy: artistic creativity may find access to otherwise inexpressible horrors.

But every artist who creates a piece of art about the Holocaust faces the important question to what degree aesthetic decisions may betray the historical reality of the Holocaust and trivialize the suffering endured by "non-Aryan" people. Is it possible that the transformation of the Holocaust into art, as Michael Wyschogrod maintains, "demeans the Holocaust and must result in poor art"?[4]

Insensitive depictions of the Holocaust do indeed gloss over and distort the pain of the victims. They are in bad taste and provoke emotional repulsion. Evidence for careless use of art can be found in the fine arts, literature, drama, and movies. Photographic depictions, even if published for the purpose of documentation, should not be excluded from this list. They too cannot escape what Langer calls the "aesthetics of atrocities."[5] Susan Sontag goes even a step further, arguing that any display of atrocities "risks being tacitly pornographic."[6] Movies are especially susceptible to aesthetics which displays atrocities in order to attract an audience. More than any other art form, they are subjected to the laws of commercialism. Although trash productions, and in particular pornographic exploitation of Nazi atrocities, are obscene and irresponsible, they are frequent occurrences in the film industry. Commercialization of the Holocaust is a slap in the face of those who survived or died in death camps.

The Holocaust raises serious questions which cannot easily be dismissed. Passing final judgements on works of art is a difficult task since the search for criteria is always tied to matters of perspective and personal taste. Studies show, however, that criteria are not completely arbitrary.[7] Negative examples cannot invalidate the important contribution of the arts in recording, expressing, and teaching the Holocaust. With each piece of art, Langer's question should be posed anew: "How should art — how can art — represent the inexpressibly inhuman suffering of the victims, without doing an injustice to that suffering?"[8]

Drama is not exempted from challenges which the Holocaust raises. In theater, immediate and subjective identification causes an active, and therefore unpredictable, interaction between audience and artistic presentation. Drama involves real people both in the audience and onstage so that, according to Robert Skloot, "the search for a style and a form for the Holocaust experience... is yet more difficult in the theater."[9] The effectiveness of a live performance is the strength of drama and the risk it has to take.

Encounters between drama and the Holocaust have been diverse and fruitful, ranging from theatrical activities in death camps to elaborate texts by modern playwrights, and from metaphorical allusions in various theatre productions to thematic incorporation in experimental drama.

What is not very well-known are the many theatrical activities by prisoners that were performed in the Nazi death camps themselves. Mostly underground, performances took place in Auschwitz, Buchenwald, Westerbork, and Dachau, to name a few.[10] Whether political or nonpolitical in nature, they constituted acts of resistance and were essential to fight spiritual defeat. Only in Theresienstadt were full-scale productions possible, due to the special nature of this camp, having been built for propaganda purposes: to show the International Red Cross that Germans had created "humane" camp environments for their enemies. With the exception of Theresienstadt where imposed entertainment created a "hell of delusion,"[11] theatrical performances were acts of defiance and sustenance, helping the prisoners to organize the means for survival.

Since 1945, many plays have been written about the *Shoah*. Rolf Hochhuth's *The Deputy*, Arthur Miller's *Incident at Vichy*, and Peter Weiss' *The Investigation* are familiar pieces, which approach the Holocaust by focusing on one particular aspect. They are not restricted to one single style or message, however, even though somewhat naturalistic and often documentary forms are prevalent. In general modern playwrights have employed a wide range of dramatic modes in order to portray life under Nazi rule.[12]

Plays dealing explicitly with the Holocaust are not the only attempt of postwar theatre to deal with this gruesome event. Often, the Holocaust is depicted by implicit references, presupposing that a general audience has some knowledge about death camps and Nazi mass murder. Thus a few symbols, images, gestures or words are considered dramatically sufficient to create specific associations, messages, and emotions. Sensitively employed, such associations can be very strong. However, the metaphorical use of the Holocaust is a perilous enterprise. Since it is dramatically so effective, it is prone to exploit and distort history, both in the aesthetic and ethical sense. The Holocaust resists metaphorical analogy to a great extent.[13] Before the *Shoah*, literary imagination was free to create hyperbolic idioms and metaphors of daemonic worlds. With the *Shoah*, however, even the most macabre literary imagination was transformed into reality. In cases where post-Holocaust literature falls back to unrestrained language, Rosenfeld speaks of the "imaginative misapprehension of atrocity."[14] If, for instance, the annihilation of the Jewish people is used as an example of the presence of ontological evil, the particular crime of the Final Solution is generalized, and consequently minimized. Victims and victimizers do have a name and an address; any elevation into a mythological realm helps to exonerate the crime. A second example: the Holocaust is often borrowed as a metaphor to emphasize the harshness of an elsewhere committed atrocity, such as sexual or racial oppression.[15] Such metaphorical borrowing becomes entangled in the ambiguous value of comparability. Drawing comparisons diffuses rather than clarifies the issue.[16]

The allusive play with the Holocaust theme in drama raises many questions which cannot be answered here. After all, language as such and especially dramatic visualization cannot manage without symbolic representation. Yet, reenacting the Holocaust bears a special responsibility which cannot be dealt with apart from its context. In a Christian dominated culture, the "Jew" always served as a symbol, as a negative foil for Christian projections. The metaphorical abuse of Jewish people constitutes both a cause and expression of anti-Semitism. The metaphorical use of the "Holocaust" is but a continuation of the symbolic "Jew." Instead of taking the endured suffering for what it is, Holocaust metaphors restrictively define Jewish people as the paradigmatic "eternal victim," which can then be applied to any other desired context and intention. Using the Holocaust apart from its victims leaves an empty shell. To fill it for the sake of dramatic effects is an inappropriate venture.

Experimental drama, as part of the avant-garde, also addresses the Holocaust. The term "experimental drama" is somewhat ambiguous.[17] For the purpose of this paper, it is sufficient to name a few of its features. As opposed to modern drama, it is not limited to a written text. It often includes biographical material of the artist-performer, relies on improvisation, invents new techniques, and works with performance scripts which emphasize movement, sounds, and images. It experiments with newly defined relations between audience and actors, and borrows eclectically and syncretically from various traditions, styles and forms. A spirit of collaborative work — and continual lack of money — complete the list.

Experimental drama is continuously expanding boundaries. It searches for nonstereotypical responses to challenges of our century. Antonin Artaud, the famous visionary of experimental drama, went so far as to proclaim that actors should be "like victims burnt at the stake, signaling through the flames."[18]

Given this desired intensity, the Holocaust theme almost suggested itself. It is hard to tell how many ensembles have worked on the subject since many of these experimental performances are poorly documented. Dramatic works such as *Berlin, Jerusalem and the Moon* (1985) by A Traveling Jewish Theatre, and *The Survivor and the Translator* (1980) by Leeny Sack, daughter of Holocaust survivors, give witness to some of the many theatrical activities which are less known to the public. The same holds true for experimental dance pieces such as *Dreams* (1979) by Anna Sokolov, and *Quarry* (1977) by Meredith Monk.[19]

The Jewish - German Dance Theatre,[20] founded in Philadelphia in November 1985, works in the tradition of experimental drama and dance. To my knowledge, it is the only performance collaboration in which (American) Jews and (Gentile) Germans together try to come to terms with the *Shoah*. The ensemble examines how the inheritance of the Holocaust affects their relationships as Jews and Germans born after the war. In May 1986, on Holocaust Remembrance Day, their original piece *But What About the Holocaust?* premiered at the Painted Bride Arts Center in Philadelphia.[21]

This project is unique in that it depends on the participation and collaboration of Jews and Germans. Though desirable for reconciliation and education, such binational collaborations are probably rare because of many difficulties, including technical, financial, and language problems. In the context of teaching the Holocaust, however, it is very important to examine the ensemble's experience with experimental drama techniques. If these techniques are sensitively applied to classroom situations, they can provide students with a deepened understanding of the ethical and emotional complexities involved in the *Shoah*.

In the next section of this paper, I highlight the preparatory phase and rehearsal periods of the Jewish-German Dance Theatre in the Spring of 1986. Most of the painstaking and exhausting work happened in this period. The performance of *But What About the Holocaust?* will be less the focus since it tells more about the art of performing, while preparation and rehearsals are more concerned with the art of teaching.

The final portion of this paper treats possible application of the work of the Jewish-German Dance Theatre to a classroom environment. As a model it can inspire other Jewish - Christian groups and can even assist in situations where encounters are less likely to happen because the "other" side is unavailable.

It should be understood, of course, that my conclusions are tentative and preliminary, and require the courage of teachers to test them carefully. As with all issues which involve and provoke strong emotional responses, hurt and healing lie close together.

Description: The Jewish - German Dance Theatre

The Preparatory Phase

Pursuit of a new idea always generates excitement. Many people attended for the first informal meeting in November 1985, to which the coordinators Lisa Green and this author invited their Jewish and German colleagues.[22] It became apparent that involvement in the project entailed a clear time commitment and the willingness to expose oneself to emotionally strenuous situations. People were hesitant to commit themselves. For the next two months it remained uncertain whether the project would be realized. By January 1986, when it became clear that any further postponement would jeopardize the entire project, a core of people started to prepare themselves.

In order to ground our work on some common knowledge, we all read Wiesel's autobiographical account *Night,* which had a deep and lasting impact on the group. A second required reading was Terrence Des Pres' *The Survivor.* We studied this book in order to understand the spiritual and humane achievements of prisoners in death camps. Reading continued on an individual basis, and we collected and shared important articles, facts, journal entries, poems, and newspaper clippings. We saw only one film together, Claude Lanzmann's nine and a half hour oral history *Shoah.* Lanzmann used no film footage from the Holocaust period itself, but limited himself to interviews with survivors, eyewitnesses, and German Nazis 40 years later. The victims still suffer from their wounds, while the perpetrators remain unrepentant for their crimes. *Shoah* illustrates once more that the JGDT's attempt to deal with the Holocaust is not a retreat into the past, but indeed, a present necessity.

Participation in the JGDT did not depend on our sharing any specific point of view. As a matter of fact, consensus was not a prerequisite, nor unity a desired goal. We came with diverse backgrounds, knowledge, and worldviews. We all changed in our own ways during the process, but never was anyone asked to adopt another's point of view. But since an ensemble has to make artistic decisions, conflicts, caused by the variety of perspectives, were inevitable.

Our first meetings were characterized by insecurity and guardedness. We did not exactly know how to enter the task before us. It soon turned out that trust and anger were the two major emotions with which we had to deal. Although we liked each other on a personal level, we did not know what to expect from each other while dealing with the Holocaust. How could we retrieve biographical and more intimate information? What level of embarrassment would the group tolerate? Would we be able to give up our need for protection and show our vulnerable spots? Would there be confidence enough to bear and express feelings of hurt, shame, blame, and anger? How would we confront prejudices? Would it be possible to distinguish between personal animosities and cultural cliches? Would we endanger our good personal relationships by lapsing into a history which defined us as victims and victimizers?

After all, we were not just dealing with raw emotions but with emotions shaped by and inherited from a different cultural consciousness. Anger provides a good example. Jewish anger and resentment towards "the Germans" was different from the Germans' wrath against their own parents and grandparents. Although it was easy for both sides to agree on anger against the Nazis, it was far from easy to confront the delicate issue of one's own family history. Uneasiness accompanied us throughout our work: having to deal with painful issues generated a certain amount of self-hate. We always took turns at wondering why we were involving ourselves with such a heavy subject. We often plunged completely into a world full of violence and despair. At the same time, we were very much afraid of doing injustice to the Holocaust; to a reality which, after all, was not ours. From time to time an ensemble member, as if emerging from a nightmare, would ask the sobering question: "But what about the Holocaust?" Did we, after strenuous hours of work, really understand what it was all about?

Another occurrence indicated the extent of our difficulties in handling anger. In the beginning, the only (verbal) fighting which took place was in-fighting: Germans arguing against Germans, Jews against Jews. Though there were good reasons for clarifying issues initially with one's own fellows, it soon became obvious that in-fighting also guaranteed more safety: rules were familiar, and possible pitfalls and hurt could be assessed. Common ground for a struggle between Jews and Germans had not yet been established. The frame for such a struggle needed to be drawn. We were learning that anger was tied to trust, and that only after we had created a firm basis of trust would anger be risked.

Besides the readings, we used a questionnaire, a guided sociodrama, physical exercise, and a meeting with a Holocaust survivor as methodological devices to enter the task ahead of us.

Questionnaire:

Early on in our work, one member with a degree in social work developed a questionnaire designed to disclose some of our prejudices. The questions were:

1. When I think of Jewish or German people, what characteristics come to mind?

2. Do I know people who fit my image of a "typical" Jew/German?

3. What do I think about each member of the group?

4. What are my interests, fears, and hopes?

The first two questions directly addressed issues of prejudice. Answers to question 1 referred to images of "the other" which each of us had accumulated through school, home, the media, and books. We were generally aware of their distortional character; a few images, however, remained in the foggy sphere in which truth and stereotype are inseparable. "Germans" for example, were described as both cosmopolitan and cruel, compulsive and cultured. For the Germans, a prevailing image of Jews consisted of memories of photographed skeletons and piles of bodies. These memories, as it turned out, reflected the situation of Germany's postwar generation which grew up with documentations of the Holocaust while never having met any living Jews.[23]

Asked to write about the "typical" Jew/German (question 2), we talked about personal encounters with "the other." Our stories revealed that Jews/Germans whom we had met prior to the JGDT, either confirmed or dissolved preconceived images. In most cases, encounters with the "other" were preconditioned by judgmental opinions. We made ourselves aware that we automatically compared preconceived image and actual person.

In the third question, we reflected upon our relationships and interactions; responses were cautious and limited to positive feedback. We stressed the individual character in each of us: Human being first, Jew/German second. Although the emphasis on individuality accurately reflected the ensemble's make-up, we were at the same time anxious not to identify the "typical" Jew/German with someone from the group.

The last question was more task-oriented. Fears and hopes about the JGDT were closely connected. We dreaded falling back on stereotypes, or worse, creating new prejudices — in spite of ourselves. We hoped to find common ground without minimizing history. We then formed and analyzed concepts: we would avoid staging a naturalistic play, and instead interweave biographical stories, historical reenactments, and our own relationships. We felt that a straight docu-drama about the Holocaust would not reflect our contemporary struggle with the past. Ultimately, we could not comprehend the *Shoah*. Our coming to terms with the Holocaust had to take place via our relationships, and both past and present ought to be part of the final performance.

Sociodrama:

The questionnaire was a good starting point but engaged us only mentally. Well-phrased formulations allowed us to hide dangerous memories and emotions unself-consciously. That changed drastically when we arranged to spend an evening with a trained, four-member sociodrama group.[24] Neither group knew the other. Ten people crowded into a small room. We started with a few simple exercises. "Be an animal!" Ten people crawled over chairs, on the floor, barked and squeaked, stretched their limbs and crept under cushions. "Affirm your rights in an overcrowded subway!" Our jostling and shoving released some tensions. "Dating" was the last situation we acted out. We pretended to be in love with another person which established a calm and intimate environment.

These impromptu exercises took no longer than 15 minutes, but we were then ready to go a step further. We gathered in a circle, and everybody was asked to conceive of a situation in Nazi Germany. We played two of these imagined situations: one about book burnings, the other about nightly arrests by the Gestapo. They did not work very well since we relied on clichés. We repeated movie scenes instead of finding personal access to conditions of fear and power. A sociodrama member then offered to play Hitler. He portrayed him as a calm, dominating figure. This rather "cruel-father-type" embodiment upset one of our Jewish members. She proceeded to play Hitler in an outburst of anger, screaming and gesticulating violently. The group was taken by surprise, and retreated into silence. Nobody was able to take up the improvisation and transform it into another scene. Frustration spread. The Jewish member felt abandoned by the entire group, and the group was overwhelmed by her. Finally, a German member uttered the wish to slip into his father's skin in order to talk to Hitler, still played by the Jewish woman. The German fellow embodied his own father's youth, and soon an independent play developed. Incorporating a double configuration (son-plays-father), he leaped back into the Nazi era. He told the group about his growing up under the Nazi regime. Since his own father (the player's grandfather) had refused to join the party due to strong Catholic beliefs, he had not been allowed to join the Hitler Youth. Consequently, he was belittled by his friends and comrades as they rose in the Hitler Youth hierarchy.

The sociodrama leader interrupted the story, and asked the player to act out his anger. But the anger — which was now simultaneously his father's as well as the player's own — could not be expressed. The session was concluded at this point (or else it would have developed into individual therapy).

It remained the only guided sociodramatic session which the JGDT attended. We had a first glimpse into the depth and impact which the Holocaust had on our lives. We realized how much this past had determined our upbringing and personalities. We all felt that a psycho- or sociodramatic method was very fruitful for our undertaking. Eventually we decided not to pursue a supervised therapeutic journey further. We wanted instead to examine a variety of methods which would help us to construct a performance. As it turned out, many of our future exercises included therapeutic and cathartic elements.

Physical Exercise:

For some, Wiesel's *Night* was the first exposure to a survivor's story. But even for those who read the book a second time, a sense of despair and sadness pervaded. We were afraid that talk would violate the story's fragile preciousness. It touched us so deeply that dancing to *Night* appeared to be a sacrilegious act.

Yet it was our task to translate words into movements. When we recalled images from Wiesel's imprisonment in Auschwitz and Buchenwald, feelings of entrapment pushed themselves to the foreground. We started improvising these images. But how do you express entrapment through movement? Our struggle to find physical expression for a condition which violated and destroyed any personal space was an accompanying contradiction to our venture. Our freedom to dance spontaneously stood so very much in contradistinction to conditions in death camps. Would not our voluntary experimentation mock the suffering of those who could not escape brutally imposed entrapment?

Like survivors, whose urge to witness is ultimately stronger than their inclination towards silence, we too had to overcome a state of paralysis. We started moving. We used our bodies as suffocating instruments. We enclosed a person with our upright stiff bodies. The person in the center absorbed the claustrophobic situation before reacting to it. Some just gave up and crouched on the floor; others tried to liberate themselves. People forming the circle were not strong enough to prevent the breaking out of an entrapped person, therefore, we changed the exercise and experimented with weight. One person would lay on the floor while the rest of us placed our full weight on top of the person. There was no escape in this configuration. The entrapped person could attempt to writhe and roll around as much as possible, but never succeed in getting free. Playing the entrapped person in turn, each of us would indicate to the group when we had had enough. Some struggled several minutes until soaked with sweat; for others, the pressure of the weight was already so scary and suffocating that they did not even move.

Right and wrong did not exist in this experiment. We learned from the entrapment exercise that defiant and forceful resistance was as much an appropriate response as immobility.

Interview:

We invited a survivor of the Warsaw Ghetto to one of our meetings.[25] We listened to her story for several hours. We were petrified. No one ate; we barely dared sip our tea to clear dry throats. Germans and Jews alike were overwhelmed — some of us cried. Exposure to her fate was one of the most powerful experiences of the JGDT. In our performance we based a solo dance, called "Rye-Bread," on an incident the survivor told us. It was winter when German soldiers once forced her to clean windows with her bare hands. It was so cold that when she splashed water on the glass, it froze immediately. When she feared losing her hands from scraping the ice, she said something in German. Because the soldiers were surprised to hear a Polish Jew speak German, they released her from the cruel work, and gave her a loaf of rye-bread. Although starving, she did not eat a single bite, but tried to smuggle it back into the ghetto to her family. At a final check-point on her way home, however, a gendarme discovered the bread, threw it in the mud, stamped on it, and said: "This bread is too good for a Jew!"

Rehearsals:

The transition from preparation to rehearsal work was marked by a four-day residency.[26] Away from the routine of daily life and worries, the ensemble could plunge into its task. We were not accompanied by any outside observer or director. We alone were responsible for anything that would happen during these days. A spirit of sharing, collaboration, and spontaneous creativity developed. Without the residency, we might not have succeeded in reaching the level of trust from which we gained the courage needed to explore the dangerous territory within which we moved.

Since no time pressure prevented us from experimenting extensively with various approaches and methods, many of the following ideas and exercises originated in the residency.

Warmups:

Every rehearsal began with warmup sessions, including Yoga, a stretching ritual, contact improvisation, work on voice and resonance, dance technique and drama exercises. Besides the different needs of each individual, the JGDT emphasized spine and sound flexibility. Tensions in the back and in the throat are not only of bodily nature but also originate in emotional strain. It is crucial to release these tensions.

To achieve flexibility, we used well-known dramatic exercises.[27] In the context of the Holocaust, simple technical exercises can be more than just warmups; they carry symbolic meaning.[28]

Chinese Mask: This exercise aims at controlling both facial muscles and emotions. It asks people to stay indifferent while inflicting and watching pain.

> Take a partner and stay approximately one foot apart. Look into each other's eyes. One person raises a hand, brings it close to the partner's face, and starts pulling or twisting one particular part of this face (nose, eye, cheek, lips, etc.). You do not actually touch the other's face, but mime a simple movement (slow motion). Nerves and muscles of the tormented facial part respond to the movement of the hand. If, for example, the hand mimes pulling the nose, full concentration is given to the nose. All facial expressions are determined by the imagined pain in the nose. When hand movement and facial expression reach their natural limit, the sequence is reversed. The tormented face slowly returns to its originally calm appearance. During this procedure, the face of the tormentor does not change at all: it should exhibit neither compassion, nor a smile of sadistic pleasure. The goal is to remain completely indifferent.

The "Chinese Mask" is emotionally difficult because it demands that one person identify with the victimizer. Especially in the context of the Holocaust, everyone resists even temporary identification with the torturer. It was, however, important for our work to be able to slip into the skin of the victimizer. Not only did we have to portray Nazis on stage, but we also had to acknowledge our potential to become perpetrators. In particular, German ensemble members had to come to terms with the probability that they would have themselves been Nazis fifty years ago. We practiced the "Chinese Mask" without any specific reference to the Holocaust. It was still frightening and embarrassing to mime the tormenting of faces of our Jewish and German partners.

Guided fantasy: This is a simple but very effective exercise.

The group decides on a question which can be a fantasy, a travel to the unconscious, or analysis of a problem. Everyone lies down on their backs, forming a circle. All heads point to the center and touch each other. Since all heads should be interconnected, no more than 6 persons should be in the circle. Eyes are closed. After a few moments of relaxation, anyone can start talking about the given subject. Each speaker is limited to a few sentences and allows others to join. A situation will be created in which each response inspires the other, and serves as a jumping-off place for the next person.

The heads touch each other. A meditative spirit makes creative listening possible.

A chain of associations leads to deeper and deeper layers of memories, or reaches dizzying heights of fantasy. Nobody in the circle should enforce an artificial ending since the exercise will find its own natural closure. Sessions can last from 15 minutes to over an hour.

When the JGDT used this exercise for the first time, we posed the question : "When did you first hear about the Holocaust?" A Jewish member was able to recall a moment in her childhood when her parents explained the Holocaust in simple terms. None of the three Germans could recall such a decisive moment. The Holocaust had sneaked into their lives, and settled unnoticed in their subconsciousness. Sometimes the Holocaust would emerge, leaving a feeling of shame and uneasiness. One German remembered being a fourth-grader and painting swastikas on a toy airplane. He remembered feeling embarrassed afterwards, although, at that age, he did not know exactly why. The only non-Jewish American of the JGDT recalled images of bad guys and good guys in movies and cartoons. As a child, he used to distinguish them by their badges: the bad guys wore swastikas, the good guys stars and stripes.

Painting: We wanted to get in touch with the issue of forgiveness, and chose painting as our methodological approach. After almost an hour, it became clear that no interaction took place. Instead of reaching out to the "other," everybody became totally enwrapped in their own painting. Frustrated, we stopped the attempt.

Both method and subject matter might explain this failure. On the other hand, painting was unsuitable for strengthening a community sense since everyone showed a somewhat possessive pride in their individual drawings. On the other hand, the theme of forgiveness was difficult to handle. We later tried to apply other methods, but we were never able to find the emotional value or bodily equivalent to this moral entity.

Empty space: A theoretical and practical achievement of experimental drama is the elimination of superfluous techniques, designs, texts, etc. This is accomplished by a return to simple, spontaneous and ritualized movements which call for authentic and nonstereotypical responses.

The "empty space" is an example of this search for authenticity. Performers sit in a large circle. The circle encloses a space which remains empty until spontaneous action takes place in it. Whoever feels moved gets up and starts an improvisation (gesture, speech, song). Each of the others may enter the action spontaneously at any point — and leave it as well, returning to the perimeter until moved to join the action again. All performers, whether in the center or on the periphery, are responsible for the kind of world being created in the "empty space."

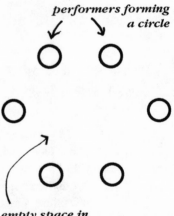

performers forming a circle

empty space in which all action takes place

The "empty space" became a favorite exercise of the JGDT. On one occasion, *Night* was placed in the center of the circle. It inspired one of the most intense improvisations: The Gentile American carefully picked up the book and opened it. A German entered the circle, closed the book, and hid it under his pants. A German woman demanded the return of the book, and started to read from it. A Jewish woman accompanied her rhythmically beating the floor with her fists. It became a haunting rhythm, full of sadness, almost a *Kaddish*. All of a sudden, everybody was in the center, piling up into a heap of bodies. "In every body, I saw myself," someone started to chant repeatedly. A few moments later, another voice was heard, singing: "In every survivor, I saw myself." Somebody got up, started jumping, clapping hands, and crying at the top of her voice: "I don't believe it, I don't believe it." The pile of bodies dissolved. Some returned to the circle, others leaned against each other in despair. The Gentile American seized the other two men, and shouted: "We have to run. Run!" He started running, dragging the two reluctant bodies. Two women started a slow dance by holding each other's hands, and humming: "It's over, it's over." The men, supporting each other, continued running in circles until exhausted. Finally, a woman stepped into the men's pathway and stopped them. The nightmare was over. We had survived. Tired, confused, with tears running down our cheeks, we huddled together, caressing each other. The improvisation had lasted for almost an hour.

We had played ourselves into a trance-like state so that we were unable to recall any of the events. Fortunately, however, the session had been videotaped. Later we reviewed and transformed it into a performance piece.

Improvisation: Most of the JGDT's improvisational work was based on an idea, an object, or a story. The following examples illustrate some of our points of departure.

Books: *Charlotte*[29] was another book which the JGDT used for improvisation. One Jewish member told us how she had immersed herself in the world of Charlotte Solomon as a child. Charlotte was a German Jew who left hundreds of paintings recording her fate. She was killed by the Nazis in southern France. The JGDT interwove both women's stories, past and present, and translated Charlotte's life and paintings into a dance.

Emotions: The feeling of abandonment and separation overshadowed many events of the Holocaust. We formed pairs and then worked in close physical proximity to each other. At a certain point the intimate bond was forcefully broken. Thus we explored the fear of losing our most intimate friend. It eventually developed into a performance dance which was accompanied by the sad tune of *"Tsvey Taybelekh"* ("Two Doves"), a Yiddish love song from the Vilna Ghetto.

Dreams: Sometimes the Holocaust pursued us in our sleep. For the first time in his life, one German member dreamed of Hitler. A Jewish member had a nightmare about a nuclear holocaust: She fled from the explosion, but everyone refused to offer her refuge in their homes. The ensemble sometimes shared and worked with these dreams.

Storytelling: Storytelling was our favorite way to connect our contemporary lives with the Holocaust. "Schnäpschen," a story remembered by a German, was the nickname of a Jewish peddler who used to come to his parents' house to sell brushes. When growing older, the German realized that this peddler had somehow survived the Holocaust. In the performance, the German gently related Schnäpschen's story to the audience, interrupted by a jarring reading of Goebbels' journal entries. The ghostly reappearance of the Nazi minister of propaganda loomed in the background of the stage.

History: "Thorough Work" is a piece about the increasing threat to and destruction of Jewish life in Nazi Germany. Since the JGDT felt uneasy about portraying plain violence — for reasons mentioned in the introduction — we experimented with violations of personal and sacred spaces. We sketched a plot in which a Jewish woman prepares a Shabbat table. Her pathway across the stage is crisscrossed by a waltzing couple, a soldierly underling, and a worker, performing mechanized gestures. The increasing speed of their walking harassed the woman. They bump into her, enclose her, push her around, and finally drag her paralyzed body away. During this interaction, a German woman is scrubbing the floor. The moment the Jewish woman is taken away, she shakes out her cloth — which is the blouse of the Jewish woman.

News: Newspapers can always serve as jumping-off places. Since *"But What About the Holocaust?"* premiered shortly after the election of Kurt Waldheim as Austria's president, we included a satirical sketch about him.

Religion: A German who had studied Protestant theology proposed a piece about the underlying anti-Semitism in Christianity. As a paradigm for Christian hostility towards Jews, he picked the Lord's Prayer. A chorus sang the prayer in the background of the stage while, in the foreground, a Jewish woman was *davvening,* chanting in Hebrew. One actor crisscrossed the stage, repeating in increasing hysteria the Lord's Prayer. He always stopped at the verse "...and forgive us our sins," while alternately covering eyes, ears, and mouth with his hands.

Culture: A Jewish member chose as her thematic jumping-off place cultural differences between Germans and Jews. She assumed that something could be learned about those differences if we would just watch each other eating. Thereupon, she took an apple, bit sensually into the fruit, and slowly consumed it. At first, the group reacted with consternation, until a German joined her improvisation. He took a knife and another apple, peeled it accurately, cut it into four equal parts, and offered the neat and clean slices to the group.

Application: Experimental Drama in the Classroom

"Acting... is a way of making testimony to what we have witnessed — a declaration of what we know and what we can imagine." Joseph Chaikin[30]

The JGDT always had doubts about the possibility of staging a performance about the Holocaust. In the beginning, we committed ourselves only to a journey with an unpredictable outcome. We expected the journey to be difficult and dangerous, but we surrendered to its capriciousness and coincidences. What encouraged us to dare it were vague promises. Our anticipations were not betrayed: despite sweat-soaked shirts , despite stomach cramps caused by tensions and anger, and despite embarrassments which led to hysterical laughter — we were rewarded by moments of authenticity, clarity, and joy.

It is a common mistake to view rehearsals only as preliminary and secondary to performance. Performance theory stresses "that the essential ritual action of theatre takes place during rehearsals."[31] Experimental drama acknowledges the importance of rehearsal periods and even goes so far as to eliminate staged performances altogether. Theatre no longer consists of actors and performers, but performer-participants who engage in ritual actions. This is not the place to discuss whether such steps ultimately contradict the very concept of theatre. What is significant is the proximity of these radical trends in theatre with educational workshops. Rehearsals/workshops provide time and space for extensive experimentation and for playing without being restricted by any pressure to perform. "The workshop is a way of playing around with reality, a means of examining behavior by re-ordering, exaggerating, fragmenting, recombining and adumbrating it. ... Workshops are more important than most people dream of."[32]

Experimental drama developed as a protest against conventional forms of theatre, reacting against the lack of relevance, authenticity, and danger in traditional theatre.[33] Experimental drama rediscovered these three lost moments. Similarities to the task of teaching the Holocaust are obvious: it is a relevant venture, it calls for authentic treatment, and it enters dangerous territory.

Relevance: The dilemma which faces the artist is not so different from that which confronts the teacher: how can suffering on a genocidal scale be adequately expressed in art or brought into the classroom? According to Skloot, modern playwrights who deal with the *Shoah* pursue five objectives: "to pay homage to the victims... ; to educate audiences... ; to produce an emotional response... ; to raise certain moral issues... and to draw a lesson from the events re-created."[34]   The strong educational element in these objectives is easily recognizable.

What needs to be clarified is the relevance of experimental drama techniques for the classroom. While modern playwrights retain text as their focal point, experimental drama stresses context. Not written plays, but free play is given priority. Students in a classroom are neither spectators of a performance, nor actors who are asked to portray a character. They become performer-participants. Their presence, not a display of tricks or technical skills, is what is important. In the context of the Holocaust, performer-participants discover themselves in relation to the Holocaust. Students' reactions to the *Shoah* have priority over preconceived concepts or scripts. Texts can be used as a starting point (the JGDT's use of *Night)*, but are superseded by improvisation. Students explore their emotions and create their own images and associations. Performer-participants are allowed to play themselves and to test out personal responses. They connect levels of their own experience to a history which is only indirectly theirs. The horror of the Holocaust remains incomprehensible, but the distance to it can be bridged. The aim, after all, is to bring the Holocaust down from a mythological and metaphorical realm. If performer-participants take their own presence seriously, they have the chance to retrieve the Holocaust from a distant past. There was nothing ontological or supernaturally predestined about the circumstances, victims, and victimizers of the Holocaust: it was human in the sense that sufferers and perpetrators were ordinary people, and that the endurance of pain or the execution of torture were real acts. Students are encouraged to discover this humanness, and though their dramatic exploration is harsh and strenuous, it entails passionate and occasionally joyful moments. "The joy in theatre comes through discovery and the capacity to discover."[35]

If each playful/dramatic action in a classroom is taken at face value, then performer-participants have to take responsibility for both their fellow students and the success of the play. Every action contributes to or disturbs the flow of improvisation and has repercussions on other students. Exercises like the "Guided Fantasy" or "Empty Space" allow practice of this responsibility since their execution depends on collaboration. At best, improvisation, attentiveness, and a high level of energy culminate in, what Victor Turner calls, "liminal" experiences.[36] Liminal phenomena occur during social transitions. Performer-participants have public permission to take their play seriously. If liminality is temporarily achieved, ambiguity, transformation, and inversion of symbolic behavior are experienced.[37] A successful workshop/rehearsal is like a rite of passage: performer-participants, like initiates, pass through transformations. Richard Schechner calls performances with liminal and transformative power, "transformances."[38]

Ideally a classroom turns into a space for anticipated transformances, for learning is not to perpetuate stereotypes but to challenge them.

Authenticity: Neither teacher/director, nor performer-participants can resolve to achieve liminality. 'Transformances' cannot be imposed — they can only happen. But conditions for their happening can be created.

Every play-process consists of three phases: entering, playing and leaving. Insensitively handled, they can be harmful. There is no formula for a 'good' play, only guidelines.

It is preferable to enter a play slowly. Calm explanations, a short meditation, or simple physical warmups are sufficient. A teacher should know exactly what he or she is doing, and at the same time stay as much in the background as possible. Since students are usually not familiar with dramatic approaches, a period of habituation is necessary in which laughter, embarrassment and a few ridiculous acts are allowed (exaggerated clowning, like immobility, are signs of insecurity). When students become confident as performer-participants, laughter will be replaced by sensitivity and self-discipline.

Normally, the transition into playing happens smoothly. Teachers have to use their skills to keep a balance between guidance and noninterference. The aim is to keep outside input at a minimum level: "The actor doesn't start out with answers about living - but with wordless questions about experience ... The stage performance informs the life performance and is informed by it."[39] Students have to become confident in the validity of their own experience. Authenticity is not achieved if performer-participants either mirror popular conceptions or follow a teacher's instructions. Only by playing one's "most intimate experience"[40] can the mistake of simply duplicating life and replaying stereotypes be avoided. A play about the Holocaust, however, cannot be completely without directives. Free improvisation and nonverbal exercises (such as "Empty Space," "Chinese Mask," or enacting of situations like "Be an animal!") are necessary for relaxation and help to counterbalance thematic intervention. At appropriate points, however, teachers and students together start looking for jumping-off places. Objects, text fragments, concrete images are introduced. Sometimes a method or thematic input may not work. In such cases, authentic responses of students and teachers are nonetheless expected. The impasse must simply be acknowledged. For example, the JGDT stopped painting when we finally realized that this method did not advance any understanding of forgiveness, while the "Empty Space" exercise continued for almost an hour because moments of authenticity kept being achieved.

During a play teachers have to apply three essential rules: sensitive interference, nonjudgmental behavior, and protection. Teachers have to be aware that students who enter a situation in which liminality can occur are extremely vulnerable. Students need time to overcome feelings of awkwardness, and a sense of safety in order to share intimate knowledge. The validity of their actions has to be reassured. Teachers have to become conscious of their role: they can contribute to or disturb the flow of improvisation by too much or too little interference. On the one hand, it is their task to protect the students, on the other hand they should keep their interference at a minimum level. A rash comment can paralyze a student's creativity, whereas a reassuring word can open up unexpected resources. Both students and teachers dread the emergence of passionate emotions. Play-processes, however, have built-in mechanisms to stop dangerous situations. Students develop a fine sensitivity for how far they can go. When a situation exceeds a bearable limit, a common reaction is laughter.[41] Teachers have to learn to trust not only the play-processes, but also the experience, strength, and creativity of their students. Even if the process advances slowly or takes unpredicted turns, teachers have to be patient and should not impose their expectations. In general, teachers tend to make the mistake of providing answers and passing judgements during a play. They should wait until after the play before they share their observations.

The delicate issue for a teacher is to find some balance between conscious interference and the trust to 'let go.' But nothing is as important as protection. Each student has a right, and the need, to be taken seriously. Even if students identify with positions which are inconvenient and conflicting, teachers have to protect them. In a situation in which, for example, a student verbally (or physically) attacks fellow performer-participants, protection is more important than noninterference. "The principle to apply as a piece of advice, and also a warning, is the following: 'First, do not harm.'"[42]

An often-neglected moment is the ending of a play. Trained actors develop their day-to-day rituals for parting. But in workshop situations with lay performer-participants, the moment of leaving a play-environment needs as much attention as the play itself. Students experience ambiguity and role confusion. This disorienting effect is cathartic and transformative only if the return to reality is facilitated by the cast. During this phase, the play has to be re-incorporated into the classroom reality. A break, a meditation, or ritualized actions (such as the JGDT's long embrace after the strenuous "Empty Space" exercise) allow performer-participants to return to their status as students. Extensive discussions and journal writing foster reintegrative processes.

Danger: After a clearly demarcated ending, a group has time to discuss its experience. Teachers listen, and gradually start sharing their observations. When making observations about the performance-participation of particular students, however, the teacher must maintain protection as the first rule.

In general, plays do not provoke conflicts but give expression to already existing problems. Once they are in the open, they can be conscious and worked with. "The workshop is a protected time/space where intra-group relationships may thrive without being threatened by inter-group aggression."[43] The great power of playing is the transformation of hidden emotions into visible and palpable images. Acting out emotions is not automatically cathartic, however, and can even result in the perpetuation of the status quo. This is especially true in regard to the Holocaust where there is a fine line between catharsis and the fostering of stereotypes. If, for example, a student decides to portray a Nazi and while doing so, attracts anger from fellow students which continues after the play is over, that student needs to be protected. Even if the teacher detects some temporary elements of genuine identification on the student's part with the Nazi role, the teacher has to distinguish clearly play from reality. If, on the other hand, a student assumes the role of an anti-Semite and uses it as a vehicle to continually insult Jewish fellow students, a teacher has to interrupt and protect the Jewish students, while at the same time allowing the player to step out of such a role with the least amount of embarrassment.

It is the JGDT's experience that trust and anger are inseparably connected. If we had never been angry, we could not have become truly reconciled. The goal is to distinguish anger from hostility. The aim is to move from unacknowledged hostility (in reality), to expression of anger (in play), and eventually to the awareness and transformation of anger (reintegrative phase). If a play has a strong frame and provides protection, the display of anger is necessary and appropriate. Hostility is anger without a frame. The delicate and crucial issue is to prevent anger (expressed in play) turning into hostility (in reality). This is the reason why the ending of a play needs so much attention. To get people to enter a play is comparatively easy. The real work, and the danger, begins thereafter.

Expression of anger is not to be confused with a naturalistic depiction of violence. The Holocaust is so brutal and harsh that it cannot be reenacted realistically without either retreating to clichés or provoking numbness.[44] Ideally, performer-participants discover for themselves that the Holocaust cannot be understood by trying to show or imitate its violence. After all, the aim of teaching the Holocaust with the help of experimental drama is not to explain — in the sense of exonerating — violence, but to prevent it from happening again. The pedagogical aim is to assist students to the point where they can identify better with conditions of power and powerlessness, separation and entrapment, indifference and fear. It is more effective to find symbolic and surrealistic expression for these conditions. In "Thorough Work," for example, the JGDT experimented with violations of intimate space, instead of displaying violence. Experimental drama emphasizes authentic responses; these emerge only when dimensions are tapped that cause existential reverberation among performer-participants.

In the 1930s, Antonin Artaud envisioned a theatre which would rediscover laughter and danger. He searched for a theatre which would have an immediate and seizing quality. "Like the plague," theatre should be a " spontaneous conflagration " and "an immense liquidation."[45] Artaud did not know that a few years later his vision for a renewal of theatre was surpassed by the chimneys of death camps. The Nazis had turned 'conflagration' and 'liquidation' into a horrible reality.

Today, we are left with Artaud's theatrical vision and the haunting memory of the Holocaust. Applying experimental drama techniques to the teaching of the Holocaust entails risks. I do not think that the danger can be eliminated — despite all pedagogical precautions. The Holocaust, after all, is dangerous knowledge.

---

[1] Wiesel, Elie, *A Jew Today,* New York: Random House, Vintage Books, 1978, p. 234.

[2] *Idem.,* "The Holocaust as Literary Imagination," *Dimensions of the Holocaust,* Evanston: Northwestern U. Press, 1967, p. 16.

[3] Alvin H. Rosenfeld, *A Double Dying: Reflections on Holocaust Literature,* Bloomington: Indiana U. Press, 1980. In order to describe the struggle between language and silence, he calls Holocaust literature "the poetics of expiration" p. 85; Terrence Des Pres, *The Survivor: An Anatomy of Life in the Death Camps,* (New York: Oxford U. Press, 1976) shows that the will to bear witness was an important factor in helping to survive death camps.

[4] Michael Wyschogrod, "Some Theological Reflections on the Holocaust," *Response* 25, (Spring 1975) p. 68. There is an ongoing debate about the relevance of art in regard to the Holocaust. See also Lawrence Langer, *The Holocaust and the Literary Imagination* (New Haven: Yale U. Press, 1975) who affirms the importance of art work dealing with the *Shoah.*

[5] Langer, *op. cit.,* p. 9.

[6] Sontag, Susan, "Syberberg's Hitler," in: *Under the Sign of Saturn,* New York: Farrar, Straus, Giroux, 1980, p. 139; see also her excellent book *On*

Photography, New York: Delta Book, 1977, esp. pp. 19-21 about photographed atrocities.

[7]The line between sensitive works of art and voyeuristic depictions of the Holocaust is a fine one. For movies, see Annette Insdorf, *Indelible Shadows: Film and the Holocaust,* New York: Vintage Book, 1983. One example of a bad movie is Lina Wertmüller's *Seven Beauties.* Another interesting example is *Sophie's Choice.* For Rosenfeld, *op. cit.,* pp. 159-165, William Styron's novel is a negative example for fictional exploitation of atrocities. The film of the book by Alan J. Pakula is considerably better realized; see Insdorf, *op. cit.,* p. 21.

[8]Langer, *op. cit.,* p. 1.

[9]Skloot, Robert, *The Theatre of the Holocaust: Four Plays,* The University of Wisconsin Press, 1982, p. 16.

[10]Goldfarb, Alvin, "Theatrical Activities in Nazi Concentration Camps," *Performing Arts Journal,* 1:2, Fall 1976.

[11]Mirko Tuma, survivor of Theresienstadt (Terezin), writes about theatre in the camp: "... the equation between artistic activities in Terezin and rebellion ... has been in most instances a myth. ... Only the graphic artists and poets captured in their works the true horror of Theresienstadt." Despite the abuse of theatre for propaganda purposes, Tuma concludes that Jewish actors knew how to use drama, "not only to survive and keep some semblance of sanity, but to grow towards universality." (*Idem.,* "Memories of Theresienstadt," *Performing Arts Journal,* 1:2, Fall 1976, pp. 17-18).

[12]For a short introduction to modern playwrights, see Skloot, *op. cit.,* pp. 10-22; for a discussion of Hochhuth and Weiss, and a selected list of modern drama see Rosenfeld, *op. cit.,* pp. 139-159 and p. 207.

[13]Rosenfeld, *op. cit.,* p. 27 even says: "There are no metaphors for Auschwitz, just as Auschwitz is not a metaphor for anything else."

[14]*Ibid.,* p. 181.

[15]Skloot, *op. cit.,* p. 16, names Myrna Lamb's play *Scyklon Z* as an example for misusing Holocaust metaphors for sexual liberation. The same can be said about Wertmüller's film *Seven Beauties.*

[16]There exists an exhaustive debate about "uniqueness versus universality" of the Holocaust; for a good response to the problem, see Emil L. Fackenheim,

"Concerning Authentic and Unauthentic Responses to the Holocaust," *Holocaust and Genocide Studies,* 1:1, 1986. As a German, I am extremely hesitant and careful in drawing comparisons.

[17]The term avant-garde is as ill-defined as experimental theatre. Richard Schechner makes a distinction between historical avant-garde and experimental performances. Under the former, 20th century movements like futurism, surrealism, dada, and post-war movements like poor theatre, environmental theatre, etc., are subsumed. The latter rather describes the rise of formalism in the mid-'70s. (*idem., The End of Humanism,* New York: Performing Arts Journal Publications, 1982). The distinction is somewhat arbitrary but recognizes the important shift of theatre in the mid-'70s. When I talk about experimental drama, I refer to the period of dramatic invention up to mid-'70s with people like Jerzy Grotowski, Joseph Chaikin, The Living Theatre, and all those who continue to work in their legacy.

[18]Artaud, Antonin, *The Theatre and Its Double,* New York: Grove Press, 1958, p. 13 (first published in 1938).

[19]A Traveling Jewish Theatre is still working in San Francisco; Leeny Sack's play is documented in: *The Drama Review (T87)* ("Jewish Theatre Issue"), 24:3, September 1980, p. 113; both Sokolov's and Monk's piece can be seen on film in the Dance Collection, New York Public Library at Lincoln Center.

[20]Ensemble: from America: Lisa Green, Sheila Zagar, Eric Schoefer; from Germany: Bjorn Krondorfer, Brigitte Heusinger von Waldegge, Martin Zeidler.

[21]The JGDT performed publically on several occasions. Short outdoor performances accompanied the ensemble's work throughout 1986. Its first major public appearance, after an intensive four-month preparation, was the May 6th performance of *"But What About the Holocaust?"* The JGDT then took a summer leave and resumed its work in September. The ensemble reworked the script for an October performance in a high security prison. Two days prior to the event, the prison chaplain cancelled the performance for dubious reasons. One of our German members who had rejoined us only for this occasion had to return to his job in Germany without having performed. This cancellation and subsequent loss of two members caused a severe crisis for the ensemble. A new dance piece about the Holocaust, *Engraved Episodes* premiered on December 17th, 1986. The reduced cast included: Lisa Green, Bjorn Krondorfer, Steve Macucci, Sheila Zagar, and Brigitte Heusinger von Waldegge (who directed the piece as part of her MEd in dance). Recently, the JGDT received an invitation to perform in 1988 in Germany, to commemorate the 50th anniversary of the *"Reichskristallnacht."*

[22]Lisa Green and I had known each other from our days with *Bat Kol,* a Jewish Modern Dance Ensemble. In the fall of 1985, she shared her idea of finding Jews and Germans willing to do a piece about the Holocaust.

[23]Since the 1960s, German curricula teach about the Nazi regime and the Holocaust. Nobody, however, teaches Judaism. There are only approximately 30,000 Jews left in West Germany, out of a population of 65 million. For postwar German generations, there is a big discrepancy between images of the destruction of European Jewry and the enormous ignorance about contemporary Jewish culture; see also: Krondorfer, Bjorn, "Holocaust Photographs: Innocence and Corruption," *Christianity & Crisis,* 46:11, Aug. 11, 1986.

[24]*Situations,* a sociodrama group in Philadelphia headed by Dan Estes.

[25]We dedicated our premiere of *"But What About the Holocaust?"* to Edith Millman, survivor of the Warsaw Ghetto.

[26]Fellowship Farms, located near Pottstown, PA, offered the JGDT a residency from March 9-12, 1986.

[27]Helpful works here include: Rubin, S. Lucille (ed.), *Movement for the Actor,* New York: Drama Book Specialists/Publishers, 1980; King, Nancy, *Theatre Movement: The Actor and his Space,* New York: Drama Book Specialists/Publishers, 1971; Penrod, James, *Movement for the Performing Artists,* Palo Alto: National Press Books, 1974.

[28]For example: simply imagine, that a heavy and large stone is placed on your back (your upper body is bent forward). You throw the stone in the air, catch it with the chest, throw it in the air, catch it with the back and so on. Given the Holocaust as thematic context, the stone can symbolize the historical burden which people have to carry.

[29]*Charlotte: Life or Theatre? An Autobiographical Play by Charlotte Solomon,* translated from German by Leila Vennewitz, New York: Viking Press, 1981.

[30]Chaikin, Joseph, *The Presence of the Actor,* New York: Atheneum, 1980, p. 2.

[31]Schechner, Richard, *Essays on Performance Theory 1970-1976,* New York: Drama Book Specialists, 1977, p. 132.

[32]*ibid.,* pp. 60-61; Schechner continues: "Both rehearsal and preparation employ the same means: repetition, simplification, exaggeration, rhythmic

action, the transformation of 'natural sequences' of behavior into 'composed sequences.' ... Thus it is in rehearsals/preparations that I detect the fundamental ritual of theatre." p. 136. Analogies to the work of the JGDT are obvious.

[33]"If people are out ot the habit of going to the theater ... it is because we have learned too well what the theater has been, namely falsehood and illusion. ... Contemporary theater ... has broken away from gravity, from effects that are immediate and painful — in a word, from danger.." Artaud, *op. cit.*, pp. 42, 76.

[34]Skloot, *op. cit.*, p. 14.

[35]Chaikin, *op. cit.*, p. 1.

[36]Turner, Victor, *From Ritual to Theatre, The Human Seriousness of Play,* New York: Performing Arts Journal Publications, 1982. He makes a clear distinction between liminal and liminoid. Liminal phenomena occur in rites of passage, in social transition, which are characterized by ambiguity and the inversion of symbolic behavior. Liminality is a collective experience (such as life cycle rituals), a necessary sociocultural construct of agrarian societies. Liminoid, in contrast, is a social phenomenon in industrialized societies (such as leisure/entertainment). It is less effective as ritual action, because it is voluntary and individualized 'rituals.' Turner's distinction is helpful, but I would not restrict liminal experiences to agrarian cultures. I think that spaces for temporary liminal experiences can be recreated in our society. Workshops/rehearsals with their focus on ritual action are such occasions. Turner himself says that "one works in the liminal, one plays with the liminoid" (p. 55). A successful rehearsal about the Holocaust, despite its play elements, is work.

[37]The JGDT's sociodrama session is one example of a temporary liminal experience. The Jewish woman portraying Hitler was a symbolic role inversion, while the German's son-father-play was an ambiguous configuration. This ritualistic role confusion triggered a transformative process.

[38]Schechner, *op. cit.*, pp. 71 and 120-125.

[39]Chaikin, *op. cit.*, pp. 71 and 120-125.

[40]Grotowski, Jerzy, *Towards a Poor Theatre,* New York: Simon and Schuster, 1968, p. 237. The Polish director who searched for a poor, authentic theatre chose the "via negativa" as acting technique — "not a collection of skills but an eradication of blocks." p. 17. He always reminded his students: "That is really the kernel of the ethical problem: do not hide that which is basic, it makes no

difference whether the material is moral or immoral; our first obligation to art is to express ourselves through our own most personal motives ... Aim always for authenticity." pp. 237, 244.

[41]Chaikin, *op. cit.,* p. 152: "Laughter is a collapse of control in response to something which can't be fitted in the file cabinet of the mind. It is a form of ecstasy, a collapse of reason into a basic clarity."

[42]Grotowski, *op. cit.,* p. 47.

[43]Schechner, *op. cit.,* p. 60.

[44]*Ibid.,* p. 123: "Violence mimetically replicated, or actualized, stimulates more violence. It also deadens peoples' abilities to intervene outside the theatre when they see violence being done."

[45]Artaud, *op. cit.,* p. 27.

Part IV

Surveys and Reports

Chapter Fourteen

The Holocaust as Non-History: Coverage in College Western Civilization Textbooks

Joel Epstein

The growth and development of Holocaust studies in colleges and universities in recent years has been a significant development. Wide varieties of courses taught in different disciplines, and from different perspectives, are offered at institutions across the country. While there is perhaps still opposition among some academics to offering specific courses on the subject, the number of Holocaust courses has grown large. I do not know if there has been any systematic study of enrollment trends in such courses — my own experience, however, at a small church-related liberal arts college is still positive. The enrollment in my course, "Nazism and the Holocaust," has remained steady since first offered in 1979. Moreover, the proliferation of resource material on the Holocaust is enormous; professors have a wide variety of books, articles, films, and video-tapes to choose from while planning their course. Holocaust studies, despite many problems (disagreement in some quarters as to what constitutes a respectable course, questions concerning necessary qualifications for teaching the subject, politization of the subject, and others) appears to have found some place in higher education. The continuing success of scholarly conferences on the Holocaust is further evidence of the impact the subject has had in academe.

The vast majority of college students, however, remain unaffected by these developments. Most students are still not interested in history courses and take only what may be required to graduate. Often that is nothing more than some variation of a Western or World Civilization survey course. How much do students learn about Hitler's "Final Solution" of the Jewish problem by reading today's standard Western and World Civilization textbooks? Is there significant focus in texts on the Holocaust as a major historical event? If there is not, then how may this best be explained? Finally, what suggestions for upgrading coverage of this important subject might be worth considering?

This essay will attempt to address these questions. It is based on an analysis of some twenty-five books, most of them Western and World Civilization texts published between 1966 and 1985. Wherever possible the latest editions have been consulted. One must keep in mind that texts published since the late 1970s might conceivably bear the influence of the proliferation of Holocaust studies. One does not even expect to see the use of the term "Holocaust" before this period. It is generally felt that the 1978 television mini-series of that name helped establish common usage of the term. One is, of course, interested in noting whether there has been significant "rub-off" effect on the general history textbook. If there has been some formidable "rub-off," then we must ask whether this has resulted in the most effective coverage of the Holocaust possible within the limitations of the general text.

One of the first problems to consider is one of perspective. An article entitled "Silence in the American Textbooks," written by Gerd Korman in 1970, confronted this issue directly.[1] His conclusions were based on a sample that included American history, European history, as well as Western and World Civilization texts. Korman argued that for American-trained historians, "Jews as such did not exist. They were nationals of Jewish persuasion." This, argued Korman, "may well have made it impossible for generation after generation of American-trained scholars of European history to recognize the significance of nineteenth and twentieth century Gentile-Jewish relations."[2] The depth of European anti-Semitism, Korman felt, was not sufficiently understood by American writers of European history. Korman went on to show how coverage of the extermination of Europe's Jews was sadly neglected in texts. He pointed out that Jews are omitted from indexes and that chronological charts of events for the years 1939 to 1945 totally omit references to the "Final Solution."[3] References to the plight of the Jews often appear as fringe information or in the context of a discussion of atrocities toward civilians in World War II. Korman does note important exceptions to such treatment, notably by H. Stuart Hughes, Solomon Bloom, and R. R. Palmer and Joel Colton.[4] He shows how texts by these authors demonstrate a genuine sensitivity to the twentieth century tragedy that befell Europe's Jews. A few historians at least showed an in-depth understanding of the "Jewish presence in European society" and integrated such material into texts in the early and mid-60s.[5]

Most of the examples considered here are from works published since Korman's article was written. One thing remains clear: There is still a problem of perspective for historians treating this topic in a general text. For many, the subject is still regarded as an "add on" to chapters on the Second World War. It is included but usually given significantly less attention than the military history of the War. In some instances historians seem more comfortable discussing Nazi anti-Semitism in Germany in the 1930s than they do writing about the "Final Solution."

An *extreme* example is that of Stipp, Dirrim and Hollister, *The Rise and Development of Western Civilization* (vol. II, 1972). Perhaps one would not expect to find a Western Civilization text that could fail to even mention the fate of the Jews during World War II. In bewilderment I made such a discovery. In their chapter dealing with the 30s, the authors refer to the Nazi ideas of an "Aryan elite," indicating "that the worst corruptions of virtuous blood were the Jews." "The implication was obvious," they go on, "as the bearers of the highest culture, Germans were under solemn obligation to harry all Jews out of the coming Aryan dominated world."[6] One thing is certain, with that statement Jews were in fact harried out of this particular textbook. The authors immediately go on (on the same page) to discuss what they call "Three Nazi Bases" — "Anti-Christianity," "Antisociety" and "Antihumanity." For some reason Anti-Semitism is omitted from this category.[7]

Inadequate coverage of Nazi anti-Semitism, however, is followed by "noncoverage" of the extermination of the Jews by the Nazis. One searches in vain for any mention of this in Chapter XV, "The World at War Again: 1939-1945." To be certain Hiroshima is referred to under a section entitled "Effects of the War." The authors indicate that "the cost in human life and suffering and in material goods is beyond any reasonable calculation." They mention an estimated 20 million military and civilian casualties in the Soviet Union, millions of Chinese casualties, and the fact that "in Germany *air raid casualties alone,* military and civilian, approximated one million; more than three million German soldiers were killed in battle."[8] Thus there is specificity in mentioning German victims of the War (I am not suggesting that there is anything wrong with that) but absolutely no mention of the main victims of Nazism — Europe's Jews. They also go on to discuss slave labor and mass abuse of the populations of Poland, Belgium, the Netherlands, and Italy. There is, however, no mention of Auschwitz or for that matter any camp and again no mention of Jews.

In writing to the authors of this text and confronting them with my finding, I stated:

"I am not writing this letter in the spirit of vindictiveness. I am a historian attempting to do research on a complex subject. While I realize that sensitivity to the dimensions of the Holocaust has increased significantly since you wrote this book, I find it hard to imagine that such a subject would be totally omitted from a Western Civilization text. I trust the omission was an oversight. If you have any recollection of why this subject was omitted I would very much appreciate hearing from you."

Professor Stipp, who wrote the part of the text in question, took issue with some of my claims, but admitted "puzzlement" at his "failure to include in the Nazi Chapter a reference, and an adequate, proper reference, to the Hitler-Himmler decision to exterminate all the Jews they could possibly exterminate." He adds, "Why I did not include proper treatment of this as a historic fact I simply don't know, to my mortification."[9]

While this was the only example of "non-coverage" of the topic, I found several that were clearly "inadequate." J. R. Major, *Civilization in the Western World* (1966) briefly refers to Nazi anti-Semitism and later states that "Jews, Communists, and other undesirables were exterminated." Auschwitz is mentioned, the extermination process is briefly described, and the author indicates that "the Jew virtually ceased to exist in central and eastern Europe." An entire paragraph is devoted to the persecution of the Slavs, and while references to the plight of the Jews appear, there is no specific treatment of the "Final Solution" as planned, deliberate government policy. This work like many relatively early texts merely *includes* Jews among those persecuted by the Nazis.[10] William McNeill, *History of Western Civilization: A Handbook* (1969) refers to Nazi ideology by stating: "A second Nazi peculiarity was extreme antisemitism justified by the assertion that Jews were of a different race from true Germans and therefore natural rivals and indeed enemies." The book's brief section on World War II makes no mention of the Jews and their fate under the Nazis. While this is a handbook rather than a full length text, one would at least hope for some recognition of the subject. Perhaps, however, one should not be surprised given the naive statement that "extreme antisemitism" was a "peculiarity."[11]

In F. Roy Willis's *Western Civilization: An Urban Perspective* (1973), Nazi policies toward Jews in the 30s are briefly mentioned and "the death of at least six million Jews" is mentioned in one sentence along with "hundreds of thousands of other victims — members, or suspected members of resistance movements, many of the East European intelligentsia, gypsies, the chronically sick."[12] Once again, Jews are included among other victims and the dimensions of Nazi policy toward them is neglected. Harrison and Sullivan, *A Short History of Western Civilization* (1979) mentions in two sentences that "the Nazis embarked upon a program to exterminate all Jews"... and "murdered 6 million... out of a world total of 15 million." Once again, however, discussion of the subject is included within the context of Nazi repressive policies, and much more time is spent discussing policies toward Christian churches than in covering the "Final Solution."[13] Thomas Greer, *A Brief History of Western Man* (1982) writes of Nazi plans for a "Final Solution," however, when discussing the process refers to a "ruthless program of extermination of all Jews and a portion of the Slavic peoples, whom they regarded as racially inferior (*Untermenschen*)." Coverage ends there. Despite the recent publication date (the book is in its 4th edition), the term "Holocaust" is not used.[14]

A widely used text, Walbank, Taylor, Bailkey, Jewsbury, Lewis and Hackett, *Civilization Past and Present*, 8th edition, (1981) has improved its coverage of the subject from earlier editions. The treatment of the persecution of the Jews by the Nazis is respectably covered and a subheading, "The Unspeakable Holocaust" is used for a concise treatment of the "Final Solution." It is pointed out that this policy "was done by educated bureaucrats and responsible officials from a civilized nation." This "made the act all the more chilling and incredible." While the coverage is still too brief, the text does contain an effective photo of Bergen Belsen.[15]

Several texts do contain adequate treatment of the topic and some even cover it reasonably well. A 1969 text, Roland N. Stromberg, *A History of Western Civilization* focuses on the "Final Solution" (the term is used) concisely, recognizing the distinctive nature of the crime against the Jews. While the number of Jewish victims is erroneously estimated at 4.5 million, the text recognizes the purpose and intensity of Nazi policy and strengthens its coverage by devoting an entire page to two potent photos.[16] The latest editions of both the Western (1984) and World Civilization (1982) texts by Edward McNall Burns contain barely adequate coverage of the topic. The narrative in these works indicates that Jews were singled out for total annihilation, although their fate is still discussed in the broader context of the fate of several groups. Coverage is far too brief and the terms "Final Solution" and "Holocaust" are not to be found. The inclusion of some good photos strengthens what must be termed very mediocre treatment in both Burns volumes.[17]

Three texts with somewhat better treatment of the subject are Kagan, Ozment, and Turner, *The Western Heritage Since 1684* (1974), Craig, Graham, Kagan, Ozment, and Turner, *The Heritage of World Civilizations* (1986) and Brinton, Christopher, Wolff and Winks, *A History of Civilization* (1984). The Kagan text has solid treatment of Nazi anti-Semitic policies of the 1930s (the actual Nuremberg Laws are included) and a short section on the extermination policy that mentions the "Holocaust" by name. Two excellent photos supplement the narrative.[18] *The World Civilization* text (Craig, Graham, Kagan, Ozment, and Turner) has the identical narrative and photos as the Kagan text, but adds a citation from an eyewitness account of mass murder of Jews in the Ukraine in 1942.[19] The 6th edition of the Brinton text solidly discusses Nazi anti-Semitism of the 30s and clearly and graphically depicts the process of the "Final Solution." It uses the term "Holocaust" and is one of the few texts to mention the "bystander" problem:

> "After the war many people would ask why Germans who knew of this systematic killing had not protested it;... why the Western Allies, who though surprised by the extent but well aware of the camps had not made them early targets of liberation; why the pope had not spoken out, especially with respect to nominally Catholic countries such as Poland and Austria; or why the Jews themselves had not organized more systematic resistance within the camps."[20]

This text's coverage clearly ranks among the best. It treats the subject intelligently, with sensitivity, and raises some important questions about outsider responsibility.

There are other works which cover the topic quite well given the limitations of a general text. A 1975 work, Eadie, Geanakoplos, Hexter, and Pipes, *Western Civilization*, refers briefly to Nazi anti-Semitism of the 30s, but includes a subheading in the chapter on World War II entitled "Mass Murder of European Jews," within which the process of the "Final Solution" is discussed solidly. "Every period has had its massacres, and every nation has been guilty at some time of spilling innocent blood. But never before had a whole ethnic or racial group been condemned to die, for no reason and without possibility of reprieve, and the sentence carried out in so meticulous and cold-blooded a manner." The uniqueness of the Holocaust is clearly recognized. In addition, the work discusses the apathy of other nations, the paucity of rescuers, and the fact that only a "fraction" of the estimated 50,000 people who participated in the Jewish slaughters were ever brought to trial. The whole subject is handled in a forthright manner.[21]

Strayer and Gatzke, *The Mainstream of Civilization Since 1660* (1984) covers the "Final Solution" by featuring an eye-witness account of mass gassing. The text narrative is too brief, but the use of this long quote from a primary source helps make the coverage above average. It should be noted, however, that despite the 1984 publication date, the term "Holocaust" is not used.[22] Perry, Chase, Jacob, Jacob, Von Laue, *Western Civilization* (1985) offers an excellent account of 1930s anti-Semitism under the sub-heading "The Jew as Devil." Nazi racist anti-Semitism is explained better than in any other text. In the chapter on World War II, under the sub-heading, "Extermination," the "Final Solution" is thoroughly handled by three long primary source quotations. The account mentions the Einsatzgruppen, the participation of "Ukrainian, Lithuanian and Latvian auxiliaries" as well as the role of German industry in the process. The "Holocaust" is defined as an event in Jewish history in an account that is perhaps slightly flawed by a failure to deal with the by-stander problem. The impact of the TV program *Holocaust* in West Germany is even mentioned in a later chapter.[23] The account of the subject in the Perry text ranks overall as the best to date. The topic is discussed solidly and with a sensitivity still lacking in many texts.

The same cannot be said of two other texts accounts by the same team of authors. The Western and World Civilization texts (published in 1983 and 1984, respectively) by McKay, Hill and Beckler contain duplicate coverage of the topic. The treatment is too brief, but recognizes the uniqueness of the Nazi policies toward the Jews and calls "the extermination of the European Jews" "the ultimate monstrosity" of Nazism. Brevity hampers the coverage in these texts, however, and despite their recent publication neither uses the term "Holocaust."[24]

In addition to the texts discussed, books on twentieth century Europe, three books on World War II, and two high school level general texts were also consulted. While I will not discuss my findings specifically in this essay, I would note that I encountered wide variations in the quality of coverage, and the treatment of the topic in the two secondary texts was better than that found in many of the college level works.[25]

What conclusions can be reached from this attempt to assess the coverage of the Holocaust in general college texts? In returning to the questions posed earlier I realize perhaps more than ever how complex a problem this is. Any suggestions for change are offered in the hope of stimulating interest in the subject and provoking reexamination of general text coverage of the Holocaust. First, it is clear that several texts have upgraded their treatment of the subject and that many works deal with it with intelligence and sensitivity. Some even offer concentrated sub-sections of chapters that discuss the "Final Solution" and its many facets and implications. If there are some good models, perhaps all that is needed is to get the other texts to emulate the better ones in future editions.

The problem, however, is far more complex and requires a more sophisticated approach. The fact remains that even in the best general text accounts, the Holocaust is not treated as a major historical event. The persecution and subsequent annihilation of Europe's Jews is discussed in chapters covering the rise of Fascism and World War II, respectively. The student reads something about the Nazi persecution of German Jews in the 1930s and one or two chapters later learns about the extermination of Europe's Jews. Text books are essentially narratives of history and the Holocaust is included in varying degrees within the narrative of the Second World War. Even the texts that cover the Holocaust solidly devote far more space to the military history of the War. For example, it is known that trains badly needed to refurnish the war effort in Russia were often used instead to deport Jews to killing centers in Poland. The extermination of the Jews was the main priority of the Nazis and the war effort suffered because of this priority. Unfortunately Western Civilization texts do not emphasize this vitally important historical fact.

Textbook writing is a process based on models established years ago. When World War II became history, it naturally found its place in texts as a monumental event in this century. No one is arguing that it does not deserve such status. The extermination of the Jews is, however, still treated as a "sub-event," to be discussed within the framework of Nazism and World War II. Other "aspects" of the Second World War such as the origins of the Cold War and the beginning of the nuclear age have spawned full-fledged topical treatment in general texts. Unfortunately, however, many in the history profession still regard courses on the Holocaust as "faddish." Moreover, I am convinced that many historians still do not realize that anti-Semitism was the very core of Nazism itself. There is still not complete realization that hatred of the Jews was to quote Lucy Dawidowicz, at the very "center of Hitler's mental world."[26] Is it any wonder that the topic is still relegated to "sub-status" in survey texts? Perhaps there still has not been enough sensitizing about the importance of the subject to bring significant changes in the way in which it is presented to the general student.

What then is a realistic prescription for change? As desirable as it may be to have an entire chapter devoted to the Holocaust in a Western Civilization text, this is not, in my view, a realistic goal. Editors would argue that our century has been saturated by mass murder and violence and claim that a general text must at least aim at being all-inclusive. Why not then have texts include an analytical chapter on the subject of violence in the twentieth century? The chapter might be called "The Cult of Violence in the Twentieth Century" or "Violence and Mass Death in the Twentieth Century." Such a chapter should come toward the end of the volume and thus encompass the century up to the present. The importance of trench warfare in World War I as a conditioning process for mass death, a process whereby human life was cheapened considerably, might introduce such a chapter.[27] Examples besides the Holocaust might include the Armenian genocide, the Stalinist collectivization and purge policies, horrors against civilians during World War II, including the controversiality of the American use of the atomic bomb, the genocide in the miniscule African nation of Burundi in the 1960s, and the more recent tragic events in Cambodia, among others. Events would be analyzed individually and carefully and *not* generally or loosely compared with one another. The purpose would *not* be to compare Hiroshima or My Lai with Auschwitz and suggest that the Americans have been as bad as the Nazis. Too much "comparative morality" takes place already and merely minimizes the scope and importance of the Holocaust, particularly in the eyes of the naive student. I am not suggesting increased trivialization. An analytical chapter on twentieth century mass violence can evaluate the importance of several events while reinforcing the fact that the twentieth century has been far and away the bloodiest in history. The Holocaust and its implications can be treated more effectively than it currently is even in the best of texts. The persecution of the Jews in Germany in the 1930s can be discussed in continuity with the "Final Solution" without a break of one or two chapters, allowing students to see more clearly the progression of Hitler's anti-Semitism. The specifics of Nazi intent, and procedure, would be carefully discussed. Furthermore the plight of non-Jewish victims of Nazism would be accurately explained. It can be made clear that while not all victims of Nazi horrors were Jews, all Jews were victims. The importance of Christian anti-Semitism, the church, the policies of the U.S. and Britain as well as the somewhat controversial issue of Jewish resistance can all be treated. Moreover, the legacy of the Holocaust for today's world can be carefully reviewed. In this latter context post-1945 examples of genocide would be discussed.

Perhaps this overall suggestion sounds too ambitious. Am I not proposing the condensation of an entire book on the Holocaust into a few pages of a Western Civilization text chapter? Words would have to be used carefully and such a chapter would require careful planning. I feel, however, that this type of analytical chapter on violence is not only possible, but would greatly strengthen today's general texts. Students would see more clearly the impact that senseless violence and mass murder has had on our times. They would also gain a better understanding of the Holocaust, the ultimate horror of our century. Textbooks have been deficient in covering this subject for too long. It is time members of the academic community pressured for significant change.

---

[1] Gerd Korman, "Silence in the American Textbooks," *Yad Vashem Studies on the European Jewish Catastrophe and Resistance,* VIII, 1970, pp. 183-202.

[2] Korman, pp. 185-86.

[3] Korman, pp. 197-98.

[4] Korman pp. 194-98. Specifically he discusses H. Stuart Hughes, *Contemporary Europe: A History* (1961), Solomon F. Bloom, *Europe and America; The Western World in Modern Times* (1961), and Palmer and Colton, *A History of the Modern World* (1965).

[5] Korman, p.198.

[6] Stipp, Dirrim and Hollister, *The Rise and Development of Western Civilization,* II, 1972, p. 652.

[7] Stipp, Dirrim and Hollister, pp. 652-54.

[8] Stipp, Dirrim and Hollister, pp. 730-32.

[9]I wrote identical letters to Professors Stipp, Dirrim and Hollister (January 15, 1986). I received replies from Stipp (January 31, 1986) and Hollister (January 29, 1986). Hollister said he wrote the medieval sections of the text and never reviewed other parts of it. "The omission," he adds, "does seem extremely peculiar. It may well have contributed to the book's dropping out of print after a few good years."

I would like to add that Professor Hollister edited a source book, *Landmarks of the Western Heritage* (Wiley, 1967), which contained a document describing Nazi medical experiments as well as an excerpt from Rudolf Hoess's testimony about his efficiency as commandant of Auschwitz. (See *Landmarks...* II 369-73).

[10]Russel Major, *Civilization in the Western World* (Lippincott, 1966), pp. 510, 580-82.

[11]William H. McNeill, *History of Western Civilization: A Handbook* (rev. ed., University of Chicago Press, 1969) p. 636.

[12]R. Ray Willis, *Western Civilization: An Urban Perspective* vol. II, (D.C. Heath, 1973), pp. 887, 906-907.

[13]John B. Harrison and Richard E. Sullivan, *A Short History of Western Civilization* II (5th ed., Knopf, 1979), pp. 662-64.

[14]Thomas P. Greer, *A Brief History of Western Man* (4th ed., Harcourt, Brace and Jovanovich, 1982), pp. 500, 509.

[15]Walbank, Taylor, Bailkey, Jewsbury, Lewis, Hackett, *Civilization Past and Present* II, (8th ed., Scott Foresman, 1981), pp. 372-73, 422-23.

[16]Roland N. Stromberg, *A History of Western Civilization* (rev. ed., Doresey Press, 1966), pp. 811-13. The famous Warsaw ghetto picture of the small boy with his hands raised is included along with one of a mass grave at Bergen Belsen.

[17]See Burns, Lerner, Mecham, *Western Civilizations* II, (10th ed., Norton, 1984), pp. 973- 1003.

Burns, Ralph, Lerner, Mecham, *World Civilizations*, II (7th ed., Norton, 1986), pp. 1126-27, 1271, 1301.

[18]Kagan, Ozment and Turner, *The Western Heritage Since 1684* (Macmillan, 1979), pp. 884-85, 910.

[19]Craig, Graham, Kagan, Ozment and Turner, *The Heritage of World Civilizations* (Macmillan, 1986), pp. 1123-24, 1153-55.

[20]Brinton, Christopher, Wolff, Winks, *A History of Civilization* II (6th ed., Prentice Hall, 1984), pp. 335-36, 407-08.

[21]Eadie, Geanakoplos, Hexter, Pipes, *Western Civilization* II, (2nd ed., Harper & Row, 1975), pp. 381, 406-08.

[22]Joseph Strayer and Hans W. Gatzke, *The Mainstream of Civilization Since 1660* (4th ed., Harcourt, Brace and Jovanovich, 1984), pp. 758-59, 778-79.

[23]Perry, Chase, Jacob, Jacob, Van Laue, *Western Civilization,* II, (2nd ed., Houghton Mifflin, 1985), pp. 774-75, 796-98, 823.

[24]See McKay, Hill and Buckler, *A History of Western Society,* II, (2nd ed., Houghton Mifflin, 1983), pp. 1040-41, 1047, 1054-56; also McKay, Hill and Buckler, *A History of World Societies,* II, (Houghton Mifflin, 1984), pp. 1340-41, 1347, 1354-56.

[25]See Frank Elweis, *New Dimensions of World History* (Van Nostrand, 1969), pp. 551-52, 564-65; also Leonard F. James, *The Western World Today,* (Pergamon Press, 1973), pp. 68-70.

[26]Lucy Dawidowicz, *The War Against the Jews* (Holt, Rinehart and Winston, 1975), p. 4.

[27]The significance of World War I in this process, and the significance of the battles of the Somme and Verdun in particular, has been argued best by Richard Rubenstein in *The Cunning of History* (Harper & Row, 1978), ch. 1, "Mass Death and Contemporary Civilization," pp. 1-21.

Chapter Fifteen

Problems Related to Knowledge Utilization in Elementary and Secondary Schools

Marilyn B. Feingold, Ed.D.

This chapter examines the relevance of the current status of research on knowledge use and school improvement for teaching about the Holocaust at the elementary and secondary levels. Knowledge use, as used here, is information based on evidence derived from scientific research, from practice, or from both. Knowledge can reside in ideas, theories, explanations, advice, and in "things," such as programs, materials or technologies (cited in Kane and Lehming, 1981).[1] Based on the current research literature, knowledge use, as employed in this paper, refers to policies or efforts to promote the applications of such knowledge in the practice setting. Several important questions need to be explored: What lessons for public policy can be drawn from the current research? In more specific terms, what does the research on diffusion mean to the Holocaust educator? How might we generate support for education about the Holocaust most effectively? The chapter further explores the role the NDN (National Diffusion Network) plays as a key federal mechanism for promoting knowledge utilization in our schools.

THE DISSEMINATION OF HOLOCAUST EDUCATION

Statement of Problem

The Holocaust, and the extent of public awareness of its meaning, became a national issue growing out of President Reagan's May 1985 visit to the World War II German Army cemetery at Bitburg. The major attention given to the issue by the media awakened sensitivity to the Holocaust and World War II. But the nature of the many comments that arose suggested limited awareness about the causes of the Holocaust, and the breadth of support for Nazism in Germany during the period of the Third Reich. While there is some excellent teaching about Nazi Holocaust in public and private elementary and secondary school classrooms across the country, Holocaust education, as critical as it is, seems nevertheless to be in a severely precarious position. One educator summed up the situation appropriately when he stated, "We are fighting an uphill battle because of some 25 years of poor teaching, of emphasizing the forces of evil fighting the forces of good, of assuming that everyone was either like Hitler or insanely racist, and of bombarding or assaulting students and the public with catalogues of atrocities both verbally and visually."[2]

Recent conference proceedings and current status reports prepared by the B'nai B'rith Anti-Defamation League emphasize that even in school systems such as New York City, Vineland (New Jersey), Brookline (Massachusetts) and Great Neck (New York) where there are individuals with the worthiest of personal and pedagogical motivations, not all that is happening in the name of Holocaust education is commendable. There are the obvious dangers of faddism, trivialization, oversimplification, preoccupation with the morbid, or the use of the Holocaust as a metaphor for all of society's ills. Despite the increasing recognition of the educational values inherent in teaching the Holocaust phenomenon, many teachers are not sufficiently knowledgeable on the topic and are not appropriately trained to deal with the sensitive material involved.

The experiences of introducing Holocaust education in Baltimore and vicinity exemplify what is true nationwide. The Baltimore City School System has prepared a booklet which is used in most of that city's schools. Baltimore County has also introduced the topic into its curriculum. Although both programs are written in manuals, implementation is difficult because teachers are not prepared. Most teachers learn about World War II in schools and do not really understand the full impact or implications of what they are teaching. In some cases a teacher will call the Baltimore Jewish Council (a local organization which is part of the Jewish Federation) for a speaker; the teacher is then referred to a Second Generation person or a survivor. When the survivor or a child of survivor asks exactly what has been taught, the usual reply is: 1) Hitler and how he came to power; b) Location of camps; c) Six million Jews were killed; d) What do you suggest? is a common question; e) Could you please come and speak — how many classes are you willing to speak to?

The guest speaker must educate and really understand what is asked of him/her. This is a very difficult undertaking because one does not know where to begin. Many guest speakers who are survivors are apprehensive and rightly so. They come to tell their story without an appropriate preparation or follow up, because of a lack of training and knowledge on the part of the teachers.

The afternoon Jewish School and Jewish Day Schools are in even worse shape with regard to Holocaust curriculum. Most Jewish schools have a *Yom HaShoah* Commemoration usually featuring a film. The students have very little background prior to seeing the film. They come in and walk out without any real understanding of the subject matter. In-class teaching of the Holocaust in most Day Schools is minimal, prepared curricula are lacking, and what exists is primarily for upper school children, leaving lower school children virtually out of the picture. In some instances, since *Yom HaShoah* is so close to *Yom Ha'atzmaut* and *Pesach*, it is totally overlooked.[3]

Many of the problems related to educating about the Holocaust derive from the fact that there are limits to what we can grasp intellectually regarding the sequence of events that led to the Final Solution. The focus of this paper is on other fundamental questions which need to be raised in regard to how best to link knowledge about the Holocaust or about the dissemination thereof with classroom practice. Whose job is it to promote the diffusion of this information? What guidelines exist to help individuals and groups determine that the information they have is accurate, and that the programs they develop have impact?

Current educational research shows that the three states in dissemination — initiation, implementation, and incorporation — involve activities and decisions and that the significance of key people and issues change as a project moves from one state to another. Frequently, the fate of an innovation depends on the complex interplay among characteristics of the innovative product itself and the institutional setting it seeks to change. How to transfer fundamental "good" teaching practices to classrooms, where traditional modes of teaching have ignored the subject of the Holocaust and have not allowed for discussion of controversy, poses many important considerations.

Much of the literature on the topic of curriculum change extols the importance of Linking Agents and Local School Facilitators. An active ongoing liaison between these individuals and the Users of the curriculum appear to be crucial to the quality of replication at each site. Our challenge is to identify and use an effective model which connects the Linking Agents with the Local School Facilitators and the Users to disseminate Holocaust education effectively.

Recently at a National Diffusion Network Conference, a presentation was made by Lee Wickline about the successes of the National Diffusion Network as a diffusion process for school improvement. This process addresses the dissemination needs outlined above by recognizing and supporting the key people involved in facilitating the process of change. National Diffusion Network activities are concerned with encouraging adoptions of proven exemplary educational projects and dissemination processes which have been identified and documented by the program. The NDN deserves close examination for potential transferability to the area of disseminating Holocaust education. To examine a possible mapping of the NDN process onto dissemination of Holocaust education programs, the next section of this paper describes the key characteristics of the NDN process.

THE NATIONAL DIFFUSION NETWORK

In 1974, the U. S. Office of Education established the National Diffusion Network (NTN) to help communities improve their local educational systems through the adoption (or adaptation) of projects that had been judged exemplary by a panel of experts.

The NDN's purpose has always been simple: to offer local schools a chance to adopt at low cost a variety of high-quality education projects that have been developed by classroom teachers and proved effective in their work with students.

As part of the process of enabling schools to make adoptions, NDN projects provide in-service training to the teachers and other educators who are responsible for making the adopted projects work in their new sites.

The NDN operates principally through its Developer/Demonstrators and the State Facilitators. Developer/Demonstrators are local school staff who have developed an "exemplary project" and who are then funded to train educators to understand and use their project. State Facilitators are located in each state to connect schools seeking new practices with potentially helpful Developer/Demonstrators. As part of their work, the State Facilitators survey school needs in their state, help arrange informational exchanges, and provide implementation assistance.

In the same way that the NDN links schools, most secondary institutions, and other organizations within and across state boundaries so that programs developed and proven effective in one locality can be used by others facing similar challenges, a national delivery system of Holocaust education would provide a mechanism with the goal of helping people in education learn about successful Holocaust programs.

For a project to achieve an exemplary rating and thus become eligible for dissemination support from the NDN, it must receive the approval of the Joint Dissemination Review Panel (or JDRP). This panel examines evidence of project effectiveness and determines whether the persuasive evidence exists consistent with the claims and goals of the project.

"JDRP," with respect to a Holocaust program, means that a program has met certain objectives. "Programs" as used here, is understood to refer to general intellectual and pedagogical frameworks and approaches for teaching the Holocaust. They allow for flexibility in terms of each unit, detail, and materials used. In general, the following objectives would be utilized: 1) to teach the uniquely Jewish experience of the Holocaust and its universal implications; 2) to document the socio-cultural processes of Nazi racism; 3) to understand human motivation to survive in extreme situations; 4) to demonstrate the results of collapse of democratic structures and the disruption of the judicial process; 5) to expose the trivialization of the Holocaust; 6) to nurture humanistic values in a depersonalized, technological society; 7) to instill a sense of mutual respect and tolerance between people of different religious affiliations and ethnic origins; and 8) to describe contemporary genocidal policies and practices (Pfefferkorn, 1984).[4]

Passing the Joint Disseminator Review Panel (JDRP) screening qualifies the "exemplary program" for dissemination funding from the NDN and other federal sources. In the case of approved Holocaust programs, dissemination funding would also be available to assure meaningful Holocaust education in the public and private schools at all levels.

PROJECT AHEAD

The work of the United States Holocaust Memorial Council and the leadership of its Office of Education is required to facilitate the implementation of high quality curricula and instruction related to the Holocaust in the schools of our nation. PROJECT AHEAD[5] refers to the services the USHMC would provide as it Assists in Holocaust Education Adoptions and Dissemination.

PROJECT AHEAD is a program of the U. S. Holocaust Memorial Council (USHMC) which seeks to broaden the role of Holocaust education in the life of a neighborhood, town, city, county, region, or state. Through PROJECT AHEAD, the Council will assist communities in determining for themselves the ways in which Holocaust education can become a more important element in the community.

PROJECT AHEAD is based on the idea that the organized interaction of a community's diverse interests is a constructive process which can result in new and exciting visions of the community's cultural environment. Thus PROJECT AHEAD seeks to stimulate and encourage many community interests to come together and explore the ways in which Holocaust education can become an integral part of community life.

GETTING EDUCATORS INVOLVED: GOALS

Among its goals, PROJECT AHEAD is intended to: 1) Initiate a process to evaluate the nature and extent of Holocaust programming, in cooperation with existing Holocaust centers and related education institutions,[6] teachers, school supervisors, community leaders and appropriate educational experts; 2) Identify criteria for assessing the effectiveness of various aspects of Holocaust programming in deepening understanding of the lessons of the Holocaust; 3) Utilize these criteria to foster local assessments of Holocaust programming; 4) Develop strategies and approaches for enhancing future Holocaust programming in public and private schools at all levels; 5) Serve as a clearinghouse for Holocaust and Genocide-related curriculum projects and materials; 6) Develop a

Speakers' Bureau which would provide access to survivors, scholars, curriculum specialists. etc., by school districts interested in developing or extending Holocaust Education; 7) Sponsor national and/or regional invitational conferences and seminars designed to provide opportunities for presenting and exchanging ideas on relevant curriculum materials, activities, resources and methodology; to serve as a forum to discuss issues related to implementation strategies, i.e., how can an interested principal/supervisor/superintendent generate local interest?; how can they provide training experiences for teachers? Undoubtedly, the prestige of the Council would serve to generate a broader and deeper interest in the subject on a national scale; 8) Commission studies and problem-solving retreats involving university and public school educators to deal with the many controversial aspects of the content. For example, comparisons between the Holocaust and the Armenian Genocide have brought sharp criticisms from Turkish Studies groups and need to be studied in the context of learning the similarities and differences between the events; Polish-American groups and some Catholic organizations object to materials which may tend to portray some of their respective group members in a negative light and these issues deserve appropriate examination. Public school teachers need clear guidance on these issues to assure that what we teach is defensible from an historical perspective; 9) Sponsor intensive teacher training programs throughout the country using prominent historians to address nuances in the interpretation of historical content, and successful public school teachers to provide the "nuts and bolts" of how to implement Holocaust Studies successfully in the classroom; 10) Recognize students and teachers who have participated in the Council essay contest; 11) Provide awards/incentives for teachers who have initiated programs of Holocaust study.

CONSUMER VALIDATION:
FOCUS ON DISSEMINATION OBJECTIVES

The emphasis needs to be on involving teachers in Holocaust education and on shifting improvements in teaching from the University/Holocaust Center setting to the children in classrooms where it must ultimately be put to the test. To accomplish this, PROJECT AHEAD would identify the Linking

Agents/Facilitators to operate under the auspices of the United States Holocaust Memorial Council Office of Education. These Linking Agents/Facilitators would help to bridge the gap between knowledge about the Holocaust (the range of professional, print and nonprint resources available) and the practitioners' use of the knowledge. The Linking Agents would accomplish their tasks through a multifaceted plan: 1) They would provide technical consultation to assist teachers in making specific matches between their needs and styles and the materials or methods available. Their ability to work would be enhanced because they would not be tied to one curriculum or concept; 2) They would provide on-going sustained communication with the teachers and their school systems. There would be a flow of information and support in the form of idea exchange and further material acquisition; 3) They would develop and disseminate a manual of "practice profiles" of Holocaust curricula.

ACTION STEPS: IMPLEMENTING PROJECT AHEAD

PROJECT AHEAD represents a system that makes exemplary educational programs available for adoption by schools, colleges and other institutions. In order for the project to work, several steps need to be taken: 1) A range of Holocaust curricula needs to be identified (Please see appendix for PROJECT AHEAD Data Base Form); 2) Linking Agents/Facilitators need to be identified by the USHMC Office of Education. Conceivably, members of The Chairman's Advisory Panel On Holocaust Education (whose work schedule allowed)[7] would be named to serve in this capacity; 3) Linking Agents/Facilitators would inform the education community about PROJECT AHEAD; 4) A panel needs to be appointed to examine evidence of effectiveness from the Holocaust programs identified. Members of CAPE[8], as well as Council members and Advisors, could serve on this panel; 5) The review procedure needs to be clarified. To be approved, a Holocaust program would meet specific criteria the panel had agreed upon; 6) Projects being disseminated through PROJECT AHEAD would be known as Developer/Demonstrators and potentially would be eligible for dissemination funds. The nature of this funding needs to be explored.

In summation, PROJECT AHEAD would strongly support the work of the United States Holocaust Memorial Council/Museum and provide a focus for its outreach programs. Approximately three-fourths of the world's population have been born since the end of World War II. From whom and what will they learn of the Holocaust? These are the key questions which PROJECT AHEAD needs to address.[9] The challenge is a large one, but it can be met.

Definition of Terms

1. *Dissemination*

Refers to activities that involve not only spread of information by a central agency, but also a two-way process of matching the needs of a target population and a range of relevant resources available to the population.

Dissemination process means a system for reviewing, selecting and providing information and materials about a specific content area, fields of professional development, or body of research, that will be of use to educational service providers.

2. *Exemplary Educational Project*

Exemplary educational project or "program" means a program, product, practice or dissemination process approved by the Joint Dissemination Review Panel of the National Diffusion Network.

3. *Linking Agent*

The Linking Agent may be a person or persons, or an agency or agencies, acting as intermediaries or "boundary spanners" between educational organizations and more distant sources of knowledge and assistance. They are sometimes referred to as Consultants, Change Agents, External Linking Agents or External Agents.

4. *Local School Facilitators*

Local School Facilitators contribute to school improvement efforts by being the contact people between the innovation users and the innovation developers. They are usually Building or District Level Administrators.

5. *Process of Change*

The process of change consists of the events and activities as the system moves from one state to another. Empirical observation suggests the division into three subprocesses. Current research indicates that different actors engage in different activities during the three subprocesses, and that these activities serve different functions for the organizational system undergoing change. The three subprocesses include initiation, implementation, and incorporation.

6. *School Improvements*

Refers to activities occurring at the school and school district levels which increase the effectiveness of teaching, curriculum, and other aspects of the school system's capacity to improve the quality of education for children.

---

[1]Michael Kane and Rolf Lehming, *Improving Schools: Using What We Know* (London: Sage Publications, 1981), page 11.

[2]Dr. Sidney Bolkosky, Professor of History at University of Michigan — Dearborn, personal letter.

[3]Sara Kaplan, interview held during meeting of the *Coalition of Alternatives In Jewish Education*, College Park, Maryland, 1986.

[4]Professor Eli Pfefferkorn, "Proposal For a Master Teachers Training Program In Holocaust Studies" submitted to the United States Holocaust Memorial Council, 1984.

[5]AHEAD is an acronym standing for Assist in Holocaust Education Adoption And Dissemination.

[6]Please see Appendix for a list of institutions.

[7]In May 1985, Chairman Elie Wiesel appointed a distinguished panel of educators to provide input into the educational planning of the Museum and outreach activities of the Council.

[8]Chairman's Advisory Panel on Education. Please see Appendix for list of members.

[9]Question asked by Dr. Alan L. Berger in *Martyrdom And Resistance,* March-April, 1986, pages 12 and 16.

APPENDIX I
REFERENCES

1. Crandall, David P. and Loucks, Susan F., "Preparing Facilitators for Implementation: Mirroring The School Improvement Process," March 1982. Presented at American Educational Research Association Annual Meeting.

2. Lehming, R. and Kane M., *Improving Schools*. London, England: Sage Publications, 1981.

3. Sutton, J., "A Proposed National Commission To Focus On the Education Of The Citizen For the 21st Century," June 1, 1986, prepared for The National Commission On the Education of the Citizen for the 21st Century.

4. U. S. Department of Education, "How To Prepare For A Joint Dissemination Review Panel Meeting," December 1983.

5. U. S. Department of Education, "Guidelines: Joint Dissemination Review Panel Purposes, Procedures, And Criteria," September 1985.

APPENDIX II
ORGANIZATIONS

Major National Educational Organizations

1. American Association for Higher Education

2. American Association of Colleges for Teacher Education

3. American Association of Community and Junior Colleges

4. American Association of School Administrators

5. American Association of University Professors

6. American Council on Education

7. American Educational Research Association

8. American Federation of Teachers, AFL-CIO

9. Association for Educational Communications and Technology

10. Association for Supervision and Curriculum Development

11. Association of American Colleges

12. Council for Advancement and Support of Education

13. Council for Exceptional Children

14. Council of Chief State School Officers

15. Council of Great City Schools

16. Education Writers Association

17. Educational Research Service, Inc.

18. Institute for Educational Leadership

19. National Art Education Association

20. National Association for Women Deans, Administrators and Counselors

21. National Association of Elementary School Principals

22. National Association of Independent Schools

23. National Association of Secondary School Principals

24. National Association of State Boards of Education

25. National Catholic Educational Association

26. National Committee for Citizens in Education

27. National Community Education Association

28. National Congress of Parents and Teachers

29. National Council for the Social Studies

30. National Council of Teachers of English

31. National Education Association

32. National Institute of Education — Regional Educational Laboratories

33. National Middle School Association

34. National School Boards Association

35. Phi Delta Kappa

Other organizations to be included in the planning phases of PROJECT AHEAD include:

1. Close-Up Foundation

2. American Council of Learned Societies

3. American Bar Association, Special Committee Youth Education for Citizenship

4. Council for American Private Education

5. Council for Basic Education

6. Education Commission of the States

7. Forum of Educational Organization Leaders

8. National Assessment of Educational Progress

9. Domestic Policy Association

10. Center for Civic Education

11. Lincoln Filene Center for Citizenship and Public Affairs

12. National Association of Independent Colleges and Universities

13. People for the American Way

14. National Institute for Citizen Education in the Law

15. Presidential Classroom for Young Americans, Inc.

16. Social Issues Resources Series, Inc.

17. Social Science Education Consortium, Inc.

18. ERIC Clearinghouse for Social Studies/Social Science Education

19. Social Studies Development Center, Indiana University

APPENDIX III

CHAIRMAN'S ADVISORY PANEL ON HOLOCAUST EDUCATION

U. S. HOLOCAUST MEMORIAL COUNCIL

Dr. Adrianne Bank — Senior Research Associate
Center for the Study of Evaluation
Los Angeles, CA

Mr. Shalmi Barmor — Director of Education
Yad Vashem
Jerusalem, Israel

Mr. Leon Bass — Principal,
Benjamin Franklin High School
Philadelphia, PA

Dr. Helmut Becker — Professor at Max Planck Institute
Berlin, West Germany

Ms. Janet Blatter — Curator & Exhibit Designer
McCord Museum
Montreal, Canada

Mr. Joel Bloom — President
Franklin Institute Science Museum
Philadelphia, PA

Dr. Harry J. Cargas — Professor, Department of Literature & Language
Webster University
St. Louis, MO

Dr. Lucjan Dobroszycki — Professor
YIVO Institute
New York, NY

Dr. Alice Eckardt — Professor, Department of Religion Studies
Lehigh University
Bethlehem, PA

Dr. Stephen Ellenwood   Professor, Division of Instructional Development
(Chairman of the Panel)   School of Education
                         Boston University
                         Boston, MA

Dr. Sidrah Ezrahi   Professor, Department of Dramatic Languages
                                 and Literature
                         Duke University
                         Durham, North Carolina

Dr. Marilyn Feingold   Consultant to Office of Education
                             U. S. Holocaust Memorial Council
                             Boston, MA

Dr. Richard Flaim   Supervisor of Social Studies
                         Vineland Public Schools
                         Vineland, NJ

Dr. Eric Goldman   Director
                         Jewish Media Service
                         New York, NY

Dr. Fran Haley   Executive Director
                         National Council for the Social Studies
                         Washington, D.C.

Dr. Henry Hausdorff   Professor, School of Higher Education
                         University of Pittsburgh
                         Pittsburgh, PA

Dr. Leon Jick   Professor
                         Brandeis University
                         Waltham, MA

Ms. Sara Kaplan   Principal
                         Oheb Shalom Religious School
                         Baltimore, Maryland

Dr. Dennis Klein   Director
                         International Center for Holocaust Studies
                                 of ADL
                         New York, N.Y.

Ms. Marcia Sachs Littel   Executive Director
The Anne Frank Institute of
Philadelphia, PA

Dr. Timothy Littlel   Associate Professor, College of Education
Michigan State University
Lansing, Mich

Dr. Leatrice Rabinsky   Teacher
Cleveland Heights High School
Cleveland, OH

Ms. Joan Rosenbaum   Director
Jewish Museum
New York, NY

Mr. Ted Sanders   Superintendent
Office of Education
State of Illinois
Chicago, IL

Dr. Alvin Schiff   Executive Vice President
Board of Jewish Education of
Greater New York
New York, NY

Dr. Robert Sperber   Special Assistant to the President
Boston University
Boston, MA

Mrs. Bea Stadtler   Teacher and Author on the Holocaust
Beachwood, OH

Dr. Jaime Wurzel   Assistant Professor, School of Education
Boston University
Boston, MA

APPENDIX IV

PROJECT AHEAD DATABASE INFORMATION FORM

Guidelines

1. *Name of Project:*

   Person in charge of implementing project: Give position.

   Institutional Affiliation:
   Name of Institution/School where project is located and type of
   institution.

   Address:
   Include street address and box if applicable as well as telephone number.

2. *Target Audience:*
   Circle each grade level your project targets. Indicate the number of
   students and teachers involved in your project.

3. *Goals & Objectives:*
   Provide here the rationale for your project.

4. *Approaches & Methods:*
   Included here should be a descriptive summary of your project's
   activities.

5. *Scope and Content:*
   Indicate here how many hours, days, weeks or months your project is
   taught. Provide key phrases which identify the main themes or topics
   of your project.

6. *Teacher Training:*
   Include here information on any in-service training or workshops that
   are offered to teachers, as well as information about the form of the
   teacher training.

7. *Evidence of Effectiveness:*
   This section concerns itself with several key questions, such as: Has a
   specific positive change occurred? What is the evidence of change?
   Can the change be attributed to the project? Is the change great enough
   and observed often enough to be statistically significant? Is the sample

large enough to be statistically significant? Is the cost reasonable, considering the magnitude and area of change? Can the project be used in other locations with comparable impact?

8. *Sponsors:*
   Identify the key organizations and major sources of funding currently supporting your project.

9. *Outreach:*
   Indicate here whether your project has been tried in settings other than your local school district or community. Statewide or interstate dissemination should be noted.

10. *Contact Person:*
    Give name, title or position, address, and phone number of individual who can provide more information about your project.

11. *Project Director's Comments:*
    Additional comments regarding parent/teacher/student reactions/misgivings about teaching the Holocaust are welcome here. Are there any special characteristics of the population your project targets?

Project Ahead Database Information Form

1. **Project Name:** _____

   Person in charge: _____

   Institutional Affiliation: _____

   Address: _____

   City: _____ **State:** _____ **Zip:** _____

   Telephone: _____

   Type of Institution: Public__ Parochial __ Private __
   Elementary (K-6) __   Jr. High (7&8) __
   High School (9-12) __ Vocational School __
   Post secondry __   Other (specify) _____

2. **Target Audience: K 1 2 3 4 5 6 7 8 9 10 11 12**
   College   Adults
   Other (specify) _____
   Number of students _____
   Number of teachers _____

3. **Goals & Objectives:**

   Briefly identify the project's rationale.

   _____
   _____
   _____

4. Approaches & Methods:

Check the methods used in teaching which apply:

__audio-visual   __discussion
__display/exhibits   __guest speakers
__interviewing   __journal keeping
__lecturing   __reading
__role-playing   __simulation
__testing   __writing
__other (specify) _____

Cite the major commercially available materials & locally developed materials used by your project. Please asterisk (in front of the title) the locally developed materials. [Indicate the following for *type:* B - Books; F - Film; S - Slides; FS - Filmstrip; P - Pamphlet; V - Video; D - Display/Exhibits; Other (specify).]

Title	Author	Publisher, Date, Type of Publication
_____	_____	_____

5. Scope and Content:

Length of Instruction:
Hrs./wk.___   Days/month___   Months/year___

The project is a self-contained course: Yes___   No___

The project is part of a larger course of study in a unit in an existing course: Yes___   No___

The project is intended to be adopted by local communities as a self-contained course or it may be integrated as a unit in a larger course: Yes___   No___

Area of study in which the Holocaust is taught:
__World History   __European History
__American History   __Social Studies
__Literature   __World Cultures
__Language   __Psychology
__Art   __Sciences
__Music   __Sociology
__Ethics   __Religion
__Other (e.g., General) _____

Main themes or topics covered:
_____
_____
_____

6. Teacher Training:

Form of teacher training and preparation:
__one workshop   __several workshops
__self preparation   __course for credit
__in-service training   __summer institute
__conference
__Other (specify) _____

7. Evidence of Effectiveness:

Is the effectiveness of your project systematically assessed?
                              Yes___   No___

If yes, which of the following types of assessment methods are used:
__student examinations   __teacher interviews
__student interviews   __on-site visits
__use of outside consultant
__other (specify) _____

Has your project been adopted by other communities?
                              Yes___   No___

If yes, do you monitor the implementation of the adoptions?
                              Yes___   No___

8. **Sponsors:**

Indicate and name the type(s) of organization(s) available to give assistance to your project.

Library _____   AV Center _____
Holocaust Center _____
Community Organization _____
College/University _____
Other Educational Institution _____
Professional Organization _____
Religious Organization _____
None _____

List major funding sources:

_____
_____
_____

9. **Outreach:**

Please indicate the kind of dissemination your project is oriented to providing:
__Local   __State   __National

Cite program brochure, newsletter or other promotional material which provides information about your project:
__brochure   __newsletter
__conference
__other (specify) _____

10.   **Contact Person:**   _____

11.   **Project Director's Comments:**

_____
_____
_____

Note: Please send in the results of any project assessments that have been done. We would also appreciate a copy of your curriculum and other relevant material you have developed.

Thank You!

Chapter Sixteen
My Papal Encyclical

Harry James Cargas

The Roman Catholic Church is not so structured that everything is decided at the papal level and then disseminated downward for implementation. While it is not a democratic institution, for the faithful masses to influence the hierarchy is not without certain precedents. The dogma of the Assumption of the Virgin Mary bodily into heaven is an example of a belief so popular that Vatican officials could not ignore it — they examined it, validated it, and made it a tenet of faith for members of its church.

One cannot say that the majority of Catholics today is clamoring for reconciliation with Jews, a reconciliation which must acknowledge the atrocities committed against Jews by Christians over the centuries, and in particular those injuries done against Jews in World War II known as having made up the Holocaust. But regardless of the lack of widespread fervor on this subject, its truth remains. Many Catholics sinned grievously in their actions and in their silence against Jews. The division caused between Catholics (and other Christians) and Jews during World War II may be irreparable. In one sense, that decision must be left up to the Jews, the victims. Nevertheless, it is morally necessary that we Christians — the persecutors — make strong and sincere attempts at harmonizing relationships with Jews through repentance for our continued historical behavior in regard to them.

Hence it would be fitting if, since the Catholic hierarchy does not appear to be making enough significant steps in this area, the faithful demanded action. In 1938, a papal encyclical condemning antisemitism was commissioned, was written by the American Jesuit John LaFarge, but was never promulgated. Now, over a generation after the Holocaust, where millions of people were systematically put to death, where over 6,000,000 were Jews, and where 1,000,000 of these latter were children, it is time that we required the publication of an up-to-date encyclical concerning the vital issue of Catholic-Jewish relationships.

Since encyclical letters are usually drafted for popes by others who are specialists in the subjects of each epistle, it may not be without value for me here to submit a suggested draft of such a letter on this topic. This is not offered in the sense of satire, once removed, or, I hope, from arrogance or an attitude of presumptuousness. Rather, it is written in hope: hope that other members of my church agree on the need for such a document, and hope that Jewish women and men throughout the world can believe in the sincerity of approach that some of us Christians have when we profess our love for them, or sorrow for certain past misdeeds and our firm purpose of amendment regarding our future relations with Jews.

A papal encyclical is usually known by the first two words of the letter, hence these words are carefully chosen. I would like this suggested work to begin with words which are very descriptive of the purpose of the letter:

Seeking reconciliation with Jews throughout the world because we are mindful of the many centuries of pain caused them by persons who called themselves good Christians, we address this document to men and women of good will everywhere, but especially to Catholics who must be concerned over the evils done by their co-religionists to the Jews. We likewise address this letter to our Jewish brothers and sisters indirectly in the hope that they may understand that our sincerity to and love for them is the motivating force of this encyclical.

Too often the relationship between Christian and Jew has been in the form of persecutor and persecuted, of torturer and tortured, of murderer and victim Whether we remember such historical periods as the Crusades, the Inquisition, pogroms, or the Holocaust, we Christians must ever acknowledge our guilt in the eyes of others and in the eyes of God for our treatment of those we have also recognized as being among His Chosen People.

Perhaps because it is closest to us in time of all the major persecutions about which we here write, and certainly because of the magnitude of the tragedy, we must particularly regret and make reparation in whatever ways possible for our role in the crime of the Holocaust. It is appropriate that we do this as a group, as a Mystical Body in which we all participate as Christians. If the virtues done by Christians, past and present, form a kind of spiritual reservoir upon which the world Christian community draws for moral sustenance, then we must also admit that the sins of Christians are not without effect on us as well. Indeed contemporary psychology seems to prove that nothing which has ever happened or been thought can ever be lost, can ever be without some influence, however small. In the case of the Holocaust, we cannot honestly speak of small effects. The word Holocaust stands for that collection of enormous evils which were perpetrated against helpless, defenseless, guiltless Jews and others — we emphasize again that the vast majority of the perpetrators was Christian.

With the foregoing ever present in our minds, then, let us consider actions which we may take toward reconciling Christians with Jews. We must do this following the examples of heroic Christians whose devotion to the entirety of humanity during the Holocaust exemplifies the finest in the followers of Christ: men and women like Franz Jagersdatter, Edith Stein, Dietrich Bonhoeffer, Pope John XXIII, Alfred Delp, Martin Niemoeller, Rufino Niccacci and the others (alas, too few) who followed the call of Christianity to its logical end in heroism.

As a sign of our total commitment to reconciliation through acknowledgement of our errors, then, we begin by the ecclesiastical powers vested in us, by belatedly excommunicating Adolf Hitler from the Catholic Church. Excommunication is a punishment for the living and since Hitler is dead it may seem meaningless to make this public pronouncement. We do not do so to perform a meaningless act. We do so in order to indicate to our Jewish brothers and sisters that we regret this not having been done in the 1930s, that Hitler was guilty of unspeakable crimes against humanity against which the Church should not have been silent, and we do so as a warning to all those who would today espouse Hitler's teachings opposed to the Jews. Such teachings are anathema and any who support them are guilty of grave sin. It must not be overlooked that this is the first time in the history of our Church that excommunication has been pronounced on a dead person. We do so because of the seriousness of his crimes and as an admission that our silence during his lifetime may itself have been contributory to these crimes.

We urge the Christian clergy throughout the world to emphasize the import of such action. Ideally, they would use this as a starting point for thoughtful, prayerful homilies on the meaning of the Holocaust for Christianity. For us, perhaps even more than for the Jews, the Holocaust is an enormous tragedy. How could we have stood by and watched it take place? How could we have participated in this monumental sin? Some have thought that the Holocaust marks the end of Christianity. It is our prayer that from the ashes of the fires at Dachau, Bergen-Belsen, Auschwitz, and other murderous locations we will see an unparalleled resurrection, as it were, of a truly meaningful Christianity which will touch all of our hearts and be evident for having done so to all people of all faiths everywhere and for all time to come.

If the homilies on the Holocaust are to be effective, they will have to admit to errors in the works of our teachers concerning the Jews. St. John Chrysostom was wrong in saying that God hates the Jews and always hated them. St. Justin was wrong when he said that the Jews had been made to suffer because they killed Christ. St. Cyprian was wrong when he said that the peoplehood of the Jews has been cancelled. St. Jerome was wrong when he spoke of the Jews as serpents, St. Abrogard was wrong to write a treatise on the superstitions of Jews. Many, far too many, such statements must be abjured. Whole theologies have been built on their foundation and since the foundation has proven false, the structure must be seen as uninhabitable.

In addition to the above, we proclaim in this letter that an annual memorial service for Jewish victims of the Holocaust be instituted in the liturgical calendar with comparable national, diocesan and parish programs to support the material. A mass should be said for this purpose on the Sabbath of each year closest to the day the Jews have chosen as the international day of remembrance of the Holocaust, *Yom Hashoah*.

We now turn to the sacred scriptures themselves to examine if they have, in some way, contributed to the persecution of Jews. By this we do not in any way imply the inauthenticity of the Christian Bible. Rather, we raise questions about the interpretations of holy writ which have caused so much grief. To question is not to judge. We must keep in mind that we have nothing to fear from truth. Rather, we welcome continual theological study of scriptures, as the Church has practiced since its beginning. This includes study of the very difficult problems as well as those which cause less difficulty. Yes, even less embarrassment we ought to say. The subject of Christian-Jewish relations, as influenced by our scriptures, is one which requires deep, prayerful, sensitive and continued probing.

Preliminary to such examinations, we must acknowledge that the Christian terminology for the scriptures is not conducive to bettering Jewish-Christian harmony. The terms Old Testament and New Testament are seen as insulting to some Jews and have even been considered as evidence of Christian arrogance. It would be extremely problematical to expect that our sincere and prayer-laden approaches to reconciliation with Jews could be deeply effective if the very core of our spiritual rootedness, the scriptures, were named in a way so as to divide us. Therefore we urge Catholic theologians, religious and the laity to abandon the terms Old Testament and New Testament in favor of more universally accepted names. The title "Hebrew Scriptures" cannot be applied to what is now known as the Old Testament since that body contains work which is outside the traditional Jewish canon. Thus the simple division of Hebrew scriptures and Christian scriptures would be inaccurate. By way of suggestion, but not insistence — theologians will do well to turn their attention to this area of nomenclature — we might consider calling the chronologically earlier portion of the Bible "Inherited Testament" with all of the respect to our religious forebears which that phrase implies, and the latter portion "Institutional Testament" with the recognition of the Church's role in solely establishing this canon being thus acknowledged. We reiterate, however, that we do not insist on these terms but rather suggest them as at least beginning points for theologians to consider.

All of this implies, of course, the essential Jewishness of Christianity. The Church must be proud of its heritage and this glory is to be ever regarded, publicly in liturgical celebrations and homilies as well as in the utterances and writings of Christians, and privately in the hearts of all Christians who will thus be fully aware that the persecution of Jews, as with the persecution of all persons, is reprehensible to God. By insisting on the basic Jewish roots of Christianity we will also readily recognize that the Jewish Nazarene worshipped by Christians as the Son of God is not to be regarded as a being who divides Christians and Jews but as a link between us. It is fitting that on this topic we recognize the wisdom of a document written in the United States under the ecumenical sponsorship of the Commission on Faith and Order of the National Council of Churches and the Secretariat for Catholic-Jewish Relations of the National Conference for Catholic Bishops. It reads in part: "The Church of Christ is rooted in the life of the people of Israel. We Christians look upon Abraham as our spiritual ancestor and father of our faith... The ministry of Jesus and the life of the early Christian community were thoroughly rooted in the Judaism of their day, particularly in the teachings of the Pharisees. The Christian Church is still sustained by the living faith of the patriarchs and prophets, kings and priests, scribes and rabbis, and the people whom God chose for his own. Christ is the link... enabling the Gentiles to be numbered among Abraham's 'offspring' and therefore fellow-heirs with the Jews according to

God's promise. It is a tragedy of history that Jesus, our bond of unity with the Jews, has all too often become a symbol and source of division and bitterness because of human weakness and pride." These words are eloquently written and reflect precisely the instruction which is meant here. It is a betrayal of the mission of Jesus Christ to regard him as divisive rather than unitive among human beings, and particularly among Christians and Jews.

With this document we wish not only to admonish and encourage but to set an example by taking action as well. Our proclamation of the excommunication of Adolf Hitler, our revision of the liturgical calendar to include a Holocaust memorial, are steps in this direction. In addition to these, we now declare that the Vatican historical archives, up to the year 1970, are hereby opened to qualified scholars throughout the world. Secrecy is unnecessary and even harmful regarding the events leading up to, and transpiring both during and after World War II. If we are sincere about reconciling ourselves with our Jewish brothers and sisters, then we must admit where we have been weak, where we have been wrong, where we have sinned against them. The Vatican archives contain much material which will shed light on these times. We must examine our mistakes so that we will learn from them and not be condemned to repeat them ever. Something else will happen, also, when the archives are studied. The names and acts of a large number of heroic Christians will be brought to public attention. While our great errors are hidden in the archives, also are our virtuous people and works who resisted the implementation of Nazi policies in saintly fashion. We do a disservice to these good people in not allowing their stories to be told and opening the archives of the Vatican will undoubtedly foster the dissemination of knowledge of their courage. We instruct the opening of the Vatican archives, up through December 31, 1969, immediately. We must hide nothing. We must admit, where admitting is necessary; we may take pride where that is justifiable.

There is another way we must be open, as well, and that is in the studying of the true meaning of Judaism. If we regard the Jewish religion only as embodying truths as a forerunner of Christianity, we can never fully understand what that religion means to its followers. Care is to be taken that we as Christians do not regard Judaism simplistically from a supercessionist point of view. It is wholly arrogant to profess that Judaism has existed solely as a predecessor to Christianity, meant only to be fulfilled in Christianity. Jews today comprise a body that we regard as God's Chosen People just as they did over two thousand years ago. Their uniqueness in this way should cause us to revere, admire, love and attempt to understand them more completely. Therefore, with this encyclical, we urge very strongly that where possible, at Catholic colleges and universities throughout the world, chairs of Judaic studies be established for the purpose of teaching us about Jews and their religion. Nor ought we fail to mention that such positions would be more appropriately filled by Jewish scholars, generally speaking, than by Christian scholars. This appears self-evident yet frequently the truths of Judaism are taught on Christian campuses by non-Jews. In some cases the results have been other than we here intend with this instruction. Where Jewish and Christian traditions come in apparent conflict, these differences must be recognized and discussed. However, they must always be discussed in an atmosphere of charity, mutual respect and a fervent desire only to pursue the truth.

In addition, we urge authorities in Catholic high schools and elementary schools to make extraordinary efforts to bring their pupils in touch with the true Judaism and with Jews in the community. Sadly necessary, also, are lessons, on all educational levels, dealing with the Holocaust. Both the failures and virtuous actions of Christians during that period of twentieth century history are to be taught.

Many of the sins against the Jews which have been committed by Christians are a result of the heavy emphasis on missionizing in which we Christians have been engaged for so long. True missionary efforts are turned inward; each of us who call ourselves Christian need to bear witness to Christ by perfecting our individual, personal lives. To try to convert others while neglecting ourselves is once again to act with sinful arrogance. We may learn from the great work done by the beloved members of the religious of the Congregation of Notre Dame De Sion, founded in France in 1846. Originally established to bring about better understanding between Christians and Jews, and for the conversion of the latter to Christianity, this remarkable religious group has changed its goals since the events of World War II. The emphasis is now on Christian-Jewish dialogue and the insistence is that proselytizing by members of the congregation is to be completely abandoned. If, in fact, we are to expect Jews to trust us when we say that we wish to offer them true friendship, the ulterior motive of conversion must be absent We urge this attitude on all of the faithful.

We submit this letter to all the world in prayerful humility, on our knees, to express a profound repentance. While addressed to Catholics of the world, it is our prayer that Jews everywhere read this letter and understand our intent. We have attempted simple, straightforward language in an open fashion. Nothing is meant to be hidden; there is no aim at ambiguity of expression. For all sins by Christians against Jews, we are truly sorry. For the future relationship between Christians and Jews, we are hopeful. We do not expect that Jews, who have for so long been victimized by unworthy Christians, will immediately embrace us and fully trust our motives. The long history that they have endured precludes that. However, we make this beginning, and while it will certainly take a long time for Jewish-Christian relations to reach the point that they should, we do make this beginning. Christians must be patient and not be disappointed if we are not quickly and totally accepted as loving sisters and brothers by the Jews. However, we know that with God's aid and a firm purpose of commitment, we can succeed.

Finally, and without amplification, the Vatican hereby officially extends the offer of full diplomatic relations with the State of Israel.

Chapter 17

The Nazi "Blood Myth" and the Holocaust

Livia Bitton-Jackson

At the Wannsee Conference in January 1942 the blueprint for the "Final Solution" was unveiled. An overall plan and methods for the murder of Europe's eleven million Jews had been worked out. Who were to be the executors of the plan? Was the German people prepared to become a nation of butchers to carry out the mass murder of their neighbors, human beings largely indistinguishable from themselves? Was the mood of a civilized nation set for such an unprecedented blood bath? How did Hitler and his henchmen conceive of imposing such a gruesome task on their people? Did they not fear a revulsion of the German psyche and an uprising against the initiators of such a monstrous idea?

The fiendish plan committed to paper could only have been a preliminary step. Without the cooperation of a large number of his countrymen, Hitler's demonic idea could not become a reality.

"Genocide in theory is one thing; but how human beings belonging to one of the most advanced countries in Europe could be found to annihilate people in their millions not in the heat of battle, but in cold blood and by the most diabolical devices, defies logical analysis," wrote R.W. Cooper in his account of the Nuremberg Trials.[1]

Justice Robert H. Jackson, in his opening speech at the Nuremberg Trials, declared: "There is no record in history of a crime perpetrated against so many victims, or carried out with such calculated cruelty."[2]

According to Hitler's former movie-maker, Franz Hippler, "The German people were not more anti-Semitic than other people. The French, for instance, were much more anti-Semitic. Hitler was not pleased with this," he revealed in a 1985 interview on WNET-TV. "He ordered us to do something about it." The mood of the Germans had to change radically: the nation's emotional soil had to be prepared for things to come. How was it to be done? Propaganda had to do it. Education had to do it.

The Ministry of Propaganda was charged with the task of creating a receptive atmosphere for the genocide of the Jews. Hitler ordered Franz Hippler to produce an "educational'" film about Jews for distribution throughout Germany, one that would make the "proper" impact on public opinion. Hippler complied, and *Der ewige Jude,* the most vicious anti-Semitic falsification, was the result of his efforts. In Hippler's words, the film incorporated Hitler's instructions: Lie big. The big lie is believed much more readily than the small lie. The methods? Simplification, Repetition, Reinforcement of things people want to hear. "The propagandist has to speak to the soul of people," Hitler taught his agents of propaganda.

Years later, a speech delivered by an *Einsatzgruppenführer* about the work of his men to a Final Solution plenary session gave some indication as to the effectiveness of Nazi "educational" methods. Professor Jacob Talmon referred to the report as "One of the most frightening documents submitted to the Jerusalem court... The speaker grew lyrical about the wonderful qualities of his men. They walk in Jewish blood up to their knees, Jewish corpses are piled up before their eyes till they reach the clouds, the cries of Jewish babies pierce their ears, and they, without faltering for a second, proceed with their work. They indeed deserve a monument... The image of the Jew had not merely been dehumanized," Professor Talmon commented, "he had become Satan incarnate or an evil subhuman breed. The imagination and the feelings of the butchers were no longer affected by signs of pain and sorrow manifested by the Jew."[3]

Had the Nazi propagandist indeed spoken to the "soul" of the German people? Had the "educational" work of the Propaganda Ministry been so devastatingly successful because it taught the German people lessons they wanted to learn? The horrifying answers are inherent in the mass of evidence presented at the various Nazi war crime trials.

The Final Solution had become a mission accomplished not only with deadly dedication, but with passionate, religious zeal: the nature of the means matched the nature of the end. In their quest to isolate and target the Jew, the Nazi propagandists went beyond devising rational educational materials to serve in the preparatory process. They reached into the realm of myth to create an intense psychological framework for their "educational" onslaught.

The portrait of the Jew as despoiler of pure Aryan blood was a central motif of Nazi propaganda. Adolf Hitler was obsessed with the image: "With satanic joy on his face, the black-haired Jew-boy lurks in wait for the unsuspecting girl whom he defiles with his blood, thus stealing her from her people. With every means he tries to destroy the racial foundations of the people he has set out to subjugate. Just as he himself systematically ruins women and girls, he does not shrink back from pulling down the blood barriers of others, even on a large scale," he wrote.[4]

Hitler was by no means the originator of this portrait; he only recast grotesque, stereotypical images of Jews within a mythical blood context lavishly produced by late nineteenth and early twentieth century anti-Semitic literature. It was this literature which provided key elements for Nazi racial philosophy based on the veneration of the blood myth. "In the doctrine of race... blood becomes the real primary cause that determines the whole personality of its bearer... Thinking is speaking with one's blood," Professor Talmon concludes.[5] "What gave the Jews such effectiveness in the eyes of their enemies? The theory of blood. When pure and undiluted, the power of the blood would never fail; its instinct would never err. Any lapse or failure, any weakening of the will, loss of bearing, or confusion, was a consequence of the adulteration of the good blood, of poison injected into it by the surrounding Jews."[6]

The medieval blood libel myth played a central role in pre-Nazi anti-Semitic literature, precursor of Nazi propaganda. One of the influential "thinkers" of the period, Father Henry Desportes, among others, revived the spectre of the bizarre myth in his *Mystere du Sang* (1889) and gave it contemporary relevance by claiming that spilling Christian blood was a Jewish racial need as well as a religious obligation. Composer Richard Wagner, in a letter to a German statesman waxed poetic in his exaltation of the Jews' demonic power of racial destruction. He wrote: "What a wonderful, incomparable phenomenon is the Jew: protean demon of humanity's decadence... I most certainly regard the Jewish race as the born enemy of pure men and of all nobility in them, and am convinced that we Germans in particular will be destroyed by them."[7]

La France Juive (1886), Edouard Drumont's judeophobic history of France, an international best-seller in its day, was based on the theme of the Jews' inherent evil and instinctive destructiveness, both basic components of Jewish blood. Wilhelm Marr's fear of the Jews' imminent triumph over German civilization was expressed in his demagogic *Der Sieg des Judentums uber das Germanenthums* (1879). Motivated by a dread of Jewish racial and cultural contamination of the Aryan race, the author in a hodgepodge of racial, religious and cultural metaphors issued dire warnings against a universal "Judaization," and appealed to the German masses to combat it by an overall struggle which he called a "Christian Emancipation."

Max Bewer, in a "scientific," religious text, *Der deutsche Christus* (1907), went so far as to claim that the color of Jewish blood differed from that of the Aryan. While Aryan blood was red, Jewish blood was dark! Jewish blood was the essence of lust; Jewish character was not only corrupt and evil: it was the essence of corruption and the principle of evil. Then the "scientist-theologian" went on to report on the result of an even more extraordinary piece of scholarly investigation. He had found that although Jesus had Semitic blood on his mother's side, on his father's side, he had Aryan blood: Jesus' forefathers stemmed from Westphalia! Although "a Hebraic turbidity might perhaps have affected his German blood,"[8] the ultimate outcome of the struggle between Jesus' German blood and Semitic blood was total victory: "God in Him had triumphed, German blood over Jewish blood."[9]

In the racial anti-Semitic doctrine, the spiritual and theological was interpreted strictly in a mythical-biological context, with blood a key word. Max Bewer gave the general Biblical admonition against consuming blood a Christian, anti-Jewish specificity, interpreting the verse, "Blood is the soul"[10] as: "In Christ and in the Jews blood against blood rises up and speaks... Everything that Christ says regarding resurrection in the spiritual sense seems to have been uttered from out of the blood that was resurrected solely in the bodily sense."[11]

The blood motif played a pivotal role also in anti-Semitic "belles lettres." Arthur Dinter's *Sin Against the Blood* (1918) seems to have spoken to the "soul of the German people" during the immediate post-World War I period: this incendiary anti-Semitic piece of fiction sold more than 100,000 copies within the first two years of its publication. The hero, an Aryan natural scientist, divorced his Jewish wife and married an Aryan woman. To his horror and dismay, the child from this union exhibits Semitic racial characteristics as a result of the Aryan mother's previous sexual contact with a Jew! Although the sexual encounter predated the birth of the child by many years, the Jew's evil blood had forever polluted her German blood. At the culmination of the novel, the Aryan hero is proclaimed not guilty by a sympathetic jury for the righteous murder of the evil Jew who had permanently defiled his wife's blood.

As a result of his dedicated research, the intrepid hero discovers that Jews had been carrying on a systematic, surreptitious sexual campaign to pollute the blood of Aryans. His undaunted investigation of his former father-in-law's correspondence, which bears a striking resemblance to the *Protocols of the Elders of Zion*, reveals that the Jew had not only defiled the blood of "pure, blond virgins," but "like a spider he sat in his Berlin office, sucking these people's marrow from body and soul — great pitiless heart, sucking human blood to convert it into gold."[12]

Even the historian Oswald Spengler, who otherwise repudiated the National Socialist racial creed, singled out Jews for condemnation as "destructive elements" and "carriers of poisonous cynicism." In his summary of the *Decline of the West,* Spengler depicted the scene of the last struggle "in which civilization reaches its final form," the struggle between money and blood, and warned, using the Nazi metaphor: "Money is overcome and eliminated only by blood... "[13] It is only fair, if one takes Dinter at his word about the conversion of blood into money by Jews, that the reverse of the process should undo the harm and redeem history which, according to the final words of Spengler's oracle, "is concerned with life, and only with life, with race and with the triumph of the will to power. History is not concerned with the victory of truths, of discoveries or of money."[14]

It is quite surprising that Hans Bluher, the philosopher of the German youth movement and its Tonangeber from 1914 till 1934, chose to provide primarily a theological, and not purely racial, rationale for Jewish destructiveness. In his pamphlet, *Secessio Judaica,* composed in 1921 in order to provide a "philosophical basis to the historical position of Jewry and of the anti-Semitic movement," Bluher maintained that Jewish destructiveness derived from the Jews' primal act of destruction — their killing of Christ, a guilt forever unatoneble. Its primary theological orientation notwithstanding, the pamphlet became an essential item in Nazi propaganda literature and underwent several editions. In the foreword to the third edition in 1933, Bluher made some uncharacteristically revealing remarks: "This pamphlet was written in 1921, when German Jewry stood at the height of its power, unopposed. At about the same time the national forces, today victorious, prepared their blow against

Jewry by propaganda means. It is difficult to say whether *Secessio Judaica* influenced this development; at any rate, present events seem to be the literal implementation of this pamphlet."[15]

Fascination with the mythical power of blood and the Jews' sinister exploitation of it formed the central theme of the philosophy of Alfred Rosenberg, Hitler's chief Nazi ideologist. The "Jewish vampire" assumed diabolic proportions in his magnum opus, *The Mythos of the Twentieth Century* (1930), where the image of the Jew is no longer that of a lusty blood-sucker, draining blood and money in equal measure from healthy, blond Aryans. In his mind and the minds of other Nazi ideologues over a decade after Dinter, the Jews had been transformed into germs of disease — creatures who not only derive profit from gorging on the blood of the weak and the vulnerable, but also through the very act that benefits them, cause fatal damage to their victims: "Whenever a wound is torn in the body of the nation, there the Jewish demon eats into the thick flesh and in parasitic fashion exploits the great of the world during their hour of weakness."[16]

In time, "Blut," with its associative myths like "Ehre" and "Rasse," moved out of the realm of Nazi creed and into the realm of Nazi worship. Alfred Rosenberg was one of the early prophets to preach the religion of "blood and race," supplanting Christianity. By his own admission, Rosenberg propagated the removal of Christianity from the midst of German civilization because he believed it to be a faith spawned by the black forces of Jewish magic: in ridding Germans of Christianity, he hoped to rid them of the taint of Judaism.[17]

Poet Dietrich Eckart shared Alfred Rosenberg's irrational fear of what he believed was the dictatorship of the Jewish mob spirit. In his major work, *Der Bolschevismus von Moses bis Lenin. Zwiegesprach zwischen Adolf* Hitler *und mir*, a dialogue with Hitler, Eckart revealed Hitler's obsession with an image of the Jew that was even more menacing in its sinister metaphysical implications than those of Rosenberg or Eckart. The poet in Eckart, in presenting his view of history to Hitler's record of evil-doings of the three great Jewish Bolsheviks — Moses, Jesus and Lenin, — all rabble-rousers and fomenters of the lowly mob against the civilized elite, proposed to "neutralize" the Jews' destructive effect by burning all the synagogues. Hitler despaired of such naïveté and dismissed the suggestion with a gesture of agonized resignation, proclaiming with prophetic anguish that even if not a single synagogue, not a single Jewish school were left, and even had there been no Old Testament, the Jewish spirit would still be there, would still exercise an impact. "It is there," Hitler declared darkly, "since the beginning of time, and there is not a Jew, not a single one, who does not embody it." In order to liberate oneself from the omnipotent presence of the Jew, Hitler preached with a passion that "the substance of flesh and blood" had to be destroyed.[18]

Hitler and the Nazis' primitive preoccupation with blood and the Jews' sinister power is a throwback to archetypal images of human sacrifice and ancient accusations of ritual murder.

Early Christianity ascribed such omnipotence of evil to the Jews as deicide, and medieval minds revived the charge of ritual murder in association with the Jews, in order to keep alive the charge of deicide. As the Church felt that the Christian world needed a constant reminder of the Jew as Christ-killer, the charge that Jews every Easter reenacted the Crucifixion by killing a Christian child was fabricated and planted as rumor in the popular mind. Known as blood libel, the diabolical fabrication transformed the image of the Jew from a figure informed by a distant mythical aura of darkness into a creature of dread whose immediate presence spelled a threat to the safety of Christian children.

In a parallel development, Christ's agony and crucifixion became the subject of widespread popular dramatization on the medieval stage. These early Passion, Mystery and Gospel plays presented the Jew as Judas, the traitor who sold Jesus to his executioners for thirty pieces of silver. It was the Jew-figure of the medieval York, Chester and Townely plays in England and the Benediktbeurn series in Germany whose betrayal of Jesus for money fixed the identification of money with blood in the popular mind. The stereotype of the traitorous, greedy Jew reinforced the blood libel.

In the dramatizations of Christ's betrayal by Judas, German poets often replaced the name Judas with the word Jude. In time, Judas-Jude not only sold but actually murdered Jesus:

"Da kam ein blinder Jud gegangen
er fuhrt ein sper an einen stangen
er fuhrts so stark in seiner faust
stach gott gegen seinen herzen auf."

With the blood libel, in the twelfth century the killer of Christ evolved into the killer of Christian children. The myth burst onto the scene of Christian-Jewish relations with whispered accusations of torture and bloodletting, a rumor that was to grow into the most durable tale of horror to plague Jewish lives through Europe for centuries to come. Literature, than as now, played a central role in perpetuating and disseminating the news and setting the mood for revenge. Matthew Paris' account of the Lincoln blood libel and its bloody repercussions was echoed in twenty-seven literary versions — ballads, folk tales, chronicles, and plays... generating afresh the lust for Jewish blood. Jews were put to death through the continent, following the celebrated blood libels of Norwich and Lincoln in England; Blois, in France (1171); Vienna (1181); Erfurt (1199); Lauda, Bischofsheim and Fulda (1234); Mainz (1283); Munich, Colmar, Krems, Magdeburg, Weissenburg (1235); Bern, Wurzburg, Posnan, Prague, Trent, Boppard, Budweis and numerous other localities in German lands.

The blood libel myth survived into the twentieth century and reached even the shores of America.

Scholars and educators added embellishments to the fantastic accounts of the chroniclers, turning the blood libel into the most colorful, tragic hoax of all time. Dominican Thomas of Cantimpre, in his book on bees, *Bonum universale de spibus* (1263), maintained that Jews spilt Christian blood as a cure against a constant flow of blood from their own bodies — a strange affliction from which only Jews suffered, as a punishment for having killed Christ. The charge that Christian blood was used for baking "matzos" came later. A popular German play, *Der religionsevefer, oder die susrottung der Juden in Deggendorf* (1337), celebrated the horrors of Jewish suffering by presenting the drama of the burning of the Jews in Deggendorf as a festive event. One of Grimms' fairytales (1462), the gruesome story of a little Christian boy's torture by Jews, had a happy ending: all the town's Jews were exterminated as punishment. Nicholas Marschalk's *Mons Stellarum* (1492) recounted the burning of the Jews of Sternberg, as a just punishment for the "desecration of the host" by one of the Jews of the town.

This libel made its appearance about a century after the emergence of the blood libel, as a satellite myth. According to this accusation, the Jews would sneak into the church and stab the host, the consecrated wafer, until it spurted blood. In the Catholic mass, the wafer is the sanctified symbol of Christ's body; the Jews' attempt to cause it to bleed was tantamount to a reenactment of the Crucifixion.

Gengenbach's epic, *Funf Juden* is about a similarly bizarre crime and equally cruel punishment of five Jews accused of having pierced the picture of the Holy

Virgin.   Michael Lindener's *Katzipori* (1558), and the plays, *Das endiger Judenspiel, Der wuchernde Jude am Pranger,* and several numbers in the repertoire of the Corpus Christi players dramatized like incidents with like consequences.   Printed broadsides and woodcuts circulated throughout the Holy Roman Empire proclaiming the miraculous cures wrought by the bones of Simon of Trent, a little child "martyred" by Jews and eventually canonized by the Vatican.   The City of Frankfurt commemorated the incident with a monument of the child surrounded by Jews in the company of the devil which was erected on a bridge over the River Main.

By the latter half of the nineteenth century, the stereotype of the Jew as a monstrous moneylender had become an extension of the blood myth; by draining the Gentile world of its money, the Jew was draining its lifeblood. Just like the Jewish vampire of Dinter, all the greedy Jewish bankers and Elders of Zion were but reincarnations of Judas, the arch-Jew, whose betrayal of Jesus for money had become equated with spilling his blood.

The money-blood equation has been a potent mythical component of the Jew-image since its origins in early Christian polemics. The dual accusation of deicide and betrayal-for-money has remained the pivotal component of Jew-mythification: the thirty pieces of silver and the blood of Christ — powerful archetypal images — have rested on Jewish heads ever since, to be utilized by an incongruous assortment of enemies, ever since.

Of all the Jews' enemies, this image had the most compelling relevance for Hitler and the Nazis. In their paranoid fascination with blood and their phobia of the Jew, this image assumed awesome proportions. The Nazis adopted the Jew-myth as an integral part of their creed, either out of genuine conviction, or because of deep-rooted psychological or other reasons; yet, they were clever enough to recognize the Jew-myth's practical propaganda potential. With a shrewd business sense, they discerned it as a highly marketable commodity; and the complex blood myth was just that: a commodity that had been successfully marketed for centuries. They were determined to exploit it to the fullest.

Judaism has been a disturbing paradox, an enigma. Jewry has been a puzzling amalgam of contradictions — a people dispersed yet united, disparate yet cohesive, adaptable yet stubborn, open to new ideas yet loyal to tradition, extraverted yet inscrutable. No set of rules applied in categorizing this strange community of religion, faith, history, ethics, ideas, culture and even nationality; no category applied.   All conclusions had to be improvised, and the improvisations almost always belonged to the realm of fantasy, often phantasmagoria.

How did this inexplicable group survive against overwhelming odds? How did it retain its unique character? Its integrity? Its dreams? Since the answers were not evident, the questioners sought them in dark hidden places... concocted them in the dark recesses of the mind:

A secret power — the devil, satan, demons, black magic — motivated and kept the Jew alive! And the Jew himself was the devil, satan, a demon, an evil spirit, a vampire, a black magician, a parasite, the Antichrist... To these dreadful, fear-inducing images of power, the Nazis added the hate-inducing element of repulsion: vermin, plague, pestilence, poison, sub-human.

"How could it all have happened?" Professor Jacob Talmon poses the question. "That systematic planning in cold blood, in well-heated offices by clean-shaven civil servants, walking upon thick and soft carpets; that scheme of tracking down every Jewish child and baby hidden in a cellar, or left to the tender mercies of Aryan Christians; that mobilization of manpower and transport for the mass murder of defenseless and anguished men, women, and children, when the total war effort was crying out for every pair of hands, and every vehicle; those mass executions upon prepared open graves, that smashing of heads of babies..."[19]

Does this evidence of a centuries-long educational campaign at dehumanizing the image of the Jew give an answer? Can a total desensitization of one soul to the suffering of another be achieved through education, no matter how cunning? What, in the final analysis, accounted for the phenomenal success of the preparatory process that led to the Final Solution? Could both the process and its outcome be duplicated? Can it happen again?

---

[1]R. W. Cooper, *The Nuremberg Trial,* Harmondsworth, 1956, p. 113.

[2]Max Weinreich, *Hitler's Professors,* N.Y. 1946, p. 6.

[3]Jacob J. Talmon, "The Universal Significance of Modern Anti-Semitism," *The Catastrophe of European Jewry,* Jerusalem, 1976, p. 172.

[4]A. Hitler, *Mein Kampf,* Boston, 1943, p. 65.

[5]J. J. Talmon, *op. cit.,* p. 55.

[6]*Ibid.,* pp. 157-158.

[7]Richard Wagner, *Das Judentum in der Musik, Gesammelte Schriften,* Leipzig, 1869.

[8]Max Bewer, *Gedanken,* Dresden, 1892, p. 31; cf. Uriel Tal, "Anti-Christian Anti-Semitism," *The Catastrophe of European Jewry,* p. 198.

[9]*Ibid.,* p. 32.

[10]"Only be steadfast in not eating the blood for the blood is the soul... " (Deut., 12:23).

[11]*Ibid.,* p. 31.

[12]Arthur Dinter, *Sin Against the Blood,* 1918; cf., Alex Bein, "The Jewish Question in Modern Anti-Semitic Literature," *The Catastrophe of European Jewry,* pp. 65-67.

[13]Oswald Spengler, *The Decline of the West,* Vol. I, 1918; II, 1922; cf. A. Bein, *op. cit.,* p. 52.

[14]*Ibid.*

[15]Hans Bluher, *Secessio Judaica;* cf., A. Bein, *op. cit.,* p. 83.

[16]Alfred Rosenberg, *The Mythos of the Twentieth Century, op. cit.,* p. 64.

[17]*Ibid.,* Both Hitler and Rosenberg were greatly influenced by Houston Stewart Chamberlain's *Die Grundlagen des 19th Jahrhunderts... (The Foundations of the Nineteenth Century,* Munich, 1889). Chamberlain, Richard Wagner's son-in-law, in turn received his inspiration from the composer's rabidly anti-Semitic ideology. According to Rosenberg, the parasitism of the Jew is "a definition of a

fundamental (biological) fact... in the very sense in which we speak of parasitical phenomena among plants and animals... " (Rosenberg, *op. cit.*, p. 459 ff).

[18]Talmon, *op. cit.*, pp. 169-170; "Deadly Jewish poison" were the last words of Adolf Hitler, according to H. R. Trevor-Roper, *The Testament of Adolf Hitler*, London, 1961, pp. 105, 109.

[19]*Ibid.*

Index

Sources

Hebrew Bible

Deuteronomy

    6:5

    7:6

    7:12,13

    10:15

    14:2

    26:18,19

    28:9

Exodus

    4:22

    13:21

    19:6

    24:7

Ezra

    8:16

Genesis

    15

Isaiah

    29:2

    29:5-8

    43:10

Job

    42:7-8

Numbers

    23:9

Zechariah

    14:9

Babylonian Talmud

Berachot

    32b

Metziah

    59a-59b